Latest Research in Bioinformatics

Volume I

Latest Research in Bioinformatics Volume I

Edited by **Christina Marshall**

New York

Published by Callisto Reference,
106 Park Avenue, Suite 200,
New York, NY 10016, USA
www.callistoreference.com

Latest Research in Bioinformatics: Volume I
Edited by Christina Marshall

International Standard Book Number: 978-1-63239-445-3 (Hardback)

Printed in the United States of America.

Contents

Preface   **VII**

Chapter 1   **Solving the 0/1 Knapsack Problem by a Biomolecular DNA Computer**   **1**
Hassan Taghipour, Mahdi Rezaei and Heydar Ali Esmaili

Chapter 2   **Maximum Recommended Dosage of Lithium for Pregnant Women Based on a PBPK Model for Lithium Absorption**   **7**
Scott Horton, Amalie Tuerk, Daniel Cook, Jiadi Cook and Prasad Dhurjati

Chapter 3   **Application of an Integrative Computational Framework in Trancriptomic Data of Atherosclerotic Mice Suggests Numerous Molecular Players**   **16**
Olga Papadodima, Allan Sirsjö, Fragiskos N. Kolisis and Aristotelis Chatziioannou

Chapter 4   **MRMPath and MRMutation, Facilitating Discovery of Mass Transitions for Proteotypic Peptides in Biological Pathways Using a Bioinformatics Approach**   **25**
Chiquito Crasto, Chandrahas Narne, Mikako Kawai, Landon Wilson and Stephen Barnes

Chapter 5   **Literature Retrieval and Mining in Bioinformatics: State of the Art and Challenges**   **35**
Andrea Manconi, Eloisa Vargiu, Giuliano Armano and Luciano Milanesi

Chapter 6   **Identification of Robust Pathway Markers for Cancer through Rank-Based Pathway Activity Inference**   **45**
Navadon Khunlertgit and Byung-Jun Yoon

Chapter 7   **Do Peers See More in a Paper Than Its Authors?**   **53**
Anna Divoli, Preslav Nakov and Marti A. Hearst

Chapter 8   **MicroRNA Response Elements-Mediated miRNA-miRNA Interactions in Prostate Cancer**   **68**
Mohammed Alshalalfa

Chapter 9   **A High-Throughput Computational Framework for Identifying Significant Copy Number Aberrations from Array Comparative Genomic Hybridisation Data**   **78**
Ian Roberts, Stephanie A. Carter, Cinzia G. Scarpini, Konstantina Karagavriilidou, Jenny C. J. Barna, Mark Calleja and Nicholas Coleman

Chapter 10   **CMD: A Database to Store the Bonding States of Cysteine Motifs with Secondary Structures**   90
Hamed Bostan, Naomie Salim, Zeti Azura Hussein, Peter Klappa and Mohd Shahir Shamsir

Chapter 11   **Efficient Serial and Parallel Algorithms for Selection of Unique Oligos in EST Databases**   95
Manrique Mata-Montero, Nabil Shalaby and Bradley Sheppard

Chapter 12   *In Silico* **Docking of HNF-1a Receptor Ligands**   101
Gumpeny Ramachandra Sridhar, Padmanabhuni Venkata Nageswara Rao, Dowluru SVGK Kaladhar, Tatavarthi Uma Devi and Sali Veeresh Kumar

Chapter 13   **Exploring Biomolecular Literature with EVEX: Connecting Genes through Events, Homology, and Indirect Associations**   106
Sofie Van Landeghem, Kai Hakala, Samuel Rönnqvist, Tapio Salakoski, Yves Van de Peer and Filip Ginter

Chapter 14   **Intervention in Biological Phenomena via Feedback Linearization**   118
Mohamed Amine Fnaiech, Hazem Nounou, Mohamed Nounou and Aniruddha Datta

Chapter 15   **BioEve Search: A Novel Framework to Facilitate Interactive Literature Search**   127
Syed Toufeeq Ahmed, Hasan Davulcu, Sukru Tikves, Radhika Nair and Zhongming Zhao

Chapter 16   **Applications of Natural Language Processing in Biodiversity Science**   139
Anne E. Thessen, Hong Cui and Dmitry Mozzherin

Chapter 17   **Gene Regulation, Modulation, and Their Applications in Gene Expression Data Analysis**   156
Mario Flores, Tzu-Hung Hsiao, Yu-Chiao Chiu, Eric Y. Chuang, Yufei Huang and Yidong Chen

Chapter 18   **On the Meaning of Affinity Limits in B-Cell Epitope Prediction for Antipeptide Antibody-Mediated Immunity**   167
Salvador Eugenio C. Caoili

Chapter 19   **Wavelet Packet Entropy for Heart Murmurs Classification**   184
Fatemeh Safara, Shyamala Doraisamy, Azreen Azman, Azrul Jantan and Sri Ranga

Chapter 20   **Detecting Cancer Outlier Genes with Potential Rearrangement Using Gene Expression Data and Biological Networks**   190
Mohammed Alshalalfa, Tarek A. Bismar and Reda Alhajj

Permissions

List of Contributors

Preface

In order to study the impactful alterations in cellular functions in different diseases, the advanced data collected must be processed to give a comprehensive understanding of the pictures obtained. It should be collaborated in such a manner that it can be later re-used for further research or comparisons. The primary function of bioinformatics is to develop software tools to produce advanced biological results. Advanced researches in the field of biology raised a considerable amount of data to be stored categorically and arranged in a certain fashion so as to be helpful in further derivations. Thus, came into existence the science of bioinformatics.

The current scenario of science is transforming it from being an exclusively laboratory based science to a more informational field of study. This transformation will revolutionize the science of biology. One of the major steps in this drastic reformation will be to train a new generation of scientists who are well-versed with both computational science and the mainstream laboratory practices. The future of biology will only prefer computational biologists. Thus, bioinformatics plays a vital role in today's world of biology.

This book provides an overview of the most important aspects of bioinformatics along with their evolution and application. We hope that this book facilitates the fruitful development of science. I would like to thank all the people associated with this book at every stage. This book would not have been accomplished without your rigorous efforts.

Editor

Solving the 0/1 Knapsack Problem by a Biomolecular DNA Computer

Hassan Taghipour,[1] Mahdi Rezaei,[2] and Heydar Ali Esmaili[1]

[1] *Department of Pathology, Tabriz University of Medical Sciences, Tabriz, Iran*
[2] *Department of Theoretical Physics and Astrophysics, University of Tabriz, Tabriz 51664, Iran*

Correspondence should be addressed to Hassan Taghipour; taghipourh@yahoo.com

Academic Editor: Bhaskar Dasgupta

Solving some mathematical problems such as NP-complete problems by conventional silicon-based computers is problematic and takes so long time. DNA computing is an alternative method of computing which uses DNA molecules for computing purposes. DNA computers have massive degrees of parallel processing capability. The massive parallel processing characteristic of DNA computers is of particular interest in solving NP-complete and hard combinatorial problems. NP-complete problems such as knapsack problem and other hard combinatorial problems can be easily solved by DNA computers in a very short period of time comparing to conventional silicon-based computers. Sticker-based DNA computing is one of the methods of DNA computing. In this paper, the sticker based DNA computing was used for solving the 0/1 knapsack problem. At first, a biomolecular solution space was constructed by using appropriate DNA memory complexes. Then, by the application of a sticker-based parallel algorithm using biological operations, knapsack problem was resolved in polynomial time.

1. Introduction

DNA encodes the genetic information of cellular organisms. The unique and specific structure of DNA makes it one of the favorite candidates for computing purposes. In comparison with conventional silicon-based computers, DNA computers have massive degrees of miniaturization and parallelism. By recent technology, about 10^{18} DNA molecules can be produced and placed in a medium-sized laboratory test tube. Each of these DNA molecules could act as a small processor. Biological operations such as hybridization, separation, setting, and clearing can be performed simultaneously on all of these DNA strands. Thus, in an in vitro assay, we could handle about 10^{18} DNA molecules or we can say that 10^{18} data processors can be executed in parallel.

In 1994, Adleman introduced the DNA computing as a new method of parallel computing [1]. Adleman succeeded in solving seven-point Hamiltonian path problem solely by manipulating DNA molecules and suggested that DNA could be used to solve complex mathematical problems.

In 1999, a new model of DNA computing (sticker model) was introduced by Roweis et al. [2]. This model has a kind of random access memory that requires no strand extension, uses no enzymes, and its materials are reusable. Sticker-based DNA computing has potential capability for being a universal method in DNA computing. Roweis et al. [2] also proposed specific machine architecture for implementing the sticker model as a microprocessor-controlled parallel robotic workstation. Thus, the operations used in sticker model can be performed on fully automated devices, which is helpful in reducing the error rates of operations.

In this paper, we applied sticker model for solving the knapsack problem which is one of the NP-complete problems.

The paper is organized as follows. Section 2 introduces the DNA structure and various DNA computing models and discusses about the sticker based DNA computing and biological operations which are used in sticker model. Section 3 introduces a DNA-based algorithm for solving the knapsack problem in sticker model.

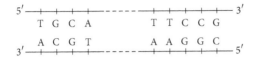

FIGURE 1: A DNA molecule.

2. Basics of DNA Computing

2.1. Structure of DNA and DNA Computing Models. DNA is a polymeric and a double-stranded molecule which is composed of monomers called nucleotides. Nucleotides are building blocks of DNA, and each of them contains three components: sugar, phosphate group, and nitrogenous base. There are four different nitrogenous bases which contribute in DNA structure: Thymine (T) and Cytosine (C) which are called pyrimidines and Adenine (A) and Guanine (G) which are called purines. Because nitrogenous bases are variable components of nucleotides, different neucleotides are distinguished by nitrogenous bases which contribute in their structure. For this reason, the name of the bases are used to refer to the neucleotides, and the neucleotides are simply represented as A, G, C, and T. The nucleotides are linked together by phosphodiester bonds and form a single-stranded DNA (ssDNA). A ssDNA molecule can be likened to a string consisting of a combination of four different symbols, A, G, C, and T. Mathematically, this means that we have a four-letter alphabet $\sum$ = {A, G, C, T} to encode information. Two ssDNA molecules join together to form a double-stranded DNA (DsDNA) based on complementary rule: "A" always pairs with "T," and likewise "C" pairs with "G." In Figure 1, a schematic picture of DNA is shown.

DNA computing was initially developed by Adleman in 1994. Adleman resolved an instance of Hamiltonian path problem just by handling the DNA molecules [1]. In 1995, Lipton presented a method for solving the satisfiability (SAT) problem [3]. Adleman-Lipton model can be used to solve different NP-complete problems. In Adleman-Lipton model, DNA splints are used for the construction of solution space. Adleman [4, 5] also presented a molecular algorithm for solving the 3-coloring problem. Chang and Guo [6–8] showed that the DNA operations in Adelman-Lipton model could be used for developing DNA algorithms to resolve the dominating set problem, the vertex cover problem, the maximal clique problem, and the independent set problem.

In 1999, Roweis et al. [2] introduced the Sticker based DNA computing model and applied it in solving the minimal set cover problem, and this model also was applied for breaking the Data Encryption Standard (DES) [9]. In our previous work, we also applied sticker based model for solving the independent set problem [10].

Other than Adleman-Lipton and Sticker based models, other various models are also proposed in DNA computing by researchers. Quyang et al. [11] solved the maximal clique problem using DNA molecules and restriction endonuclease enzymes. Amos et al. [12, 13] described a DNA computation model using restriction endonuclease enzymes instead of successive cycles of separation by DNA hybridization, which

can reduce the error rate of computation. Hagiya et al. [14] proposed a new method of DNA computing that involves a self-acting DNA molecule containing both the input, program, and working memory. In this method, a single-stranded DNA molecule consists of an input segment on the $5'$ end, followed by a formula (program) segment, followed by a spacer, and finally with a "head" on the $3'$ end that moves and performs the computation. Another method for DNA computation is "computation by self-assembly." Winfree et al. [15–17] introduced a linear and 2-dimensional self-assembly model.

The surface-based model was introduced by Liu et al. [18]. This model uses DNA molecules attached to a solid surface, instead of DNA molecules floating in a solution. The surface-based model was used by Taghipour et al. for solving the dominating set problem [19]. The computing by blocking was introduced by Rozenberg and Spaink [20]. This model uses a novel approach to filter the DNA molecules. Instead of separating the DNA strands to distinct tubes, or destroying and removing the DNA molecules that do not contribute to finding a solution, it blocks (inactivates) them in a way that the blocked strands can be considered as nonexistent during the subsequent steps of computation.

2.2. Sticker-Based DNA Computation. The sticker model was introduced by Roweis et al. [2]. In this model, there is a memory strand with N bases in length subdivided into K nonoverlapping regions each M bases long ($N \geq MK$). M can be, for example, 20. The substrands (bit regions) are significantly different from each other. One sticker is designed for each subregion; each sticker has M bases long and is complementary to one and only one of the K memory regions. If a sticker is annealed to its corresponding region on memory strand, then the particular region is said to be *on*. If no sticker is annealed to a region, then the corresponding bit is *off*. Each memory strand along with its annealed stickers is called memory complex. In sticker model, a tube is a collection of memory complexes, composed of large number of identical memory strands each of which has stickers annealed only at the required bit positions. This method of representation of information differs from other methods in which the presence or absence of a particular subsequence in a strand corresponded to a particular bit being *on* or *off*. In sticker model, each possible bit string is represented by a unique association of memory strands and stickers. This model has a kind of random access memory that requires no strand extension and uses no enzymes [2]. Indeed, in the sticker model, memory strands are used as registers, and stickers are used to write and erase information in the registers.

Another conception in sticker model is (K, L) library. Each (K, L) library contains memory complexes with K bit regions, the first L bit regions are either on or off, in all possible ways, whereas the remaining K-L bit regions are off. The last K-L bit regions can be used for intermediate data storage. In every (K, L) library, there are at least 2^L memory complexes. In Figure 2, a memory complex with 7 bit regions representing the binary number 1100101 is shown.

FIGURE 2: A memory complex representing 1100101.

FIGURE 3: Memory strand with at least $n + W + V$ bit regions.

2.3. Biological Operations in Sticker Model. There are four principal operations in sticker model: combination, separation, setting, and clearing [2]. We also defined a new operation called "divide" which is used in the construction of solution space [10]. Here, we briefly discuss about these operations.

(1) *Combine* $(T_0, T_1,$ and $T_2)$. The memory complexes from the tubes T_1 and T_2 are combined to form a new tube, T_0, simply the contents of T_1 and T_2 are poured into the tube T_0. $(T_0 = T_1 \cup T_2)$.

(2) *Separate* $(T_0, i) \rightarrow (T^+, T^-)$. This operation creates two new tubes T^+ and T^-; T^+ contains the memory complexes having the ith bit on $(T^+ = +(T_0, i))$, and T^- contains the memory complexes having the ith bit off $(T^- = -(T_0, i))$.

(3) *Set* (T_0, i). The ith bit region on every memory complex in tube T_0 is set to 1 or turned on.

(4) *Clear* (T_0, i). The ith bit region on every memory complex in tube T_0 is set to 0 or turned off.

(5) *Divide* $(T_0, T_1,$ and $T_2)$. By this operation, the contents of tube T_0 is divided into two equal portions and poured the tubes T_1 and T_2.

3. Solving the 0/1 Knapsack Problem in Sticker-Based DNA Computers

3.1. Definition of the Knapsack Problem. Knapsack problem is one of the classical optimization problems which have two variants: the 0/1 and fractional knapsack problems.

The 0/1 knapsack problem is posed as follows.

There are n items $I_1, I_2, I_3, \ldots, I_n$; each item I_j has a weight W_j and a value V_j, where W_j and V_j are integers. We have a knapsack which its capacity (weight) is C, where C is also an integer. We want to take the most valuable set of items that fit in our knapsack. Which items should we take? This is called the 0/1 or binary knapsack problem because each item must either be taken or left behind; we cannot take a fractional amount of an item.

In the fractional knapsack problem, the setup is the same, but we can take fractions of items, rather than having to make a binary (0-1) choice for each item. The fractional knapsack problem is solvable by a greedy strategy, where as the 0/1 knapsack problem is not. The 0/1 knapsack problem has been proved to be an NP-complete problem [21].

3.2. Construction of Sticker Based DNA Solution Space for Knapsack Problem

3.2.1. Designing Appropriate DNA Memory Complexes. As discussed before, there are n items $I_1, I_2, I_3, \ldots, I_n$; each item I_j has a weight W_j and a value V_j, where W_j and V_j are integers. Let us consider that the total weight of items is W and total value of items is V.

$$W = W_1 + W_2 + W_3 + \cdots + W_n = \sum_{j=1}^{n} W_j,$$

$$V = V_1 + V_2 + V_3 + \cdots + V_n = \sum_{j=1}^{n} V_j \tag{1}$$

n = total number of items.

We start with 2^n or more identical memory strands, which each of them has at least $n + W + V$ bit regions. (Figure 3) The first n bit regions (bit regions 1 to n) are used to represent n items, the middle W bit regions (bit regions $n + 1$ to $n + W$) represent the total weight of items W, and the next V bit regions (bit regions $n + W + 1$ to $n + W + V$) represent the total value of items V. Each bit region, for example can have 20 neucleotides, furthermore, every memory strand at least contains 20 $(n + W + V)$ neucleotides.

3.2.2. Production of DNA Memory Complexes Which Represent All Possible Subsets of Items. It is clear that a set of n items has 2^n subsets and each of these subsets has its own weight and value. For construction of solution space, it is essential to represent all subsets of items by appropriate DNA memory complexes. Furthermore, by using at least 2^n or more memory strands and making the first n bit regions *on* or *off* in all possible ways, we represent all 2^n subsets of items by DNA memory complexes. On the other hand, simply we design a $(n + W + V, n)$ library. For this purpose, (Procedure 1) is proposed.

Procedure 1 has n divide, n set and n combine operations. At the end of procedure, tube T_0 contains all of the memory complexes which each of them represent one of the subsets of items.

3.2.3. Representing the Weight and Value of Each Subset on DNA Memory Complexes. In this step, based on the items which are present in subsets, and by annealing corresponding stickers in W and V regions of memory strands, the total weight and value of subsets are represent on memory complexes. Note, each item I_j has a weight W_j and a value V_j, thus,

```
(1) Input (T_0), where T_0 contains 2^n or more memory strands with at least (n + W + V) bit regions.
(2) For i = 1 to n, where n is the total number of items
        (a) Divide (T_0, T_1, T_2)
        (b) Set (T_1, i)
        (c) Combine (T_0, T_1, T_2)
    End for
```

PROCEDURE 1

```
For i = 1 to n
{
        Separate (T_0, i)  →  (T^+, T^-)
        For j = 1 to W_i
            Set (T^+, n + Σ_{k=1}^{i-1} W_k + j)
        For j = 1 to V_i
            Set (T^+, n + Σ_{k=1}^{n} W_k + Σ_{k=1}^{i-1} V_k + j)
        Combine (T_0, T^+, T^-)
}
```

PROCEDURE 2

for each item I_j, W_j numbers of stickers are annealed to W region and V_j numbers of stickers are annealed to V region on memory strands. Furthermore, the numbers of annealed stickers in W and V regions represent the weight and value of corresponding subset, respectively. Procedure 2 is proposed for representing the weight and value of each subset.

Now, our solution space is completely produced and contains at least 2^n memory complexes, which each of them represent one of the subsets of items, and the numbers of annealed stickers in W and V regions represent the weight and value of corresponding subset, respectively.

3.3. DNA Algorithm for Solving the 0/1 Knapsack Problem. Algorithm 1 is proposed for solving the 0/1 knapsack problem.

According to the steps in the algorithm, the knapsack problem can be resolved by sticker based DNA computation in polynomial time.

By the execution of step 1, the memory complexes without any annealed stickers in W region (represent the subset ∅) are placed in tube T_0, the memory complexes with only one annealed sticker (represent the subsets of items which their weight are 1) are placed in tube T_1, the memory complexes with 2 annealed stickers (represent the subsets of items which their weight are 2) are placed in tubes T_2, the memory complexes with 3 annealed stickers (represent the subsets of items which their weight are 3) are placed in tube T_3, and finally, the tube T_W contains the memory complexes witch all bit regions located in W region are turned to "on" (represent the subset which contains all items). On the other hands, step 1 is a sorting procedure and sorts memory complexes according to the number of annealed stickers in W region. In this step, $W + 1$ tubes are produced ($T_0, T_1, T_2, \ldots, T_W$), and number of every tube indicate the number of annealed

stickers in W region. Step 1 contains $W(W + 1)/2$ separate and $W(W + 1)/2$ combine operations, or totally it contains $W(W + 1)$ operations.

In step 2 of algorithm, the contents of tubes $T_{c+1}, T_{c+2}, T_{c+3}, \ldots, T_W$ are discarded, because memory complexes which are present in these tubes, represent subset of items that their weight are exceeded the capacity of knapsack. Then, the contents of tubes $T_0, T_1, T_2, \ldots, T_c$ are mixed together and transferred to tube T_0. Now, tube T_0 contains memory complexes which represent the subsets of items that their weight are not exceeded the capacity of knapsack. Furthermore, at the end of step 2, the memory complexes which represent the subsets of items that their weight are exceeded the capacity of knapsack, removed from solution space and only remain memory complexes representing subsets that fit in our knapsack. It is clear that the step 2 contains only 2 operations.

By the execution of step 3, sorting of memory complexes are performed according to the number of annealed stickers in V region. During this step, $V + 1$ tubes are produced ($T_0, T_1, T_2, \ldots, T_V$). The memory complexes without any annealed stickers in V region (represent the subset ∅) are placed in tube T_0, the memory complexes with only one annealed sticker (represent the subsets of items which their value are 1) are placed in tube T_1, the memory complexes with 2 annealed stickers (represent the subsets of items which their value are 2) are placed in tubes T_2, the memory complexes with 3 annealed stickers (represent the subsets of items which their value are 3) are placed in tube T_3, and finally, the tube T_V contains the memory complexes with all bit regions located in V region are turned to "on" (represent the subset which contains all items). Step 3 contains $V(V + 1)/2$ separate and $V(V + 1)/2$ combine operations, or totally it contains $V(V + 1)$ operations.

(1) For $i = n$ to $n + W - 1$

    For $j = i$ down to n

        Separate $(T_{j-n}, i+1) \rightarrow (T_{(j-n+1)'}, T_{j-n})$

        Combine $(T_{j-n+1}, T_{j-n+1}, T_{(j-n+1)'})$

(2) The capacity of knapsack is C,

    Discard tubes $T_{c+1}, T_{c+2}, T_{c+3}, \ldots, T_W$

    Combine $(T_0, T_0, T_1, T_2, \ldots, T_c)$

(3) For $i = n + W$ to $n + W + V - 1$

    For $j = i$ down to $n + W$

        Separate $(T_{j-n-W}, i+1) \rightarrow (T_{(j-n-W+1)'}, T_{j-n-W})$

        Combine $(T_{j-n-W+1}, T_{j-n-W+1}, T_{(j-n-W+1)'})$

(4) Read T_V; else if it was empty then:

    Read T_{V-1}; else if it was empty then:

    Read T_{V-2}; else if it was empty then:

    $\vdots$

    Read T_2; else if it was empty then:

    Read T_1;

ALGORITHM 1

In step 4, all of tubes (from T_V to T_1) are evaluated for presence of memory complexes, and the first tube which is not empty and contains memory complexes represent the most valuable set. Step 4, maximally contains V Read operations.

Finally, it is clear that the total number of operations in our algorithm is: $W^2 + V^2 + W + 2 * V + 2$.

4. Conclusion

In this paper, the sticker based DNA computing was used for solving the 0/1 knapsack problem. This method could be used for solving other NP-complete problems. There are four principal operations in sticker model: Combination, Separation, Setting and Clearing. We also defined a new operation called "divide" and applied it in construction of solution space.

As mentioned earlier, one of the important properties of DNA computing is its real massive parallelism, which makes it a favorite and powerful tool for solving NP-complete and hard combinatorial problems. In sticker model, as in other DNA based computation methods, the property of DNA molecules to making duplexes is used as main biological operation. The main difference between the sticker model and Adleman-Lipton model is that in the sticker model there is a kind of Random access memory and the computations do not depend on DNA molecules extension as seen in Adleman-Lipton model.

References

[1] L. Adleman, "Molecular computation of solutions to combinatorial problems," *Science*, vol. 266, pp. 1021–1024, 1994.

[2] S. Roweis, E. Winfree, R. Burgoyne et al., "A sticker based model for DNA computation," in *Proceedings of the 2nd Annual Workshop on DNA Computing, Princeton University*, L. Landweber and E. Baum, Eds., Series in Discrete Mathematics and Theoretical Computer Science, DIMACS, pp. 1–29, American Mathematical Society, 1999.

[3] R. J. Lipton, "DNA solution of hard computational problems," *Science*, vol. 268, pp. 542–545, 1995.

[4] L. M. Adleman, *On Constructing a Molecular Computer*, Department of Computer Science, University of Southern California, 1995.

[5] L. M. Adleman, "On constructing a molecular computer," in *DNA Based Computers*, R. J. Lipton and E. B. Baum, Eds., pp. 1–22, American Mathematical Society, 1996.

[6] W.-L. Chang and M. Guo, "Solving the dominating-set problem in Adleman-Liptons Model," in *Proceedings of the 3rd International Conference on Parallel and Distributed Computing, Applications and Technologies*, pp. 167–172, Kanazawa, Japan, 2002.

[7] W.-L. Chang and M. Guo, "Solving the clique problem and the vertex cover problem in Adleman-Lipton's model," in *IASTED International Conference, Networks, Parallel and Distributed Processing, and Applications*, pp. 431–436, Tsukuba, Japan, 2002.

[8] W.-L. Chang and M. Guo, "Solving NP-complete problem in the Adleman-Lipton Model," in *Proceedings of The International Conference on Computer and Information Technology*, pp. 157–162, 2002.

[9] L. Adleman, P. Rothemund, S. Roweis, and E. Winfree, "On applying molecular computation to the data encryption standard," in *Proceedings of the 2nd DIMACS wWorkshop on DNA Based Computers, Princeton University*, pp. 24–48, 1996.

[10] H. Taghipour, A. Taghipour, M. Rezaei, and H. Esmaili, "Solving the independent set problem by sticker based DNA computers," *American Journal of Molecular Biology*, vol. 2, no. 2, pp. 153–158, 2012.

[11] Q. Ouyang, P. D. Kaplan, S. Liu, and A. Libchaber, "DNA solution of the maximal clique problem," *Science*, vol. 278, no. 5337, pp. 446–449, 1997.

[12] M. Amos, A. Gibbons, and D. Hodgson, "Error-resistant implementation of DNA computations," in *Proceedings of the 2nd DIMACS Workshop on DNA Based Computers*, 1996.

[13] M. Amos, A. Gibbons, and D. Hodgson, "A new model of DNA computation," in *Proceedings of the 12th British Colloquium on Theoretical Computer Science*, 1996.

[14] M. Hagiya, M. Arita, D. Kiga, K. Sakamoto, and S. Yokoyama, "Towards parallel evaluation and learning of boolean μ-formulas with molecules," *DIMACS Series in Discrete Mathematics and Theoretical Computer Science*, vol. 48, pp. 57–72, 1999.

[15] E. Winfree, "Simulations of computing by self-assembly," in *Proceedings of the 4th International Meeting on DNA Based Computers*, pp. 213–239, 1998.

[16] E. Winfree, F. Liu, L. A. Wenzler, and N. C. Seeman, "Design and self-assembly of two-dimensional DNA crystals," *Nature*, vol. 394, no. 6693, pp. 539–544, 1998.

[17] E. Winfree, X. Yang, and N. Seeman, "Universal computation via self-assembly of DNA: some theory and experiments," in *Proceedings of the 2nd DIMACS Workshop on DNA Based Computers*, 1996.

[18] Q. Liu, Z. Guo, A. E. Condon, R. M. Corn, M. G. Lagally, and L. M. Smith, "A surface-based approach to DNA computation," in *Proceedings of the 2nd Annual Meeting on DNA Based Computers, Princeton University*, 1996.

[19] H. Taghipour, M. Rezaei, and H. Esmaili, "Applying surface-based DNA computing for solving the dominating set problem," *American Journal of Molecular Biology*, vol. 2, no. 3, pp. 286–290, 2012.

[20] G. Rozenberg and H. Spaink, "DNA computing by blocking," *Theoretical Computer Science*, vol. 292, no. 3, pp. 653–665, 2003.

[21] M. R. Garey and D. S. Johnson, *Computer and Intractability: a Guide to the Theory of NP-Completeness*, Freeman, San Francisco, Calif, USA, 1979.

Maximum Recommended Dosage of Lithium for Pregnant Women Based on a PBPK Model for Lithium Absorption

Scott Horton,[1] Amalie Tuerk,[1] Daniel Cook,[1] Jiadi Cook,[2] and Prasad Dhurjati[1]

[1] Colburn Laboratory, Department of Chemical and Biomolecular Engineering, University of Delaware, Newark, DE 19716, USA
[2] Resident in the Department of Family Medicine, Christiana Care Health Services, Wilmington, DE 19805, USA

Correspondence should be addressed to Daniel Cook, djcook@udel.edu

Academic Editor: Huixiao Hong

Treatment of bipolar disorder with lithium therapy during pregnancy is a medical challenge. Bipolar disorder is more prevalent in women and its onset is often concurrent with peak reproductive age. Treatment typically involves administration of the element lithium, which has been classified as a class D drug (legal to use during pregnancy, but may cause birth defects) and is one of only thirty known teratogenic drugs. There is no clear recommendation in the literature on the maximum acceptable dosage regimen for pregnant, bipolar women. We recommend a maximum dosage regimen based on a physiologically based pharmacokinetic (PBPK) model. The model simulates the concentration of lithium in the organs and tissues of a pregnant woman and her fetus. First, we modeled time-dependent lithium concentration profiles resulting from lithium therapy known to have caused birth defects. Next, we identified maximum and average fetal lithium concentrations during treatment. Then, we developed a lithium therapy regimen to maximize the concentration of lithium in the mother's brain, while maintaining the fetal concentration low enough to reduce the risk of birth defects. This maximum dosage regimen suggested by the model was 400 mg lithium three times per day.

1. Introduction

Bipolar disorder, which affects approximately 1% of the population (mostly women), is a type of mood disorder which has periods of manic behavior and periods of depressive behavior. An overly joyful or overexcited state characterizes manic behavior; extremely sad and hopeless states characterize depressive behavior [1]. A standard treatment for bipolar disorder involves treatment with the element lithium, which was the first mood-stabilizing medication approved for treatment of "mania," which later came to be known as bipolar disorder, in 1970 [2]. The brand names of bipolar lithium treatment drugs are Eskalith and Lithobid, which deliver lithium as lithium carbonate (Li_2CO_3). The typical size of a dose of lithium drug ranges from 900 to 1800 mg Li_2CO_3/day (if administered in 2 divided doses a day) and 900 to 2400 mg Li_2CO_3/day (if administered in 3-4 divided doses a day) [3]. Although the mechanism by which lithium mitigates the symptoms of bipolar disorder is not completely understood, lithium is thought to affect sodium transfer in the brain [4]. High doses can cause lithium poisoning

and side effects such as the inability to control movement, blackouts, seizures, hallucinations, severe headaches, and acute renal failure [3, 5].

In women, bipolar disorder typically manifests prior to the age of 30, which coincides with the timing of a woman's peak reproduction age [4]. Unfortunately, lithium is also classified as one of only thirty known teratogenic drugs (i.e., substances associated with causing birth defects) [6]. Therefore, the treatment of pregnant women for bipolar disorder with lithium presents a major risk for the safety of the fetus. Lithium crosses the human placenta freely [2] and affects vasculature formation in the fetus [4]. Because the majority of vasculature forms during the first trimester, lithium affects the development of the fetus most in the first trimester [7]. The most common birth defects associated with 30 babies exposed to lithium during pregnancy were hypotonia (43%); cardiac problems (40%); respiratory distress syndrome and cyanosis (30%); poor feeding ability, lethargy, and depressed Moro and suck reflexes (27%) [2].

Although lithium treatment concurrent with pregnancy has the potential to cause serious birth defects, there is little guidance toward appropriate lithium treatment regimens for pregnant women. Current FDA-approved packaging for Lithobid states, "If this drug is used in women of childbearing potential, or during pregnancy, or if a patient becomes pregnant while taking this drug, the patient should be apprised by their physician of the potential hazard to the fetus" [8]. The extent of the current guidance by physicians is to avoid lithium if possible during the first trimester of pregnancy; if this is not possible, and during the second and third trimesters, the lowest effective dose of lithium should be used [3].

It would be beneficial to quantitatively establish a maximum acceptable dosage regimen that will not cause teratogenic effects on the fetus. However, measuring the actual concentration in the fetus is prohibitively difficult and has a potential to cause damage to the fetus. Furthermore, a large dataset associating actually administered lithium therapy regimens correlated with instances and noninstances of birth defects would be required in order to conclusively establish a correlation of lithium exposure with birth defect incidence; this data is not currently available. Additionally, animal models describing fetal lithium toxicity or teratogenic effects are lacking.

In lieu of these experimental methods, lithium concentration in various organs can be predicted by the construction of a pharmacokinetic model, such as that presented by Bischoff et al. [9]; this provides a means to predict lithium concentration within the fetus during various dosage regimens based upon the concentrations in other parts of the mother's body which are easier and safer to sample. By modeling the effect of dosage regimens previously associated with high incidence of birth defects, improved dosage regimens with lower likelihoods of causing birth defects can be proposed. To this end, we have employed a modified version of the biological model first proposed by Bischoff et al. [9] (the Physiologically Based Pharmacokinetic (PBPK) model). PBPK models have been developed and validated for a variety of applications since they were first introduced, including predicting organophosphate insecticide concentration in humans [10], modeling toxicology of complex mixtures [11], and drug discovery [12]. This work applies a modified PBPK model to the problem of impaired fetal development due to maternal lithium treatment in order to propose maximum recommended dosage regimens.

2. Basis and Development of Model

2.1. General Assumptions of the Model. A few assumptions and features of this model warrant discussion. First, this mass-transfer-based model includes organ "compartments"; each compartment represents a "lumped" region of organs/tissues with similar physiochemical properties. All properties of the "compartment" (volume, blood flow rate, etc.) have independently verifiable anatomical significance [13]. Another assumption employed in the model development was an assumption of flow-limited conditions; this implies that the blood leaving a tissue/organ is in diffusion equilibrium with the tissue/organ, such that the perfusion

rate is rate controlling rather than the diffusion rate. The rationale and justification for this assumption is discussed in detail in Bischoff et al. [13]. Finally, in this model, each compartment is modeled as a continuously stirred tank reactor (CSTR), with constant volume, constant inflow and outflow rates, and a blood permeable partitioning membrane through which lithium enters the organ/tissue along with the blood. Each organ/tissue has a specific membrane partition constant to characterize the relative partitioning of the drug between the blood, which delivers the drug, and the tissue; this parameter can also be described as the tissue to plasma equilibrium distribution ratio. These values are contained in Table 1. These distribution ratios were found from published literature for all compartments except the fetus, for which data was not available. In addition, there is no published literature that provides absolute fetal lithium concentrations associated with lithium therapy regimens. However, dosage regimens which have resulted in birth defects have been documented [2]. Without a correlation of fetal concentrations to these known pathological dosage regimens, the value of the fetal compartment partition coefficient (R_F) can be chosen arbitrarily; this allowed us to explore the effect of different lithium therapy regimens on relative fetal concentration. Since the fetal lithium concentrations reported by the simulation are relative to pathological cases, any value chosen for R_F will simply give scaled results leading to the same conclusions. This makes selecting a particular value for R_F arbitrary. We selected a value of 0.8 as the fetal partition coefficient to use in our model.

The original model of Bischoff et al. [9] predicted concentrations of the anticancer drug methotrexate in different organs in the body. Because methotrexate is metabolized in the liver and secreted through the colon without a concentration buildup in the upper organs, Bischoff et al. [9] modeled only the lower organs in the body. Our model, however, deals with lithium, for which the brain is a primary site of lithium activity and accumulation. Furthermore, as we are specifically modeling the lithium exposure of pregnant women, the fetus and the uterus are additional physiological regions for which lithium concentrations should be predicted. Therefore, we have modified the original PBPK model to better reflect our system by adding compartments for the brain, the uterus, and the fetus, and modifying the compartment connectivity accordingly (see Figure 1). In our model, we assumed that the fetus was in the first trimester, when lithium exposure is most damaging to its development. Due to the lower development of the fetus at this point in the pregnancy, we modeled the fetus as a single compartment. Our model also included thyroid, gastrointestinal (GI) tract, kidneys, and bone compartments.

2.2. Physiological Considerations of the Model. In order to investigate the effect of lithium dosage regimens on maternal organ and fetal concentrations, data on lithium partitioning between blood plasma and the relevant organs and tissues is required. This enables the model to predict which organs/tissues preferentially uptake and concentrate lithium. We obtained partitioning coefficients directly from

TABLE 1: Model parameters.

Conversion factor for lithium content of drug dose	8/300	mEq (mmol) Li/mg dose	[3]
Bone mass	8	kg	[14]
Bone density	1.1	g/mL	[15]
Kidney clearance rate (kk)	20	mL/min	[3]
Physiological volumes of organ/tissue compartments			
Plasma (V_P)	5200	mL	[16]
Bone (V_B)	7273	mL	Calculated from bone mass and bone density
Kidney (V_K)	280	mL	[16]
Uterus (V_U)	1000	mL	[7]
Gastrointestinal (GI) tract (V_G)	1650	mL	[16]
Thyroid (V_T)	13	mL	[16]
Brain (V_{Br})	1450	mL	[16]
Fetus, 1st Trimester (V_F)	150	mL	[7]
Blood flow to organs			
Bone (Q_B)	272	mL/min	Calculated from bone perfusion and bone mass [14]
Kidney (Q_K)	1240	mL/min	[16]
Uterus (Q_U)	475	mL/min	[7]
GI Tract (Q_G)	1100	mL/min	[16]
Thyroid (Q_T)	60	mL/min	Modeled based on similar sized organs
Brain (Q_{Br})	700	mL/min	[16]
Fetus, 1st trimester (Q_F)	300	mL/min	[7]
Tissue to plasma equilibrium distribution ratios for lithium			
Bone (R_B)	1.5		[3]
Kidney (R_K)	1		[3]
Uterus (R_U)	0.4		[3]
GI Tract (R_G)	1		[3]
Thyroid (R_T)	1.5		[3]
Brain (R_{Br})	1.5		[3]
Fetus (R_F)	0.8		Estimated; see rationale in text

the medical database Lexi-Comp Online [3] for all organs except the fetus, for which data was not available. The kidneys are the main source of lithium clearance from the body; approximately 99% of the lithium in the body is removed through the urine, while the remaining 1% passes through feces. Therefore this model assumes that the lithium clearance through the feces is negligible and only considers kidney clearance for lithium removal. The GI tract is included because an oral mode of delivery is employed for lithium-containing bipolar drugs, thus lithium is ingested and absorbed through the GI tract.

Lexi-Comp Online indicated that lithium accumulates in the brain, thyroid, and bone tissue. Therefore, these organs have the possibility to significantly affect the concentrations in important organs by absorbing a majority of lithium when

blood plasma concentrations are high or releasing lithium even when blood plasma concentrations are low.

The connectivity of the model, as shown in Figure 1, is based on clinical physiology. Each compartment represents an organ with a certain partition coefficient, denoted by a dashed line, through which blood flows. The box marked "Plasma" can be viewed as the aorta, or the main pathway for blood flow through the body; within the aorta, mixing of the blood/plasma is assumed to occur so that the blood exiting this compartment, destined to the other organs of the body, has a single concentration at any point in time (C_P). The plasma splits into two pathways; the upper pathway proceeds to the thyroid and brain, while the lower pathway proceeds to the GI tract, kidneys, uterus, and bone. As in the body, blood flows through these organs in parallel. Since the

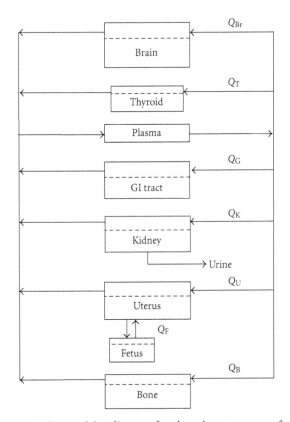

Figure 1: Connectivity diagram for the relevant organs of the PBPK model for lithium accumulation in a pregnant woman. Each compartment represents an organ with a certain partition coefficient, denoted by a dashed line, through which blood flows.

fetus is connected to the mother through the uterus, the flow of blood to and from the fetus travels through the uterus. According to Kozma [2], lithium crosses the human placenta freely, and the concentrations in fetal serum are equal to that of maternal serum; this enables us to assume that the concentration of lithium in the blood passing entering the fetus has the same concentration as that of the blood leaving the uterus. Because our model assumes a fetus in the first trimester, the renal system was assumed to be immature such that renal clearance of lithium from the fetus would be negligible [2]. Therefore the only route for lithium to exit the fetus is partitioning back from the fetus to the plasma. This has the additional effect of causing a delayed clearance of lithium from the fetus (and accumulation of lithium within the fetus), so that toxic levels of lithium may be experienced by the fetus even though the concentration of lithium for the mother may be within the therapeutic range [2].

2.3. Mathematical Considerations of the Model-Coupled Differential Equations.
The following coupled differential equations describe the time dependence of lithium concentrations in the compartments from Figure 1. Based upon a general mass balance, the rate of accumulation of lithium ($(d/dt)(V_iC_i)$) within the control volume (V_i) of a general physiological compartment i is equal to the rate of lithium entering the compartment minus the rate of lithium leaving the compartment minus the rate of lithium clearance from the system plus the rate of lithium absorption to the system, as shown in (1).

General organ/tissue mass balance:

$$\frac{d}{dt}(V_iC_i) = r_{Li,\text{entering}} - r_{Li,\text{exiting}} - r_{Li,\text{clearance}} + r_{Li,\text{absorption}} \tag{1}$$

For a general compartment i (exceptions are discussed below), the rate of lithium entering the compartment is the product of the plasma flow rate to the compartment (Q_i) and the concentration of lithium in the plasma (C_P); the rate of lithium leaving a general compartment is the product of the plasma flow out of the compartment (which is equivalent to the flow in, Q_i) and the concentration of lithium in the blood flowing out. The concentration of lithium in the blood exiting an organ will be a function of the concentration of lithium in the organ (C_i) divided by the partitioning coefficient R_i that characterizes the distribution of lithium between the plasma and the organ/tissue. The mass of lithium leaving the organ is often lower than entering due to the tissue to plasma equilibrium distribution ratio, resulting in lithium accumulation in that tissue. For all organs (except the kidneys), the rate of lithium clearance within the organ is negligible, and the only mode of lithium removal is through partitioning of lithium back from the tissue to the blood. Therefore, the general mass balance presented above in (1) can be modified with these described adjustments, resulting in the following.

General compartment mass balance without clearance or absorption:

$$\frac{d}{dt}(V_iC_i) = Q_iC_P - Q_i\frac{C_i}{R_i} \tag{2}$$

Assuming that the volume of each compartment is constant, the time-dependent concentration of lithium in the general tissue compartment i can be expressed as follows.

Constant-volume compartment mass balance without clearance or absorption:

$$\frac{dC_i}{dt} = Q_i\left(C_P - \frac{C_i}{R_i}\right)\frac{1}{V_i} \tag{3}$$

This general form applies to the brain, the thyroid, and the bone; the differential equations characterizing lithium concentration in these compartments are described in (4), (5), and (6) below.

Brain (brain compartment mass balance):

$$\frac{dC_{\text{Br}}}{dt} = Q_{\text{Br}}\left(C_P - \frac{C_{\text{Br}}}{R_{\text{Br}}}\right)\frac{1}{V_{\text{Br}}} \tag{4}$$

Thyroid (thyroid compartment mass balance):

$$\frac{dC_{\text{T}}}{dt} = Q_{\text{T}}\left(C_P - \frac{C_{\text{T}}}{R_{\text{T}}}\right)\frac{1}{V_{\text{T}}} \tag{5}$$

Bone (bone compartment mass balance):

$$\frac{dC_B}{dt} = Q_B\left(C_P - \frac{C_B}{R_B}\right)\frac{1}{V_B} \tag{6}$$

The connectivity between the uterus and the fetus, the clearance of lithium from the kidneys, the absorption of lithium into the gut, and the contribution of all tissues to the plasma concentration lead to additional terms in the differential equations for these compartments; further discussion is provided below for each compartment with a form modified from the general one provided above in (3).

Uterus (uterus compartment mass balance):

$$\frac{dC_U}{dt} = \left(Q_U\left(C_P - \frac{C_U}{R_U}\right) + Q_F\left(\frac{C_F}{R_F} - \frac{C_U}{R_U}\right)\right)\frac{1}{V_U} \tag{7}$$

Blood flow to the uterus comes from both the plasma compartment (at flow rate Q_U and at the plasma lithium concentration C_P) as well as from the fetus compartment (at flow rate Q_F and at the lithium concentration leaving the fetus, C_F/R_F), and so there are two inflow terms in the uterus mass balance, as can be seen in (7). Furthermore, the flow exiting the uterus is at a lithium concentration of C_U/R_U, and it exits at flow rate Q_F (to the fetus) and at flow rate Q_U (back to the plasma compartment), providing two outflow terms to the uterus compartment mass balance.

Fetus (fetus compartment mass balance):

$$\frac{dC_F}{dt} = Q_F\left(\frac{C_U}{R_U} - \frac{C_F}{R_F}\right)\frac{1}{V_F} \tag{8}$$

Because the fetus is connected through the body only through the uterus, and not directly to the plasma compartment, the blood entering and leaving the fetus passes first through the uterus, as shown above in (8). The partition function for the fetus, R_F, also describes the partitioning between the fetus compartment and the plasma.

Kidneys (kidney compartment mass balance):

$$\frac{dC_K}{dt} = \left(Q_K\left(C_P - \frac{C_K}{R_K}\right) - kk\frac{C_K}{R_K}\right)\frac{1}{V_K} \tag{9}$$

In the kidney compartment mass balance (9), the term kk refers to the kidney clearance rate (Table 1). The term $kk *$ C_K/R_K gives the rate at which lithium is cleared from the body through the kidneys.

GI tract (GI tract compartment mass balance):

$$\frac{dC_G}{dt} = \left(Q_G\left(C_P - \frac{C_G}{R_G}\right) + G(t)\right)\frac{1}{V_G} \tag{10}$$

The parameter $G(t)$ is the rate (mEq/minute) of lithium absorption into the blood through the GI tract. In this study, we assumed all lithium drug was delivered orally as a time-release capsule. This term is only nonzero during the release

of lithium from an active drug dosing time period. Assuming that the time-release format of the drug delivery would result in a constant rate of absorption over the course of the drug dissolution time, the absorption term $G(t)$ in (10) above was calculated as follows.

Drug absorption term:

$$G(t) = \frac{m_D(\text{mEq } Li/\text{mg drug})}{\Delta t} \tag{11}$$

In (11), m_D is the mass of the drug dose in mg, mEq Li/mg drug is the conversion factor for lithium active ingredient contained in each mg of drug, and Δt is the time over which the constant rate absorption of the time-release capsule occurs. According to [3], peak serum concentrations occur 4–12 hours after dosing with controlled release lithium drug. Logically, this implies that the last of the lithium drug is delivered to the system 4–12 hours after the dose is administered. By utilizing the lower end of this range of drug absorption time, a "worst-case" scenario for peak tissue concentration with a time-release drug regimen will be obtained. Therefore, the default assumption for the duration of drug absorption during administration was to use $\Delta t = 4$ hours in (11). The timing of the predicted peak in plasma lithium concentration in the model that corresponds to this $G(t)$ is four hours, confirming that the peak concentration corresponds with the end of drug release and absorption in our model.

Plasma (plasma compartment mass balance):

$$\frac{dC_P}{dt} = \left[Q_G\frac{C_G}{R_G} + Q_K\frac{C_K}{R_K} + Q_B\frac{C_B}{R_B} + Q_U\frac{C_U}{R_U} + Q_T\frac{C_T}{R_T} \right.$$
$$\left. + Q_{Br}\frac{C_{Br}}{R_{Br}} - (Q_G + Q_K + Q_B + Q_U + Q_T + Q_{Br})C_P\right]\frac{1}{V_P} \tag{12}$$

The mass balance on the plasma compartment includes the sum of all the outflows from and inflows to each of the individual compartments included in the model.

3. Results

All simulations were performed using the MATLAB software suite. In the medical literature, bodily lithium concentrations are reported in milliequivalents lithium/mL tissue volume (mEq/mL); the unit mEq is equivalent to a millimol. In this paper, we utilize the units mEq to report bodily concentrations to be consistent with the medical literature. Dosages of lithium drugs are reported in milligram of the total drug, which is lithium carbonate (Li_2CO_3) for the brand name drugs Eskolith and Lithobid. Therefore, for example, a 300 mg tablet contains 8 mEq lithium.

3.1. Lithium Concentration Profiles for a Single 900 mg Dose of Lithium Drug (as Li_2CO_3). A typical dosage regimen for an individual suffering from bipolar disorder is to administer 900 mg of lithium drug twice daily. The lithium concentration time course (in mEq Li/mL) resulting from a single 900 mg dose of lithium drug, delivered via two simultaneously administered 450 mg controlled release capsules, results in the concentration profiles shown in Figure 2. The organs shown in Figure 2(b) are important for the aim of this study, which was to provide better guidance for safe lithium dosing for fetal development; the concentration profiles shown in Figure 2(c) are other organs included in the model but less critical for the aim of this study. The drug release occurs over four hours, as described above, in conjunction with the mass-balance development for the GI Tract; after the last of the delivered drug has absorbed into the system, all concentrations decay due to loss of lithium through the urine via kidney clearance. Our simulation uses a flow rate of urine containing lithium of 20 mL/minute; this value is consistent with the standard accepted values of 20–40 mL/minute [3].

The concentration in each organ is based on the tissue to plasma equilibrium distribution ratio, R_i. For example, the concentration in the uterus is less than half that of the plasma because the ratio for lithium partitioning into the uterus from the plasma (R_U) is 0.4 [3].

These concentration profiles fit the known data. There is a peak in plasma lithium concentration at approximately 4 hrs, concurrent with the end of drug dissolution from the time-release capsule. The half-life of lithium can be approximated as the time it takes for the lithium in the plasma to decrease 50% from its maximum value. In our model, this half-life is approximately 12 hours, which is consistent with the reported serum half-life of lithium for pregnant women [4].

3.2. Lithium Concentration Profiles for Dosage Regimens Known to Cause Birth Defects.

Lithium is known to cause birth defects in infants; although there have been no clinical trials to ascertain the exact dosage that causes harm. There are, however, several reported cases of women who continued to take lithium during their pregnancy, gave birth to a baby with birth defects, and the doctors reported the dosage regimen. One-dosage regimen that has been documented to cause birth defects was two capsules daily, 450 mg in the morning followed by 900 mg in the evening [2]. There are numerous sources, including the International Register of Lithium Babies, that document birth defects as a result of treatment with lithium. However, the dosage regimens used are not reported or accessible. The standard dosage of two 900 mg doses daily was used to describe the dosage profiles for these cases. The predicted lithium concentrations over time associated with these dosing regimens are shown in Figure 3 for the brain, plasma, fetus, and the uterus.

For both dosage regimens, the figure shows the concentration profile after the patient has been taking the drug for a long period of time; this means that every two-dose cycle has the exact same profile, which will be referred to as the terminal profile. The first regimen with alternating dosage sizes resulted in a concentration profile of high and low peaks. The maximum fetus concentration associated with the 450 mg/900 mg regimen is 1.4 mEq/mL, with an average

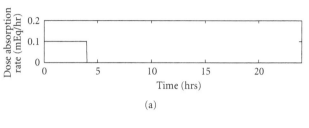

(a)

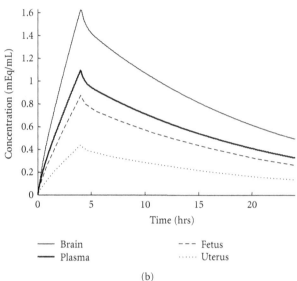

(b)

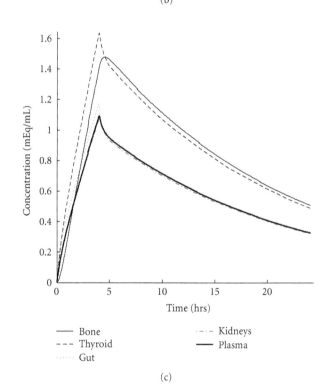

(c)

FIGURE 2: Concentration profiles in all physiological compartments resulting from a single, time-release 900 mg dosage of lithium drug. Initial lithium concentration in the body is 0 mEq/mL. (a) Profile of drug release pulse. (b) Lithium concentration time courses in the most important compartments for the study, with fetus labeled. (c) Lithium concentration profiles for less critical compartments.

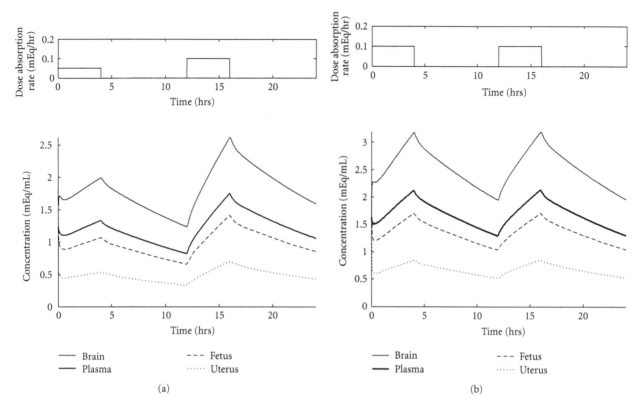

FIGURE 3: Terminal concentration profiles in selected physiological compartments for dosage regimens that are known to cause birth defects. In this case, lithium medication is administered twice daily and controlled-release tablets release lithium over 4 hours. A pulse function corresponding to the drug absorption is shown above each figure. (a) One dose of a 450 mg tablet (12 mEq lithium) with a subsequent 900 mg (24 mEq lithium) dose. (b) Two doses of a 900 mg tablet (24 mEq lithium).

concentration of 0.97 mEq/mL. For the second regimen of two 900 mg doses daily, the peak fetus concentration is 1.7 mEq/mL and an average concentration of 1.3 mEq/mL. Both peaks and means were found using a terminal profile.

Birth defects could be caused by either the maximum concentration experienced by the fetus, or the average concentration of lithium in the fetus over the gestation period; the data presently available does not conclusively point to either of these as the primary cause of the birth deformations. While this information cannot be utilized to recommend a "safe" dosage regimen that can guarantee a defect-free fetus, there are two useful conclusions from these results.

The first and most useful output from this analysis is to provide, from the 450 mg/900 mg dosage regimen, the following concentrations which should not be exceeded during lithium treatment of a pregnant woman:

(1) a *maximum* peak fetal lithium concentration,

(2) an *average* fetal lithium concentration.

These standards can be used to identify lithium therapy regimens likely to exceed these known pathological concentrations, so that their administration to pregnant patients can be prevented.

The second output is the ability to now use the model to suggest dosage regimens that will result in fetal concentrations that fall significantly below the known pathological levels, while still maintain high enough concentrations to be effective for the mother; this is the topic of the next section.

3.3. Lithium Dosage Regimens Eliminated Based on Model Results. The previously documented pathological cases are primarily useful in ruling out other potential dosage regimens. To this end, we selected two dosing regimens within the therapeutic dose range where the effect on the fetus is unknown. The first dosage regimen we modeled is two 700 mg doses, 12 hrs apart (denoted 700/700). The next dosage regimen is a 1000 mg dose followed by a 300 mg dose 12 hrs later. The results of these simulations are shown in Figure 4.

The 700/700 dosage regimen gives a higher average concentration than the pathological dosage, while maintaining a lower peak concentration. This is because the doses are more "spread out" across the day. The 1000/300 dosage regimen gives a higher peak than the pathological dosage, while maintaining a lower average. Neither of these regimens should be considered for pregnant women because they cross the pathological dosage either average or peak concentration and therefore have the potential to cause birth defects. The power behind this conclusion is that the model used clinical

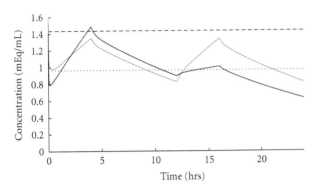

--- Maximum fetal concentration value from pathological dosage
...... Average fetal concentration value from pathological dosage
——— 700 mg/700 mg dosage regime
——— 1000 mg/300 mg dosage regime

FIGURE 4: Model-predicted pathological dosage regimens. The maximum and average fetus concentrations from the 450/900 dosage regimen are plotted along with two new dosage regimens. A 300/1000 dosage regimen is shown in black and a 700/700 dosage regimen is shown in blue.

pathological data to eliminate dosing regimens that have an unknown/undocumented effect on a fetus.

3.4. Model-Suggested Reduced Risk Lithium Dosage Regimens. In order to find safer dosage regimens, we modeled several regimens to find ones with peak and average concentrations below the pathological dosage. Drug ingestion does not have to occur only twice daily, and the regimens we tested reflect this. However, we did not consider the effect of nonevenly spaced dosages which, due to its complexity and questionable clinical relevance, is beyond the scope of the current work. We modeled the following regimens: 300/300, 600/600, 300/300/500, 400/400/400, and 300/300/300/300 (all in mg). We included the 300/300 dosage regimen because this has been suggested as an average lowest effective dosage regimen [2]. Although this varies for each patient, it is a good starting value for minimum effective dose. The 300/300/500 dosage regimen simulates two low doses with breakfast and lunch and a slightly higher dosage with dinner to go through the night. Figure 5 show the results of several of these simulations. Table 2 shows the maximum and average concentration values of these dosage regimens.

All of the dosage regimens modeled show both a lower peak concentration and average concentration than the pathological dosage. We noticed several interesting aspects when evaluating these simulations. First, fewer doses per day give a higher peak concentration at constant daily dosage. For example, the 600/600 regimen (not shown) has a peak concentration of 1.141 mEq/mL. The 400/400/400 regimen, however, has a peak concentration of 1.019 mEq/mL. Second, higher peak concentrations do not necessarily mean a higher average concentration. The data from the three 1200 mg/day dosages (300/300/300/300, 400/400/400, and 600/600) show that predicting average fetus concentration from total dosage, number of doses, or peak fetus concentration can be difficult or nonintuitive.

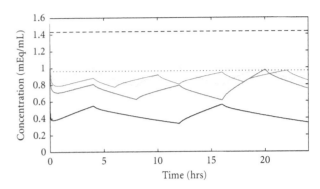

--- Maximum fetal concentration value from pathological dosage
...... Average fetal concentration value from pathological dosage
——— 300 mg/300 mg/500 mg dosage regime
    400 mg/400 mg/400 mg dosage regime
——— 300 mg/300 mg/300 mg/300 mg dosage regime
——— 300 mg/300 mg dosage regime

FIGURE 5: Model-predicted reduced risk dosage regimens. The maximum and average fetus concentrations from the 450/900 dosage regimen are plotted along with two new dosage regimens. The values for average and peak concentrations are listed in Table 2.

TABLE 2: Average and maximum fetal concentrations (mEq/mL) for suggested dosage regimens compared with the pathological case. All dosages are over a 24 hour period.

Dosage regimen	Average fetal concentration (mEq/mL)	Maximum fetal concentration (mEq/mL)
450 mg/900 mg (pathological)	0.965	1.434
300 mg/300 mg/500 mg	0.796	1.021
300 mg/300 mg	0.419	0.570
300 mg/300 mg/300 mg/300 mg	0.867	0.960
400 mg/400 mg/400 mg	0.860	1.019
600 mg/600 mg	0.886	1.141

In order to find a recommended maximum reduced risk regimen, we need to consider both the peak and average concentrations. All of the dosage regimens displayed in Figure 5 show average and peak concentrations below the pathological dosage; therefore, they are all acceptable from a quantitative viewpoint. The "best" recommended dosage regimens to reduce risk are the 300/300/300/300 and 400/400/400 regimens. The 300/300/300/300 regimen is the best quantitatively. The average concentration is only slightly less than the pathological dosage, but no peak goes above the pathological dosage average. The downfall of this dosage regimen, however, is that four doses per day may be difficult for patients to reasonably take. For compliant patients who are concerned with the welfare of the child and need high lithium dosages, the 300/300/300/300 dosage regimen is the best maximum regimen. For any other patient, a dosage regimen that allows for taking the drug with meals will be much more convenient and likely to succeed in a clinical setting. The best maximum regimen for most patients will therefore be the 400/400/400 dosage regimen. This regimen keeps the average concentration slightly lower than the 300/300/300/300 regimen, and the peaks in the concentration profile go slightly above the Pathological Dosage average concentration. However, since only the peaks are higher than the pathological dosage average concentration, there should still be reduced risk associated with this dosing regimen. It should be noted that this best dosage regimen was determined from the results of a simulation which has not been validated by animal or clinical trials; furthermore the treatment of patients deals with individuals. Because individuals respond to drugs differently and have many different medical histories, the optimum dose (and even the maximum safe dose) will vary with individual patients. The results of this study should therefore be taken as a guide to safely treat patients rather than universal canon.

4. Conclusion

This model has taken the first steps toward predicting the maximum acceptable lithium dosage regimen for pregnant bipolar women. Based on our simulation results and on clinical patient compliance, we recommend a maximum dosage regimen of three doses of 400 mg lithium evenly spaced over a 24-hour period. It is important to note that the maximum dosages recommended from the model are not necessarily nonpathological. These recommended dose regimens simply lower the average and peak values below concentrations known to be pathological. It is still important to take the lowest effective dosage of lithium to minimize the risk of birth defects. Hopefully, this paper has shed some light on what the maximum doses in a dosage regimen should look like to lower the risk of birth defects. Future research to improve the model could include determination of the fetal tissue to plasma lithium equilibrium ratio and collecting data on "safe" dosages of lithium that do not cause birth defects.

Authors' Contribution

The authors Scott Horton, Amalie Tuerk, Daniel Cook contributed equally to this work.

Acknowledgment

Amalie Tuerk was supported by a National Science Foundation Graduate Research Fellowship (Grant No. 0750966).

References

[1] National Institute of Mental Health, "Bipolar Disorder," NIH Publication 09-3679, U.S. Department of Heath and Human Services, National Institutes of Health, 2009.

[2] C. Kozma, "Neonatal toxicity and transient neurodevelopmental deficits following prenatal exposure to lithium: another clinical report and a review of the literature," *American Journal of Medical Genetics*, vol. 132, no. 4, pp. 441–444, 2005.

[3] Lexi-Comp Online, *Formulary and Drug Therapy Guide: Lithium*, Lexi-Comp, Hudson, Ohio, USA, 2011.

[4] L. D. Blake, D. N. Lucas, K. Aziz, A. Castello-Cortes, and P. N. Robinson, "Lithium toxicity and the parturient: case report and literature review," *International Journal of Obstetric Anesthesia*, vol. 17, no. 2, pp. 164–169, 2008.

[5] H. Bendz, S. Schön, P. O. Attman, and M. Aurell, "Renal failure occurs in chronic lithium treatment but is uncommon," *Kidney International*, vol. 77, no. 3, pp. 219–224, 2010.

[6] S. T. Blackburn, *Maternal, Fetal, & Neonatal Physiology: A Clinical Perspective*, Elsevier Saunders, St. Louis, Mo, USA, 2nd edition, 2007.

[7] F. G. Cunningham, K. J. Leveno, S. Bloom, J. C. Hauth, D. Rouse, and C. Spong, *Williams Obstetrics*, McGraw-Hill, New York, NY, USA, 23rd edition, 2009.

[8] U.S. National Library of Medicine. Lithobid (lithium carbonate) tablet, film coated, extended release [Internet]. Daily Med: Current Medication Information, 2011, http://dailymed.nlm.nih.gov/dailymed/lookup.cfm?setid=ea4 ece7f-e81f-48de-b262-577db5b6fe6c.

[9] K. B. Bischoff, R. L. Dedrick, D. S. Zaharko, and J. A. Longstreth, "Methotrexate pharmacokinetics," *Journal of Pharmaceutical Sciences*, vol. 60, no. 8, pp. 1128–1133, 1971.

[10] C. Timchalk, R. J. Nolan, A. L. Mendrala, D. A. Dittenber, K. A. Brzak, and J. L. Mattsson, "A physiologically based pharmacokinetic and pharmacodynamic (PBPK/PD) model for the organophosphate insecticide chlorpyrifos in rats and humans," *Toxicological Sciences*, vol. 66, no. 1, pp. 34–53, 2002.

[11] R. Tardif, G. Charest-Tardif, J. Brodeur, and K. Krishnan, "Physiologically based pharmacokinetic modeling of a ternary mixture of alkyl benzenes in rats and humans," *Toxicology and Applied Pharmacology*, vol. 144, no. 1, pp. 120–134, 1997.

[12] H. M. Jones, I. B. Gardner, and K. J. Watson, "Modelling and PBPK simulation in drug discovery," *AAPS Journal*, vol. 11, no. 1, pp. 155–166, 2009.

[13] K. B. Bischoff, R. L. Dedrick, and D. S. Zaharko, "Preliminary model for methotrexate pharmacokinetics," *Journal of Pharmaceutical Sciences*, vol. 59, no. 2, pp. 149–154, 1970.

[14] A. Schoutens, J. Arlet, J. W. M. Gardeniers, and S. P. F. Hughes, Eds., *Bone Circulation and Vascularization in Normal and Pathlogical Conditions*, vol. 247 of *NATO Advanced Science Institutes Series A: Life Sciences*, Springer, 1st edition, 1993.

[15] "The skeletal system," in *Oxford Textbook of Medicine*, D. J. Weatherall, J. G. G. Ledingham, and D. A. Warrell, Eds., vol. 3, p. 3066, Oxford University Press, New York, NY, USA, 1996.

[16] B. Davies and T. Morris, "Physiological parameters in laboratory animals and humans," *Pharmaceutical Research*, vol. 10, no. 7, pp. 1093–1095, 1993.

3

Application of an Integrative Computational Framework in Trancriptomic Data of Atherosclerotic Mice Suggests Numerous Molecular Players

Olga Papadodima,[1] Allan Sirsjö,[2] Fragiskos N. Kolisis,[3] and Aristotelis Chatziioannou[1]

[1] Metabolic Engineering and Bioinformatics Program, Institute of Biological Research and Biotechnology, National Hellenic Research Foundation, 48 Vas. Constantinou Avenue, 11635 Athens, Greece
[2] Division of Clinical Medicine, School of Health and Medical Sciences, Örebro University, Örebro SE-701 82, Sweden
[3] Biotechnology Laboratory, School of Chemical Engineering, Zografou Campus, National Technical University of Athens, 15780 Athens, Greece

Correspondence should be addressed to Allan Sirsjö, allan.sirsjo@oru.se and Aristotelis Chatziioannou, achatzi@eie.gr

Academic Editor: Konstantina Nikita

Atherosclerosis is a multifactorial disease involving a lot of genes and proteins recruited throughout its manifestation. The present study aims to exploit bioinformatic tools in order to analyze microarray data of atherosclerotic aortic lesions of ApoE knockout mice, a model widely used in atherosclerosis research. In particular, a dynamic analysis was performed among young and aged animals, resulting in a list of 852 significantly altered genes. Pathway analysis indicated alterations in critical cellular processes related to cell communication and signal transduction, immune response, lipid transport, and metabolism. Cluster analysis partitioned the significantly differentiated genes in three major clusters of similar expression profile. Promoter analysis applied to functional related groups of the same cluster revealed shared putative cis-elements potentially contributing to a common regulatory mechanism. Finally, by reverse engineering the functional relevance of differentially expressed genes with specific cellular pathways, putative genes acting as hubs, were identified, linking functionally disparate cellular processes in the context of traditional molecular description.

1. Introduction

Atherosclerosis is the leading pathological contributor to cardiovascular morbidity and mortality worldwide, characterized by the progressive accumulation of lipid and fibrous depositions in the vessel wall of medium-sized and large arteries. Although it has traditionally been viewed as simple deposition of lipids within the vessel wall, it is now assumed that atherosclerosis is a multifactorial disease that involves several genes and proteins, activated during its genesis, progress, and phenotypic manifestation. During atherogenesis, a complex endothelial activation and dysfunction induced by elevated and modified low-density lipoproteins and many other factors leads to a compensatory inflammatory response [1]. Current evidence supports a central role for inflammation, in all phases of the atherosclerotic process. Substantial biological data implicate inflammatory pathways in early atherogenesis, in the progression of lesions, and finally in the thrombotic complications of this disease [2].

Clinical investigations, population studies, and cell culture experiments have provided important clues to the pathogenesis of atherosclerosis. However, the use of animal models has had a crucial contribution in the research of the atherosclerotic course. Atherosclerosis will not be developed in laboratory mice under normal conditions. However, targeted deletion of the gene for Apolipoprotein E (ApoE knockout mice) leads to severe hypercholesterolemia

Application of an Integrative Computational Framework in Trancriptomic Data of Atherosclerotic Mice
Suggests Numerous Molecular Players

17

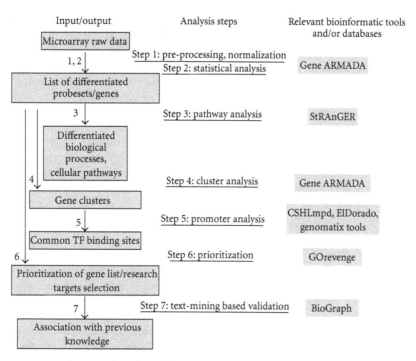

FIGURE 1: Schematic representation of the proposed workflow. Arrows depict the various analysis steps. The bioinformatic tools and databases used for the implementation of each step are also shown.

and spontaneous atherosclerosis [3]. For this reason, ApoE deficient mice are widely used to study atherosclerosis [4]. ApoE is a ligand for receptors that clear chylomicrons and very low-density lipoprotein remnants. Furthermore, a number of population studies suggest that ApoE genotype predicts the risk of developing atherosclerosis and related diseases [5].

In this study, we propose a framework for efficient translational bioinformatic analysis showcased on a microarray dataset concerning biological specimen from ApoE knockout mice. Gene expression data of wild type and ApoE knockout 6-, 32-, and 78-week-old mice have been utilized. This dataset was previously presented in a detailed work studying atherosclerosis and inflammatory pathways during aging [6]. The proposed workflow comprises seven basic steps (Figure 1): raw data pre-processing and normalization, statistical selection, pathway analysis, clustering, promoter analysis, gene list prioritization, exploiting network centrality criteria enabling identification of interesting research targets, and finally intelligent text-mining based validation of the selected molecular targets from the broader biomedical literature. Aim here is to combine several bioinformatic tools, in a unique, generic, computational workflow, appropriate for batch processing, able to confer reliable functional knowledge, regarding different aspects of the biological mechanism investigated, in order to highlight critical, underlying, molecular determinants governing it. Besides an algorithmic proposition, the workflow presented here is currently in the phase of implementation, regarding the seamless integration of its constituent modules, exploiting

the web service technology [6], accessible through a user-friendly web application, and enabling automated extraction of consolidated biological knowledge, in the form of concrete functional scenario, from high-volume data omic datasets. Nowadays, several tools are available for the implementation of each analysis step. For instance, Bioconductor [7] represents one of the richest repositories of statistical algorithms and has become, by all means, a standard for microarray data analysis but its command line interface limits its usability to many, wet-lab oriented, biological experts. To overcome this limitation, user friendly software packages for normalization, statistical analysis, and visualization of microarray expression data have been developed, like Gene ARMADA [8] and FlexArray [9]. Regarding pathway analysis, multiple software tools are exploiting ontological vocabularies to target the issue of detecting over-represented terms in microarray datasets, aiming to indicate possibly altered molecular processes [10–14]. Regarding promoter analysis, it remains one of the most intricate issues regarding the efficient mining of gene lists derived from transcriptomic experiments. Different promoter sequence databases [15, 16] and bioinformatic tools [17, 18] have been developed but still elucidation of gene transcription regulating networks remains a great challenge. The derivation of functional information regarding gene function, exploiting semantic similarity criteria, represents a promising, yet fuzzy and increasingly bewildering in its interpretation, approach. Several criteria and measures have been proposed [19], however it is GOrevenge [20], which instead of focusing in the neighboring genes, it highlights linker genes, associated with discrete cellular functions (distant in terms of semantic similarity). Finally BioGraph [21] is a data integration and data mining platform for the exploration and discovery of biomedical information. The platform offers prioritizations of putative disease genes, supported by functional hypotheses. BioGraph can retrospectively confirm recently discovered disease genes and identify potential susceptibility genes, without requiring prior domain knowledge, outperforming from other text-mining applications in the field of biomedicine. In the present analysis we show that integration of different analysis snapshots, as obtained through bioinformatic analyses, results in reliable, prioritized and informative lists of differentiated genes, and/or molecular pathways.

2. Materials and Methods

2.1. Microarray Data. The mouse dataset used is the GSE 10000, available at Gene Expression Omnibus (GEO) database. Microarrays were prepared following MIAME guidelines, as described in [22]. Briefly, RNA from aortic tissue of ApoE knockout and wild type animals was hybridized on Affymetrix 430 2.0 Arrays. Three different ages were studied: 6, 32, and 78 weeks.

2.2. Microarray Data Analysis and Statistical Analysis. Microarray data analysis was performed in Gene ARMADA [8]. Briefly, background correction was performed employing its gcRMA method followed by Quantile Normalization. Data were log2 transformed to comply with the normality assumption. Differentially expressed genes in at least one among all the experimental conditions were identified using Gene ARMADA, by performing 1-way ANOVA on log2 transformed fold changes. The resulting gene list was obtained by setting the P value threshold to 0.01, the False Discovery Rate (FDR) threshold to 0.05 and by removing genes that presented a fold change below |1|, in log2 scale, in all conditions.

2.3. Prioritized Pathway/Functional Analysis. Statistical enrichment analysis was performed using StRAnGER [8], in order to highlight biological processes including statistically significant numbers of the ANOVA derived genes. In order to expand our knowledge regarding the functional implication of genes in various cellular processes, prioritizing them according to their centrality, we used the online tool GOrevenge [20] with the following settings: Aspect: BP (Biological Process), Distance: Resnik, Algorithm: BubbleGene, and Relaxation: 0.15.

2.4. Cluster and Promoter Analysis. The list derived from ANOVA was subjected to hierarchical clustering (linkage method: Average, distance: Cosine) in Gene ARMADA. Promoter sequences from −700 to +300, relative to transcription start site, were downloaded for mouse and human from Cold Spring Harbor Laboratory Mammalian Promoter Database (CSHLmpd) [16]. In the cases that alternative promoters were given for the same gene, we selected the one defined as the "best" at [16]. For promoters that we

could not detect in this database, we additionally searched the ElDorado database [15]. In the case of genes with multiple promoters supported by different transcripts, we selected the one corresponding to the Reference Sequence of NCBI. To analyze each promoter set for common TF binding sites, we used the MatInspector software [18]. The parameters used were as follows: Library version: Matrix Library 8.0, Matrix group: Vertebrates, Transcription Factor sites common to: 85% of input sequences, Core similarity: 0.75, Matrix similarity: Optimized, and P value cut-off was set at 0.01. Among the identified TF sites only those that were present in both species were considered.

3. Results

3.1. Statistically Significant Differentiated Genes. To obtain the aortic gene expression profile of ApoE deficient mice in 6-, 32-, and 78-week-old mice we analyzed the GSE 10000 dataset, containing expression data of aortic tissue from wild type and ApoE knockout mice. Specifically, in order to identify significant alterations among all three tested ages, 1-way ANOVA was applied to expression fold changes between expression in ApoE knockout and wild type animals (P value <0.01 and FDR <0.05) coupled with further filtering on fold change (> |1| in at least one condition in log2 scale). A list of 1033 significantly differentiated probesets was obtained (Supplementary Table 1; see supplementary material available online at doi:10.1155/2012/453513), depicted per time point using a volcano plot representation (Figure 2). These 1033 probesets correspond to 852 annotated genes. It is characteristic that in 6 weeks old mice the number of significantly altered genes is very limited, in 32 weeks old mice the majority of differentiated genes are upregulated, while in 78 weeks old mice we have the greater number of differentiated genes.

3.2. Pathway Analysis. For the scope of gaining further insight concerning the biological functionalities of gene expression alterations in a more systematic way, the list of 852 significantly differentiated genes yielded from ANOVA was subjected to statistical enrichment analysis using StRAnGER, exploiting GO terms and Kegg pathways for the task of the functional annotation of the interrogated genes. GO-based analysis, focused on the categories of "Biological Process" with a hypergeometric P value <0.001, suggested several processes as possibly differentiated, which are presented in Table 1. A lot of central molecular mechanisms emerge as altered, as indicated by the GO categories listed in Table 1, like differentiation, proliferation (inferred by cell cycle and cell division GO terms), apoptosis, cell adhesion, signal transduction, and immune response. Kegg pathway-based analysis also indicates alterations in cytokine signaling, cell adhesion, and signal transduction (Supplementary Table 2). It is important to note that in conformity to the well established relationship of atherosclerosis and inflammation, the majority (29 out of 32) of the genes under the category "immune response" are upregulated suggesting a stimulation of the immunological mechanisms (Table 2).

Application of an Integrative Computational Framework in Trancriptomic Data of Atherosclerotic Mice
Suggests Numerous Molecular Players

19

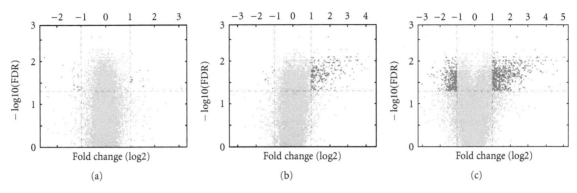

(a) (b) (c)

FIGURE 2: Volcano plots of the gene list as yielded by ANOVA. Each panel represents filtered and normalized data from each experimental condition (3, 6, and 78 weeks old mice). The horizontal axes depict the fold change ratio between ApoE deficient and wild type mice, for each age in log2 scale, while the vertical axes represent statistical significance by depicting the −log10 (FDR).

TABLE 1: GO-analysis. The list of 852 significantly altered genes was submitted to GO analysis elucidating over-represented GO terms. GOT P value represents the hypergeometric test P value score for each GO term. Enrichment represents the ratio of the number of times a GO term occurs in the 852 gene list to the number of times this GO term exists in the list of the Affymetrix 430 2.0 array.

GO annotation	GOT P value	Enrichment
Ion transport	0.00000000003	33/498
Signal transduction	0.00000000004	44/803
Cell differentiation	0.00000000005	36/480
Immune response	0.00000000005	32/250
Metabolic process	0.00000000007	38/542
Cell adhesion	0.00000000011	36/387
Protein amino acid phosphorylation	0.00000000059	32/497
Multicellular organismal development	0.00000000128	41/770
Proteolysis	0.00000000690	25/358
Apoptosis	0.00000010814	24/383
Lipid metabolic process	0.00000328813	15/212
Protein transport	0.00003352383	22/465
G-protein coupled receptor signaling	0.00028681297	19/436
Oxidation reduction	0.00034119987	21/510
Cell cycle	0.00043684087	18/417
Cell division	0.00050194998	12/231

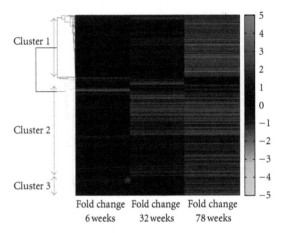

FIGURE 3: Hierarchical clustering of the 1033 statistically significant differentiated probesets. Fold changes between the gene expressions in ApoE knockout as compared to age-matched wild type mice are grouped in three major clusters.

3.3. Cluster Analysis.

3.3. Cluster Analysis. In order to identify groups of genes presenting similar expression and possibly comprising regulated "waves" of transcription, the list of 1033 significantly differentiated probesets was subjected to hierarchical clustering (Figure 3). Three major clusters can be distinguished: the first one (323 probesets) contains transcripts downregulated in 78 week old mice, while their expression remains close to the control (wild type) level at 6 and 32 weeks. The second cluster (526 probesets) groups genes which are upregulated at 32 weeks and their expression at ApoE knockout mice remains at high levels, as compared to wild type, also at 78 weeks. The third cluster (110 probesets) groups genes whose expression is late upregulated at 78 week old ApoE knockout, as compared to age-matched wild type mice.

Based on these three major clusters, we performed GO-analysis to the genes of each cluster separately. Genes under cluster 1 are functionally connected to processes involved in cell differentiation, adhesion, and signal transduction. Cluster 2 contains the greatest number of genes, which are related mainly to mechanisms involved in immune and inflammatory response as well as lipid metabolism. These processes emerge as significantly altered specifically in the case of cluster 2. Cluster 2 genes are also connected to key cellular processes like signal transduction, apoptosis, cell cycle, and differentiation. Cluster 3 genes are mainly related to mechanisms concerning gene transcription.

3.4. Promoter Analysis. Next, we focused our analysis on small groups of genes presenting similar expression profile, as indicated by cluster analysis, and also being functional relevant, as suggested by GO analysis. In order to investigate

TABLE 2: Expression of genes under the GO term immune response. Values in the three last columns depict fold changes between ApoE knockout and age-matched wild type mice in log2 scale. The majority of genes at 32 and 78 weeks are upregulated.

Symbol	Description	6 weeks	32 weeks	78 weeks
Ccl6	Chemokine (C-C motif) ligand 6	−0.17	2.25	2.23
Cd74	CD74 antigen (invariant polypeptide of major histocompatibility complex, class II antigen-associated)	0.29	1.56	1.43
C1qb	Complement component 1, q subcomponent, beta polypeptide	−0.23	2.28	2.43
H2-Ab1	Histocompatibility 2, class II antigen A, beta 1	−0.25	1.94	2.77
C1qa	Complement component 1, q subcomponent, a polypeptide	−0.08	1.98	2.18
Tlr2	Toll-like receptor 2	0.14	0.99	1.38
Ccl7	Chemokine (C-C motif) ligand 7	−0.98	1.59	4.42
C4b	Complement component 4B (Childo blood group)	0.23	1.2	1.74
Cblb	Casitas B-lineage lymphoma b	0.2	0.34	1.36
Fcgr2b	Fc receptor, IgG, low affinity IIb	−0.1	1.93	2.19
Cd300lb	CD300 antigen like family member B	−0.46	2.83	2.87
Susd2	Sushi domain containing 2	0.22	−0.08	−1.07
Ccl8	Chemokine (C-C motif) ligand 8	0.33	2.92	3.01
Cd14	CD14 antigen	−0.14	1.52	2.44
Fcgr1	Fc receptor, IgG, high affinity I	−0.05	1.82	2.03
Cadm1	Cell adhesion molecule 1	−0.57	1.5	2.01
C2	Complement component 2 (within H-2S)	−0.81	1.02	−0.03
Clec7a	C-type lectin domain family 7, member a	0.15	3.52	3.86
Procr	Protein C receptor, endothelial	−0.25	0.77	1.02
C1qc	Complement component 1, q subcomponent, C chain	−0.22	2.22	2.25
Ccl19	Chemokine (C-C motif) ligand 19	−0.71	1.07	1.64
Enpp3	Ectonucleotide pyrophosphatase/phosphodiesterase 3	0.24	−0.00	−1.28
Cx3cl1	Chemokine (C-X3-C motif) ligand 1	0.18	1.71	1.87
Ccl9	Chemokine (C-C motif) ligand 9	−0.46	1.74	2.19
H2-Eb1	Histocompatibility 2, class II antigen E beta	0.19	1.62	2.17
H2-Aa	Histocompatibility 2, class II antigen A, alpha	0.95	2.39	2.34
Cxcl12	Chemokine (C-X-C motif) ligand 12	−0.34	1.1	1.95
Enpp1	Ectonucleotide pyrophosphatase/phosphodiesterase 1	0.14	0.37	1.08
Rnf19b	Ring finger protein 19B	−0.29	0.73	2.58
Prg4	Proteoglycan 4	0.16	3.33	3.99
Irf8	Interferon regulatory factor 8	0.28	1.9	2.61
Cxcl1	Chemokine (C-X-C motif) ligand 1	−0.46	1.77	2.66

whether there are common regulatory transcriptional mechanisms in such groups of genes, we performed a representative promoter analysis in genes of cluster 2 belonging to the GO category of "immune response" either "inflammatory response." We selected these categories because they appear as significantly altered, scoring at the top of GO analysis prioritization list. We combined the genes of these two groups, resulting at a total number of 36 genes in both categories, because they are functionally relevant, as they represent genes involved in immunological mechanisms. In order to find common putative transcription factor (TF) binding sites in at least a subset of this group, proximal promoter sequences from both mouse and human genomes were extracted from available databases and analyzed as described in Methods. Only common TF binding sites

among the two species were considered. Table 3 summarizes statistically significant TF motif families common in at least 80% of promoter sequences, sorted in descending order in terms of statistical significance. The P values, representing the probability to obtain a greater or equal number of sequences with a match in a random sample of the same size as the input sequence set, are precalculated for each binding site and depend on its definition.

We then examined whether among the significantly differentiated genes we could identify TFs possibly recognizing binding sites presented at Table 3 and thus being involved in the regulation of the relevant genes. Interestingly, among the upregulated genes there are Klf4 and Irf8 TFs, whose binding sites are found at 100% and 86% of the tested promoters, respectively. In particular, Klf4 shows an increased expression

Application of an Integrative Computational Framework in Trancriptomic Data of Atherosclerotic Mice
Suggests Numerous Molecular Players

21

TABLE 3: Common TF motif families in the promoters of 36 genes belonging to cluster 2 and to the categories "immune response" and "inflammatory response." The percentage column depicts the percentage of genes whose promoters have at least one match with the respective motif family. Percentages and P value calculations are based on mouse promoters.

Family	Description	P value	%
V$CTCF	CTCF and BORIS gene family	0.00000185	86
V$MZF1	Myeloid zinc finger 1 factors	0.00000878	89
V$EGRF	EGR/nerve growth factor induced protein C and related factors	0.00011981	86
V$SRFF	Serum response element binding factor	0.00012387	83
V$PLAG	Pleomorphic adenoma gene	0.00015650	86
V$GREF	Glucocorticoid responsive elements	0.00016410	92
V$KLFS	Krueppel like transcription factors	0.00024104	100
V$GLIF	GLI zinc finger family	0.00170920	81
V$STAT	Signal transducer and activator of transcription	0.00177177	92
V$PAX5	PAX-2/5/8 binding sites	0.00246076	89
V$E2FF	E2F-myc activator/cell cycle regulator	0.00400401	86
V$XBBF	X-box binding factors	0.00470139	89
V$GATA	GATA binding factors	0.00499105	94
V$PAX6	PAX-4/PAX-6 paired domain binding sites	0.00504198	89
V$ETSF	Human and murine ETS1 factors	0.00646776	100
V$GCMF	Chorion-specific TFs with a GCM DNA binding domain	0.00921126	83
V$HEAT	Heat shock factors	0.01639280	92
V$RXRF	RXR heterodimer binding sites	0.01834270	97
V$FKHD	Fork head domain factors	0.02095320	94
V$IRFF	Interferon regulatory factors	0.02221250	86
V$HAND	Twist subfamily of class B bHLH transcription factors	0.03199970	94
V$ABDB	Abdominal-B type homeodomain transcription factors	0.04170260	89

at ApoE knockout mice as compared to age-matched wild type both at 36 and 78 weeks (0.62 and 1 fold increase, in log2 scale, resp.) while in 6 weeks the expression of KLf4 is moderately decreased as compared to wild type (-0.46, log2 scale). The expression of Irf8 at ApoE knockout mice is significantly increased both at 36 and 78 weeks (1.9 and 2.61 fold increase, in log2 scale, resp.), while at 6 weeks it remains at the wild type levels. Thus the upregulation of these factors could partially account for the observed upregulation of the immune-related group of genes.

3.5. Identification of Candidate Hub-Genes. In order to expand our knowledge regarding which genes have critical role, taking into consideration their centrality as described in the GO tree, we used the online tool GOrevenge [20]. The list of 852 differentiated genes was submitted to GOrevenge and the analysis was performed based on GO annotations for *Mus musculus* as described in materials and methods section. The derived list of genes, containing candidate linker genes, that is genes participating in many different cellular processes, was partitioned to include only the genes that have been also identified, as statistically significantly differentiated. The derived list (Table 4) contains genes that were identified as significant both by ANOVA and by GOrevenge analysis. The list of genes is prioritized according to the centrality of each gene, as it is reflected by the number

of GO biological processes related terms remaining after GOrevenge pruning [20]. Significant molecules involved in signaling and developmental mechanisms emerge as central players. In order to evaluate the relation of these genes with atherosclerosis, which is a principle phenotypic characteristic of ApoE knockout mice, we used the BioGraph platform [21] which utilizes data mining algorithms that exploit textual terms to build a network of heterogeneous relations which link genes with a specific concept (such as genes, proteins, diseases as described in [21]). The resultant BioGraph network describes associations in *Homo sapiens*. By setting atherosclerosis as concept, the relation of each gene with atherosclerosis was assessed and the top 20 genes obtained by GOrevenge were prioritized as shown in Table 5 by BioGraph algorithm. The genes are prioritized according to their score which is a statistical enrichment measure of the relevance of each gene with the inquired context (here specified as atherosclerosis) to the total relations (references) of the gene in the universe of terms. In this way, the user can derive which of its genes are already associated and in what extent with a given disease or generally biological term, and which of them represent novel findings with respect to the investigated pathological phenotype. Since the list of gene symbols used as input to BioGraph represent *Mus musculus* genes, while BioGraph refers to *Homo sapiens* genes, some of them could have different symbol in each species. In the case that a gene symbol was not recognized by BioGraph, we searched the NCBI HomoloGene database [23] in order to find the homologous gene in *Homo sapiens* (e.g., FOXF1 of Table 5 corresponds to Foxf1a of Table 4).

4. Discussion

In this study, we presented a detailed, multi-stage, translational bioinformatic analysis of ApoE knockout mice, exploiting different methods in order to identify critical altered molecular mechanisms and important central players. Our approach was to apply a generic computational framework, which exploits rigorous statistical or computational measures at every analytical step, for the efficient systems level interpretation of the results of ApoE dataset. The workflow proposed here integrates various software products, in a unified translational pipeline, able to cope with versatile, high-volume investigation tasks, and at the same time provide a reliable systemic interpretation for the biological mechanism studied. In this way, a powerful translational backbone is set, which connects the wet-lab part with the theoretical knowledge for the biological problem interrogated, as rescued in molecular databases, controlled ontological vocabularies or the literature. The workflow presented in this study, currently in the phase of implementation as regards to its software components integration, represents an efficient and highly innovative effort, either in terms of speed of analytical performance, as well as real biological value of the results. This is so because it provides results which are qualified from a composite framework that combines ideally both individual and group quality measures, together with an insightful comprehension of the underlying topological networks, actively involved in the mechanism studied. The correlation of the results of the molecular analysis with literature-derived associations manages to highlight and propose promising, novel candidates that have not been studied in the context of the given pathology. They could thus represent ideal targets for further biological experimentation. Maximizing the total information gain encompassing all analytical steps of the proposed workflow represents a critical parameter regarding the implementation of the web application. However as the derivation of automated statistical thresholds for such high-volume data processing in an unsupervised manner both in terms of performance and computational speed is a very challenging task, this still remains an open issue for extensive research work and testing, representing an important point for future work.

Computational technologies are complementary to conventional "wet lab" gene discovery technologies in that they can support the prioritization and comprehension of high-volume molecular data (i.e., omic datasets from a microarray or novel sequencing technologies, associated regions from genome wide association or linkage studies) enabling the efficient selection of the top candidates, under a range of criteria, for further study. In recent years, there are popular tools and environments in the scientific computing realm (data-mining, artificial intelligence, hyper-computing), like the Taverna workflow manager [24] or

the RapidMiner solution, formerly known as YALE [25], which enable efficient workflow integration and deployment, exploiting versatile web service repositories, containing hundreds of operators implementing various analytical tasks. Especially Taverna workflow manager, through myExperiment (http://www.myexperiment.org) [26] and Biocatalogue (http://www.biocatalogue.org) [27], integrates an impressive number of workflows and web services all accessible through Taverna, for a very wide range of disparate bioinformatics tasks. However, to the best of our knowledge, the workflow showcased in this work addresses in a sequential, unsupervised fashion disparate tasks enabling and empowering decisively the translational procedure, in a completely innovative yet efficient way.

Applying the proposed workflow to a dataset from ApoE knockout and wild type mice, it was shown that the gene expression profile in atherosclerotic plaques containing arteries of ApoE knockout mice is profoundly different from wild type. Specifically, 852 genes were found as differentially expressed and the majority of them appear after the age of 32 weeks. The indicated altered processes, as revealed by ontology-based enrichment analysis, include adhesion and signal transduction, differentiation, apoptosis, and immune response, reflecting the cellular and molecular complexity of atherosclerosis and the cross-talk of endothelial and immune cells in aortic lesions. Cluster analysis revealed three major groups of genes with similar expression profiles, which were further analyzed, in order to find functional (GO-based) subgroups in each cluster. In agreement with the notion that atherosclerosis is an inflammatory disease [2], immune response and inflammation were the prominent categories indicated as significantly altered in the case of cluster 2, which contains genes upregulated both in 36- and 78-weeks-old mice. Promoter analysis of the genes under these categories revealed common binding elements that could contribute to a common transcriptional regulation. In particular, all of the tested genes (100%) contain cis-elements of the KLF and RXR family. The KLF family groups binding sites recognized by Krueppel like transcription factors (KLFs) [28] which are involved in many physiological and pathological processes, such as cell differentiation, proliferation, cell growth, and apoptosis during normal development or under different disease conditions. It is noteworthy that KLFs have been implicated in acute and chronic inflammatory disease states, such as atherosclerosis, diabetes, and airway inflammation [29]. It is important to note that despite the identification of KLF cis-acting elements, Klf4 TF was also found upregulated, suggesting that this factor could be involved in the regulation of the observed stimulation of the immune response related mechanisms. Klf4 has been found to regulate monocyte differentiation and to activate the macrophages to induce inflammation [30]. Furthermore, Klf4 regulates the proliferation and differentiation in vascular smooth muscle cells after injury to the vessel [31]. However, Klf4 seems to have an anti-inflammatory role in endothelial cells [28]. Regarding RXR family, it groups together motifs related to the receptors of retinoids, which are recognized by various heterodimers of retinoid X receptors (RXRs) and retinoic acid receptors. Interestingly, RXR has been reported to

Application of an Integrative Computational Framework in Trancriptomic Data of Atherosclerotic Mice
Suggests Numerous Molecular Players

23

TABLE 4: GOrevenge prioritization. The second column refers to the number of GO terms remaining after Gorevenge pruning, reflecting the centrality of each gene, while the third column refers to the original number of biological process category GO terms of each gene. Values in the three last columns depict fold changes between ApoE knockout and age-matched wild type mice in log2 scale. All presented genes are also differentially expressed. Top 20 genes are shown.

Gene symbol	Remaining GO terms	Original GO terms	6 weeks	32 weeks	78 weeks
Wnt5a	63	112	0.04	−0.38	−1.9
Fgfr2	56	92	0.15	−0.39	−1.05
P2rx7	38	73	0.02	0.61	1.84
Igf1	34	56	−0.23	0.77	1.39
Thbs1	30	42	−0.02	1.59	1.99
Ptgs2	30	37	−0.27	1.76	1.7
Foxf1a	28	34	0.09	−0.63	−1.41
Psen2	25	37	−0.4	0.23	1.02
Ccnd1	24	37	−0.01	0.67	1.07
Slc11a1	24	40	−0.16	1.29	1.9
Lyn	24	33	−0.01	1.07	2.26
Cebpa	24	30	−0.3	0.21	1.77
Tlr2	21	47	0.14	0.99	1.38
Osr1	21	33	0.09	0.08	−1.41
Hexb	19	23	−0.04	0.67	1
Col1a1	19	29	0.02	0.57	1.01
Socs3	19	27	0.58	1.59	3.19
Adam17	18	29	−0.22	0.27	1.07
Cd44	18	20	0.15	1.46	1.63
Cln8	18	26	0.37	0.85	1.71

TABLE 5: Prioritization of the genes presented in Table 4 by Bio-Graph exploiting unsupervised methodologies for the identification of causative disease-associated genes.

Gene symbol	Score
PTGS2	0.003895
CCND1	0.000566
CD44	0.000279
COL1A1	0.000194
ADAM17	0.000168
IGF1	0.000116
FGFR2	0.000116
THBS1	0.000097
LYN	0.000088
SOCS3	0.000087
CEBPA	0.000054
TLR2	0.000048
PSEN2	0.000045
P2RX7	0.000038
WNT5A	0.000035
lSLC11A1	0.000024
CLN8	0.000007
FOXF1	0.000006
HEXB	0.000005
OSR1	0.000002

regulate several genes related to metabolic homeostasis and inflammation [32]. RXR form heterodimers with many different nuclear receptors, PPARs, LXR, and FXR affecting different aspects of cholesterol metabolism in macrophages, something known to be important in the development of atherosclerosis [32]. In addition, among the identified putative TF binding sites there are interferon regulatory factors-related elements (IRFs) in the 86% of the promoters, as well as glucocorticoid responsive elements (GREs) in the 92% of the tested promoters. In agreement, Irf8, a transcription factor involved in modulation of immune response and as a central element in the IFN signaling cascade, was found significantly overexpressed, suggesting that Irf8, together with Klf4, could be involved in the upregulation of the immune response related genes. Regarding GREs, it is well known that glucocorticoid receptors play important roles in both physiological and pathological conditions involving immunity and inflammation and that they are involved in the pathology of cardiovascular diseases [33]. Finally, Table 4 includes several genes implicated to various aspects of the disease. It is noteworthy to mention Tlr2, a member of the Toll-like receptors family, which plays a fundamental role in activation of innate immunity [34]. Furthermore, the identification of Psen2 (presenillin 2), a gene implicated in Alzheimer's disease, as candidate hub gene is interesting because genes implicated in Alzheimer's have been reported to affect cholesterol or lipoprotein function and have also been implicated in atherosclerosis [35].

Concluding, this bioinformatic analysis of ApoE knock-out mice revealed critical altered cellular mechanisms governing atherosclerosis and indicated important molecular players that could be important targets for treatment of this complex disease.

References

[1] G. Stoll and M. Bendszus, "Inflammation and atherosclerosis: novel insights into plaque formation and destabilization," *Stroke*, vol. 37, no. 7, pp. 1923–1932, 2006.

[2] G. K. Hansson, "Mechanisms of disease: inflammation, atherosclerosis, and coronary artery disease," *The New England Journal of Medicine*, vol. 352, no. 16, pp. 1685–1695, 2005.

[3] S. H. Zhang, R. L. Reddick, J. A. Piedrahita, and N. Maeda, "Spontaneous hypercholesterolemia and arterial lesions in mice lacking apolipoprotein E," *Science*, vol. 258, no. 5081, pp. 468–471, 1992.

[4] R. W. Mahley and S. C. Rall Jr., "Apolipoprotein E: far more than a lipid transport protein," *Annual Review of Genomics and Human Genetics*, vol. 1, no. 2000, pp. 507–537, 2000.

[5] Y. Song, M. J. Stampfer, and S. Liu, "Meta-analysis: apolipoprotein E genotypes and risk for coronary heart disease," *Annals of Internal Medicine*, vol. 141, no. 2, pp. 137–147, 2004.

[6] E. Newcomer and G. Lomow, *Understanding SOA with Web Services*, Addison-Wesley, New York, NY, USA, 2004.

[7] R. C. Gentleman, V. J. Carey, D. M. Bates et al., "Bioconductor: open software development for computational biology and bioinformatics," *Genome Biology*, vol. 5, no. 10, article R80, 2004.

[8] A. Chatziioannou, P. Moulos, and F. N. Kolisis, "Gene ARMADA: an integrated multi-analysis platform for microarray data implemented in MATLAB," *BMC Bioinformatics*, vol. 10, article 354, 2009.

[9] M. M. Michal Blazejczyk and R. Nadon, "FlexArray: a statistical data analysis software for gene expression microarrays," Génome Québec, Montreal, Canada, 2007, http://genomequebec.mcgill.ca/FlexArray.

[10] G. Dennis Jr., B. T. Sherman, D. A. Hosack et al., "DAVID: database for annotation, visualization, and integrated discovery," *Genome Biology*, vol. 4, no. 5, article P3, 2003.

[11] D. A. Hosack, G. Dennis Jr., B. T. Sherman, H. C. Lane, and R. A. Lempicki, "Identifying biological themes within lists of genes with EASE," *Genome Biology*, vol. 4, no. 10, article R70, 2003.

[12] B. Zhang, S. Kirov, and J. Snoddy, "WebGestalt: an integrated system for exploring gene sets in various biological contexts," *Nucleic Acids Research*, vol. 33, no. 2, pp. W741–W748, 2005.

[13] Q. Zheng and X. J. Wang, "GOEAST: a web-based software toolkit for gene ontology enrichment analysis," *Nucleic Acids Research*, vol. 36, pp. W358–W363, 2008.

[14] A. A. Chatziioannou and P. Moulos, "Exploiting statistical methodologies and controlled vocabularies for prioritized functional analysis of genomic experiments: the StRAnGER web application," *Frontiers in Neuroscience*, vol. 5, article 8.

[15] Genomatix, http://www.genomatix.de.

[16] Z. Xuan, F. Zhao, J. Wang, G. Chen, and M. Q. Zhang, "Genome-wide promoter extraction and analysis in human, mouse, and rat," *Genome Biology*, vol. 6, no. 8, article R72, 2005.

[17] A. Essaghir, F. Toffalini, L. Knoops, A. Kallin, J. van Helden, and J. B. Demoulin, "Transcription factor regulation can be accurately predicted from the presence of target gene signatures in microarray gene expression data," *Nucleic Acids Research*, vol. 38, no. 11, article e120, 2010.

[18] K. Cartharius, K. Frech, K. Grote et al., "MatInspector and beyond: promoter analysis based on transcription factor binding sites," *Bioinformatics*, vol. 21, no. 13, pp. 2933–2942, 2005.

[19] C. Pesquita, D. Faria, A. O. Falcão, P. Lord, and F. M. Couto, "Semantic similarity in biomedical ontologies," *PLoS Computational Biology*, vol. 5, no. 7, Article ID e1000443, 2009.

[20] K. Moutselos, I. Maglogiannis, and A. Chatziioannou, "GOrevenge: a novel generic reverse engineering method for the identification of critical molecular players, through the use of ontologies," *IEEE Transactions on Biomedical Engineering*, vol. 58, no. 12, pp. 3522–3527, 2011.

[21] A. M. L. Liekens, J. de Knijf, W. Daelemans, B. Goethals, P. de Rijk, and J. Del-Favero, "Biograph: unsupervised biomedical knowledge discovery via automated hypothesis generation," *Genome Biology*, vol. 12, no. 6, article R57, 2011.

[22] R. Gräbner, K. Lötzer, S. Döpping et al., "Lymphotoxin β receptor signaling promotes tertiary lymphoid organogenesis in the aorta adventitia of aged ApoE-/- mice," *Journal of Experimental Medicine*, vol. 206, no. 1, pp. 233–248, 2009.

[23] HomoloGene, http://www.ncbi.nlm.nih.gov/homologene.

[24] T. Oinn, M. Addis, J. Ferris et al., "Taverna: a tool for the composition and enactment of bioinformatics workflows," *Bioinformatics*, vol. 20, no. 17, pp. 3045–3054, 2004.

[25] I. Mierswa, M. Scholz, R. Klinkenberg, M. Wurst, and T. Euler, "YALE: rapid prototyping for complex data mining tasks," in *Proceedings of the 12th ACM SIGKDD International Conference on Knowledge Discovery and Data Mining*, pp. 935–940, August 2006.

[26] C. A. Goble, S. Bhagat, S. Aleksejevs et al., "myExperiment: a repository and social network for the sharing of bioinformatics workflows," *Nucleic Acids Research*, vol. 38, no. 2, pp. W677–W682, 2010.

[27] J. Bhagat, F. Tanoh, E. Nzuobontane et al., "BioCatalogue: a universal catalogue of web services for the life sciences," *Nucleic Acids Research*, vol. 38, no. 2, pp. W689–W694, 2010.

[28] A. Hamik, Z. Lin, A. Kumar et al., "Kruppel-like factor 4 regulates endothelial inflammation," *The Journal of Biological Chemistry*, vol. 282, no. 18, pp. 13769–13779, 2007.

[29] Z. Cao, X. Sun, B. Icli, A. K. Wara, and M. W. Feinberg, "Role of Krüppel-like factors in leukocyte development, function, and disease," *Blood*, vol. 116, no. 22, pp. 4404–4414, 2010.

[30] J. K. Alder, R. W. Georgantas, R. L. Hildreth et al., "Kruppel-like factor 4 is essential for inflammatory monocyte differentiation in vivo," *Journal of Immunology*, vol. 180, no. 8, pp. 5645–5652, 2008.

[31] T. Yoshida, Q. Gan, and G. K. Owens, "Krüppel-like factor 4, Elk-1, and histone deacetylases cooperatively suppress smooth muscle cell differentiation markers in response to oxidized phospholipids," *American Journal of Physiology*, vol. 295, no. 5, pp. C1175–C1182, 2008.

[32] A. Nohara, J. Kobayashi, and H. Mabuchi, "Retinoid X receptor heterodimer variants and cardiovascular risk factors," *Journal of Atherosclerosis and Thrombosis*, vol. 16, no. 4, pp. 303–318, 2009.

[33] P. W. F. Hadoke, J. Iqbal, and B. R. Walker, "Therapeutic manipulation of glucocorticoid metabolism in cardiovascular disease," *British Journal of Pharmacology*, vol. 156, no. 5, pp. 689–712, 2009.

[34] S. Borrello, C. Nicolo, G. Delogu, F. Pandolfi, and F. Ria, "TLR2: a crossroads between infections and autoimmunity?" *International Journal of Immunopathology and Pharmacology*, vol. 24, no. 3, pp. 549–556.

[35] C. J. Carter, "Convergence of genes implicated in Alzheimer's disease on the cerebral cholesterol shuttle: APP, cholesterol, lipoproteins, and atherosclerosis," *Neurochemistry International*, vol. 50, no. 1, pp. 12–38, 2007.

MRMPath and MRMutation, Facilitating Discovery of Mass Transitions for Proteotypic Peptides in Biological Pathways Using a Bioinformatics Approach

Chiquito Crasto,[1] Chandrahas Narne,[2] Mikako Kawai,[3] Landon Wilson,[4] and Stephen Barnes[1,3,4,5]

[1] *Department of Genetics, University of Alabama at Birmingham, Birmingham, AL 35294, USA*

[2] *Department of Computer and Information Sciences, University of Alabama at Birmingham, Birmingham, AL 35294, USA*

[3] *Department of Pharmacology and Toxicology, University of Alabama at Birmingham, Birmingham, AL 35294, USA*

[4] *Centers for Nutrient-Gene Interactions, University of Alabama at Birmingham, Birmingham, AL 35294, USA*

[5] *Targeted Metabolomics and Proteomics Laboratory, University of Alabama at Birmingham, Birmingham, AL 35294, USA*

Correspondence should be addressed to Chiquito Crasto; chiquito@uab.edu

Academic Editor: Erchin Serpedin

Quantitative proteomics applications in mass spectrometry depend on the knowledge of the mass-to-charge ratio (m/z) values of proteotypic peptides for the proteins under study and their product ions. MRMPath and MRMutation, web-based bioinformatics software that are platform independent, facilitate the recovery of this information by biologists. MRMPath utilizes publicly available information related to biological pathways in the Kyoto Encyclopedia of Genes and Genomes (KEGG) database. All the proteins involved in pathways of interest are recovered and processed *in silico* to extract information relevant to quantitative mass spectrometry analysis. Peptides may also be subjected to automated BLAST analysis to determine whether they are proteotypic. MRMutation catalogs and makes available, following processing, known (mutant) variants of proteins from the current UniProtKB database. All these results, available via the web from well-maintained, public databases, are written to an Excel spreadsheet, which the user can download and save. MRMPath and MRMutation can be freely accessed. As a system that seeks to allow two or more resources to interoperate, MRMPath represents an advance in bioinformatics tool development. As a practical matter, the MRMPath automated approach represents significant time savings to researchers.

1. Introduction

A feature of the last two decades of biomedical research has been the generation of "–omics" data, a result of the pursuit of *discovery*. The introduction of soft ionization techniques for analysis of peptides and proteins by mass spectrometry in the 1980s [1, 2] led to a plethora of applications related to the identification of proteins from a wide variety of proteomes, from microorganisms to plants to mammals. These studies largely defined the *measurable* peptidome and by implication the proteome. They were also designed to "discover" significant protein changes, such as abundance and modifications. Because of the complications resulting from multiple hypotheses testing, however, detecting differences between treated and control samples has often met with limited success [3]. Concern has been expressed, for example, over the failure of different participating laboratories to systematically determine the same proteins that distinguish cancer patients from controls [4].

The next phase of proteomics is moving towards targeted, hypothesis-driven experiments. It integrates knowledge from previous proteomics discovery endeavors (2D-gel/peptide mass fingerprinting, MuDPIT, and GeLC-tandem mass spectrometry), microarray analysis (DNA, mRNA and microRNA chips, as well as DNA deep sequencing and RNA Seq), from the general scientific literature (particularly signal transduction pathways), or from the detailed study of one or several proteins in a known complex or a biological pathway. Figure 1

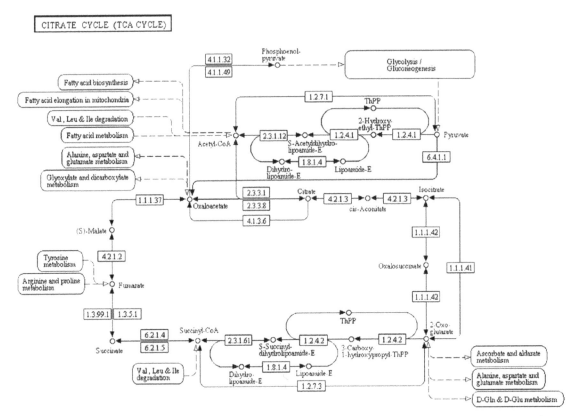

FIGURE 1: The figure represents the pathway for the citrate tricarboxylic acid cycle for humans as seen at the KEGG resource. The components, proteins, and reagents, highlighted in green, are those involved in the pathway for humans. The components not highlighted are part of the generic TCA cycle pathway. If another species is selected then only those components that contribute to the pathway are highlighted. The figure is a screen capture from the URL, http://www.genome.jp/kegg-bin/show_pathway?org_name=mmu&mapno=00062.

represents the tricarboxylic acid (TCA) cycle for humans as visualized through the KEGG (Kyoto Encyclopedia of Genes and Genomes: http://www.KEGG.jp/).

The development of targeted analysis of proteins has been facilitated by the use of multiple reaction ion monitoring (MRM), a mass spectrometry technique commonly used for the quantitative analysis of drugs and their metabolites [5]. If trypsin is used as the protease to cleave proteins into peptides, the resulting tryptic peptides, many of which consist of seven to 25 amino acids, would be suitable for analysis by MRM-MS on a triple quadrupole mass spectrometer. The molecular ion of the tryptic peptide ion (usually doubly charged) is selected by the first quadrupole, fragmented by collision with neutral gas in the second quadrupole, and specific, peptide sequence-dependent product ions are selected by the third quadrupole. The ion intensity resulting in this double selection process is typically measured for 20–30 msec at a time. Then another molecular ion/product ion combination representing a second tryptic peptide is examined. This process can be repeated 30–50 times a second before cycling back to the molecular ion/product ion combination for the tryptic peptide for the first protein. If the signal intensities of the analytes being measured are strong enough, the period for each channel can be shortened and as many as 500 transitions a second can be monitored.

The process of ensuring that a peptide from a specific protein in a biological pathway is proteotypic, especially when done manually, is prohibitive. It involves (1) selecting protein(s) involved in a biological (disease, metabolic, etc.) pathway, clicking on the source-link for the protein(s), and accessing the web page that contains information about the protein(s), or from other sources; (2) obtaining their amino acid sequences in the FASTA format; (3) submitting the sequences for *in silico* enzymatic digestion; (4) organizing the peptides that may be suitable for analysis, (5) carrying out a BLAST search for each.

Other attempts to identify suitable tryptic peptides for quantitative LC-MRM-MS analysis have either been based on a pragmatic approach (by inspection of peptide MS/MS data collected on instruments in investigators' laboratories), or on predictive tools based on a peptide training set. The latter increases the chance of selecting high intensity peptide ions. Skyline (https://brendanx-uwl.gs.washington.edu/labkey/project/home/software/Skyline/begin.view), a downloadable tool that performs many of the above steps, is available for investigators and end-users on the Windows platform. Skyline, for a given protein or peptide, calculates the masses of tryptic peptides and their fragment ions and includes provisions to filter out oxidizable groups and to allow biochemical posttranslational modifications. While Skyline is an excellent tool for investigators with experience in the use and applications of peptide mass spectrometry, it nonetheless represents a barrier for biologists who have identified areas of biochemistry where identification of changes (by western

MRMPath and MRMutation, Facilitating Discovery of Mass Transitions for Proteotypic Peptides in Biological
Pathways Using a Bioinformatics Approach

27

blotting or DNA/RNA measurements) in a critical element of a pathway prompts a thorough investigation of all the components of the pathway and in some cases neighboring pathways. MRMPath and MRMutation allow the biologist to accurately recover the peptide and associated mass spectral data about the proteins in the biological pathway(s) so that the information can be transferred to the domain of mass spectrometry.

The present study therefore has two goals: (1) to create a freely-accessible, web-based software tool (MRMPath), that is, Internet browser accessible and hence not subject to dependence on the computer operating system. This software would dynamically retrieve and process known pathways of metabolism and protein signaling using an automated bioinformatics approach. Peptides that can be evaluated for their proteotypic character using BLAST searches would be extracted using this software. Any investigator would be able to access MRMPath and download and store results; and (2) the creation of a second web-based tool (MRMutation) that dynamically accesses all the known mutations (germline, somatic, and experimental) of a given protein in order to identify those tryptic peptides which would contain the mutation.

2. Methods

The proteins associated with human diseases and other processes, including metabolic and cellular processes in many species in which the genome sequences are known, are cataloged in a publicly available web resource, the Kyoto Encyclopedia of Genes and Genomes (KEGG) (URL http://www.genome.jp/kegg/). This resource is well visited by researchers the world over. It provides information related to pathways which are categorized according to metabolic, genetic information processing, environmental information processing, cellular processes, organismal systems, and human diseases. The individual pathways include the complement of proteins that are involved in them. Figure 1 is a screen capture, for the TCA (tricarboxylic acid) cycle in humans, presented through KEGG's web interface. The result of a user query in the KEGG for a specific pathway is a generic, non clickable representation of all the components involved in a pathway. For a pathway, a user can then choose the one appropriate for each species catalogued by KEGG. When a user chooses a species, for example, *Homo sapiens*, the proteins and other components that are specifically involved in the pathway for humans become "live" or clickable links. In Figure 1, these boxes are colored green.

For proteins and enzymes (which are represented using the Enzyme Commission nomenclature), the user is taken to a page where additional information is available related to the protein, which includes alternative nomenclature for that protein in other resources, the DNA sequence from which the protein sequence is intuitively translated, the family from which the protein arises, and the link to that protein in the FASTA format (which is accessed in MRMPath), among other information.

MRMPath facilitates the collection of the protein amino acid sequence data presented by KEGG. It is freely available

on the Internet (http://tmpl.uab.edu/MRMPath/). Only an Internet browser is needed to access and use MRMPath. The system was designed for free use, mitigating the need for platform-specific computer operating systems, or to download and install software.

On accessing MRMPath and clicking on the "MRMPath" link, a user is offered three choices that involve deploying MRMPath by (1) processing proteins involved in a pathway stored in KEGG; (2) processing a protein from EXPASY (formerly, SWISSPROT) by entering the EXPASY protein ID; (3) cutting and pasting the protein sequence into a text box. Figure 2, a screen capture of the MRMPath home page, illustrates the choices that are available for protein sources.

2.1. MRMPath and KEGG. The first option allows users to use a drop-down menu to select among the pathways that are available in KEGG. When a user clicks on the pathway of choice, the system automatically populates a second drop-down menu which identifies only the species for which the selected pathway is available in KEGG. When the user clicks the "Submit" button, the system automatically downloads and represents the pathway to the investigator just as the user would see in KEGG, that is, with only the components (proteins) from the pathway highlighted in green as they are relevant to the species. This pathway is downloaded dynamically from the KEGG web resources and presented to the MRMPath user as a virtual webpage (precluding the need to store information); its HTML (hypertext markup language) webpage is processed and modified (on the UAB servers). The page illustrating the biological pathway for a species appears to the user exactly as it would appear to a KEGG user. The links for specific "live" components—proteins involved in the pathway for that species—are changed such that clicking on these links now deploys the MRMPath software for that protein, instead of leading to the webpage that contains additional information for that protein in KEGG.

2.2. MRMPath Processing. The amino acid sequence for the protein involved in the pathway is recovered in the FASTA format and subjected to *in silico* trypsin digestion (MRMPath also allows users to perform digestions using chymotrypsin, Arg-C, Lys-C, and Glu-C). Following a tryptic digest, cleavage occurs on the C-terminal side of arginine and lysine residues except when the next amino acid is proline. The mass-to-charge (m/z) values for the monoisotopic, doubly charged tryptic peptides are determined from the empirical formula for each peptide residue, using the elemental masses for carbon (12.00000000), hydrogen (1.00782503), nitrogen (14.00307401), and oxygen (15.99491462) [6]. Peptides with less than seven amino acids or more than 25 amino acids are not considered. Peptides containing cysteine or methionine resides are filtered out because of modifications that may arise from nonbiological events during sample processing. These peptides thus filtered are processed to calculate m/z values for b-ions and y-ions. Typically, these are larger than the m/z of the doubly charged molecular ion. In general, peptides chosen for MS/MS are doubly or triply charged; therefore, their higher mass, singly charged product ions

MRMPath

- **Analysis of Protein Mass Fragments from Pathways: Metabolism, Genetic, Environmental, Cellular, Organismal, Human**

Presented here is a methodology that allows the user to select individual proteins from the pathways associated with a disease process in a given species. Once the sequence of the protein is recovered, it is subjected to in silico digestion with trypsin to determine peptides that are suited to multiple reaction ion monitoring. For each fragment, the m/z values of the b and y ions are presented (only those with values greater than the doubly charged parent ion are included). For each tryptic peptide, an automated BLAST search is deployed, which results in a list of the highest similarity hits, each with the links to GENBANK. The resulting data can be exported to a comma-delimited file.

┌─ **Analysis of Protein Mass Fragments from Pathways** ──────────────
│ [Citrate cycle (TCA cycle)   ‡] [‡] [Submit]
│
│ ⊙ Trypsin ○ Arg-C ○ Lys-C ○ Chymotrypsin ○ Glu-C
└──

- **Analysis of Protein Mass Fragments**

Presented here is a methodology that allows the user to select individual proteins and perform a tryptic digest in silico to determine peptides that are suited to multiple reaction ion monitoring. The only input required is the SWISSPROT Accession ID (or) a protein sequence. For each fragment, the m/z values of the b- and y- ions are presented (only those with values greater than the doubly charged parent ion are included). For each tryptic peptide, an automated BLAST search is deployed, which results in a list of the highest similarity hits, each with the links to GENBANK. The resulting data can be exported to a comma-delimited file.

┌─ **Protein ID** ──
│ Protein ID (EXPASY): [   ] ⊙ Trypsin ○ Arg-C ○ Lys-C ○ Chymotrypsin ○ Glu-C [Submit] [Reset] (Example: P63276)
└──

┌─ **Protein Sequence** ─────────────────────────────────────
│ Protein   ┌──────────────────────────────────┐
│ Sequence: │   │
│   │   │
│   └──────────────────────────────────┘
│   ⊙ Trypsin ○ Arg-C ○ Lys-C ○ Chymotrypsin
│ ○ Glu-C   [Submit] [Reset]
│
│ (Example: MAKLTAVPLSALVDEPVHIQVTGLAPFQVVCLQASLKDEKGNLFSSQAFYRASEVGEVDL)
└──

FIGURE 2: Front page of the Targeted Metabolomics and Proteomics Laboratory website. This is the home page for MRMPath and MRMutation. The three input choices for MRMPath—processing of peptides of proteins involved in biological pathways via KEGG, through Accession IDs in UniProt and direct input of a protein sequence—are illustrated.

have m/z values that could not arise from a singly charged molecular ion at the same m/z value as the doubly or triply charged peptide ion. The filtered tryptic amino acid sequences are subjected to automated BLAST analysis at NCBI (http://blast.ncbi.nlm.nih.gov/Blast.cgi). This is carried out either on a single tryptic peptide or on all the selected tryptic peptides for a given protein.

The following specific example illustrates the specific data-mining steps that the system deploys following a user query. When a user chooses a pathway and a species, MRMPath automatically creates a URL (Universal Resource Locator) which a user would otherwise manually type to access that pathway for that species. For example, consider the link http://www.genome.jp/kegg-bin/show_pathway?org_name=mmu&mapno=00062. The organism's

name is identified by the three-letter species code "mmu" (*Mus musculus*). The numerical representation "0062" refers to the pathway, "fatty acid elongation." In KEGG, this pathway is represented under the category "Metabolism," and subcategory "Lipid Metabolism." We initially recovered and stored the codes for all the organisms and pathways in KEGG.

One of the components of this pathway is the mitochondrial trans-2-enoyl-CoA reductase (EC: 1.3.1.38). Within KEGG, when this component is clicked, it takes the user to information about that enzyme in KEGG through the URL (http://www.genome.jp/dbget-bin/www_bget?mmu:26922). Through MRMPath, when the pathway is downloaded and processed, each link within the downloaded file is modified. The KEGG link for mitochondrial trans-2-enoyl-CoA reductase would be automatically modified

MRMPath and MRMutation, Facilitating Discovery of Mass Transitions for Proteotypic Peptides in Biological
Pathways Using a Bioinformatics Approach

29

to http://www.genome.jp/dbget-bin/www_bget?-f+-n+a+ mmu:26922, which is the link to the FASTA file for this protein. The FASTA formatted protein sequence is then further processed.

Leveraging pathways published at the KEGG resource is an innovative aspect of MRMPath. MRMPath can process proteins involved in pathways and makes them all available to mass spectrometry specialists.

For the two other deployment strategies available in MRMPath, the above description is the same, except that only one protein at a time is processed.

2.3. EXPASY. The EXPASY Bioinformatics Resource Portal (http://www.expasy.org/) contains the world's most comprehensive and highly curated repository for proteins. In addition to information related to protein sequences, this resource is constantly updated with tools and subdata bases for different aspects of the analysis of proteins. The database within EXPASY that stores and allows access to proteins is UniProtKB (http://www.uniprot.org/). This resource allows access to proteins on the database through a keyword search or a descriptor search or by using the UniProt accession ID.

MRMPath uses web-accessibility techniques that were discussed previously to download a pathway or a FASTA-formatted protein sequence from KEGG. For example, consider a protein with a UniProt Accession ID, P47888. Clicking on the link associated with this Accession ID, http://www.uniprot.org/uniprot/P47888, allows a user to access additional information about this protein. MRM-Path manipulates this link such that its algorithms can automatically access and download the FASTA formatted sequence from this protein through the webpage with the link, http://www.uniprot.org/uniprot/P47888. The sequence is thus downloaded and can be processed further by MRM-Path, as described in the section on MRMPath and KEGG.

2.4. User Supplied Sequences. The third option, shown at the bottom of Figure 2, is a text box, which allows the user to cut and paste a protein sequence. This could be an entire protein as well as a fragment. This protein sequence is then processed through MRMPath in the same way as described when a FASTA formatted protein sequence is automatically downloaded from KEGG or from UniProt.

2.5. MRMPath's Process. As illustrated in the above section, the input for MRMPath is a protein or peptide sequence. This sequence can be automatically extracted for a protein involved in a biological pathway from KEGG, or a protein that is stored in the proteomics repository at EXPASY, or a user-supplied sequence. MRMPath processes a sequence as follows.

Enzymatic Digest. The sequence is first processed to create peptides following a theoretical enzymatic digest. MRMPath allows a user to choose between trypsin (cleaves on the carboxyl side of Arg and Lys), chymotrypsin (cleaves on the carboxyl side of Phe, Tyr, and Trp), AspN (cleaves the amino side of aspartate residues), GluC (cleaves the carboxyl side

of aspartate and glutamate residues), LysC (cleaves on the carboxyl side of Lys residues), and ArgC (cleaves on the carboxyl side of Arg).

Selectivity for Met and Cys. The peptides obtained by the above user-determined enzymatic digest are processed to delete any that contain methionine or cysteine amino acid residues since these are susceptible to oxidation during sample processing and may not reflect the biology that is under investigation. A peptide containing methionine or cysteine may exist in several oxidized forms in addition to the unmodified peptide, rendering uncertainty in quantitative analysis.

Selection by Peptide Sizes. The resulting peptides are then filtered for the total number of amino acid residues. Only those peptides having seven or more, but not more than 25, residues are selected for further processing. Peptides with fewer than seven residues are unlikely to be proteotypic, whereas those with more than 25 residues become harder to detect or exceed the mass range of the quadrupole mass filter. The latter would have doubly charged ions that would be greater than m/z 1300.

Theoretical MS/MS Spectrum. For each of the resulting peptides from a protein, their multiply charged precursor ion can be collisionally dissociated producing b- and y-product ions. The y-ion masses (following cleavage at the amide bonds and containing the C-terminal residue) and b-ion masses (caused by cleaving the amide bonds and retaining from the N-terminal residue) are determined and tabulated. The m/z ratio for the peptide precursor ion is also calculated. These results are displayed on a browser following MRMPath's use (Figure 3).

2.6. BLAST Searching. Figure 4 shows that a BLAST search is also included for each fragment in the results of the webpage. When a user clicks this button, an automated BLAST search is initiated. The steps involved in the BLAST search are identical to a manual BLAST search for proteins on the webpages of NCBI BLAST (http://blast.ncbi.nlm.nih.gov/). During the manual search, a user will choose the type of BLAST, protein, nucleotide, and so forth, against a specific genomics resource (RefSeq—http://www.ncbi.nlm.nih.gov/RefSeq/ e.g.). A prompt appears on the webpage indicating after how long the search is likely to be completed. The results are then presented pictorially with color codes indicating the closeness of the BLAST results. The color red indicates a high similarity, the color black indicates lower than 40 percent similarity.

In MRMPath's automated BLAST search, the process is similar to the manual web-based BLAST search (http://blast.ncbi.nlm.nih.gov/), however, without manually entering the protein sequence (using NCBI's unique identifying number for the protein, the FASTA- or free-formatted protein sequence). MRMPath's BLAST search occurs in two steps. First, following a BLAST request for a peptide, the algorithm creates a URL. Embedded into this URL are query parameters: these include the peptide sequence, number of hits to return, and data source to search (NCBI). MRMPath then scans the NCBI BLAST server to identify a Process

Click here to download this into an Excel sheet
NOTE: Please click on the 'YES' button if a warning appears when you try to open the excel sheet

hsa:3417 IDH1, IDCD, IDH, IDP, IDPC, PICD; isocitrate dehydrogenase 1 (NADP+),
soluble (EC:1.1.1.42); K00031 isocitrate dehydrogenase [EC:1.1.1.42] (A)

BLAST ALL FRAGMENTS

Sequence	m/z Parent Ion	B Ion Mass	Y > Parent Ions
		227.1760	801.4921
		413.2553	688.4080
BLAST	457.792	542.2979	502.3287
IIWELIK		655.3819	
		768.4660	
		896.5609	
		227.1760	2293.1551
		374.2444	2180.0710
		471.2971	2033.0026
		634.3605	1935.9499
		733.4289	1772.8865
		862.4715	1673.8181
		975.5556	1544.7755
		1090.5825	1431.6915
		1203.6666	1316.6645
BLAST	1203.6235	1340.7256	
LIFPYVELDLHSYDLGIENR		1427.7576	
		1590.8209	
		1705.8479	
		1818.9320	
		1875.9535	
		1989.0376	
		2118.0801	
		2232.1231	
		2388.2241	

FIGURE 3: A screen capture of MRMPath results (truncated) shows the peptides for a chosen protein (isocitrate dehydrogenase) from the TCA cycle pathway. The peptides are a result of a tryptic digest, the precursor ion values and the b- and y-ions whose masses are greater than that of the precursor ion identified. The link towards the top of the page allows users to download the processing result to an Excel spreadsheet. The buttons that allow BLAST searching of individual peptides as well all peptides from the chosen protein are also illustrated in the figure.

hsa:3417 IDH1, IDCD, IDH, IDP, IDPC, PICD; isocitrate dehydrogenase 1 (NADP+),
soluble (EC:1.1.1.42); K00031 isocitrate dehydrogenase [EC:1.1.1.42] (A)

Sequence	Blast results
IIWELIK	This fragment is found only in protein **hsa:3417 IDH1, IDCD, IDH, IDP, IDPC, PICD; isocitrate dehydrogenase 1 (NADP+), soluble (EC:1.1.1.42); K00031 isocitrate dehydrogenase [EC:1.1.1.42] (A)** and does not show significant similarity with other proteins!
LIFPYVELDLHSYDLGIENR	This fragment is found only in protein **hsa:3417 IDH1, IDCD, IDH, IDP, IDPC, PICD; isocitrate dehydrogenase 1 (NADP+), soluble (EC:1.1.1.42); K00031 isocitrate dehydrogenase [EC:1.1.1.42] (A)** and does not show significant similarity with other proteins!

FIGURE 4: The result of a BLAST search of the tryptic peptide, the first peptide from Figure 3, shows that no results are found. The *m/z* for the parent ion of this peptide is also illustrated. If sequences similar to the peptide were identified, the top ten results would appear with links back to the GenBank resource for each similar sequence in the third column in the figure.

ID created by the BLAST system and the time it will take for the BLAST search to be completed. The program then automatically suspends processing for that amount of time (this might typically last from four to five seconds, longer if the BLAST servers are busy). After this "wait" time has elapsed, the program creates a second URL which includes the Process ID and dynamically extracts the BLAST results. One difference between the automated and manual searches is that results with very small sequence similarity will not be returned in the automated system as viable results.

The top ten BLAST results are returned to the user. If strong similarities are not found, then the program informs the user that the peptide does not have significant similarity with other proteins. The top ten BLAST results (if available)

are then presented to the user in a webpage, with links to the sources of the proteins in GenBank.

2.7. Comprehensive Processing in MRMPath. In Figure 4, at the top right hand corner is a button, "BLAST ALL FRAGMENTS." This facility allows users to perform BLAST searches on all the peptides that result from the MRMPath filter at the same time. As has been explained previously, given that there is a wait time while BLAST searching occurs, users are likely to have to wait for several minutes for all BLAST searching on all the fragments to be complete. This process would be lengthened even more if done manually, where every fragment would have to be individually entered into the BLAST query "box."

MRMPath and MRMutation, Facilitating Discovery of Mass Transitions for Proteotypic Peptides in Biological
Pathways Using a Bioinformatics Approach

31

When a user chooses to process a protein from a pathway through KEGG, MRMPath allows the option of processing all the proteins involved in a pathway for a particular species at the same time. Each protein involved in the pathway for a user-queried species will be processed in the same way as a single protein would, user-defined enzymatic digest and selection for peptide length (7–25 amino acid residues) and peptide sequences lacking methionine and cysteine residues.

In addition to the results being published on MRMPath's results webpage, where they can be downloaded, the results are also automatically written to an Excel spreadsheet. A new spreadsheet is generated with every MRMPath use. The same results that are available on the results web page are stored in the spreadsheet. We have placed, and continue to endeavor to place, information in the spreadsheet in the right format such that it can automatically, entered as input into the setup of manufacturer software such as Midas and MRMPilot for LC-MRM-MS analysis.

2.8. MRMutation. MRMutation was developed as a companion system to MRMPath, primarily because it involves several processing features that have been described for proteins (either cut and paste, or a protein from EXPASY, or proteins in a pathway stored in KEGG). MRMutation is available at the same resource that houses MRMPath. A user can deploy the software by entering a protein as its EXPASY Accession Number or by a descriptor for the protein, for example, TP53 human. In the latter case, the software accesses the EXPASY UniProt page for this entry.

The user must select the appropriate protein record. Protein accession numbers with a "P" as the first character are the most informative about the known mutations of the protein. The unique identifiers for each of these mutations are then retrieved and the information for the protein is processed. Processing involves subjecting each protein (obtained as the protein's FASTA formatted sequence) to a tryptic digest. This is to determine whether peptides with mutations are suited to multiple reaction ion monitoring. An output similar to the one for each protein in MRMPath is produced, except that it only contains the peptides that contain mutations. Figure 5 illustrates this table, where the mutated amino acid residue is highlighted. A table is generated that lists b- and y-ions whose masses are greater than the parent peptide ion m/z ratio. In addition, just as for results in MRMPath, the results of MRMutation are also available for download in a Microsoft Excel spreadsheet.

3. Discussion

The success of proteomics requires the development of informatics tools to enable the investigator to design targeted mass spectrometry experiments that answer specific biological hypotheses. Because of the immense amount of information involved, it has become important to create methods whereby biologists, in addition to mass spectrometry experts/operators, can contribute to the process. In the present study, MRMPath and MRMutation have successfully been put into practice to empower biologists to find those parts of a protein's sequence that are suitable for MRM

analysis. These programs are also valuable to the mass spectrometry expert.

The value of the approach taken in creating MRMPath is driven by the extensiveness of the information available in the KEGG database. While manually searching for information on a single protein in this database is feasible, when confronted by 20–30 members of an entire pathway, it became obvious that an automated approach was necessary. MRMPath allows the investigator to select the pathway and the species of interest and then uses a data mining approach to filter information that is associated with each protein. Once captured, the protein sequence information is processed on local computers that automatically "cut" the protein into smaller peptide sequences obeying the biochemical rules set by the protease that would be used. Peptide analysis using the MRM approach is more specific for peptides that have seven or more amino acid residues. On the other hand much larger peptides (>25 amino acids) are harder to detect in most current mass spectrometers. The MRMPath software filters the peptides from a given protein to create a list of those that have 7–25 amino acids. There are many posttranslational modifications to proteins (and hence peptides) in biological and pathologic systems. Some of these, particularly oxidations, can occur after the sample has been taken and while it is being processed, in preparation for analysis. The sulfur atoms in cysteine and methionine residues are particularly prone to this—in the case of cysteine, many investigators block its free sulfhydryl group with an alkylating agent prior to analysis. Since controlling this oxidation is difficult and variable, MRMPath automatically filters out peptides that contain cysteine or methionine residues.

MRMPath software takes each filtered peptide and calculates the m/z of its precursor (molecular) ion and the product b- and y-ions. The latter are restricted to those that have values (singly charged) that are larger than the m/z of doubly charged precursor ion. The higher m/z values ensure that a singly charged precursor ion cannot contribute to the analysis of the doubly charged peptide.

It is important to verify the specificity of the peptide as a surrogate for the parent protein. Although a BLAST search could be done manually, MRMPath makes it a simple, clickable action. Indeed, the user can click just once to carry out a BLAST search on all peptides from a protein, although it may take several minutes for the BLAST search to be completed. The result of the MRMPath BLAST search may reveal that there is only one protein record that matches the peptide sequence, or it may indicate that there are multiple protein records. The latter may nonetheless be all the same protein since the NCBI database has many duplicate records for each protein. To assist the investigator, MRMPath-generated BLAST table of results contains a link to the full protein record. It should be noted that although MRMPath in combination with the BLAST search may indicate that a protein is specific in alphabetic space, the MRM-MS analysis is carried out in mass space and therefore the possibility remains of peptides with similar sequences that match the m/z of the precursor ion and the selected product ion. This would occur when a peptide had the same amino acids (i.e.,

MRMMut

- ### Analysis of Protein Mutations

MRMutation is a methodology that allows the user to select individual proteins and determine whether they have known mutations. This is determined by examining the EXPaSY.org database. Each of the protein sequences is subjected to trypsin digestion in silico to determine whether peptides with mutations are suited to multiple reaction ion monitoring. The input required is the UNIPROT Accession ID. The output spreadsheet contains the m/z values of the first three 'b' and 'y' ions (only those with values greater than the doubly charged parent ion are included), the start and end residues of the peptide with respect to the parent protein and the mutation.

Protein ID
Protein ID (EXPASY): [p53] | Submit | Reset | (Example: P04632)

(a)

Restrict term "p53" to protein family (479), gene name (106), gene ontology (1,026), protein name (782), strain (42), taxonomy (42), web resource (1)

Entry	Entry name	Status	Protein names	Gene names	Organism	Length
P04637	P53_HUMAN		Cellular tumor antigen p53	TP53 P53	Homo sapiens (Human)	393
P02340	P53_MOUSE		Cellular tumor antigen p53	Tp53 P53 Trp53	Mus musculus (Mouse)	387
P10361	P53_RAT		Cellular tumor antigen p53	Tp53 P53	Rattus norvegicus (Rat)	391
Q29537	P53_CANFA		Cellular tumor antigen p53	TP53 P53	Canis familiaris (Dog) (Canis lupus familiaris)	381
P79892	P53_HORSE		Cellular tumor antigen p53	TP53 P53	Equus caballus (Horse)	280

(b)

Uniprot entry for P04637

sp|P04637|P53_HUMAN Cellular tumor antigen p53 OS=Homo sapiens GN=TP53 PE=1 SV=4

NOTE: Entire information (B-Ion, Y-Ion masses etc.) is available in the excel sheet

Sequence	m/z Parent Ion
MEEPhSDPSVEPPLSQETFSDLWK	1393.1396
MEEPQlDPSVEPPLSQETFSDLWK	1401.6655
MEEPQShPSVEPPLSQETFSDLWK	1399.6554
MEEPQSDSSVEPPLSQETFSDLWK	1383.6291
MEEPQSDPSiEPPLSQETFSDLWK	1395.6473
MEEPQSDPSVKPPLSQETFSDLWK	1388.1656
MEEPQSDPSVQPPLSQETFSDLWK	1388.1475
MEEPQSDPSVEPPLr	855.9067
MEEPQSDPSVEPPLSlETFSDLWK	1381.1522
MEEPQSDPSVEPPLSQdTFSDLWK	1381.6316

(c)

FIGURE 5: (a) The user interface for MRMutation. A user can input a free text search of the Accession ID of a UniProt entry. (b) The results (truncated) of a search in the interface identified records with the keyword "p53." (c) Clicking the first link results in the creation of a tryptic digest of the protein identified through Accession ID P04637. The mutated amino acid residues are highlighted in the tryptic peptide sequence, along with the m/z of the parent peptide ion.

the same molecular weight), but in a different order. In that case, there is value in obtaining the whole mass spectrum of product ions to verify the identity of the peptide. Although this is not easily obtained on a triple quadrupole (qqq) mass spectrometer, high sensitivity Qq-TOF mass spectrometers can provide this information.

As biomedical science moves into more and more use of DNA deep sequencing methods based on direct sequencing rather than hybridization to "known" sequences, it is becoming apparent that there is far more sequence variation in genes and hence proteins than previously realized. For some genes, the variation in sequence can occur between

tissues in the same person. While germ-line DNA information is copied faithfully from parents to their children with little error, somatic tissues can have >1500 mutations in the whole genome [7]. This suggests that the so-called canonical sequence of a gene or protein may be subject to more variation than hitherto. Because of their potential involvement in disease, certain genes/proteins have been subject to considerable attention. One of these is the human protein p53, a regulator of the G_1/S cell cycle checkpoint that is associated with many cancers.

MRMutation allows an investigator to capture known information about mutations for a specific protein. It data mines the UniProtKB/SwissProt database, part of the EXPASY suite of programs. The investigator can either provide the protein accession number if they already know it, or they can describe the protein (e.g., "human" and "p53" would be the search terms). In the latter case, a table of proteins normally generated by the EXPASY software appears. For both, it is best to select the protein record that starts with a "P" since these records contain a compilation of all the known mutations and greatly facilitate the recovery of the required information. In the case of human p53 (P04637), there are currently (as of the preparation of this paper) mutations that lead to 1248 peptides that are different from those in wild-type human p53. At certain residue positions in this 393 amino acid protein, there are more than 10 different amino acids. For the human low-density lipoprotein receptor (P01130) there are 129 mutated peptides, whereas for NADP-dependent isocitrate dehydrogenase only two have been described. In contrast, pyruvate kinase (P30613) has 94 peptide mutations.

While there is some overlap between the utilities provided by MRMPath and Skyline software, there are also some distinct and significant differences. The principal ones are that MRMPath leverages the results of pathway analysis and is Internet browser driven. While Skyline provides detailed analysis of mass spectrometric data that is more extensive than MRMPath, its primary input is the output of a mass spectrometry experiment, namely, the DDA (data-dependent acquisition) file and therefore is not in the domain of a biologist. Skyline is capable of processing the results of and/or data from several commercial vendors. However, Skyline is available as a standalone system that only works on the Windows operating system. Furthermore, it has to be downloaded and installed. This is an advantage for those who wish to use its tools privately and offline.

From a bioinformatics and software development standpoint, the novel aspects of MRMPath and MRMutation are advancement of the notion of interoperability [8] in the realm of proteomics [9]. Interoperability is defined as the automated exchange of knowledge and data between resources that are repositories of heterogeneous (or heterogeneously stored) information. Interoperability has seen a significant rise that keeps up with the burgeoning information available online. Interoperability seeks to create a platform for information exchange while precluding the need to recreate information that is already available at the different resource.

MRMPath and MRMutation programs access the resources, EXPASY and KEGG. The software development notions employed here are innovative because it involves access to and manipulation of information available online to better serve the users of the MRM resources. Use of MRMPath and MRMutation avoids the need to transfer and store all the protein information (from EXPASY) or all the pathway protein information (from KEGG) on local servers since the stored information would have to be continually updated. In addition, use of a dynamic mode of accessing BLAST avoids the storage of a local BLAST server.

The methods discussed in this paper are easily extensible to applications in other domains [10]. In MRMPath, the web page related to a biological pathway is downloaded and the URLs of the links therein are manipulated so that MRMPath can be deployed. The KEGG pathway downloaded by the investigator is a single webpage without additional burdens being placed on the KEGG servers. All processing is done at the UAB servers. MRMPath also represents a significant boon to mass spectrometrists, who wish to obtain surrogate peptides for proteins in any pathway in the KEGG databases.

For MRMutation, if the investigator enters a UniProtKB Accession Identifier in the text field, the URL that directs the browser to the full protein record in UniProt is modified so as to extract only the FASTA formatted protein sequence of the mutant, which is then subject to further processing. On the other hand, if a protein name is entered, MRMutation will access all the UniProt protein records that include the name. The expert user must then select the appropriate record for processing by MRMutation.

The value of MRMPath and MRMutation is that they leverage existing information (without having to recreate it). There is, on the other hand, the practical matter of the use of bioinformatics-based methodologies to rapidly and efficaciously process biological knowledge (particularly knowledge that is stored remotely and heterogeneously). Performing the same manually would be overwhelming from the standpoints of efficiency, accuracy of information processed and results obtained, and the time spent.

MRMPath and MRMutation serve researchers over a range of biomedical domains. These include anybody with a proteomics-based interest in any pathway that is currently stored in KEGG. From the time an investigator enters a protein sequence into MRMPath (in one of the three ways discussed in Section 2), results will be obtained in a matter of a few seconds; the only barriers are the time taken for BLAST results. If an investigator wishes to perform MRMPath's task manually, he or she would have to access KEGG, chose a path for a species, click on the link for a specific protein, click on the FASTA formatted file for that protein, and download the FASTA file; depending on the choice of enzyme, he or she would have to create peptide fragments, filter them according to the specifications for additional processing, manually calculate y- and b-ions, take each peptide fragment and enter it into a BLAST search, and then process the final results. It is more than likely that manually performing all the steps that MRMPath would complete in a few seconds would take a few hours. If the same procedure was to be carried out for all the proteins in a pathway for a species, it would take several man-days of work, not accounting for fatigue and the consequent errors. For MRMutation, processing of proteomic data is even more efficient.

MRMPath and MRMutation are therefore an advantageous not just from the developmental standpoint, of an interoperability-based software, but also for their simplicity of use and significant advantage over manually accomplishing the same task. These software are freely accessible and need not be downloaded and installed. The only requirements are an Internet browser; hence, the systems are platform independent. All the processing takes place on the server side, and the graphical user interface for querying the system and the results are available instantly and dynamically on the same browser MRMPath and MRMutation can be freely accessed at http://tmpl.uab.edu/MRMPath/.

4. Conclusion

In summary, MRMPath and MRMutation are bioinformatics tools that will have great value in the design of experiments in quantitative proteomics, particularly in the analysis of biomarkers.

Acknowledgments

This study was supported in part by a Grants-in-Aid (R21 AT004661, S. Barnes, PI) from the National Center for Complementary and Alternative Medicine as a supplement provided under the American Recovery and Reinvestment Act, from the National Institute on Deafness and Other Communication Disorders, National Institutes of Health (1R21DC011068, C. Crasto, PI), and from UAB Center for Clinical and Translational Science (5UL1RR025777).

References

[1] F. Hillenkamp and M. Karas, "Mass spectrometry of peptides and proteins by matrix-assisted ultraviolet laser desorption/ionization," *Methods in Enzymology*, vol. 193, pp. 280–295, 1990.

[2] J. B. Fenn, M. Mann, C. K. Meng, S. F. Wong, and C. M. Whitehouse, "Electrospray ionization for mass spectrometry of large biomolecules," *Science*, vol. 246, no. 4926, pp. 64–71, 1989.

[3] A. P. Diz, A. Carvajal-Rodríguez, and D. O. F. Skibinski, "Multiple hypothesis testing in proteomics: a strategy for experimental work," *Molecular and Cellular Proteomics*, vol. 10, no. 3, 2011.

[4] D. F. Ransohoff, "Proteomics research to discover markers: what can we learn from netflix?" *Clinical Chemistry*, vol. 56, no. 2, pp. 172–176, 2010.

[5] S. A. Gerber, J. Rush, O. Stemman, M. W. Kirschner, and S. P. Gygi, "Absolute quantification of proteins and phosphoproteins from cell lysates by tandem MS," *Proceedings of the National Academy of Sciences of the United States of America*, vol. 100, no. 12, pp. 6940–6945, 2003.

[6] http://www.nist.gov/pml/data/comp.cfm/.

[7] D. F. Conrad, J. E. M. Keebler, M. A. Depristo et al., "Variation in genome-wide mutation rates within and between human families," *Nature Genetics*, vol. 43, no. 7, pp. 712–714, 2011.

[8] K. H. Buetow, "Cyberinfrastructure: empowering a "third way" in biomedical research," *Science*, vol. 308, no. 5723, pp. 821–824, 2005.

[9] M. Cannataro, "Computational proteomics: management and analysis of proteomics data," *Briefings in Bioinformatics*, vol. 9, no. 2, pp. 97–101, 2008.

[10] W. Litwin, L. Mark, and N. Roussopoulos, "Interoperability of multiple autonomous databases," *Computing surveys*, vol. 22, no. 3, pp. 267–293, 1990.

5

Literature Retrieval and Mining in Bioinformatics: State of the Art and Challenges

Andrea Manconi,[1] Eloisa Vargiu,[2,3] Giuliano Armano,[2] and Luciano Milanesi[1]

[1] Institute for Biomedical Technologies, National Research Council, Via F.lli Cervi, 93, 20090 Segrate, Italy
[2] Department of Electrical and Electronic Engineering, University of Cagliari, Piazza d'Armi, 09123 Cagliari, Italy
[3] Barcelona Digital Technological Center, C/Roc Boronat 117, 08018 Barcelona, Spain

Correspondence should be addressed to Andrea Manconi, andrea.manconi@itb.cnr.it

Academic Editor: Jörg Hakenberg

The world has widely changed in terms of communicating, acquiring, and storing information. Hundreds of millions of people are involved in information retrieval tasks on a daily basis, in particular while using a Web search engine or searching their e-mail, making such field the dominant form of information access, overtaking traditional database-style searching. How to handle this huge amount of information has now become a challenging issue. In this paper, after recalling the main topics concerning information retrieval, we present a survey on the main works on literature retrieval and mining in bioinformatics. While claiming that information retrieval approaches are useful in bioinformatics tasks, we discuss some challenges aimed at showing the effectiveness of these approaches applied therein.

1. Introduction

Nowadays, most of the scientific publications are electronically available on the Web, making the problem of retrieving and mining documents and data a challenging task. To this end, automated document management systems have gained a main role in the field of intelligent information access [1]. Thus, research and development in the area of bioinformatics literature retrieval and mining is aimed at providing intelligent and personalized services to biologists and bioinformaticians while searching for useful information in scientific publications. In particular, the main goal of bioinformatics text analysis is to provide access to unstructured knowledge by improving searches, providing automatically generated summaries, linking publications with structured resources, visualizing contents for better understanding, and guiding researchers to formulate novel hypotheses and to discover knowledge.

In the literature, several methods, systems, and tools to retrieve and mine bioinformatics publications have been proposed and adopted, some of them being currently available on the Web. In this paper, we provide a survey of existing end-user-oriented literature retrieval and/or mining solutions for bioinformatics, together with a short discussion on open challenges. The rest of the paper is organized as follows: Section 2 illustrates the main topics addressed in this paper, that is, information retrieval, text mining, and literature retrieval and mining. In Section 3, the state of the art on literature retrieval and mining in bioinformatics is presented. Section 4 discusses some relevant open problems and challenges. Section 5 ends the paper.

2. Background

Supporting users in handling the huge and widespread amount of Web information is becoming a primary issue. Information retrieval is the task of representing, storing, organizing, and accessing information items. Information retrieval has considerably changed in recent years: initially with the expansion of the World Wide Web and the advent of modern and inexpensive graphical user interfaces and mass storage [2], and then with the advent of modern Internet technologies [3] and of the Web 2.0 [4].

Information retrieval can cover various and heterogeneous kinds of data and information problems beyond that specified in the core definition above. More generally, an information retrieval system does not inform (i.e., does not change the knowledge of) the user on the subject of her/his inquiry. It merely informs on the existence (or nonexistence) and whereabouts of documents relating to her/his request. According to [5], information retrieval is defined as the task of finding material (usually documents) of an unstructured nature (usually text) that satisfies an information need, from large collections (usually stored on computers). Nowadays, information retrieval solutions rely on the adoption of Web services and suitable Semantic Web approaches, such as ontologies. Indeed, Semantic Web inference can improve traditional text search, and text search can be used to facilitate or augment Semantic Web inference [6].

Text Mining is an information retrieval task aimed at discovering new, previously unknown information, by automatically extracting it from different text resources [7]. In fact, the term "text mining" is generally used to denote any system that analyzes large quantities of natural language text and detects lexical or linguistic usage patterns in an attempt to extract probably useful (although only probably correct) information [8]. Automatic extraction of metadata (e.g., subjects, language, authors, key-phrases) is a prime application of text mining techniques. Although contemporary automatic document retrieval techniques bypass the metadata creation stage and work directly on the full-text of the documents, text mining has been largely applied to learn metadata from documents. Language identification is a relatively simple mining task aimed at providing an important piece of metadata for documents in international collections. A simple representation for document categorization is to characterize each document by a profile that consists of "n-grams," that is, sequences of n consecutive words, that appear in it. Occurrence probabilities of common words are then compared with the most frequent words of the text data. Author's metadata is one of the primary attributes of most documents, and it is usually known. However, in some cases, authorship is uncertain and must be guessed from the text. Text mining is also applied to provide summaries of documents or groups of documents. Text summarization is aimed at producing a condensed representation of its input, intended for human consumption [9]. Earliest instances of research on summarization of scientific documents extract salient sentences from text using features like word and phrase frequency [10], positions in the text [11], and key phrases [12]. Various works published since then had concentrated on other domains, mostly on newswire data [13] and contextual advertising [14]. Overall, summarization techniques can be divided in two groups [15]: those that extract text containing the most relevant information from the source documents (*extraction-based approaches*) and those that perform paraphrasing on the source documents (*abstraction-based approaches*).

Document clustering is an unsupervised learning technique in which there is no predefined category or class, but groups of documents that belong together are sought. For example, document clustering may assist in retrieval tasks by creating links between similar documents, which in turn allows related documents to be retrieved once one of the documents has been deemed relevant to a query [16]. Although they do not require training data to be preclassified, clustering techniques are generally often more computation intensive than supervised schemes [17]. Nevertheless, clustering has been largely applied in text mining applications. Trials of unsupervised schemes include the work by Aone et al. [18], who use the conceptual clustering scheme COBWEB [19] to induce natural groupings of close-captioned text associated with video newsfeeds; Liere and Tadepalli [20], who explore the effectiveness of AutoClass [21] in producing a classification model for a portion of the Reuters corpus; Green and Edwards [22], who use AutoClass to cluster news items gathered from several sources into *stories* (i.e., groupings of documents covering similar topics). One of the main subfields of text mining is information extraction, that is, the task of filling templates from natural language input [23]. Typical extraction problems address simple relationships among entities, such as finding the predicate structure of a small set of predetermined propositions. Machine learning has been applied to the information extraction task by seeking pattern-match rules that extract fillers for slots in the template [24–27]. Extracted information can be used in a subsequent step to learn rules that characterize the content of the text itself.

In the academic area, online search engines are used to find out scientific resources, as journals and conference proceedings. However, finding and selecting appropriate information on the Web is still difficult. To simplify this process, several frameworks and systems have been developed to retrieve scientific publications from the Web. Bollacker et al. [28] developed CiteSeer (http://citeseer.ist.psu.edu/), the well-known automatic generator of digital libraries of scientific literature. Being aimed at eliminating most of the manual effort of finding useful publications on the Web, CiteSeer uses sophisticated acquisition, parsing, and presentation methods. In particular, CiteSeer uses a three-stage process: database creation and feature extraction; personalized filtering of new publications; personalized adaptation and discovery of interesting research and trends. These functions are interdependent: information filtering affects what is discovered, whereas useful discoveries tune the information filtering. In [29], the authors study how to recommend research publications using the citation between publications to create a user-item matrix. In particular, they test the ability of collaborative filtering to recommend citations that could be additional references for a target research publication. Janssen and Popat [30] developed UpLib, a personal digital library system that consists of a full-text indexed repository accessed through an active agent via a Web interface. UpLib is mainly concerned with the task of collecting personal collections comprising tens of thousands of documents. In [31], Mahdavi et al. start from the assumption that trend detection in scientific publication retrieval systems helps scholars to find relevant, new and popular special areas. To this end, they developed a semiautomatic system based on a semantic approach.

3. State of the Art

A great deal of biological information accumulated through years is currently available in online text repositories such as Medline. These resources are essential for biomedical researchers in their everyday activities to plan and perform experiments and verify the results.

Among other kinds of information, let us concentrate on publications and scientific literature, largely available on the Web for any topic. As for bioinformatics, the steady work of researchers, in conjunction with the advances in technology (e.g., high-throughput technologies), has arisen in a growing amount of known sequences. The information related with these sequences is daily made available as scientific publications. Digital archives like BMC Bioinformatics (http://www.biomedcentral.com/bmcbioinformatics/), Pub-Med Central (http://www.pubmedcentral.gov/) and other online journals and resources are more and more searched for by bioinformaticians and biologists, with the goal of retrieving publications relevant to their scientific interests. For researchers, it is still very hard to find out which publications are of interest without an explicit classification of the relevant topics they describe. Thus, these resources must provide adequate mechanisms for retrieving the required information.

3.1. Literature Retrieval in Bioinformatics. Discovering and accessing the appropriate bioinformatics resource for a specific research task has become increasingly important, as suggested in earlier reports [32]. To address this issue, various significant projects and initiatives have been carried out, leading to several pioneering indexes of bioinformatics resources that are currently available on the Internet. Available search engines can be categorized according to different criteria. In particular, in agreement with [33], search engines can be categorized in three groups, depending on the way a query is performed: (i) those that perform the query only in the fields of citations; (ii) those that perform the query in the full text article; (iii) those that further process the retrieved citations to organize them and/or to retrieve further information.

As for the first category, let us recall here RefMed [34], MedlineRanker [35], and iPubMed [36]. RefMed (http://dm.postech.ac.kr/refmed/) is a search engine for PubMed that provides relevance ranking. It is widely known that ranking according to the global importance often does not meet the user interests. Given a starting keyword-based query, an initial list of results is presented to the user, who analyzes the proposed documents and passes judgment on their relevance. Then, RefMed induces a new ranking according to the user judgment by exploiting a machine learning algorithm (i.e., RankSVM [37]). MedlineRanker (http://cbdm.mdc-berlin.de/tools/medlineranker/) and iPubMed (http://ipubmed.ics.uci.edu/) are search engines for Medline. For a given topic, the former learns the most discriminative

words by comparing a set of abstracts provided by the user with the whole Medline (or a subset). Then, it ranks abstracts according to the learned discriminative words. The latter, which implements the *search-as-you-type* paradigm, has the main advantage to provide results on the fly, which allows users to dynamically modify their query.

eTBLAST [38] and QUERTLE [39] belong to the second category. eTBLAST (http://etest.vbi.vt.edu/etblast3/) allows searching for both citations (i.e., Medline) and full-text articles (i.e., PubMed Central). To retrieve useful documents, it performs a text-similarity search by comparing documents in a target database with an input text. In doing so, it finds the documents that best match the keywords extracted from the query by analyzing the word alignment.

QUERTLE (http://www.quertle.info/) is a new semantic search engine able to perform queries on PubMed, Toxline, National Institutes of Health Re-PORTER, PubMed Central and BioMed Central. Unlike the above-mentioned systems, QUERTLE is able to perform queries based on the meaning and the context of documents. It exploits a meta-database of subject-verb-object relationships asserted by the authors and automatically extracted using semantic-based linguistics. The search engine matches the user query against these relationships.

Finally, GoPubMed [40], XploreMed [41], EBIMed [42], and iHOP [43] are search engines that belong to the third category. GoPubMed allows (http://www.gopubmed.com/web/gopubmed/) submitting keywords to PubMed, extracts Gene Ontology (GO) terms from the retrieved abstracts (GO is becoming a standard for gene/protein function annotation), and supplies the user with the relevant ontology for browsing. It indexes PubMed search results with ontological background knowledge, such as GO and MeSH. The approach to search can also help to answer questions. In particular, the summary of important terms in "top five & more" is a most helpful feature for answering questions or reducing the big initial result to a smaller set of relevant publications in one click. XploreMed (http://www.ogic.ca/projects/xplormed/) filters PubMed results according to the eight main MeSH (http://www.nlm.nih.gov/mesh/) categories and then extracts topic keywords and their cooccurrences, with the goal of extracting abstracts. EBIMed (http://www.ebi.ac.uk/Rebholz-srv/ebimed/) combines information retrieval and extraction from Medline. It analyzes retrieved Medline abstracts to highlight associations among UniProtKB/Swiss-Prot proteins, GO terms, drugs, and species. All identified terms, sentences, and abstracts are displayed in tables, and all terms are linked to their entries in biomedical databases. iHOP (http://www.ihop-net.org/UniPub/iHOP/) uses genes and proteins as hyperlinks among sentences and abstracts. It converts the information in PubMed into navigable resources. The navigation along gene network allows a stepwise and controlled exploration of the information space. Each step through the network produces information about one single gene and its interactions.

3.2. Literature Mining in Bioinformatics. Given the growth of biomedical information on the Internet, Web-based tools capable of mining the public databases and of highlighting their relevant information in a well-organized and coherent manner are more and more required. Tanabe et al. [44] have proposed MedMiner (MedMiner is no longer available), an Internet-based hypertext program able to filter and organize large amounts of textual and structured information returned from public search engines—like GeneCards (http://www.genecards.org/) and PubMed. Med-Miner offered a potentially significant new aid for coping with the torrent of molecular biology data confronting today researchers. By filtering and organizing material retrieved from high-quality Internet sites, it makes complex database searches much easier to execute and digest. MedMiner successfully integrated public and local databases, using a local database as a "proxy" to the (much larger) public ones. Additional databases could be merged into the system, integrating a wider variety of filters with a consistent user interface. PubCrawler (http://pubcrawler.gen.tcd.ie/) is a free alerting service that scores daily updates to the NCBI Medline [45] and GenBank databases. PubCrawler can keep scientists informed of the current contents of Medline and GenBank by listing new database entries that match their research interests.

To facilitate retrieval and analysis of the huge amount of data contained in documents on biological and medical data, several researchers developed dedicated information extraction systems that attempt to simplify the underlying tasks. Most of the corresponding works use the abstract only, owing to the convenience of access and the quality of data.

As abstracts provide a concise summarization of a publication, very useful to categorize it. On the other hand, analyzing full text is essential to detect all detailed information (e.g., methods, tables, and figures). Abstracts are generally available through central collections with easy direct access (e.g., PubMed). Full texts are distributed across many locations (e.g., publishers websites, journal websites, and local repositories), making their access more difficult [46].

Interactions between proteins are very important to understand their functions and biological processes. Several approaches and tools have been defined to deal with this challenge. Thomas et al. [47] present a system aimed at extracting occurrences of protein interactions from Medline abstracts, producing a database of protein pairs characterized by a type of interaction. To this end, the authors customized the Highlight system, a general purpose information extraction engine for commercial applications [47]. The main customizations of highlight consist of (i) adapting the natural language component to make it able to correctly recognize the relevant entities and events (ii) developing a set of templates or outlines of the kinds of relevant information, and (iii) developing patterns aimed at deciding how to slot items and events into templates. PPI Finder (liweilab.genetics.ac.cn/tm/) [48] is a web application aimed at mining human protein-protein interactions from PubMed abstracts. It is able to (i) find the genes related to the gene of interest based on their cooccurrence frequencies and (ii) extract the semantic descriptions of interactions

from the co-occurring literature by computational linguistic methods. Moreover, PPI Finder maps the known interactions from the widely used PPI databases, with the aim to distinguish between novel and known interactions. PIE (http://pie.snu.ac.kr/) (Protein Interaction information Extraction) is a web application to extract protein-protein interaction sentences from PubMed abstracts as well as user-provided articles. To extract hidden interactions, PIE exploits natural language processing and machine learning techniques.

Another important challenge is to automatically translate biomedical literature text into a structured form. Due the huge increase of biomedical literature, manual annotation databases are often incomplete and inconsistent with the literature [49]. In this perspective, Craven and Kumlien [50] applied machine learning techniques to automatically map information from text sources to structured representations. In particular, the goal of their research is to develop methods that can accurately map information from scientific text sources to structured representations, such as knowledge bases or databases. To this end, they developed a system to automatically extract key facts from scientific texts. Their system could be used as a support to construct and update databases and knowledge bases. The authors used the system in the development of an ontology of localization patterns and to populate the corresponding database with text-extracted facts describing localization patterns of individual proteins. Another application of this system is to provide structured summaries of what is known about biological objects. Moreover, according to Swanson and Smalheiser [51], the system can be used to extract relationships among entities by automatically eliciting information from the literature. PreBIND (http://bind.ca) [52] is a system developed to solve a very specific problem. It has been devised to curate the BIND database. BIND is a database aimed at curating and archiving protein-protein interaction from the literature using a standard data representation. In doing so, PreBind exploits both statistical and rule-based methods. Statistical methods are used to retrieve relevant documents, whereas rule-based methods are used for biomolecule name recognition, with the aim to find statements about protein interactions. Wiegers et al. [53] proposed another tailored solutions. The authors presented a text-mining prototype to curate the Comparative Toxicogenomics Database (CTD), a publicly available resource that promotes understanding about the etiology of environmental diseases. It provides manually curated chemical-gene/protein interactions and chemical- and gene-disease relationships from the peer-reviewed published literature. The goals of the research reported here were to establish a baseline analysis of current CTD curation, develop a text-mining prototype from readily available open-source components, and evaluate its potential value in augmenting curation efficiency and increasing data coverage. PathText [54] is an integrated environment for combining standards compliant biological pathway models and original publications regarding selected parts of the pathway, through the use of text mining technology and tools, to facilitate the creation of manual annotations. PathText integrates three knowledge sources indispensable for systems biology: (i) external databases, such as SwissProt, EntreGene, Flybase, HUGO; (ii) text databases such as MEDLINE and full publications; (iii) pathways as organized interpretations of biological facts. PathText successfully provides integration of text to pathways and has been used by three groups that make research on biological topics at the Systems Biology Institute, the University of Tokyo [55], and the Manchester Centre for Integrative Systems Biology in the UK [56]. Karamanis et al. [57] apply natural language processing techniques to develop a generic tool aimed at assisting FlyBase curators. Kiritchenko et al. [58] proposed a tool aimed at retrieving Medline publications that mention genes. After being retrieved, publications are categorized according to the GO codes. The purpose of their work is to retrieve the known functionality of a group of genes from the literature and translate it into a controlled vocabulary. The categorization process can be used for automatic or semiautomatic database curation and maintenance. At the same time, it can be used as a stage in gene expression analysis. After that microarray experiments have been performed and gene expression data have been preprocessed and clustered, the information on gene functions can be added as background knowledge. Literature-Based Discovery (LBD for short) is another relevant research area that applies text-mining with the goal of finding new relationships from knowledge typically available on the Web, in terms of scientific documents, books, and papers. The technique was pioneered by Don R. Swanson in the 1980s and has been widely studied afterwards. It is worth pointing out that LBD techniques do not generate knowledge by means of experiments. Rather, they seek to connect existing knowledge from empirical results by searching and highlighting relationships not yet put into evidence. The pioneering work of Swanson [59] hypothesized the role of fish oil in clinical treatment of Raynaud's disease, combining different pieces of information from the literature, and the hypothesis was later confirmed with experimental evidence. Swanson was using the so-called ABC model of discovery, which asserts that, in the event A and B are related and B and C are related, then A and C might be (indirectly) related. Swanson's ABC model can be implemented in accordance with two different discovery processes: closed and open. The former tries to identify existing links between a hypothesis and the existing literature, whereas the latter generalizes the closed approach by rendering the hypothesis a "free variable" in the discovering task. Hence, a closed discovery process is characterized by the elaboration of a hypothesis, whereas an open discovery process is also concerned with hypothesis generation. LBD has been extensively investigated and applied to many areas of biomedicine, mainly using textual information derived from MedLine (typically in terms of titles, abstracts, and MeSH headings). Among relevant tools and systems proposed and/or experimented in this research field (for a review, see, e.g., [60]), let us recall the work of Hristovski et al. [61]. The authors use semantic predications to enhance cooccurrence-based open discovery systems. Predications are produced by using two natural language processing systems in combination that is, BioMedLEE [62] and SemRep [63], together with

the BITOLA system. BITOLA is an open discovery system, compliant with the Swanson's approach, which uses MeSH terms instead of title words and employs association rules instead of word frequencies to relate medical concepts. The authors include also domain-specific knowledge, as they use information in the form of chromosome location and gene expression localization.

Corney et al. [64] propose BioRAT (http://bioinf.cs.ucl.ac .uk/software_downloads/biorat/) (Biological Research Assistant for Text mining), an information extraction tool specifically tailored for biomedical tasks. Able to access and analyze both abstracts and full-length publications, it incorporates a domain specific document search ability. BioRAT uses natural language processing techniques and domain-specific knowledge to search for patterns in documents, with the aim of identifying interesting facts. These facts can then be extracted to produce a database of information, which has a higher *information density* than a pile of publications. PolySearch (http://wishart.biology.ualberta.ca/polysearch/) [65] is a web application aimed at extracting and analyzing text-derived relationships between human diseases, genes, proteins, mutations (SNPs), drugs, metabolites, pathways, tissues, organs, and subcellular localizations. To this end, it analyzes documents and data from several sources, including PubMed, OMIM, DrugBank, SwissProt, HMDB, HGMD, and Entrez SNP. The system has been designed to address queries of the form "*Given a single X, find all Y's*," where X and Y are biomedical terms (e.g., diseases, tissues, cell compartments, and gene/protein names). Metabolic and signaling pathways are an increasingly important part of organizing knowledge in systems biology. They serve to integrate collective interpretations of facts scattered throughout the literature. Biologists construct a pathway by reading a large number of publications and interpret them as a consistent network, but most of the models currently lack direct links to those publications. Biologists who want to check the original publications have to spend substantial amounts of time to collect relevant publications and to identify the sections relevant to the pathway [66]. PathwayAssist [67] is a software application developed to navigate and analyze biological pathways, gene regulation networks, and protein interaction maps. PathwayAssist enables researchers to create their own pathways and produces pathway diagrams. For visualization purposes, pathways are represented as a graph with two types of nodes: those reserved for proteins, small molecules, and cellular processes and those that represent events of functional regulation, chemical reactions, and protein-protein interactions. PathwayAssist comes with a database of molecular networks automatically assembled from scientific abstracts. The database has been populated by using the text-mining tool MedScan on the whole PubMed. MedScan preprocesses input text to extract relevant sentences, which undergo natural language processing. The preprocessing step uses a manually curated dictionary of synonyms to recognize biological terms. Sentences that do not contain at least one matched term are filtered out. The natural language processing kernel deduces the syntactic structure of a sentence and establishes logical relationships between concepts. Finally, results are matched against the functional ontology to produce the biological interpretation. SciMiner (http://jdrf.neurology.med.umich.edu/SciMiner/) [68] is a web-based literature mining and functional analysis tool aimed at analyzing Medline abstracts and full-text articles to identify genes and proteins. Gene and proteins are extracted and ranked by the number of documents in which they appear. Moreover, they are further analyzed for their enrichments in GO terms, pathways, Medical Subject Heading (MeSH) terms, and protein-protein interaction networks based on external annotation resources. Anni 2.0 (http://biosemantics.org/anni) [69] retrieves documents and associations for several classes of biomedical concepts. It exploits an ontology-based interface to MEDLINE that defines concepts and their relations. Anni finds related concepts based on their associated sets of texts. Peregrine [70] is a concept recognition software, that has been used in Anni to identify references to concepts in text. Texts can be also related to a concept by using manually curated annotation databases. Texts related with a concept are characterized by a concept profile, which consists of a list of concepts used to infer functional associations between genes, between genes and GO codes, to infer novel genes associated with the nucleolus, and to identify new uses for drugs and other substances in the treatment of diseases. FACTA (http://text0.mib.man.ac.uk/software/facta/) [71] is a text search engine aimed at browsing biomedical concepts that are potentially relevant to a query. FACTA differs from other similar tools for its ability to deliver real-time responses and to accept flexible queries.

4. Open Problems and Challenges

As already pointed out, the steady work of researchers has brought a huge increase of publications in life sciences. This amount of scientific literature requires an extra work by researchers, typically involved in keeping up-to-date all information related to their favorite research topics. This effort mainly depends on two aspects: the continuous increase of the scientific production and the poor amount of communication among life science disciplines [72]. In this scenario, devising suitable strategies, techniques, and tools aimed at supporting researchers in the task of automatically retrieving relevant information on the Web (in particular, from text documents), has become an issue of paramount importance.

The research field of literature retrieval and mining in bioinformatics is intrinsically manifold, which makes more complex the task of identifying open problems and challenges. However, in our view, some specific issues deserve the attention of researchers more than others, along the way that leads to significant improvements. Without claiming exhaustiveness, let us briefly point out some of them: (i) encoding/preprocessing techniques; (ii) intrinsic complexity of literature retrieval and mining problems; (iii) standards and requirement for further standardization; (iv) assessment of existing tools.

Encoding/Preprocessing Techniques. Roughly speaking, preprocessing techniques can be divided according to the following dimensions: (i) natural language processing (NLP), (ii) lexical techniques, and (iii) semantic techniques. Currently, NLP does not guarantee to come up with effective solutions able to account for the virtually infinite set of variations concerning the way relevant information is "deployed" in text documents. However, this field may become of primary importance in the next future, due to its great potential. Lexical techniques, focused on finding relevant terms able to characterize documents, are usually simpler to implement, no matter whether they are actually framed in a perspective based on frequencies or information theory. As a matter of fact, they should be considered only a starting point, as preprocessing made using purely lexical techniques (e.g., TFIDF [2]) appears not suitable for typical literature retrieval and mining problems. To some extent, semantic techniques lie in the middle between NLP and lexical techniques. A usual schema adopted while applying semantic techniques is to enrich lexical information with additional knowledge, which can be obtained in several ways. Just to cite few: (i) any given text document can be mapped to an existing taxonomy/ontology, with the goal of identifying relevant concepts and attach them to the document itself, to facilitate further processing; (ii) specific term disambiguation techniques (e.g., latent semantic indexing, synset analysis, or NER analysis) may be applied, with the goal of improving the significance of candidate terms, to be used for representing (together with other terms) a given document; (iii) space transformation techniques (e.g., feature extraction) may be applied, with the goal of limiting the amount of information required for disambiguating text documents. Based on singular value decomposition, Latent Semantic Indexing (LSI) [73] is a technique used to compute document and term similarities according to a "soft" term matching rule. In doing so, terms and documents can be expressed as vectors of statistically independent factors, so that the similarity of any two terms can be better estimated by the cosine of their vector expressions. Synsets have become popular with the advent of WordNet [74], a lexical database for the English language. In Wordnet, English words are grouped into sets of synonyms called synsets, each containing all synonyms related to a specific concept. Named Entity Recognition (NER) [75] is aimed at detecting all instances of a biological term (e.g., protein name, gene name, drug name) in an article or a in a collection.

Intrinsic Complexity of Literature Retrieval and Mining Problems. Beyond the difficulties related to the task of identifying the "right" encoding/preprocessing technique to be adopted, some tasks are in fact inherently complex. For instance, let us consider a generic open discovery processes, framed in the subfield of LBD, which requires to select the hypothesis to be investigated. Even under the assumption that the corresponding task is guided by suitable heuristics aimed at restricting the set of candidate hypotheses, the complexity in time of an open discovery process remains very high and requires specific AI techniques and algorithms. Besides, at least in principle, complexity issues hold also for closed discovery processes, as they can be framed in the general context of abduction.

Standards and Requirements for Further Standardization. Life sciences are evolving very quickly. To this end, a wide agreement by the scientific community on describing biological concepts is more and more required. On one hand, resolving names, abbreviations, and acronyms is very difficult, due to the fact that different entities could be referenced through the same (or similar) names, abbreviations, and acronyms. On the other hand, it is difficult to detect when a composite name begins and ends in a text. In our opinion, these problems strictly depend on the lack of standard nomenclature and software tools. Fortunately, a good initiative aimed at promoting standardization has been the Unified Medical Language System (UMLS), which brings together many health and biomedical vocabularies and standards—with the goal of enabling interoperability between computer systems. The UMLS has three tools: Metathesaurus (which contains terms and codes from many vocabularies), Semantic Network (able to navigate throughout relevant categories and their relationships), and Specialist (equipped with language processing tools). However, several other problems are still open—due to a lack of standardization. In our opinion, one of the most challenging problems is the need for automatically fusing literature and biological databases. Indeed, the activities of bioinformaticians are unrelated from those of database curators. In this scenario, standard tools able to facilitate the tasks of extracting text and relationships from the literature and to facilitate database curators in the task of identifying relevant literature for annotation would greatly contribute to make the problem less severe or even absent. Other challenging problems are strongly related to the structure of scientific publications. Indeed, although it is quite easy to detect relationships between sentences by analyzing an abstract, the same it is not true while analyzing a full-text publication. This happens because the ability of a software system to detect relationships within a publication is closely related to the structure therein. In particular, each section may be in charge of addressing a specific topic. For instance, the *Introduction* is devoted to describe and analyze the problem; the *Methods* section is aimed at illustrating and explaining the methodological approach, whereas *Results* and *Discussion* are devoted to report experimental results and to discuss whether the initial goals have been achieved. This implies that different concepts (e.g., entity names, experimental conditions, and results) might be located at different sections of a publication [76]. As a consequence, a term could be related to different concepts, depending of the section(s) in which it appears. For example, the name of a gene in the *Introduction* can be related to results published in previous works rather than to novel discoveries presented in the document under analysis. The same might happen for sentences belonging to different sections of the same publication. To solve these problems, recent advances in literature retrieval and mining, together with the increase of open-access journals, are propelling publishers to provide

structured version of full-text publications (usually as XML files). We completely agree that the adoption of suitable standards able to represent documents in a structured way would greatly improve the effectiveness of text mining procedures.

Assessment of Existing Tools. Nowadays, the scientific community is strongly concerned with finding how the proposed techniques can provide better access to the existing literature. Some competitions have been organized with the aim of assessing to which extent new approaches allow to navigate and mine the literature. A good example in this direction is given by the critical assessment of text mining methods in molecular biology (BioCreAtIvE) [77, 78]. This competition, which gets together every two years many researchers, is aimed at comparing methods devised to detect: (i) biologically significant entities and their association to existing database entries and (ii) entity-fact associations (e.g., protein-functional term associations). In our view, further initiatives in this direction could promote the sharing of relevant knowledge and skills, while pushing researchers to make a step forward in their specific topics of interest.

5. Conclusions

Research and development in the analysis of bioinformatics literature aims to provide bioinformaticians with effective means to access and exploit the knowledge contained in scientific publications. Although the majority of scientific publications are nowadays electronically available, keeping up to date with recent findings remains a tedious task hampered by the difficulty of accessing the relevant literature. Bioinformatics text analysis aims to improve the access to unstructured knowledge by alleviating searches, providing auto-generated summaries, linking publications with structured resources, visualizing content for better understanding, and supporting researchers in the task of formulating novel hypotheses and of discovering knowledge. Research over recent years has improved fundamental methods in bioinformatics text mining, ranging from document retrieval to the extraction of relationships. Consequently, more and more integrative literature analysis tools have been put forward, targeting a broad audience of life scientists. In this paper, after briefly introducing information retrieval, text mining, and literature retrieval and mining, we first recalled the state of the art on literature retrieval and mining in bioinformatics. In the second part of the paper, we discussed some challenges deemed worth of further investigation, with the goal of improving bioinformatics literature-retrieval-and-mining tools and systems. Summarizing, the scientific community is strongly involved in addressing different problems in literature retrieving and mining, and several solutions have been currently proposed and adopted. Nevertheless, they will remain largely ineffective until the scientific community will make further significant steps towards common standards concerning the way existing knowledge is published and shared among researchers—with particular emphasis on the structure of the scientific publications.

Acknowledgments

This work has been supported by the Italian Ministry Education and Research through the Flagship "InterOmics," ITALBIONET (RBPR05ZK2Z), Bioinformatics analysis applied to Populations Genetics (RBIN064YAT 003), and the European "SHIWA" projects.

References

[1] G. Armano, M. de Gemmis, G. Semeraro, and E. Vargiu, *Intelligent Information Access*, vol. SCI 301 of *Studies in Computational Intelligence*, Springer, Heidelberg, Germany, 2010.

[2] R. A. Baeza-Yates and B. Ribeiro-Neto, *Modern Information Retrieval*, Addison-Wesley Longman, Boston, Mass, USA, 1999.

[3] M. Kobayashi and K. Takeda, "Information retrieval on the web," *ACM Computing Surveys*, vol. 32, no. 2, pp. 165–173, 2000.

[4] S. Bao, G. Xue, X. Wu, Y. Yu, B. Fei, and Z. Su, "Optimizing web search using social annotations," in *16th International World Wide Web Conference (WWW '07)*, pp. 501–510, New York, NY, USA, May 2007.

[5] C. D. Manning, P. Raghavan, and H. Schtze, *Introduction to Information Retrieval*, Cambridge University Press, New York, NY, USA, 2008.

[6] J. Mayfield and T. Finin, "Information retrieval on the semantic web: Integrating inference and retrieval," in *Proceedings of the SIGIR Workshop on the Semantic Web*, August 2003.

[7] M. W. Berry, *Survey of Text Mining*, Springer, New York, NY, USA, 2003.

[8] F. Sebastiani, "Machine learning in automated text categorization," *ACM Computing Surveys*, vol. 34, no. 1, pp. 1–47, 2002.

[9] I. Mani, *Automatic Summarization*, John Benjamins, Amsterdam, The Netherlands, 2001.

[10] H. Luhn, "The automatic creation of literature abstracts," *IBM Journal of Research and Development*, vol. 2, pp. 159–165, 1958.

[11] P. Baxendale, "Machine-made index for technical literature—an experiment," *IBM Journal of Research and Development*, vol. 2, pp. 354–361, 1958.

[12] H. P. Edmundson, "New methods in automatic extracting," *Journal of ACM*, vol. 16, pp. 264–285, 1969.

[13] A. Nenkova, "Automatic text summarization of newswire: lessons learned from the document understanding conference," in *Proceedings of the 20th National Conference on Artificial Intelligence*, vol. 3, pp. 1436–1441, AAAI Press, 2005.

[14] G. Armano, A. Giuliani, and E. Vargiu, "Studying the impact of text summarization on contextual advertising," in *Proceedings of the 8th International Workshop on Text-based Information Retrieval*, 2011.

[15] A. Kołcz, V. Prabakarmurthi, and J. Kalita, "Summarization as feature selection for text categorization," in *Proceedings of the 10th ACM International Conference on Information and Knowledge Management (CIKM '01)*, pp. 365–370, New York, NY, USA, November 2001.

[16] J. Martin, "Clustering full text documents," in *Proceedings of the Workshop on Data Engineering for Inductive Learning at (IJCAI '95)*, 1995.

[17] P. Willett, "Recent trends in hierarchic document clustering: a critical review," *Information Processing and Management*, vol. 24, no. 5, pp. 577–597, 1988.

[18] C. Aone, S. W. Bennett, and J. Gorlinsky, "Multi-media fusion through application of machine learning and nlp," in *AAAI Spring Symposium Working Notes on Machine Learning in Information Access*, 1996.

[19] D. H. Fisher, "Knowledge acquisition via incremental conceptual clustering," *Machine Learning*, vol. 2, no. 2, pp. 139–172, 1987.

[20] R. Liere and P. Tadepalli, "Active learning with committees for text categorization," in *Proceedings of the 14th National Conference on Artificial Intelligence (AAAI '97)*, pp. 591–596, July 1997.

[21] P. Cheeseman, J. Kelly, M. Self, J. Stutz, W. Taylor, and D. Freeman, *Readings in Knowledge Acquisition and Learning, chap. AutoClass: A Bayesian Classification System*, Morgan Kaufmann, San Francisco, Calif, USA, 1993.

[22] C. Green and P. Edwards, "Using machine learning to enhance software tools for internet information management," in *Proceedings of the AAAI Workshop on Internetbased Information Systems*, pp. 48–55, 1996.

[23] D. E. Appelt, "Introduction to information extraction," *AI Communications*, vol. 12, no. 3, pp. 161–172, 1999.

[24] S. Soderland, D. Fisher, J. Aseltine, and W. Lehnert, "Crystal inducing a conceptual dictionary," in *Proceedings of the 14th International Joint Conference on Artificial Intelligence*, vol. 2, pp. 1314–1319, Morgan Kaufmann, San Francisco, Calif, USA, 1995.

[25] S. B. Huffman, "Learning information extraction patterns from examples," in *Connectionist, Statistical, and Symbolic Approaches to Learning for Natural Language Processing*, pp. 246–260, Springer, London, UK, 1996.

[26] M. E. Califf and R. J. Mooney, "Relational learning of pattern-match rules for information extraction," in *Proceedings of the 16th National Conference on Artificial Intelligence (AAAI '99), 11th Innovative Applications of Artificial Intelligence Conference (IAAI '99)*, pp. 328–334, July 1999.

[27] D. Freitag, "Machine learning for information extraction in informal domains," *Machine Learning*, vol. 39, pp. 169–202, 2000.

[28] K. D. Bollacker, S. Lawrence, and C. L. Giles, "Discovering relevant scientific literature on the Web," *IEEE Intelligent Systems and Their Applications*, vol. 15, no. 2, pp. 42–47, 2000.

[29] S. M. McNee, I. Albert, D. Cosley et al., "On the recommending of citations for research papers," in *Proceedings of the 8th Conference on Computer Supported Cooperative Work (CSCW '02)*, pp. 116–125, New York, NY, USA, November 2002.

[30] W. C. Janssen and K. Popat, "UpLib: a universal personal digital library system," in *Proceedings of the 2003 ACM Symposium on Document Engineering*, pp. 234–242, fra, November 2003.

[31] F. Mahdavi, M. A. Ismail, and N. Abdullah, "Semi-automatic trend detection in scholarly repository using semantic approach," in *Proceedings of the World Academy of Science, Engineering and Technology*, pp. 224–226, Amsterdam, The Netherlands, 2009.

[32] N. Cannata, E. Merelli, and R. B. Altman, "Erratum: time to organize the bioinformatics resourceome," *PLoS Computational Biology*, vol. 2, no. 2, p. 112, 2006.

[33] A. K. Bajpai, S. Davuluri, H. Haridas et al., "In search of the right literature search engine(s)," *Nature Preceding*, 2011.

[34] H. Yu, T. Kim, J. Oh, I. Ko, S. Kim, and W. S. Han, "Enabling multi-level relevance feedback on PubMed by integrating

rank learning into DBMS," *BMC Bioinformatics*, vol. 11, supplement 2, p. S6, 2010.

[35] J. F. Fontaine, A. Barbosa-Silva, M. Schaefer, M. R. Huska, E. M. Muro, and M. A. Andrade-Navarro, "MedlineRanker: flexible ranking of biomedical literature," *Nucleic Acids Research*, vol. 37, no. 2, pp. W141–W146, 2009.

[36] J. Wang, I. Cetindil, S. Ji et al., "Interactive and fuzzy search: a dynamic way to explore MEDLINE," *Bioinformatics*, vol. 26, no. 18, Article ID btq414, pp. 2321–2327, 2010.

[37] R. Herbrich, T. Graepel, and K. Obermayer, "Large margin rank boundaries for ordinal regression," in *Advances in Large Margin Classifiers*, Smola B. and Schoelkopf S., Eds., MIT Press, Cambridge, Mass, USA, 2000.

[38] J. Lewis, S. Ossowski, J. Hicks, M. Errami, and H. R. Garner, "Text similarity: an alternative way to search MEDLINE," *Bioinformatics*, vol. 22, no. 18, pp. 2298–2304, 2006.

[39] P. Coppernoll-Blach, "Quertle: the conceptual relationships alternative search engine for pubmed," *Journal of Medical Library Association*, vol. 99, no. 2, pp. 176–177, 2011.

[40] A. Doms and M. Schroeder, "GoPubMed: exploring PubMed with the gene ontology," *Nucleic Acids Research*, vol. 33, no. 2, pp. W783–W786, 2005.

[41] C. Perez-Iratxeta, A. J. Pérez, P. Bork, and M. A. Andrade, "Update on XplorMed: a web server for exploring scientific literature," *Nucleic Acids Research*, vol. 31, no. 13, pp. 3866–3868, 2003.

[42] D. Rebholz-Schuhmann, H. Kirsch, M. Arregui, S. Gaudan, M. Riethoven, and P. Stoehr, "EBIMed—text crunching to gather facts for proteins from Medline," *Bioinformatics*, vol. 23, no. 2, pp. e237–e244, 2007.

[43] R. Hoffmann and A. Valencia, "A gene network for navigating the literature," *Nature Genetics*, vol. 36, no. 7, p. 664, 2004.

[44] L. Tanabe, U. Scherf, L. H. Smith, J. K. Lee, L. Hunter, and J. N. Weinstein, "MedMiner: an internet text-mining tool for biomedical information, with application to gene expression profiling," *BioTechniques*, vol. 27, no. 6, pp. 1210–1217, 1999.

[45] T. Greenhalgh, "How to read a paper. The medline database," *BMJ*, vol. 315, no. 7101, pp. 180–183, 1997.

[46] A. S. Yeh, L. Hirschman, and A. A. Morgan, "Evaluation of text data mining for database curation: lessons learned from the KDD Challenge Cup," *Bioinformatics*, vol. 19, pp. i331–339, 2003.

[47] J. Thomas, D. Milward, C. Ouzounis, S. Pulman, and M. Carroll, "Automatic extraction of protein interactions from scientific abstracts," *Pacific Symposium on Biocomputing*, pp. 541–552, 2000.

[48] M. He, Y. Wang, and W. Li, "PPI finder: a mining tool for human protein-protein interactions," *PLoS ONE*, vol. 4, no. 2, Article ID e4554, 2009.

[49] M. Berardi, D. Malerba, R. Piredda, M. Attimonelli, G. Scioscia, and P. Leo, *16 Biomedical Literature Mining for Biological Databases Annotation*, 2008.

[50] M. Craven and J. Kumlien, "Constructing biological knowledge bases by extracting information from text sources," in *Proceedings of the 7th International Conference on Intelligent Systems for Molecular Biology*, pp. 77–86, 1999.

[51] D. R. Swanson and N. R. Smalheiser, "An interactive system for finding complementary literatures: a stimulus to scientific discovery," *Artificial Intelligence*, vol. 91, no. 2, pp. 183–203, 1997.

[52] I. Donaldson, J. Martin, B. de Bruijn et al., "PreBIND and Textomy—mining the biomedical literature for protein-protein interactions using a support vector machine," *BMC Bioinformatics*, vol. 4, no. 1, p. 11, 2003.

[53] T. C. Wiegers, A. P. Davis, K. B. Cohen, L. Hirschman, and C. J. Mattingly, "Text mining and manual curation of chemical-gene-disease networks for the comparative toxicogenomics Database (CTD)," *BMC Bioinformatics*, vol. 10, article 326, 2009.

[54] B. Kemper, T. Matsuzaki, Y. Matsuoka et al., "PathText: a text mining integrator for biological pathway visualizations," *Bioinformatics*, vol. 26, no. 12, Article ID btq221, pp. i374–i381, 2010.

[55] K. Oda, J. D. Kim, T. Ohta et al., "New challenges for text mining: mapping between text and manually curated pathways," *BMC Bioinformatics*, vol. 9, supplement 3, p. S5, 2008.

[56] M. J. Herrgård, N. Swainston, P. Dobson et al., "A consensus yeast metabolic network reconstruction obtained from a community approach to systems biology," *Nature Biotechnology*, vol. 26, no. 10, pp. 1155–1160, 2008.

[57] I. Karamanis, R. Lewi, R. D. Seal, and B. E, "Integrating natural language processing with flybase curation," in *Proceedings of the Pacific Symposium on Biocomputing*, pp. 245–256, Maui, Hawaii, USA, 2007.

[58] S. Kiritchenko, S. Matwin, and A. F. Famili, "Hierarchical text categorization as a tool of associating genes with gene ontology codes," in *Proceedings of the 2nd European Workshop on Data Mining and Text Mining for Bioinformatics*, pp. 26–30, 2004.

[59] D. R. Swanson, "Fish oil, Raynaud's syndrome, and undiscovered public knowledge," *Perspectives in Biology and Medicine*, vol. 30, no. 1, pp. 7–18, 1986.

[60] P. Bruza and M. Weeber, *Literature-based Discovery*, vol. 15, Springer, Heidelberg, Germany, 2008.

[61] D. Hristovski, B. Peterlin, J. A. Mitchell, and S. M. Humphrey, "Using literature-based discovery to identify disease candidate genes," *International Journal of Medical Informatics*, vol. 74, no. 2–4, pp. 289–298, 2005.

[62] L. Chen and C. Friedman, "Extracting phenotypic information from the literature via natural language processing," *Medinfo*, vol. 11, no. 2, pp. 758–762, 2004.

[63] P. Srinivasan and T. Rindflesch, "Exploring text mining from MEDLINE," *Proceedings of the AMIA Symposium*, pp. 722–726, 2002.

[64] D. P. A. Corney, B. F. Buxton, W. B. Langdon, and D. T. Jones, "BioRAT: extracting biological information from full-length papers," *Bioinformatics*, vol. 20, no. 17, pp. 3206–3213, 2004.

[65] D. Cheng, C. Knox, N. Young, P. Stothard, S. Damaraju, and D. S. Wishart, "PolySearch: a web-based text mining system for extracting relationships between human diseases, genes, mutations, drugs and metabolites," *Nucleic Acids Research*, vol. 36, pp. W399–W405, 2008.

[66] S. Ananiadou, D. B. Kell, and J. I. Tsujii, "Text mining and its potential applications in systems biology," *Trends in Biotechnology*, vol. 24, no. 12, pp. 571–579, 2006.

[67] A. Nikitin, S. Egorov, N. Daraselia, and I. Mazo, "Pathway studio—the analysis and navigation of molecular networks," *Bioinformatics*, vol. 19, no. 16, pp. 2155–2157, 2003.

[68] J. Hur, A. D. Schuyler, D. J. States, and E. L. Feldman, "SciMiner: web-based literature mining tool for target identification and functional enrichment analysis," *Bioinformatics*, vol. 25, no. 6, pp. 838–840, 2009.

[69] R. Jelier, M. J. Schuemie, A. Veldhoven, L. C. J. Dorssers, G. Jenster, and J. A. Kors, "Anni 2.0: a multipurpose text-mining tool for the life sciences," *Genome Biology*, vol. 9, no. 6, article R96, 2008.

[70] M. Schuemie, R. Jelier, and J. K. J, "Peregrine: lightweight gene name normalization by dictionary lookup," in *Proceedings of*

the 2nd BioCreative Challenge Evaluation Workshop, pp. 131–140, 2007.

[71] Y. Tsuruoka, J. Tsujii, and S. Ananiadou, "Facta: a text search engine for finding associated biomedical concepts," *Bioinformatics*, vol. 24, no. 21, pp. 2559–2560, 2008.

[72] M. Weeber, H. Klein, A. R. Aronson, J. G. Mork, L. T. de Jong-van den Berg, and R. Vos, "Msc: Text-based discovery in biomedicine: the architecture of the DAD-system," *Proceedings of the AMIA, the Annual Conference of the American Medical Informatics Association*, pp. 903–907, 2000.

[73] S. C. Deerwester, S. T. Dumais, T. K. Landauer, G. W. Furnas, and R. A. Harshman, "Indexing by latent semantic analysis," *JASIS*, vol. 41, no. 6, pp. 391–407, 1990.

[74] G. A. Miller, "Wordnet: a lexical database for english," *Communications of the ACM*, vol. 38, no. 11, pp. 39–41, 1995.

[75] M. Krauthammer and G. Nenadic, "Term identification in the biomedical literature," *Journal of Biomedical Informatics*, vol. 37, no. 6, pp. 512–526, 2004.

[76] P. K. Shah, C. Perez-Iratxeta, P. Bork, and M. A. Andrade, "Information extraction from full text scientific articles: where are the keywords?" *BMC Bioinformatics*, vol. 4, article no. 20, 2003.

[77] L. Hirschman, A. Yeh, C. Blaschke, and A. Valencia, "Overview of BioCreAtIvE: critical assessment of information extraction for biology," *BMC Bioinformatics*, vol. 6, no. 1, article S1, 2005.

[78] M. Krallinger, A. Morgan, L. Smith et al., "Evaluation of text-mining systems for biology: overview of the second biocreative community challenge," *Genome Biology*, vol. 9, no. 2, article no. S1, 2008.

6

Identification of Robust Pathway Markers for Cancer through Rank-Based Pathway Activity Inference

Navadon Khunlertgit and Byung-Jun Yoon

Department of Electrical and Computer Engineering, Texas A&M University, College Station, TX 77843-3128, USA

Correspondence should be addressed to Byung-Jun Yoon; bjyoon@ece.tamu.edu

Academic Editor: Hazem Nounou

One important problem in translational genomics is the identification of reliable and reproducible markers that can be used to discriminate between different classes of a complex disease, such as cancer. The typical small sample setting makes the prediction of such markers very challenging, and various approaches have been proposed to address this problem. For example, it has been shown that pathway markers, which aggregate the gene activities in the same pathway, tend to be more robust than gene markers. Furthermore, the use of gene expression ranking has been demonstrated to be robust to batch effects and that it can lead to more interpretable results. In this paper, we propose an enhanced pathway activity inference method that uses gene ranking to predict the pathway activity in a probabilistic manner. The main focus of this work is on identifying robust pathway markers that can ultimately lead to robust classifiers with reproducible performance across datasets. Simulation results based on multiple breast cancer datasets show that the proposed inference method identifies better pathway markers that can predict breast cancer metastasis with higher accuracy. Moreover, the identified pathway markers can lead to better classifiers with more consistent classification performance across independent datasets.

1. Introduction

Advances in microarray and sequencing technologies have enabled the measurement of genome-wide expression profiles, which have spawned a large number of studies aiming to make accurate diagnosis and prognosis based on gene expression profiles [1–4]. For example, there has been significant amount of work on identifying markers and building classifiers that can be used to predict breast cancer metastasis [2, 4]. Many existing methods have directly employed gene expression data without any knowledge of the interrelations between genes. As a result, the predicted gene markers often lack interpretability and many of them are not reproducible in other independent datasets.

To overcome this problem, several different approaches have been proposed so far. For example, a recent work by Geman et al. [3] proposed an approach that utilizes the relative expression between genes, rather than their absolute expression values. It was shown that the resulting markers are easier to interpret, robust to chip-to-chip variations, and more reproducible across datasets. Another possible

way to address the aforementioned problem is to interpret the gene expression data at a "modular" level through data integration [5–11]. These methods utilize additional data sources and prior knowledge—such as protein-protein interaction (PPI) data and pathway knowledge—to jointly analyze the expression of interrelated genes. This results in modular markers, such as *pathway markers* and *subnetwork markers*, which have been shown to improve the classification performance and also to be more reproducible across independent datasets [8–11]. In order to utilize pathway markers, we need to infer the pathway activity by integrating the gene expression data with pathway knowledge. For example, Guo et al. [6] used the mean or median expression value of the member genes (that belong to the same pathway) as the activity level of a given pathway. Recently, Su et al. [10] proposed a probabilistic pathway activity inference method that uses the log-likelihood ratio between different phenotypes based on the expression level of each member gene.

In this work, we propose an enhanced pathway activity inference method that utilizes the ranking of the member genes to predict the pathway activity in a probabilistic manner. The immediate goal is to identify better pathway markers that are more reliable, more reproducible, and easier to interpret. Ultimately, we aim to utilize these markers to build accurate and robust disease classifiers. The proposed method is motivated by the relative gene expression analysis strategy proposed in [3, 12] and it builds on the concept of probabilistic pathway activity inference proposed in [10, 11]. In this study, we focus on predicting breast cancer metastasis and demonstrate that the proposed method outperforms existing methods. Preliminary results of this work have been originally presented in [13].

2. Materials and Methods

2.1. Study Datasets. Six independent breast cancer microarray gene expression datasets have been used in this study: GSE2034 (USA) [4], NKI295 (The Netherlands) [14], GSE7390 (Belgium) [15], GSE1456 (Stockholm) [16], GSE15852, and GSE9574. The Netherlands dataset uses a custom Agilent chip and it has been obtained from the Stanford website [17]. All datasets have been profiled using the Affymetrix U133a platform and they have been downloaded from the Gene Expression Omnibus (GEO) website [18].

The above datasets have been used in our study both with and without (re)normalization. To test the reproducibility of pathway markers, we selected the USA dataset and the Belgium dataset, both of which were obtained using the Affymetrix platform. The raw data for these two datasets have been normalized by utilizing the microarray preprocessing methods provided in the Bioconductor package [19]. We applied three popular normalization methods—RMA, GCRMA, and MAS5—with default setting.

The pathway data have been obtained from the MSigDB 3.0 Canonical Pathways [20]. This pathway dataset consists of 880 pathways, where 3,698 genes in these pathways intersect with all datasets.

2.2. Gene Ranking. In this study, we utilize "gene ranking" or the relative ordering of the genes based on their expression levels within each profile [3]. Consider a pathway that contains n member genes $\mathcal{G} = \{g_1, g_2, \ldots, g_n\}$ after removing the genes that are not included in all datasets. Given a sample $\mathbf{x}_k = \{x_k^1, x_k^2, \ldots, x_k^n\}$ that contains the expression level of the member genes, the gene ranking $\mathbf{r}_k$ is defined as follows:

$$\mathbf{r}_k = \left\{ r_k^{i,j} \mid 1 \leq i < j \leq n \right\}, \tag{1}$$

where

$$r_k^{i,j} = \begin{cases} 1, & \text{if } x_k^i < x_k^j, \\ 0, & \text{otherwise.} \end{cases} \tag{2}$$

The resulting gene ranking $\mathbf{r}_k$ is a binary vector representing the ordering of the member genes based on their expression values in the kth sample $\mathbf{x}_k$. To preserve the gene ranking in each sample, we do not employ any between-sample normalization.

2.3. Pathway Activity Inference Based on Gene Ranking. To infer the pathway activity, we follow the strategy proposed in [10], where the activity level a_k of a given pathway in the kth sample is predicted by aggregating the probabilistic evidence of all the member genes. The main difference between the strategy proposed in this work and the original strategy [10] is that we estimate the probabilistic evidence provided by each gene based on its ranking rather than its expression value. More specifically, the pathway activity level is given by

$$a_k = \sum_{1 \leq i < j \leq n} \lambda_{i,j}\left(r_k^{i,j}\right), \tag{3}$$

where $\lambda_{i,j}(r_k^{i,j})$ is the log-likelihood ratio (LLR) between the two phenotypes (i.e., class labels) for the ranking $\mathbf{r}_k$. The LLR $\lambda_{i,j}(r_k^{i,j})$ is defined as

$$\lambda_{i,j}\left(r_k^{i,j}\right) = \log\left[\frac{f_{i,j}^1\left(r_k^{i,j}\right)}{f_{i,j}^2\left(r_k^{i,j}\right)} \right], \tag{4}$$

where $f_{i,j}^1(r)$ is the conditional probability mass function (PMF) of the ranking of the expression level of gene g_i and gene g_j under phenotype 1 and $f_{i,j}^2(r)$ is the conditional PMF of the ranking of the expression level of gene g_i and gene g_j under phenotype 2.

In practice, the number of possible gene pairs ($\binom{n}{2}$) may be too large when we have large pathways with many member genes (i.e., when n is large). To reduce the computational complexity, we prescreen the gene pairs based on the mutual information [21] as follows. For every gene pair (i, j), we first compute the mutual information between the ranking $r_k^{i,j}$ and the corresponding phenotype c_k. Then we select the top 10% gene pairs with the highest mutual information and use only these gene pairs for computing the pathway activity level defined in (3). Although we selected the top 10% gene pairs for simplicity, this may not be necessarily optimal and one may also think of other strategies for adaptively choosing this threshold.

In a practical setting, we may not have enough training data to reliably estimate the PMFs $f_{i,j}^1(r)$ and $f_{i,j}^2(r)$. For this reason, we normalize the original LLR $\lambda_{i,j}(r_k^{i,j})$ as follows to decrease its sensitivity to small alterations in gene ranking:

$$\widehat{\lambda}_{i,j}\left(r_k^{i,j}\right) = \frac{\lambda_{i,j}\left(r_k^{i,j}\right) - \mu\left(\lambda_{i,j}\right)}{\sigma\left(\lambda_{i,j}\right)}, \tag{5}$$

where $\mu(\lambda_{i,j})$ and $\sigma(\lambda_{i,j})$ are the mean and standard deviation of $\lambda_{i,j}(r_k^{i,j})$ across all $k = 1, \ldots, n$. Figure 1 illustrates the overall process.

2.4. Assessing the Discriminative Power of Pathway Markers. In order to assess the discriminative power of a pathway marker, we compute the t-test statistics score, which is given by

$$t(\mathbf{a}) = \frac{\mu_1 - \mu_2}{\sqrt{\sigma_1/K_1 + \sigma_2/K_2}}, \tag{6}$$

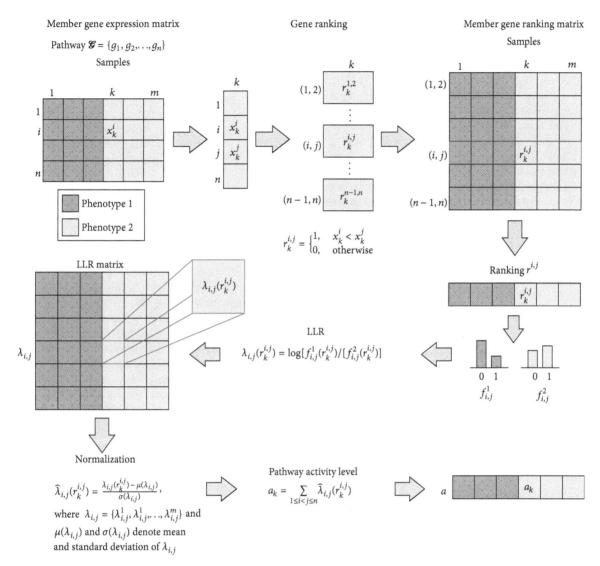

FIGURE 1: Probabilistic inference of rank-based pathway activity. For a given pathway, we first compute the ranking of the member genes for each individual sample in the dataset. Then we estimate the conditional probability mass function (PMF) of the gene ranking under each phenotype. Next, we transform the gene ranking into log-likelihood ratios (LLRs) based on the estimated PMFs and normalize the LLR matrix. Finally, the pathway activity level is inferred by aggregating the normalized LLRs of the member genes.

where $\mathbf{a} = \{a_k\}$ is the set of inferred pathway activity levels for a given pathway, μ_ℓ and σ_ℓ represent the mean and the standard deviation of the pathway activity levels for samples with phenotype $\ell \in \{1, 2\}$, respectively, and K_ℓ represents the number of samples in the dataset with phenotype ℓ. This measure has been widely used in previous studies to evaluate the performance of pathway markers [9, 10].

2.5. Evaluation of the Classification Performance. In order to evaluate the classification performance, we use the AUC (Area under ROC Curve). Many previous studies [8–11] have utilized AUC due to its ability to summarize the efficacy of a classification method over the entire range of specificity and sensitivity. We compute the AUC based on the method proposed in [22]. Given a classifier, let $x_1, x_2, \ldots, x_m$ be the output of the classifier for m positive samples and let

$y_1, y_2, \ldots, y_n$ be the output for n negative samples. The AUC of the classifier can be computed as follows:

$$A = \frac{1}{mn} \sum_{i=1}^{m} \sum_{j=1}^{n} I\left(x_i > y_j\right), \quad (7)$$

where

$$I\left(x_i > y_j\right) = \begin{cases} 1, & \text{if } x_i > y_j, \\ 0, & \text{otherwise.} \end{cases} \quad (8)$$

3. Results and Discussion

3.1. Discriminative Power of the Pathway Markers Using the Proposed Method. In order to assess the performance of the rank-based pathway activity inference method proposed in this paper, we first evaluated the discriminative power of the pathway markers following a similar setup that was adopted in a number of previous studies [9, 10]. For comparison, we also evaluated the performance of the mean and median-based schemes proposed in [6] and the original probabilistic pathway activity inference method (we refer to this method as the "LLR method" for simplicity) presented in [10]. As explained in Materials and Methods, the discriminative power of a pathway marker was measured based on the absolute t-test score of the inferred pathway activity level. Then the pathway markers were sorted according to their t-score, in a descending order.

Figure 2 shows the discriminative power of the pathway markers on the six datasets using different activity inference methods. On each dataset, we computed the mean absolute t-test statistics score of the top $P\%$ pathways for each of the four pathway activity inference methods. The x-axis corresponds to the proportion ($P\%$) of the top pathway markers that were considered and the y-axis shows the mean absolute t-test score for these pathway markers. As we can see from Figure 2, the proposed method clearly improves the discriminative power of the pathway markers on all six datasets that we considered in this study. In order to investigate the effect of normalization on the discriminative power of the pathway activity inference methods, we repeated this experiment using the USA and the Belgium datasets, where we first normalized the raw data using three different normalization methods (RMA, GCRMA, and MAS5) and then evaluated the discriminative power of the pathway markers. The results are summarized in Figure S1 (see Supplementary Material available online at http://dx.doi.org/10.1155/2013/618461), where we can see that the proposed rank-based scheme is not very sensitive to the choice of the normalization method and performs consistently well in all cases.

Next, we investigated how the top pathway markers identified on a specific dataset perform in other independent datasets. We first ranked the pathway markers based on their mean absolute t-test statistics score in one of the datasets and then estimated the discriminative power of the top $P\%$ markers on a different dataset. These results are shown in Figure 3, where the first dataset is used for ranking the markers and the second dataset is used for assessing the discriminative power. As we can see from Figure 3, the pathway markers identified using the mean- and the median-based schemes do not retain their discriminative power very well in other datasets. Both the LLR method [10] and the proposed rank-based inference method perform well across different datasets, where the proposed method clearly outperforms the previous LLR method. It is interesting to see that the discriminative power of the markers is retained even when we consider datasets that are obtained using different platforms. For example, USA/Belgium datasets are profiled on the U133a platform and The Netherlands dataset is profiled on a custom Agilent chip, but Figure 3 shows that pathway markers identified using the proposed method retain their discriminative power across these datasets. As before, we repeated these experiments after normalizing the datasets using different normalization methods. The results are depicted in Figure S2, where we can see that the proposed method works very well, regardless of the normalization method that was used. Interestingly, this is also true even

when the first dataset and the second dataset are normalized using different methods, as shown in Figures S3 and S4.

Another interesting observation is that the rank-based method can overcome one of the limitations of the previous LLR method. For example, normalization of the Belgium dataset using GCRMA results makes the LLR method fail, as some of the genes loose variability and some of the LLR values become infinite. We can see this issue in Figures S1(d), S2(c), S3(a), and S3(f). However, this limitation is easily overcome by the proposed method through the use of gene ranking and the preselection of informative gene pairs based on mutual information.

3.2. Classification Performance of the Pathway Markers Using the Proposed Method.
Next, we evaluated the classification performance of the proposed rank-based pathway activity inference method. For this purpose, we performed fivefold cross validation experiments, following a similar setup used in previous studies [8–11]. We first performed the within-dataset experiments for each of the six datasets. First, a given dataset was randomly divided into fivefolds, where fourfolds (training dataset) were used for constructing an LDA (Linear Discriminant Analysis) classifier and the remaining fold (testing dataset) was used for evaluating its performance. To construct the classifier, the training dataset was again divided into threefolds, where twofolds (marker-evaluation dataset) were used for evaluating the pathway markers and the remaining onefold (feature-selection dataset) for feature selection. The entire training dataset was used for PDF/PMF estimation. The overall setup is shown in Figure 4(a).

In order to build the classifier, we first evaluated the discriminative power of each pathway on the marker-evaluation dataset. The pathways were sorted according to their absolute t-test statistics score in a descending order and the top 50 pathways were selected as potential features. Initially, we started with an LDA-based classifier with a single feature (i.e., the pathway marker that is on the top of the list) and continued to expand the feature set by considering additional pathway markers in the list. The classifier was trained using the marker-evaluation dataset and its performance was assessed on the feature-selection dataset by measuring the AUC. Pathway markers were added to the feature set only when they increased the AUC. Finally, the performance of the classifier with the optimal feature set was evaluated by computing the AUC on the testing dataset. The above process was repeated for 100 random partitions to ensure reliable results, and we report the average AUC as the measure of overall classification performance.

Figure 5 shows how the respective classifiers that use different pathway activity inference methods perform on different datasets. As we can see in Figure 5, among the four inference methods, the proposed rank-based scheme typically yields the best average performance across these datasets. We also performed similar experiments based on the USA and the Belgium datasets after normalizing the raw data using different normalization methods. These results are summarized in Figure S5. We can see from Figure S5 that the proposed method yields the best performance on the

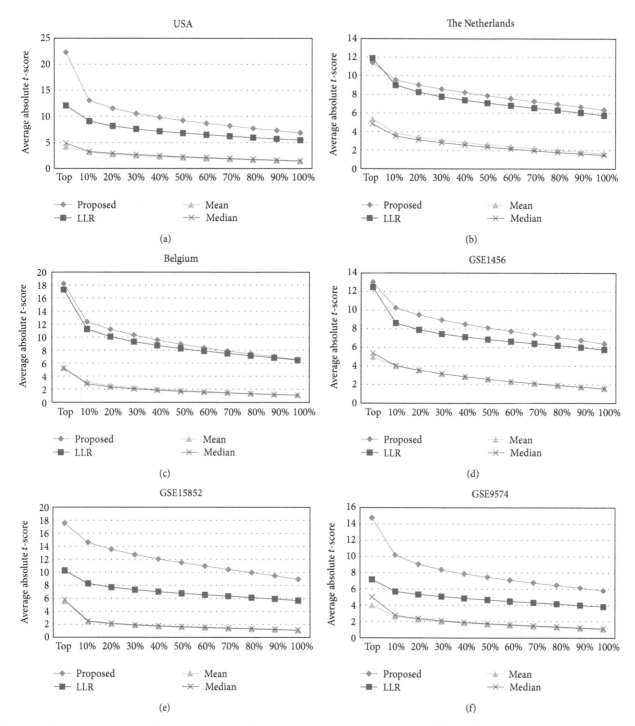

FIGURE 2: Discriminative power of pathway markers. We computed the mean absolute t-score of the top P% markers for each dataset without any further normalization.

USA dataset for all three normalization methods. On the Belgium dataset, the proposed method yields good consistent performance that is not very sensitive to the normalization method.

3.3. Reproducibility of the Pathway Markers Identified by the Proposed Method. To assess the reproducibility of the pathway markers, we performed the following cross-dataset

experiments based on a similar setup that has been utilized in previous studies [8–11]. In this experiment, we used one of the breast cancer datasets for selecting the best pathway markers (i.e., only for feature selection) and a different dataset for building the classifier (using the selected pathways) and evaluating the performance of the resulting classifier. More specifically, we proceeded as follows. The first dataset was first divided into threefolds, where twofolds were used for

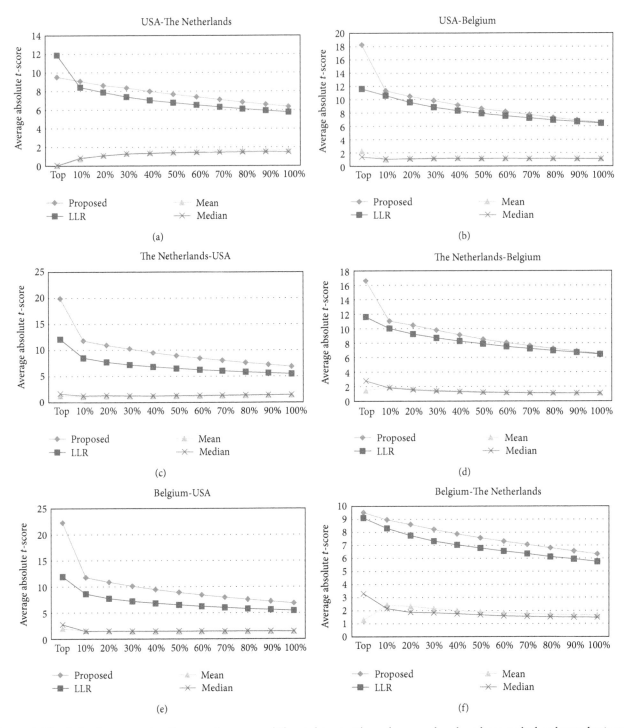

FIGURE 3: Discriminative power of pathway markers across different datasets. The pathway markers have been ranked and sorted using the first dataset, and their discriminative power has been reevaluated using the second dataset. As before, the mean absolute t-score was used for assessing the discriminative power.

marker evaluation and the remaining fold was used for feature selection. The second dataset was randomly divided into fivefolds, where fourfolds were used to train the LDA classifier, using the features selected from the first dataset, and the remaining fold was used to evaluate the classification performance. The overall setup is shown in Figure 4(b). To obtain reliable results, we repeated this experiment for

100 random partitions (of the second dataset) and report the average AUC as the performance metric. For these experiments, we used the three largest breast cancer datasets (USA, The Netherlands, and Belgium) among the six.

The results of the cross-dataset classification experiments are shown in Figure 6. As we can see from this figure, the proposed rank-based inference scheme typically outperforms

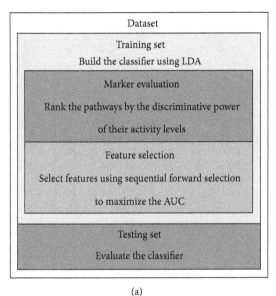

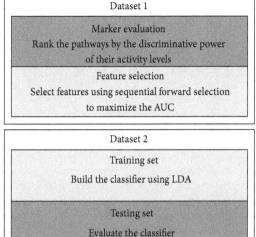

(a)   (b)

FIGURE 4: Experimental setup for evaluating the classification performance. (a) The setup for the within-dataset experiment. (b) The setup for the cross-dataset experiment.

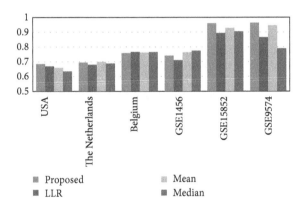

FIGURE 5: Classification performance for within-dataset experiments. The bars show the classification performance (average AUC) of different pathway activity inference methods evaluated on various breast cancer datasets.

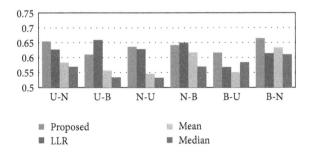

FIGURE 6: Classification performance for cross-dataset experiments. The bars show the cross-dataset classification performance (average AUC) of different pathway activity inference methods. The first dataset was used for selecting the pathway markers and the second dataset was used for training and evaluation of the classifier. The three largest breast cancer datasets were used: USA (U), The Netherlands (N), and Belgium (B).

other methods in terms of reproducibility. Furthermore, we can also observe that the proposed method yields consistent classification performance across experiments, while the performance of other inference methods is much more sensitive on the choice of the dataset. Next, we repeated the cross-dataset classification experiments based on the USA and the Belgium datasets after normalizing the raw data using RMA, GCRMA, and MAS5. As shown in Figure 7, the proposed method yields consistently good performance, regardless of the normalization method that was used.

Finally, we performed additional cross-dataset experiments after normalizing the USA and the Belgium datasets using different normalization methods. These results are summarized in Figures S6 and S7. We can see that the proposed pathway activity inference scheme is relatively robust to "normalization mismatch." Moreover, these results also show that the proposed scheme overcomes the problem of the previous LLR-based scheme [10] when used with GCRMA (see Figures 7, S6, and S7).

4. Conclusions

In this work, we proposed an improved pathway activity inference scheme, which can be used for finding more robust and reproducible pathway markers for predicting breast cancer metastasis. The proposed method integrates two effective strategies that have been recently proposed in the field: namely, the probabilistic pathway activity inference method [10] and the ranking-based relative gene expression analysis approach [3]. Experimental results based on several breast cancer gene expression datasets show that our proposed inference method identifies better pathway markers that have higher discriminative power, are more reproducible, and can lead to better classifiers that yield more consistent performance across independent datasets.

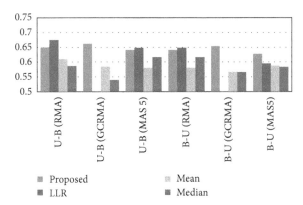

FIGURE 7: Classification performance for cross-dataset experiments. We repeated the cross-dataset experiments based on the USA and the Belgium datasets after normalizing the raw data using different normalization methods.

Acknowledgment

N. Khunlertgit has been supported by a scholarship from the Royal Thai Government.

References

[1] M. West, C. Blanchette, H. Dressman et al., "Predicting the clinical status of human breast cancer by using gene expression profiles," *Proceedings of the National Academy of Sciences of the United States of America*, vol. 98, no. 20, pp. 11462–11467, 2001.

[2] L. J. Van't Veer, H. Dai, M. J. Van de Vijver et al., "Gene expression profiling predicts clinical outcome of breast cancer," *Nature*, vol. 415, no. 6871, pp. 530–536, 2002.

[3] D. Geman, C. D'Avignon, D. Q. Naiman, and R. L. Winslow, "Classifying gene expression profiles from pairwise mRNA comparisons," *Statistical Applications in Genetics and Molecular Biology*, vol. 3, no. 1, article 19, 2004.

[4] Y. Wang, J. G. M. Klijn, Y. Zhang et al., "Gene-expression profiles to predict distant metastasis of lymph-node-negative primary breast cancer," *The Lancet*, vol. 365, no. 9460, pp. 671–679, 2005.

[5] L. Tian, S. A. Greenberg, S. W. Kong, J. Altschuler, I. S. Kohane, and P. J. Park, "Discovering statistically significant pathways in expression profiling studies," *Proceedings of the National Academy of Sciences of the United States of America*, vol. 102, no. 38, pp. 13544–13549, 2005.

[6] Z. Guo, T. Zhang, X. Li et al., "Towards precise classification of cancers based on robust gene functional expression profiles," *BMC Bioinformatics*, vol. 6, article 58, 2005.

[7] C. Auffray, "Protein subnetwork markers improve prediction of cancer outcome," *Molecular Systems Biology*, vol. 3, article 141, 2007.

[8] H. Y. Chuang, E. Lee, Y. T. Liu, D. Lee, and T. Ideker, "Network-based classification of breast cancer metastasis," *Molecular Systems Biology*, vol. 3, article 140, 2007.

[9] E. Lee, H. Y. Chuang, J. W. Kim, T. Ideker, and D. Lee, "Inferring pathway activity toward precise disease classification," *PLoS Computational Biology*, vol. 4, no. 11, Article ID e1000217, 2008.

[10] J. Su, B. J. Yoon, and E. R. Dougherty, "Accurate and reliable cancer classification based on probabilistic inference of pathway activity," *PloS ONE*, vol. 4, no. 12, Article ID e8161, 2009.

[11] J. Su, B. J. Yoon, and E. R. Dougherty, "Identification of diagnostic subnetwork markers for cancer in human protein-protein interaction network," *BMC Bioinformatics*, vol. 11, no. 6, article 8, 2010.

[12] J. A. Eddy, L. Hood, N. D. Price, and D. Geman, "Identifying tightly regulated and variably expressed networks by Differential Rank Conservation (DIRAC)," *PLoS Computational Biology*, vol. 6, no. 5, Article ID e1000792, 2010.

[13] N. Khunlertgit and B. J. Yoon, "Finding robust pathway markers for cancer classification," in *Proceedings of the IEEE International Workshop on Genomic Signal Processing and Statistics (GENSIPS '12)*, 2012.

[14] M. J. Van De Vijver, Y. D. He, L. J. Van 'T Veer et al., "A gene-expression signature as a predictor of survival in breast cancer," *New England Journal of Medicine*, vol. 347, no. 25, pp. 1999–2009, 2002.

[15] C. Desmedt, F. Piette, S. Loi et al., "Strong time dependence of the 76-gene prognostic signature for node-negative breast cancer patients in the TRANSBIG multicenter independent validation series," *Clinical Cancer Research*, vol. 13, no. 11, pp. 3207–3214, 2007.

[16] Y. Pawitan, J. Bjohle, L. Amler, and A. L. Borg, "Gene expression profiling spares early breast cancer patients from adjuvant therapy: derived and validated in two population-based cohorts," *Breast Cancer Research*, vol. 7, pp. R953–R964, 2005.

[17] H. Y. Chang, D. S. A. Nuyten, J. B. Sneddon et al., "Robustness, scalability, and integration of a wound-response gene expression signature in predicting breast cancer survival," *Proceedings of the National Academy of Sciences of the United States of America*, vol. 102, no. 10, pp. 3738–3743, 2005.

[18] R. Edgar, M. Domrachev, and A. E. Lash, "Gene Expression Omnibus: NCBI gene expression and hybridization array data repository," *Nucleic Acids Research*, vol. 30, no. 1, pp. 207–210, 2002.

[19] R. C. Gentleman, V. J. Carey, D. M. Bates et al., "Bioconductor: open software development for computational biology and bioinformatics," *Genome Biology*, vol. 5, no. 10, p. R80, 2004.

[20] A. Liberzon, A. Subramanian, R. Pinchback, H. Thorvaldsdóttir, P. Tamayo, and J. P. Mesirov, "Molecular signatures database (MSigDB) 3.0," *Bioinformatics*, vol. 27, no. 12, pp. 1739–1740, 2011.

[21] T. M. Cover and J. A. Thomas, *Elements of Information Theory*, Wiley Interscience, New York, NY, USA, 2006.

[22] T. Fawcett, "An introduction to ROC analysis," *Pattern Recognition Letters*, vol. 27, no. 8, pp. 861–874, 2006.

7

Do Peers See More in a Paper Than Its Authors?

Anna Divoli,[1] Preslav Nakov,[2] and Marti A. Hearst[3]

[1] *Pingar Research, Pingar, Auckland 1010, New Zealand*
[2] *Qatar Computing Research Institute, Qatar Foundation, Tornado Tower, Floor 10, P.O. Box 5825, Doha, Qatar*
[3] *School of Information, University of California at Berkeley, CA 94720, USA*

Correspondence should be addressed to Anna Divoli, annadivoli@gmail.com

Academic Editor: Goran Nenadic

Recent years have shown a gradual shift in the content of biomedical publications that is freely accessible, from titles and abstracts to full text. This has enabled new forms of automatic text analysis and has given rise to some interesting questions: How informative is the abstract compared to the full-text? What important information in the full-text is not present in the abstract? What should a good summary contain that is not already in the abstract? Do authors and peers see an article differently? We answer these questions by comparing the information content of the abstract to that in *citances*—sentences containing citations to that article. We contrast the important points of an article as judged by its authors versus as seen by peers. Focusing on the area of molecular interactions, we perform manual and automatic analysis, and we find that the set of all citances to a target article not only covers most information (entities, functions, experimental methods, and other biological concepts) found in its abstract, but also contains 20% more concepts. We further present a detailed summary of the differences across information types, and we examine the effects other citations and time have on the content of *citances*.

1. Introduction

Text mining research in biosciences is concerned with how to extract biologically interesting information from journal articles and other written documents. To date, much of biomedical text processing has been performed on titles, abstracts, and other metadata available for journal articles in PubMed[1], as opposed to using full text. While the advantages of full text compared to abstracts have been widely recognized [1–5], until relatively recently, full text was rarely available online, and intellectual property constraints remain even to the present day. These latter constraints are loosening as open access (OA) publications are gaining popularity and online full text is gradually becoming the norm. This trend started in October 2006, when the Wellcome Trust[2], a major UK funding body, changed the conditions of grants, requiring that "research papers partly or wholly funded by the Wellcome Trust must be made freely accessible via PubMed Central[3] (PMC) (or UK PubMed Central once established) as soon as possible, and in any event no later than six months after publication" [6]. Canadian Institutes of Health Research followed, as did the National Institute of Health (NIH) in the USA in April 2008.[4] Moreover, many publishers founded and promoted OA initiatives, namely, BioMed Central[5] (BMC) and the Public Library of Science[6] (PLoS). PubMed now offers access to all OA publications via PMC. The availability of OA publications has allowed several recent text mining and information retrieval competitions turning to use full-text corpora, for example, BioCreAtIvE since 2004, the TREC Genomics Track since 2006, and the BioNLP shared task since 2011.

The rise of full text, which differs in length (both overall length and average sentence length), structure (e.g., use of parenthesized text, tables, and figures), and content from abstracts, has posed many new challenges for biomedical text processing, for example, standard tools like part-of-speech and gene mention taggers were found to perform much worse on article bodies than on abstracts [7]. The availability of full text has further opened up some more general interrelated questions.

(1) *How informative is the abstract compared to the full text?*

(2) *What important information in the full text does not appear in the abstract?[7]*

(3) *What should an ideal summary of the full text contain that is not already in the abstract?*

(4) *What are the differences in the way authors and peers see an article?*

We explore these questions indirectly, using an under-explored information source: the sentences containing the citations to a target article or *citances*. While cocitation analysis is commonly-used for determining the popularity, and by association, the importance of a publication [8–15], our focus here is on the *contents* of the sentences containing the citations, that is, the citances.

In particular, we compare the information content of the abstract of a biomedical journal article to the information in all citances that cite that article, thus contrasting the important points about it as judged by its authors versus as seen by peer researchers over the years following its publication. Put another way, we use citances as an indirect way to access important information in the full text[8]. The idea is that (1) any information not mentioned in the abstract but referred to in citances should be coming from the full text, and (2) entities and concepts mentioned in a citance should be important and somewhat representative of their source.

To give an example, here is the abstract of an article (PubMed ID 11346650):

Multiple Mechanisms Regulate Subcellular Localization of Human CDC6.

CDC6 is a protein essential for DNA replication, the expression and abundance of which are cell cycle-regulated in Saccharomyces cerevisiae. We have demonstrated previously that the subcellular localization of the human CDC6 homolog, HsCDC6, is cell cycle-dependent: nuclear during G(1) phase and cytoplasmic during S phase. Here we demonstrate that endogenous HsCDC6 is phosphorylated during the G(1)/S transition. The N-terminal region contains putative cyclin-dependent kinase phosphorylation sites adjoining nuclear localization sequences (NLSs) and a cyclin-docking motif, whereas the C-terminal region contains a nuclear export signal (NES). In addition, we show that the observed regulated subcellular localization depends on phosphorylation status, NLS, and NES. When the four putative substrate sites (serines 45, 54, 74, and 106) for cyclin-dependent kinases are mutated to alanines, the resulting HsCDC6A4 protein is localized predominantly to the nucleus. This localization depends upon two functional NLSs, because expression of HsCDC6 containing mutations in the two putative NLSs results in predominantly cytoplasmic distribution. Furthermore, mutation of the four serines to phosphate-mimicking aspartates (HsCDC6D4) results in

strictly cytoplasmic localization. This cytoplasmic localization depends upon the C-terminal NES. Together these results demonstrate that HsCDC6 is phosphorylated at the G(1)/S phase of the cell cycle and that the phosphorylation status determines the subcellular localization.

And here are some citances pointing to it:

Much of the soluble Cdc6 protein, however, is translocated from the nucleus to the cytoplasm when CDKs are activated in late G1 phase, thus preventing it from further interaction with replication origins [#C, #C and #TC].

To ensure that the pre-RC will not re-form in S or G2, Cdc6p is phosphorylated and degraded in yeast (#C; #C; #C) or exported to the cytoplasm in higher organisms (#TC; #C; #C; #C; #C).

It is phosphorylated by cyclin A-cdk2 at the G1-S transition and this modification causes some, but not all, of the Cdc6 to be exported out of the nucleus (#TC; #C; #C and #C).

Cdc6CyΔ has a mutation in a cyclin binding motif that is an essential part of the substrate recognition signal for cdks (#TC).

After entry into S phase, phosphorylation of HsCdc6, probably by cyclinA/CDK2, leads to its export from nucleus to the cytoplasm via NES [#TC].

Once replication begins, Cdc6 is degraded in yeast (#C, #C, #C, #C, #C), whereas for mammals it has been suggested that Cdc6 is translocated out of the nucleus during S phase in a cyclin A-Cdk2- and phosphorylation-dependent manner (#C, #TC, #C,-#C, #C) and then subject to degradation by the anaphase-promoting complex (#C, #C, #C).

In the above examples, #TC refers to the publication we are comparing against (the target citation: PubMed ID 11346650), whereas #C refers to other publications. Throughout this paper, we will refer to these citation sentences to other publications as *adjoining citations*.

Previous studies have discussed some of the potential of the use of *citances* for literature mining [16, 17]. Similar to anchor text on the web (visible, clickable text in a webpage, clicking on which navigates the user to another webpage), they are votes of confidence about the importance of a research article. Collectively, they also summarize the most important points about the target article, which makes them a potential surrogate for its full text [18] and an important knowledge source when generating a survey of scientific paradigms [19].

While previous work has focused on the *words* in citances, we compare their contents to the contents of the abstracts using coarse-grained biologically meaningful *concepts* such as entities, functions, and experimental methods.

Focusing on the area of molecular interactions, we perform careful *manual* analysis, and we present detailed summary of the differences across information types. We further study the effects that other citations and temporal measures have on the contents of citances. Finally, we verify these manual results with a large-scale automatic analysis.

In the remainder of this paper, we first discuss related work, then we describe our concept annotation scheme, we perform manual and automatic analysis, and we summarize the results, aggregating them over information types. Finally, we discuss the findings and we point to some promising directions for future work.

2. Related Work

In the bioscience literature, several studies focused on comparing the information structure of abstracts to that of full-text. Schuemie et al. [4], building on work by Shaw [3], looked into the density (the number of instances found divided by the number of words) of MeSH terms and gene names in different sections of full text articles. They found that the density was highest in the abstract and lowest in the Methods and the Discussion sections. They further found that nearly twice as many biomedical concepts and nearly four times as many gene names were mentioned in the full text compared to the abstract. In a related study, Yu et al. [2] compared abstracts and full text when retrieving synonyms of gene and protein names and found more synonyms in the former. A more comprehensive study on the structural and content difference of abstracts versus full text can be found in [7].

There has been extensive work on automatically generating an article abstract from full text, which studies the relationship between sentences in full text to those in abstracts [1, 5]. However, this work does not consider citances.

A lot of work on citation analysis has focused on citation links and counts, which have been used to determine the relative importance of publications within a field and to study the interaction between different fields [11–14, 20]. Today, this kind of analysis is at the core of a number of scholarly sites, including CiteSeerX[9], DBLP[10], Google Scholar[11], Microsoft Academic Search[12], ACM Digital Library[13], IEEE Xplore[14], ACL Anthology[15], and ArnetMiner[16], to mention just a few. There have been also specialized research tools for exploring citation networks, for example, [21].

In natural language processing (NLP), research has focused in a different and arguably more interesting direction, using citations as an (additional) information source to solve various text processing problems. The growing interest in the research community on the topic culminated in 2009 in a specialized workshop on Text and Citation Analysis for Scholarly Digital Libraries (collocated with the 2009 Conference on Empirical Methods on Natural Language Processing[17]).

An early overview of this general research direction was presented by White [16], who described three main lines of research.

First, citation sentences can be *categorized*, for example, as conceptual versus operational, organic versus perfunctory, and so forth. For example, Teufel and Moens [22] identified and classified citations in scientific articles and used them as features for classifying noncitance sentences, for the purpose of text summarization.

Second, *context analysis* is concerned with identifying recurring terms in citances and using them to help solve information retrieval tasks. For example, Nanba et al. [23] used citances as features to help classify papers into topics. Similarly, Bradshaw [24] indexed articles with the terms in the citances that cite them. Mercer and Di Marco [25] applied a similar idea to biomedical documents. Tbahriti et al. [26] used paper cocitation as a similarity measure when evaluating a biomedical information retrieval system. Rosario and Hearst [27] demonstrated that using citances to a publication can yield higher accuracy compared to using other sentences for the problem of multiway relation classification, applied to the identification of the interactions between proteins in bioscience text. Similarly, Kolchinsky et al. [28] improved protein-protein interaction extraction using citation network features. Aljaber et al. [29] used citances text as an additional input to improve document clustering, and Aljaber et al. [30] used the text contained in citances as an additional information source to improve the assignment of Medical Subject Headings (MeSH) terms, which are commonly-used in PubMed and other databases administered by the National Library of Medicine.

The third line of research, according to White, is concerned with *citer motivation*, that is, with identifying the reason authors cite earlier work, and why some work is more cited than other. Lehnert et al. [31] created a taxonomy of 18 citation types, such as method, attribution, fact, example, critisism, and built a system to classify citations in these types. Similarly, Teufel et al. [32] annotated citation sentences from computational linguistics papers according to their rhetorical functions (e.g., contrast/comparison in goals or methods, contrast/comparison in results, weakness of cited approach, neutral description, etc.), and Teufel et al. [33] and Teufel and Kan [34] described algorithms to automatically assign such rhetorical functions.

Another informative early overview can be found in Nakov et al. [17], who also proposed the use of *citances* (they coined this neologism to refer to citation sentences) for bioscience papers for various semantic processing tasks, including summarization of target papers, synonym identification and disambiguation, and as a way to generate candidate sentences for manual curation. They further applied text paraphrase techniques to normalize the myriad forms of expression of citances in order to determine which of them express the same subsets of concepts. This last objective was later facilitated by the work of Schwartz et al. [35] using multiple sequence alignment and conditional random fields with posterior decoding.

More importantly, Nakov et al. [17] proposed to use citances as an information source for automatic summarization of the scientific contributions of a research publication, which is somewhat related to the idea of using the information in hyperlinks to summarize the contents of a web page [36, 37]. This direction has been explored by a number of researchers thereafter.

Schwartz and Hearst [38] hypothesized that in many cases, as time goes by, citances can indicate the most important contributions of a paper more accurately than its original abstract.

Qazvinian and Radev [39] used citation summaries and network analysis techniques to produce a summary of the important contributions of a research paper. A related technique for the same problem was proposed by Mei and Zhai [40], who relied on language modeling techniques. In a subsequent extension, Qazvinian and Radev [41] have proposed a general framework to pick the sentence(s) from a target paper that a citance in another paper is most likely referring to.

More closely related to the present work, Elkiss et al. [18] compared the information contained in the set of all citances citing a given biomedical paper and the abstract for that paper, using a lexical similarity metric called *cohesion*. They found significant overlaps but also many differences since citances focus on different aspects than abstracts.

Mohammad et al. [19] compared and contrasted the usefulness of abstracts and of citances in automatically generating a technical survey on a given topic from multiple research papers from the ACL Anthology. They found that while abstracts are undoubtedly useful, citances contain important additional information. They further noted that abstracts are author-biased and thus complementary to the broader perspective inherent in citances.

There has been also work that goes in the opposite direction: instead of trying to summarize a document using the textual content of multiple citances to it, Wan et al. [42] built a system that summarizes it using its full text in order to provide the reader with a summary relevant to a given citance in another document.

Hoang and Kan [20] introduced another interesting task: automatic related work summarization. Given multiple articles (e.g., conference/journal papers) as input, they created a topic-biased summary of related work that is specific to a given target paper.

Citations, citances, and links between them are similar to hyperlinks and hypertext on the web. Anchor text has been used in most search engines for indexing and retrieval of web pages. Applications of anchor text include identification of home pages of people and companies [43], classification of web pages [44, 45], Web crawlers [46], improved ranking of search results [47], and web page summarization [36]. See [24] for an overview of the uses of anchor text.

Our present work is more general and more quantitative than that in the above publications. First, we do not restrict ourselves to a particular application, while most work above was limited to, for example, summarization. Second, we study the degree of overlap between the information contained in abstracts and citances from a biomedical perspective focusing on molecular interactions and using biomedically meaningful semantic units (rather than words) such as entities, functions, dependencies, characteristics, locations, species, time, experimental methods, chemicals, and disorders. Third, we use and/or map our annotations to

MeSH[18], a standardized hierarchical resource, thus allowing for further comparisons and applications. Fourth, we study the effect of time on the way papers are cited. We further investigate the effect of the presence of adjoining citations. Finally, we report the results from both small and focused manual analysis and from large-scale automatic analysis.

3. Methods

We performed small-scale detailed manual analysis and large-scale fully automatic comparison of the information contained in citances and abstracts.

In the manual analysis, we considered 6 abstracts from PubMed in the molecular interaction domain, published during 1996–2002, and 136 citances to them, which we carefully annotated with the mentions of entities, functions, experimental methods, and other biological concepts. More details about the dataset can be found in Table 1. We used this dataset to compare the set of concepts that appear in the abstract of an article to the set of concepts that appear in the citances to that article. We also looked at the concepts mentioned in the citances over a six-year period to study changes over time.

In the automatic comparison, we analyzed 104 journal publications in PubMed (this included the six articles used for the manual analysis), again from the molecular interaction domain, published during 1995–2002, which received a total of 11,199 citances in the period 1995–2005. We annotated the MeSH terms in the abstracts of these publications and in the corresponding citances, and we mapped these terms to broad biomedical concepts; then, we proceeded with the manual analysis. MeSH is a comprehensive controlled vocabulary created for the purpose of indexing journal articles and cataloging books in the life sciences, and it is commonly used for annotations in the biomedical domain. We chose MeSH for our automatic annotations because it is a formal established resource that has a relatively simple structure, allowing for intuitive, pragmatic analysis.

3.1. Data Selection. Our goal was to find articles that are highly cited and are in an area of biology that has attracted a lot of text mining interest. The "Molecular Interaction Maps" NIH website[19] lists a number of annotations and references for each interaction map that the site covers. We selected 104 target articles from the "Replication Interaction Maps" collection and used the ISI citation service[20] to find which articles cite the targets. We downloaded them and used the code developed by Nakov et al. [17] to extract the citances. We further collected the abstracts and the full text as well as the MeSH terms and the substances indexed by PubMed for these articles. Six of the 104 articles were used for manual analysis.

3.2. Manual Annotation. We performed detailed manual analysis of the mentions of various biologically meaningful concepts in the abstracts of the target six articles and in 136 citances to them. For one target article, we considered all 46 available (in our dataset) citances, and for another one, we

TABLE 1: Summary of the data used for the manual analysis.

PubMed ID Of the target	Year of publication	Number of sentences analyzed		Number of annotations in		Number of papers the citances are derived from
		Abstract	Citances	Abstract	Citances	
8939603	1996	17	51	192	728	27
11346650	2001	11	45	141	761	24
11125146	2000	8	10	91	144	10
11251070	2001	12	10	142	128	10
11298456	2001	9	10	146	178	9
11850621	2002	8	10	132	157	8
All		65	136	844	2096	88

selected a comparable number of 51 citances, whereas for each of the remaining four articles, we analyzed 10 randomly selected citances to ensure some variation. We annotated a total of 844 concepts in the six abstracts and 2,096 in the 136 citances. See Table 1 for more detail.

The goal of the annotation was to represent as much of the important contents of the citances as possible. Table 2 describes the different types of concepts we annotate, and Figure 1 shows an example of an annotated citance.

Table 2 shows the categories for manual annotation. All datasets used in this study were annotated manually following a number of rules. Every unit (word or short phrase) was assigned an ID, and any matching unit within the same set was given the same ID. A few categories of units were decided for each set; they were reflected in the first part of the ID by a capital letter. The IDs, whenever possible, were very simple: composed of a single letter and a number. However, sometimes we tried to capture more complex units, for example, if "*Xenopus*" = "S1", "*orc*" = "E1" and "*antibody*" = "E10", then "*anti-Xorc1*" = "E10.E1.S1.1", and if "*DNA*" = "H1" and "*synthesis*" = "F1", then "*DNA synthesis*" = "H1.F1" so "*DNA*" is given the IDs: "H1, H1.P1" and "*synthesis*" is assigned "P1, H1.P1". The last column shows the corresponding MeSH IDs, which were used for the automatic annotation.

We identified the distinct semantic units, words or phrases, and we assigned them annotation IDs, which had different prefixes (E, H, etc.) for different types of information. We assigned suffixes for subtypes (e.g., E2), and we represented complex concepts by combining IDs (e.g., E2.2). We used the same rules to annotate the citances (given below).

Manual Annotation Rules

(1) Try to identify units (words or phrases) that convey information in one of the annotation categories (Table 2). Use words as annotation units, whenever possible.

(2) Compare units by trying to match them to parts of other citances within the set.

(3) If an entity (category E) is comprised of more than one word, consider the words as one unit and assign the same ID to each word.

(4) Try to group entities together (extending to protein complexes and families) if used in the same context throughout the citances for a target document. Use subtypes when necessary to keep related concepts similarly labeled (.a, .b, .c... or .1, .2, .3).

(5) If an entity is complex, use "·" to join IDs, but keep the main entity in the front. For example, if *Xenopus* = S1, *orc* = E1 and antibody = E10, then the annotation for anti−*Xorc1* is E10.E1.S1.1 and for Xorc2 is E1.S1.2.

(6) Annotate individual word units, but also consider complex concepts (e.g., *DNA replication*). Similarly to entities, capture concepts that are made of more than one unit by concatenating their IDs with "·".

(7) When annotating complex concepts, annotate each unit of the concept with the unit's ID followed by a comma, followed by the concept ID.

(8) Consider *opposite* information units (e.g., competent-incompetent, increase-decrease). Capture these in the IDs by adding ".o".

(9) Consider subcategories of IDs by appending .a, .b, ... or .1, .2,... extensions if appropriate for the same citance set, for example, *prevent and inhibit*.

3.3. *Data Analysis.* The annotations of the citances and abstract sentences shown in Table 1 enabled us to run a number of comparisons between the content of the abstract and the corresponding citances, the outcomes of which are presented in the next section.

In our automatic analysis, we relied on MeSH, the U.S. National Library of Medicine's controlled hierarchical vocabulary. There are 15 main subtrees in MeSH, each corresponding to a major branch of the biomedical terminology, for example, subtree A corresponds to *anatomy*, subtree B to *organisms*, subtree C to *diseases*, and so forth. Down the MeSH hierarchy, concepts are assigned one or more positional codes, for example, A (*anatomy*), A01 (*body regions*), A01.456 (*head*), A01.456.505 (*face*), and A01.456.505.420 (*eye*). Note that MeSH is not a tree, but a lattice, and thus multiple paths are possible for the same concept, for example, *eye* is ambiguous, and it has one additional code: A09.371 (A09 represents *sense organs*).

TABLE 2: Categories used in the manual annotation.

Categories	Description	Examples	MeSH Tree IDs
E (entities)	Genes and proteins	MCM, protein, ORC, Skp2	D06, D08, D12, and D23.529
F (function)	Biological function or process	Regulation, pathway, and function	G, F01, F02
D (dependency)	Relationship type	Involve, cause	N/A
X (characteristic)	Modifier	Unstable, common, and ionizing	N/A
L (location)	Cellular or molecular part	C-terminal, cytosol, and motif	A
S (species)	Any taxonomic description	Human, mammal, and *S. cerevisiae*	B
T (time)	Temporal information	During, after, and following	N/A
M (exp methods)	Methods and their components	Recombination, transfect	E
H (chemicals)	Not including genes/proteins	DNA, thymidine, and phosphoryl	D (except: D06, D08, D12, and D23.529)
R (disorders)	Names and associated terms	Cancer, tumor, and patient	C, F03
Special Types:			
IDs with subtypes	Subtype of a BASIC type	Retain-change, common-distinct	
IDs with opposite	Opposite of a BASIC type	Cell cycle—G phase, CDK–CDK2	
Complex IDs	Combination of BASIC types	Radio-resistant DNA synthesis	

We used an in-house MeSH term recognizer and normalizer tool, which we originally developed for our participation in the first Genomics Track [48], but which we significantly expanded thereafter. We used a version of the tool developed for the Second BioCreAtIvE Challenge [49]. The tool uses normalization rules in order to allow for the following variations in form: (1) removal of white space, for example, "BCL 2"⇒"BCL2," (2) substitution of nonalpha-numerical characters with a space, for example, "BCL-2"⇒"BCL2," and (3) concatenation of numbers to the preceding token, for example, "BCL 2"⇒"BCL2." All possible normalizations and expansions of all known MeSH terms and their synonyms were generated offline and then matched against a normalized version of the input text using an exact, first-longest-string-matching measure. The matches were then mapped back to the original unnormalized text, and the corresponding MeSH IDs were assigned.

Once the MeSH terms were identified, we considered (1) the whole MeSH tree ID and (2) the MeSH tree tag truncated to maximum 2 levels (xxx.xxx) in abstracts and citances[21]. We performed automatic analysis and mapping to identify different MeSH annotation groups (shown in Figure 2) and their counts in abstracts, corresponding citances, and their overlap. We also looked at annotations in citances with 0 adjoining citations (whose contents must have come from the target article) and how they compare to the annotations in abstracts. Finally, we looked at citances' annotations appearing in the same year as the original publication, as well as at additional/new annotations appearing in the following year, and additional annotations appearing 2, 3, and 4+ years later, and how they compare to annotations from the abstracts.

3.4. Category Mapping. There are a few distinct annotation categories in each manual and automatic schemata. However,

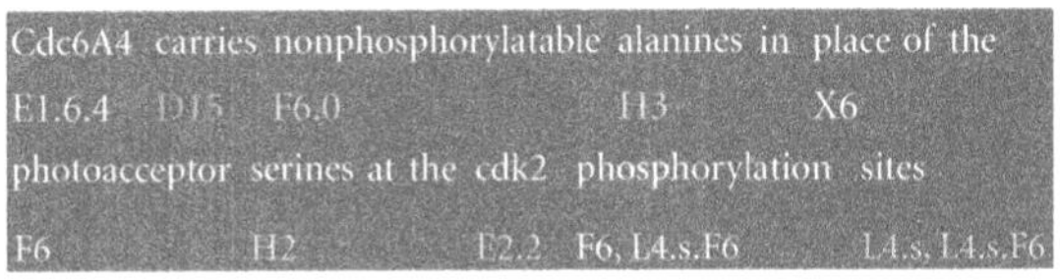

FIGURE 1: Example of an annotated citance. The citance is for PMID 11346650, demonstrating different categories of annotation (e.g., E, D; F; H...), subtypes (e.g., E1.64; L4.s; E2.2...), opposite concepts (e.g., F6.o), and complex IDs (e.g., L4.s.F6).

for most categories of interest for the area of molecular interactions, the semantic annotations overlap. We provide the mapping in Figure 2.

4. Results

Here we describe the results of our manual and automatic analysis, trying to answer the research questions posed in the introduction. We further study the effect of the presence of adjoining citances and of the passage of time.

4.1. Differences between Abstracts and Citances. In order to examine the differences in the contents of abstracts and citances, we compared the distributions of the ten categories of concepts that we considered in the manual analysis (see Table 2). Figure 3 shows these distributions (a) over abstracts and (b) over citances. It further presents these distributions (i) for all six articles, and (ii) for one article only, namely, the one with PubMed ID 11346650.

In Figure 3, we can see that there are generally higher proportions of "entities" and "experimental methods" annotations in citances than in abstracts. The difference for experimental methods was statistically significant for the two

Anatomy Organisms Diseases Chemicals Drugs Chemicals Entities Experim. Methods Psyc. Functions Psyc. Disorders Processes Functions

	Annotation group	Mapped MeSH tree IDs	Manual analysis	Automatic analysis
1	Anatomy	[A]	✓	✓
2	Organisms	[B]	✓	✓
3	Diseases	[C]	✓	✓
4	Chemicals-Drugs	[D]: 01-05, 09-10, 13, 20, 23 (not: 23.529)	✓	✓
5	Chemicals-Entities	[D]: 06, 08, 12, 23.529	✓	✓
6	Experimental Methods	[E]	✓	✓
7	Psych. Functions	[F]: 01-02	✓	✓
8	Psych.-Disorders	[F03]	✓	✓
9	Processes-Functions	[G], [F]: 01-02	✓	✓
10	Disciplines/Occupations	[H]		✓
11	Anthr./Educ./Social	[I]		✓
12	Technol./Indus./Agric.	[J]		✓
13	Humanities	[K]		✓
14	Information Science	[L]		✓
15	Named Groups	[M]		✓
16	Health Care	[N]		✓
17	Publication Character.	[V]		✓
18	Geographicals	[Z]		✓
19	Dependency	n/a (involve, cause...)	✓	
20	Characteristic	n/a (unstable, common, ionizing...)	✓	
21	Time	n/a (during, after, following...)	✓	

Disciplines Occup. Anthropol. Educ./Soc. Technology Indus./Agr. Humanities Information Science Named Groups Health Care Publication Character. Geographic.

FIGURE 2: Semantic annotation groups. This figure depicts all different annotation types associated with abstract sentences and with citances. The overlap and, where possible, the mapping of automatic and manual annotations categories are also shown. See also Table 2 for details on the mapping of MeSH IDs to categories from the manual annotation.

larger sets, corresponding to PubMed IDs 11346650 and 8939603.

The top of Figures 4 and 5 use Venn diagrams to show the overlap of unique (i.e., each ID was counted just once regardless of how many times it actually occurred) semantic annotations between abstracts and citances for the large-scale automatic analysis. Figure 4 shows the overlap over MeSH annotation categories that can be mapped (see Figure 2) to the manually assigned annotations, that is, those categories that were included in both the automatic and the manual analysis, whereas Figure 5 presents the overlap over annotation categories that were studied in the automatic but not in the manual analysis.

We see that indeed the categories in Figure 4, which we considered important for our dataset and used for the manual annotation, have a lot more unique annotations than the categories in Figure 5 that are largely less pertinent for molecular interactions (see Figure 2 for more details on the categories). We do see, however, that across all categories in both figures, citances carry a lot more annotations than abstracts with the overlap between the two being at least 50% of the abstract's unique annotations (with the exception of

psychological disorders, representing a very small portion of the annotations). For most categories, the overlap is about 75–80%.

4.2. The Effect of Adjoining Citations and the Differences between Abstracts and Citances. Looking more closely at the data in Figure 3, we found that every annotation in our six manually annotated abstracts could be found in at least one citance. For the four articles for which we only consider 10 citances, we had to look for additional unannotated citances to get complete coverage for some of the concepts.

The contrary, however, was not true: some concepts found in citances were not mentioned in the abstract. Before describing this point in detail, we would like to note that very often in bioscience journal articles, a citation sentence backs up its claims with more than one reference. As we mentioned earlier, we call the references that appear in addition to the target *adjoining citations*. Our analysis has shown that citances containing adjoining citations are the source of most of that extra information. Thus, we decided to have a closer look at the clean cases of citances with zero adjoining citations (referred to as "zero adjoining citations"

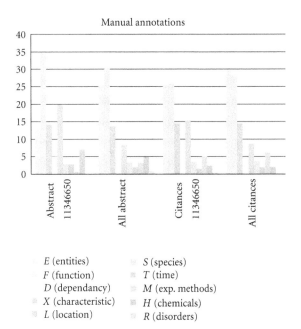

E (entities)   S (species)
F (function)   T (time)
D (dependancy)   M (exp. methods)
X (characteristic)   H (chemicals)
L (location)   R (disorders)

FIGURE 3: Distribution (in %) of the manually annotated categories for abstracts and citances. Shown are results for all abstracts and for the one with PubMed ID 11346650.

or "cit_0" below), that is, those that cited our target article only. Citances that refer to only one paper should really contain information that can be found in the citing paper.

In the manual analysis, we examined 23 citances with no adjoining citations, which corresponded to five of our target papers, and we found 73 distinct annotation types in the citances that did not appear in the abstracts. First, we checked whether the annotations conveyed biological meaning; if not, they were marked as "n/a." Then we tried to find the extra annotations in the full text of the targets, and we examined the "MeSH/substances" that the target article was indexed with in PubMed. After all these checks, a few annotations were still "not found." The distribution for each of the six articles is shown in Table 3.

Table 3 and Figure 6 (manual evaluation) show that most of the concepts that abstracts do not contain fall under the entities or the experimental methods categories. Two others were mentioned in figures of the full text paper (PMID: 11298456) as part of describing an experimental technique. Two more were actually found in the full text (PMID: 8939603) as restriction enzymes, which are commonly used in experiments to cut *dsDNA*. Some other distinct annotation types missed by abstracts were also related to Methods, for example, *plasmid*, which was annotated as a chemical; in fact, plasmids are commonly-used in genetic engineering as vectors.

Some other entities had subtypes (e.g., *Wee1A*) and although the main type was matched in the full text, the specific subtype was not. In the species category, a sentence from cit_0 for the target PubMed ID 11251070 was referring to the animal category, which was not mentioned in the abstract. The full text mentioned *eukaryotes* and *various*

organisms, but it was indexed with the more general MeSH term *animals*.

We further analyzed how adjoining citations affect the number of distinct annotation types by grouping the citances into five groups: cit_0, which cites the target paper only, cit_1/cit_2/cit_3, with one/two/three adjoining citations, and cit_4+, with four or more adjoining citations. In order to compare the effect of the adjoining citation, we took the abstract of each set (representing the minimum number of distinct annotation types), and we added each of the above groups separately as well as together (the abstract and the citances representing the maximum number of distinct annotation types). The results are shown in Table 4. We can see that the more references a citance has, the more distinct the annotation types that are introduced. The effect is most clearly pronounced for the two papers with a larger set of citances, those with PubMed IDs 8939603 and 1346650.

We also studied the effect of the adjoining citations in the larger dataset, which we used for the automatic analysis. Figure 4 shows the effect that adjoining citations have on the semantic annotation content of citances. We can see that "zero adjoining citances" contain much less annotations in comparison to all citances, but the overlap of annotations with the abstracts' annotations are, proportionately, much larger.

4.3. The Effect of Time. Next, we studied how the concepts mentioned in the citances changed over time. For each target article in our large dataset, we grouped the citances per year of citation, from cited in the same year of publication to cited up to 4+ years thereafter.

Our results (see Figure 7) show that with every year passing, new annotations are being assigned to the target paper via its citances. The majority of citances' annotations that overlap with abstracts' annotations appear within the first couple of years, but more are constantly added each following year. This is quite uniform across all categories. It would be of interest to conduct more in-depth analysis to see if these new annotations are representative of the research trends progression across the biomedical literature.

5. Discussion

In this section, we discuss the effect of the internal structure of the sentences on our methodology. We further provide a critical overview of our combination of manual and automatic analysis. Finally, we discuss the significance of our results and how they can be applied in a number of areas aiming at improving literature-mining solutions for life sciences research.

5.1. The Internal Structure of Citances. As we have seen above, the relationship between citances and citations is not always 1 : 1, for example, in some cases, a citance would contain citations to multiple target articles. While we acknowledged and analyzed the issue, we still treated citances as *atomic* from the viewpoint of the target article(s), assuming that the whole citance was commenting on it/them.

Automatic analysis-unique annotations

Comparison of abstracts and citances

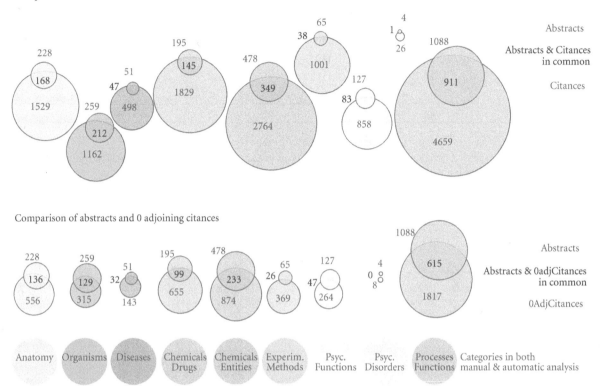

FIGURE 4: Number of unique concepts found in abstracts, all citances, and citances with 0 adjoining citations. Also shown is the overlap between all citances and abstracts.

Automatic analysis – unique annotations

Comparison of abstracts and citances

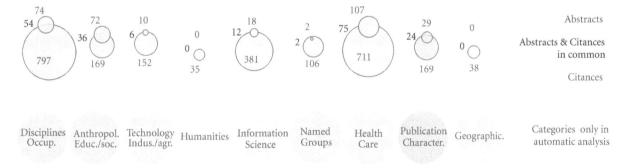

FIGURE 5: Unique Annotations found in abstracts, citances, and their overlap for the annotation categories defined only in the automatic analysis.

Things are more complicated though: it is often the case that only part of a citance is really relevant. This is similar to HTML pages, where only part of a sentence containing a hyperlink is actually included in the hyperlink. Unfortunately, research publications, unless published in some hyperlink-friendly format, do not use such precise mechanisms for pointing out the relevant part of a citance.

Yet, authors of research articles do use citations that refer to part of a citance, which poses interesting challenges to research on citances. See [50] for an overview. Below we list and illustrate three ways in which authors use references:

Type 1. Use separate citations for different parts of the citance.

TABLE 3: Comparison of the number of distinct annotation types in abstracts and citances with zero adjoining citations. We used all sentences from the 6 abstracts and all 23 citances that were only citing one paper for this analysis.

PubMed ID	Abstract	Abstract and citances_0	Difference	n/a	In full text	In MeSH or substances	Not found
8939603	52	65	13	1	10		2
11346650	52	75	23	3	14		6
11251070	57	73	16	2	3	2	9
11298456	60	71	11		6		5
11850621	61	71	10		9		1
Total	282	355	73	6	42	2	25

TABLE 4: Number of citances with a different number of adjoining citations in each article and the number of distinct annotation types they contain. These statistics are for the manual analysis. For the automatic analysis, see Figure 4 and the supplementary material.

PMID	Citance number						Distinct annotation types (abstract and citances)					
	All cit.	Cit_0	Cit_1	Cit_2	Cit_3	Cit_4+	All cit.	Cit_0	Cit_1	Cit_2	Cit_3	Cit_4+
8939603	51	3	8	12	10	18	121	65	68	63	87	85
11346650	45	7	3	4	7	24	170	75	66	66	73	144
11125146	10	0	6	3	1	0	80		67	65	43	
11251070	10	7	0	0	0	3	88	73				73
11298456	10	3	3	2	0	2	96	71	72	66		70
11850621	10	3	4	1	0	2	98	71	76	67		71
Total	136	23	24	22	18	49	653	355	349	327	203	443

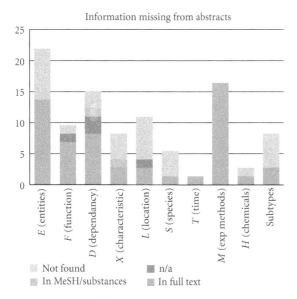

FIGURE 6: Categories of distinct manual annotation types not found in abstracts.

Example. Subsequently, it has been observed that a similar motif is present also in substrates like Cdc6 [21] and retinoblastoma family of proteins [22] and the activator Cdc25A [13].

Type 2. Use citation(s) for part of the citance only.

Example. The nucleosolic or nonutilized Cdc6 then could either be translocated to the cytoplasm (10, 11, 16, 28, 33) or have its affinity for chromatin reduced but still remain in the nucleus (as our immunohistochemical and biochemical data would suggest); this would prevent inappropriate pre-RC formation and reinitiation of DNA replication.

Type 3. List multiple references together at the end of the citance.

Example. These and other biochemical and genetic studies in Drosophila and Xenopus demonstrate that the ORC functions in chromosomal DNA replication in multicellular eukaryotes, just as it does in yeast (25, 28–30, 48, 49).

Citances of Type 2 might have been the reason that a number of biological concepts mentioned in citances were not found in the full text of the target citations. Additionally, we could have used citances of Type 1 to detect more accurately the origin of the information in citances.

Notwithstanding that having considered this variation in citance structure would had enabled us to determine the source of information more accurately, as we discussed in the related work section, a lot of work has been done on the basis that references that appear together are related. Therefore, any additional information from other references can be used to augment the information from the target citation.

Finally, we should note that even knowing when a sentence contains a citation is a challenging task by itself since citation markers can differ in style. Moreover, even after a citation has been identified in text, resolving its target article is not a trivial task. For a further discussion on these issues, see [51–53].

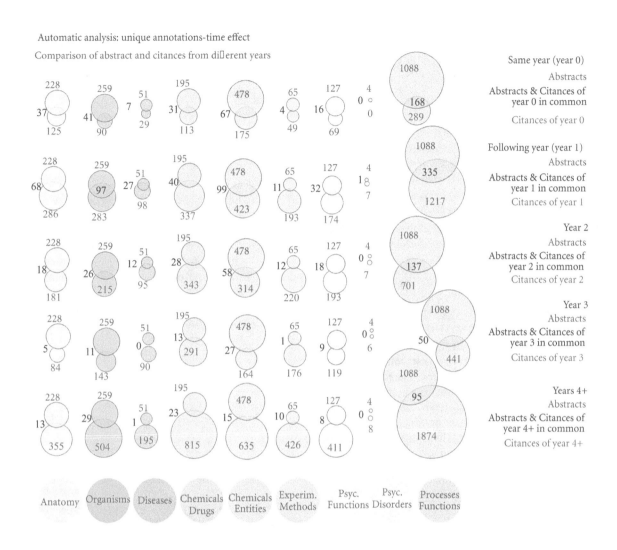

FIGURE 7: The effect of time. We show the unique semantic categories mentioned in the citances from the same publication year as the original target paper and how they overlap with the semantic categories matched in the target abstracts. Semantic annotations and overlap with the abstract for the following 1, 2, 3, and 4+ years are also shown. Note that only *new* unique semantic annotations are counted, for example, annotations of "citances of year 2" do not include any annotations that already appeared in years 0 or 1.

5.2. Combining Manual and Automatic Analysis. We strived to map the categories of our manual schema to the automatic annotation schema the best possible way, while keeping them pertinent to the area of molecular interactions. Despite the significant overlap between these two schemata, the mapping was not ideal, as Figure 2 shows. For example, we could not use MeSH to automatically generate concepts covering events and relations, which were present in the manual annotation. To compensate for this, we added a number of additional concept categories that were easy to identify in MeSH, for example, disciplines, humanities, healthcare, and so forth (see Table 2, Figure 2).

Another issue with the automatic analysis was that the 1 : 1 mapping to the concept categories for the manual annotation was not possible since MeSH categories did not always align perfectly to our concepts. On the positive side,

we relied on MeSH, which is a standard resource that is widely used in biomedical text mining. It provides many variants and synonyms for the concepts it covers, which allows us to handle the variety in expression that is inherent in natural language. Moreover, the MeSH concepts are organized in a hierarchical structure, which allows for a very easy mapping of whole subtrees to predefined categories; in the ideal case, all that is needed to define the mapping is to find the correct level of generalization in MeSH. Table 2 shows how this was done in our case.

5.3. Using Semantic Annotations Found in Citances to Augment Annotations in Abstracts. While studying the effect of adjoining citations, we found that the majority of citances' unique annotation IDs that overlap with unique annotations found in the original target abstract can indeed be found in citances with 0 adjoining citations. This means that citances that cite multiple papers can be used to complement the abstract of each citing paper with more annotations. Imagine that an abstract with 20 semantic annotations assigned to it has 0adj_citances with 30 annotations and 15 of them overlap with the abstract annotations. Now, we have 15 more annotations that can be mapped to the abstract. The target paper is about to have 1+adj_citances that can be associated with a larger number of annotations, say 60; these new annotations can now also be associated with the original paper.

Much like modern media's social boosting from users assigning tags, these new annotations provided by expert peers can be used to help various NLP tasks. Here we propose utilization of these annotations for document summarization, document ranking, and automatic biological database annotation.

In the case of document summarization where most related work has concentrated on, we observe the following opportunities (1) A way to expand information by combining (union) the citances, which contain the best representative information from the full text (rich peer-produced resource), with the abstract (author-produced resource)—this would offer the best complete, inclusive summary. (2) A way to narrow down the information by using the intersection of the information found in citances and abstracts, especially years later—this would offer the most distilled, concentrated summary. (3) A way to generate a summary for a paper, even when its abstract and/or full text are not available in electronic form—that is, use just the citances.

In the case of document/sentence ranking, the density of these annotations in a sentence (or, alternatively, the category/type of annotation, or the relationship of the annotations to the original source) can be used to boost a weight-based ranking system.

Furthermore, our approach can be extended to other standardized resources (e.g., GO and UMLS) that are often used in biomedical databases to automatically map normalized entities and concepts to each other as well as to articles.

5.4. The Four Questions. Let us now go back to the four original research questions, keeping in mind that our dataset focused on molecular interactions, a very hot area for literature mining, as it is the main resource for constructing molecular networks and thus answering systems biology questions.

(1) *How informative is the abstract compared to the full text?* We have shown that the information contained in the abstract and in the citances overlap to a large extent. Yet, there is information in the full text that is important enough to be referred to in citances, but it is not included in the abstract. Thus, abstracts cannot substitute the full text since peers cite information from the full text that is not always included in the abstract.

(2) *What important information in the full text does not appear in the abstract?* We have shown that citances contain additional information that does not appear in abstracts. Since this information appears in a citance, then (1) it should come from the full text, and (2) it should be seen by peers as important. We studied several categories of biologically meaningful concepts and we found that citances contained more information for each of these categories; still, the differences were most pronounced for biological entities and experimental methods.

(3) *What should a summary of the full text contain that is not already in the abstract?* We believe that a good summary of an article should combine the information from its abstract and from citances. Citances give the viewpoint of multiple peers and are thus a very valuable information source. Our study has found that citances tend to mention more biological entities and to care more about experimental methods than authors do in their abstracts. Thus, we would recommend that summaries pay more attention to molecular entities and even consider including information on methods.

(4) *What are the differences in the way authors and peers see an article?* Authors' viewpoint is summarized in the articles abstract, while peers' viewpoint is reflected in the citances to that article. Thus, articles are author-biased, while the set of citances, which are produced by many peers, is more objective. Moreover, citances are written years after the article was published, which also contributes to a more objective view to the contribution of an article: we have seen that, in the first year peers largely agreed with the authors, while differentiation was observed later when the citances have become arguably more divergent in content than the original target paper. The overlapping information though (found both in abstracts and in citances from years later) can be perceived as the most interesting, as it remains pertinent scientifically years later. Overall, we have found that authors focused in their abstracts on a smaller number of concepts compared to their peers. Moreover, peers tended to pay more attention to experimental methods compared to authors.

5.5. Future Directions. In future work, we would like to do a more careful study that would cover more and finer-grained categories in MeSH; trying resources like UMLS and GO is another attractive option. Looking at facts of larger granularity than just concepts, for example, looking at predicate-argument relations is another interesting direction for future work. We further plan to analyze the internal structure of citances, so that we can identify which part of the citance is relevant to a given citation. It would be also interesting to try similar analysis for other disciplines and areas of science, where the way research publications are written and the number of citations a publication receives may differ a lot from what we observe in life sciences.

Another interesting aspect is the passage of time. We have seen that while early citations tend to agree with the authors, later ones tended to diverge more from the original abstract. It would be interesting to see whether this means that later citations are really more objective. An important tool in this respect would be to look at the repetitiveness of citations, which we ignored in our present study, where we focused on unique concept mentions instead: if many peers stated the same fact, then maybe it should be deemed not only more important, but also more objective. Peer motivation for citing an article is important as well, for example, citations that cite a fact would probably agree with the abstract more than those that criticize it.

Last but not least, we are interested in using citances to help NLP applications. While previous work has already shown a number of such examples including information retrieval [24, 25], document summarization [19, 39, 40], document categorization [23], document clustering [29], MeSH terms assignment [30], relation extraction [27], and automatic paraphrasing [17], we believe that this list can be extended significantly.

6. Conclusion

Citances tell us what peers see as contributions of a given target article, while abstracts reflect the authors viewpoint on what is important about their work. Unlike citances, which typically focus on a small number of important aspects, abstracts serve a more general purpose: they not only state the contributions, but also provide a summary of the main points of the paper; thus, abstracts tend to be generally broader than citances. Yet, our manual and automatic comparison of abstracts and citances for articles describing molecular interactions has shown that, collectively, citances contain more information than abstracts.

We performed manual evaluation, which revealed that while all concepts in an article's abstract could be found in the citances for that article (provided that the article has already accumulated enough citations), the reverse was not true: citances mentioned about 20% more concepts than abstracts. Assuming that any information that is not mentioned in the abstract but is important enough to be referred to in citances should be coming from the full text, we can conclude that full text contains important information that is not mentioned in the abstract. We did not detect any significant changes in concept mentions over time.

The automatic analysis verified the results of the manual analysis on a larger scale, using MeSH terms, which were automatically mapped to the biological concepts from the manual analysis. These experiments confirmed our findings that most concepts mentioned in abstracts can be also found in citances. They further confirmed that citances contained some additional information, which in our case was primarily related to biological entities and experimental methods. The large-scale analysis has shown that the manual analysis could indeed be automated; the approach can be extended to other commonly-used biomedical resources such as GO and UMLS, which allow for uniform representation of concepts, that is, useful information about the semantic relationship between abstracts and citation sentences and among concepts themselves.

Overall, our results show that citances are good surrogates of the information contained in a biomedical journal article. The set of all citances citing a given research publication can be seen as concise summaries of its important contributions and thus using them can be preferable to the full text in a variety of scenarios. For example, they allow text mining applications to concentrate on potentially useful sentences without the need to deal with the full text, which is long, has a complex structure, and often would not be available at all, for example, for older publications. Since our work was based on biologically meaningful semantic concepts, it provides quantitative justification of their usefulness for text mining as it has been observed in previous work [17, 27, 30].

We can conclude that, with the recent growth of free access to journal articles and open access publications, full text should be seriously considered for yet another reason: it contains citances with information on the publications referenced therein. Peers cite (mention and comment) information that they see as important even if it is not mentioned in the original publication's abstract. We would further like to draw special attention to citances, as a good source of concise, verifiable information on molecular interaction networks. To answer the question posed by our title "Do Peers See More in a Paper than its Authors?": yes they do, and we should leverage this information.

Acknowledgments

The authors would like to thank the anonymous reviewers for their constructive comments, which has led to great improvements in this paper. This research was funded in part by NSF Grant DBI-0317510.

Endnotes

1. http://www.ncbi.nlm.nih.gov/pubmed/

2. http://www.wellcome.ac.uk/

3. http://www.ncbi.nlm.nih.gov/pmc/

4. http://grants.nih.gov/grants/guide/notice-files/NOT-OD-08-033.html

5. http://www.biomedcentral.com/

6. http://www.plos.org/

7. Our study also helps answer the question: *what abstract claims are not (strongly) supported by the full text?* We hypothesize that these would be those claims that are cited very infrequently or not cited at all, but a separate study is required to answer this question.

8. Note that here we assume that peers base their citations on full text and not only on the abstract. While this is a strong assumption, we believe that it generally holds in the research community. Our previous studies have shown that biomedical researchers like to verify reported results, for example, by looking at the methods that were used and by exploring the images and the

tables in the full text. This has also motivated us to create a specialized search engine, the BioText Search Engine (http://biosearch.berkeley.edu/), for searching the figures and tables contained in open access journals, which is described in [54, 55].

9. CiteSeerX: http://citeseer.ist.psu.edu/

10. DBLP: http://www.informatik.uni-trier.de/~ley/db/

11. Google Scholar: http://scholar.google.com/

12. Microsoft Academic Search: http://academic.research .microsoft.com/

13. ACM Digital Library: http://dl.acm.org/

14. IEEE Xplore Digital Library: http://ieeexplore.ieee.org/ Xplore/

15. ACL Anthology: http://aclweb.org/anthology-new/

16. ArnetMiner: http://arnetminer.org/

17. EMNLP 2009: http://conferences.inf.ed.ac.uk/emnlp09/

18. http://www.nlm.nih.gov/mesh/

19. http://discover.nci.nih.gov/mim/index.jsp

20. http://isiknowledge.com/

21. The data on the analysis considering the extended tree IDs can be found in the supplementary material available online at doi:10.1155/2012/750214. The majority of results discussed in this paper refer to higher MeSH level annotation representing broader entities and concepts.

References

[1] I. Mani and M. Maybury, *Advances in Automatic Text Summarization*, MIT Press, 1999.

[2] H. Yu, V. Hatzivassiloglou, C. Friedman, A. Rzhetsky, and W. Wilbur, "Automatic extraction of gene and protein synonyms from MEDLINE and journal articles," in *Proceedings of the AMIA Symposium (AMIA '02)*, pp. 919–923, 2002.

[3] P. K. Shah, C. Perez-Iratxeta, P. Bork, and M. A. Andrade, "Information extraction from full text scientific articles: where are the keywords?" *BMC Bioinformatics*, vol. 4, article 20, 2003.

[4] M. J. Schuemie, M. Weeber, B. J. A. Schijvenaars et al., "Distribution of information in biomedical abstracts and full-text publications," *Bioinformatics*, vol. 20, no. 16, pp. 2597–2604, 2004.

[5] H. T. Dang, "Overview of DUC 2005," in *Proceedings of the HLT/EMNLP Workshop on Text Summarization DUC*, 2005.

[6] M. Walport and R. Kiley, "Open access, UK PubMed central and the wellcome trust," *Journal of the Royal Society of Medicine*, vol. 99, no. 9, pp. 438–439, 2006.

[7] K. B. Cohen, H. L. Johnson, K. Verspoor, C. Roeder, and L. E. Hunter, "The structural and content aspects of abstracts versus bodies of full text journal articles are different," *BMC Bioinformatics*, vol. 11, article 492, 2010.

[8] E. Garfield, "Can citation indexing be automated," *National Bureau of Standards Miscellaneous Publication*, vol. 269, pp. 189–192, 1965.

[9] M. Liu, "Progress in documentation. the complexities of citation practice: a review of citation studies," *Journal of Documentation*, vol. 49, no. 4, pp. 370–408, 1993.

[10] M. Moravcsik and P. Murugesan, "Some results on the function and quality of citations," *Social Studies of Science*, vol. 5, pp. 86–92, 1975.

[11] E. Garfield, "Citation indexes for science," *Science*, vol. 122, no. 3159, pp. 108–111, 1955.

[12] C. L. Giles, K. D. Bollacker, and S. Lawrence, "CiteSeer: an automatic citation indexing system," in *Proceedings of the 3rd ACM Conference on Digital Libraries*, pp. 89–98, ACM Press, June 1998.

[13] F. Menczer, "Correlated topologies in citation networks and the Web," *European Physical Journal B*, vol. 38, no. 2, pp. 211–221, 2004.

[14] M. E. J. Newman, "The structure of scientific collaboration networks," *Proceedings of the National Academy of Sciences of the United States of America*, vol. 98, no. 2, pp. 404–409, 2001.

[15] C. Duy, V. Hoang, and M.-Y. Kan, "Towards automated related work summarization," in *Proceedings of the 23rd International Conference on Computational Linguistics (COLING '10)*, pp. 427–435, Posters, 2010.

[16] H. D. White, "Citation analysis and discourse analysis revisited," *Applied Linguistics*, vol. 25, no. 1, pp. 89–116, 2004.

[17] P. Nakov, A. Schwartz, and M. Hearst, "Citances: citation sentences for semantic analysis of bioscience text," in *Proceedings of the Workshop on Search and Discovery in Bioinformatics (SIGIR '04)*, 2004.

[18] A. Elkiss, S. Shen, A. Fader, G. Erkan, D. States, and D. Radev, "Blind men and elephants: what do citation summaries tell us about a research article?" *Journal of the American Society for Information Science and Technology*, vol. 59, no. 1, pp. 51–62, 2008.

[19] S. Mohammad, B. Dorr, M. Egan et al., "Using citations to generate surveys of scientific paradigms," in *Proceedings of Human Language Technologies: The Annual Conference of the North American Chapter of the Association for Computational Linguistics (NAACL '09)*, pp. 584–592, Boulder, Colo, USA, 2009.

[20] H. D. White and B. C. Griffith, "Author cocitation: a literature measure of intellectual structure," *Journal of the American Society for Information Science*, vol. 32, no. 3, pp. 163–171, 1981.

[21] A. Aris, B. Shneiderman, V. Qazvinian, and D. Radev, "Visual overviews for discovering key papers and influences across research fronts," *Journal of the American Society for Information Science and Technology*, vol. 60, no. 11, pp. 2219–2228, 2009.

[22] S. Teufel and M. Moens, "Summarizing scientific articles: experiments with relevance and rhetorical status," *Computational Linguistics*, vol. 28, no. 4, pp. 409–445, 2002.

[23] H. Nanba, N. Kando, and M. Okumura, "Classification of research papers using citation links and citation types: towards automatic review article generation," in *Proceedings of the American Society for Information Science SIG Classification Research Workshop: Classification for User Support and Learning*, pp. 117–134, 2000.

[24] S. Bradshaw, "Reference directed indexing: redeeming relevance for subject search in citation indexes," in *Proceedings of the 7th European Conference on Research and Advanced Technology for Digital Libraries*, 2003.

[25] R. Mercer and C. Di Marco, "A design methodology for a biomedical literature indexing tool using the rhetoric of science," in *Proceedings of the BioLink Workshop in Conjunction with NAACL/HLT*, pp. 77–84, 2004.

[26] I. Tbahriti, C. Chichester, F. Lisacek, and P. Ruch, "Using argumentation to retrieve articles with similar citations: an inquiry into improving related articles search in the MEDLINE digital library," *International Journal of Medical Informatics*, vol. 75, no. 6, pp. 488–495, 2006.

[27] B. Rosario and M. Hearst, "Multi-way relation classification: application to protein-protein interactions," in *Proceedings of the Conference on Human Language Technology and Empirical Methods in Natural Language Processing (HLT '05)*, 2005.

[28] A. Kolchinsky, A. Abi-Haidar, J. Kaur, A. A. Hamed, and L. M. Rocha, "Classification of protein-protein interaction full-text documents using text and citation network features," *IEEE/ACM Transactions on Computational Biology and Bioinformatics*, vol. 7, no. 3, pp. 400–411, 2010.

[29] B. Aljaber, N. Stokes, J. Bailey, and J. Pei, "Document clustering of scientific texts using citation contexts," *Information Retrieval*, vol. 13, no. 2, pp. 101–131, 2010.

[30] B. Aljaber, D. Martinez, N. Stokes, and J. Bailey, "Improving MeSH classification of biomedical articles using citation contexts," *Journal of Biomedical Informatics*, vol. 44, no. 5, pp. 881–896, 2011.

[31] W. Lehnert, C. Cardie, and E. Riloff, "Analyzing research papers using citation sentences," in *Proceedings of the 12th Annual Conference of the Cognitive Science Society*, pp. 511–518, Lawrence Erlbaum Associates, 1990.

[32] S. Teufel, A. Siddharthan, and D. Tidhar, "An annotation scheme for citation function," in *Proceedings of Sigdial-06*, Sydney, Australia, 2006.

[33] S. Teufel, A. Siddharthan, and D. Tidhar, "Automatic classification of citation function," in *Proceedings of EMNLP-06*, Sydney, Australia, 2006.

[34] S. Teufel and M. Y. Kan, "Robust argumentative zoning for sensemaking in scholarly documents," in *Advanced Language Technologies for Digital Libraries*, vol. 6699 of *Lecture Notes in Computer Science*, pp. 154–170, Springer, Berlin, Germany, 2011.

[35] C. Schwartz, A. Divoli, and M. Hearst, "Multiple alignment of citation sentences with conditional random fields and posterior decoding," in *Proceedings of the Joint Conference on Empirical Methods in Natural Language Processing and Computational Natural Language Learning (EMNLP-CoNLL '07)*, pp. 847–857, 2007.

[36] E. Amitay and C. Paris, "Automatically summarising web sites: is there a way around it," in *Proceedings of the 9th International Conference on Information and knowledge Management*, pp. 173–179, ACM Press, 2000.

[37] J. Y. Delort, B. Bouchon-Meunier, and M. Rifqi, "Enhanced web document summarization using hyperlinks," in *Proceedings of the 14th ACM Conference on Hypertext and Hypermedia*, pp. 208–215, August 2003.

[38] A. Schwartz and M. Hearst, "Summarizing key concepts using citation sentences," in *Proceedings of the Workshop on Linking Natural Language Processing and Biology: Towards Deeper Biological Literature Analysis (BioNLP '06)*, pp. 134–135, New York, NY, USA, 2006.

[39] V. Qazvinian and D. Radev, "Scientific paper summarization using citation summary networks," in *Proceedings of the 22nd International Conference on Computational Linguistics (COLING '08)*, vol. 1, pp. 689–696, Manchester, UK, 2008.

[40] Q. Mei and C. Zhai, "Generating impact-based summaries for scientific literature," in *Proceedings of the 46th Annual Meeting of the Association for Computational Linguistics (ACL '08)*, pp. 816–824, Columbus, Ohio, USA, 2008.

[41] V. Qazvinian and D. Radev, "Identifying non-explicit citing sentences for citation-based summarization," in *Proceedings of the 48th Annual Meeting of the Association for Computational Linguisticsproceedings of (ACL '10)*, pp. 555–564, 2010.

[42] S. Wan, C. Paris, and R. Dale, "Whetting the appetite of scientists: producing summaries tailored to the citation context," in *Proceedings of theACM/IEEE Joint Conference on Digital Libraries (JCDL '09)*, pp. 59–68, June 2009.

[43] N. Craswell, D. Hawking, and S. Robertson, "Effective site finding using link anchor information," in *Proceedings of the 24th Annual International ACM SIGIR Conference on Research and Development in Information Retrieval*, pp. 250–257, ACM Press, 2001.

[44] S. Chakrabarti, B. Dom, P. Raghavan, S. Rajagopalan, D. Gibson, and J. Kleinberg, "Automatic resource compilation by analyzing hyperlink structure and associated text," in *Proceedings of the 7th International Conference on World Wide Web 7*, pp. 65–74, Elsevier Science Publishers B.V., 1998.

[45] J. Fürnkranz, "Exploiting structural information for text classification on the www," in *Proceedings of the 3rd International Symposium on Advances in Intelligent Data Analysis*, pp. 487–498, Springer, 1999.

[46] J. Rennie and A. McCallum, "Using reinforcement learning to spider the web efficiently," in *Proceedings of the 16th International Conference on Machine Learning*, pp. 335–343, Morgan Kaufmann Publishers, 1999.

[47] M. Richardson and P. Domingos, "The intelligent surfer: probabilistic combination of link and content information in pagerank," in *Proceedings of the Advances in Neural Information Processing Systems*, vol. 14, MIT Press, 2002.

[48] G. Bhalotia, P. Nakov, A. Schwartz, and M. Hearst, "BioText team report for the TREC, 2003 Genomics track," in *Proceedings of the 13th Text REtrieval Conference (TREC '04)*, Gaithersburg, Md, USA, 2004.

[49] P. Nakov and A. Divoli, "BioText report for the second BioCreAtIvE challenge," in *Proceedings of BioCreAtIvE II Workshop*, Madrid, Spain, April 2007.

[50] A. Ritchie, S. Teufel, and S. Robertson, "How to find better index terms through citations," in *Proceedings of the Workshop on How Can Computational Linguistics Improve Information Retrieval?* pp. 25–32, Sydney, Australia, 2006.

[51] D. Bergmark, "Automatic extraction of reference linking information from online documents," Technical Report CSTR 2000-1821, Cornell Digital Library Research Group, 2000.

[52] D. Bergmark, P. Phempoonpanich, and S. Zhao, "Scraping the ACM digital library," *SIGIR Forum*, vol. 35, no. 2, pp. 1–7, 2001.

[53] B. Powley and R. Dale, "Evidence-based information extraction for high-accuracy citation extraction and author name recognition," in *Proceedings of the 8th RIAO International Conference on Large-Scale Semantic Access to Content*, 2007.

[54] M. A. Hearst, A. Divoli, H. H. Guturu et al., "BioText Search Engine: beyond abstract search," *Bioinformatics*, vol. 23, no. 16, pp. 2196–2197, 2007.

[55] A. Divoli, M. A. Wooldridge, and M. A. Hearst, "Full text and figure display improves bioscience literature search," *PLoS ONE*, vol. 5, no. 4, Article ID e9619, 2010.

8

MicroRNA Response Elements-Mediated miRNA-miRNA Interactions in Prostate Cancer

Mohammed Alshalalfa[1, 2]

[1] *Department of Computer Science, University of Calgary, 2500 University Dr. NW, Calgary, AB, Canada T2N 1N4*
[2] *Biotechnology Research Center, Palestine Polytechnic University, Hebron, Palestine*

Correspondence should be addressed to Mohammed Alshalalfa, msalshal@ucalgary.ca

Academic Editor: Ramana Davuluri

The cell is a highly organized system of interacting molecules including proteins, mRNAs, and miRNAs. Analyzing the cell from a systems perspective by integrating different types of data helps revealing the complexity of diseases. Although there is emerging evidence that microRNAs have a functional role in cancer, the role of microRNAs in mediating cancer progression and metastasis remains not fully explored. As the amount of available miRNA and mRNA gene expression data grows, more systematic methods combining gene expression and biological networks become necessary to explore miRNA function. In this work I integrated functional miRNA-target interactions with mRNA and miRNA expression to infer mRNA-mediated miRNA-miRNA interactions. The inferred network represents miRNA modulation through common targets. The network is used to characterize the functional role of microRNA response element (MRE) to mediate interactions between miRNAs targeting the MRE. Results revealed that miRNA-1 is a key player in regulating prostate cancer progression. 11 miRNAs were identified as diagnostic and prognostic biomarkers that act as tumor suppressor miRNAs. This work demonstrates the utility of a network analysis as opposed to differential expression to find important miRNAs that regulate prostate cancer.

1. Introduction

MicroRNAs (miRNAs) are small (18–24) nucleotide long noncoding RNAs that play a major regulatory role in a broad range of biological processes and complex diseases. Since the discovery of microRNAs [1], they emerged as a new layer of gene regulation that dramatically influence genes by binding to its 3'UTR and inactivate it by promoting its degradation or translational repression [2]. Computational predictions estimated that there are around 1700 miRNAs in human and each targets hundreds of mRNAs and over 50% of the human protein coding genes are regulated by miRNAs [3]. The area of miRNA genetics has rapidly expanded from identifying miRNAs to exploring their function and their potential as therapeutic options. Several studies have demonstrated that miRNAs are key players in the initiation and progression of cancer including prostate cancer and they act as oncogenes and tumor suppressors [4–6]. Examination of prostate

tumor miRNA expression has revealed widespread dysregulation of miRNAs in primary and metastatic compared with normal prostate tissue [7]. Profiling miRNAs in various types of cancer provided evidence that miRNAs are diagnostic and prognostic biomarkers [8] that may stratify prostate tumors based on specific genetic profiles and thereby improve aspects of patient management such as staging and treatment [9, 10].

A big body of research has been focusing on identifying the functional association between miRNAs and mRNA targets. Several factors affect the association between miRNAs and targets. The first is the degree of complementarity between the miRNA and the target [11]. Several computational methods have been proposed to identify miRNAs sequence and their target based complementary sequence and thermodynamics stability with mRNA target [11, 12]. The problem with computational predictions is that they are false positive prone methods and they are not functional. The second factor is the functional association between miRNAs and targets. Since miRNA promote target degradation, a negative correlation between a miRNA and its targets is anticipated [13, 14]. Considerable body of research has concentrated on the area of integrating sequence-based miRNA target prediction and expression data to identify functional miRNA-target interactions and find miRNA-target modules. Several tools and algorithms have been developed in this respect. GenMiR++ and GenMiR3 [15] are two such tools; GenMiR3 is the modified version of GenMiR++; it combines the results of miRNA target prediction programs like TargetScanS with paired miRNA-mRNA expression data. The algorithm scores each miRNA-mRNA pair by a Bayesian approach. It evaluates whether the expression of the miRNA explains the expression level of mRNA. Target pairs get high score when miRNA or mRNA is highly expressed while the other molecule is downregulated. The third factor is endogenous RNA competition. Recently, several studies have characterized the power of miRNAs as a communication language between noncoding RNAs [16, 17]. Considerable body of research has emerged to characterize the function of noncoding RNA and the regulatory function of coding mRNAs. Results revealed that the MRE of RNAs is an important part of RNA that can play a key role in gene regulation by competing for miRNA. RNAs (coding or noncoding) that share similar MRE showed an ability modulate each other by buffering targeting miRNAs and compete for miRNA and thus influence its availability [16, 17].

Gene expression techniques are witnessing a revolution in the last decade that lead to produce very large amount of high throughput gene expression data to study cellular systems, but the drawback of these techniques is that they study individual components of the system. A major challenge in systems biomedicine is not only understanding the function of individual elements in the system, but rather understanding the function of elements as a system. There is a big gap between the biological techniques to generate high-throughput data and computational biologists who use this data to build models to explain the data. Thus a more statistical and systematic methods integrating gene expression with biological networks to have high-level understanding of biological systems function is needed. miRNA and mRNAs are two cellular molecules that interact together and regulate each other's expression. miRNAs regulate mRNAs expression by downregulating them; on the other hand, mRNA regulates miRNA by modulating its availability. Thus a new layer of gene regulation has emerged that affect mRNA expression based on miRNA language. However, how mRNA can influence and play the modulator role in miRNA regulation has not been investigated.

This study focuses on the role of MRE or 3′UTR in mediating the interactions among miRNAs. I hypothesize that MRE can modulate miRNA-miRNA interactions activity and that miRNAs can influence each other through MREs. Sponge modulators include both messenger RNAs (mRNAs) and noncoding RNAs, which contains multiple miR-binding sites for distinct miRNAs are key player in modulating miRNA availability. Depending on their expression levels and

on the total number of functional miR-binding sites that they harbour, sponge modulators can decrease the number of free miR molecules available to repress other functional targets. When modulators expression is high, miRNAs targeting them will get decreased. miRNAs that share a modulator and have similar expression profile given the expression of the modulator are anticipated to be functionally related and form a posttranscriptional regulatory network. In this work a 3′UTR-mediated miRNA-miRNA in prostate cancer is constructed to identify key miRNA players that influence each other.

2. Materials and Methods

2.1. miRNA Targets Interactions. Human miRNA target predictions for miRNA with conserved 3′UTR were taken from TargetScan 5.1 [11] (PredNet), and experimentally validated miRNAs and their targets were taken from mirTarBase [8] and miRecord [20]. I used the union of mirTarBase and miRecord as a source of experimentally validated miRNA-target interactions (ExpNet). PredNet and ExpNet will constitute the miRNA-target interaction networks that will be used to associate miRNAs with their targets.

2.2. Expression Datasets. MRNA and miRNA expression data from the MSKCC Prostate Oncogenome Project, that is, available at the Gene Expression Omnibus (GEO accession number: GSE21032) [21], was used in this study. The data contains expression levels of 26443 genes across 179 samples (131 primary cancer, 19 metastatic, and 29 normal samples), and expression of 370 miRNAs across 140 samples. The expression data of 139 samples with both mRNA and miRNA data for our analysis was used in this study. I also used localized prostate cancer miRNA expression data from independent prostate patient cohort (GSE23022 [22]) to further validate the predicted function of miRNAs. Taylor data was used to build the network of miRNAs and GSE23022 data was used to further characterize the diagnostic role of the network results.

2.3. MRE-Mediated miRNA-miRNA Network Construction. Here I describe the mathematical model used to build mRNA-mediated miRNA-miRNA interaction network as illustrated in Figure 1. I hypothesize that the expression of mRNA(m) can modulate interactions between miRNAs (miR1, miR2) that have miR-binding site in the MRE of the mRNA (m). The model requires miRNA-target interaction data (PredNet or ExpNet) and expression profiles of miRNAs and targets from the same sample set. To find the mRNA(m)-mediated miRNA-(miR1-) miRNA(miR2) interactions, I used conditional mutual information as described in [17]. Mutual information between miR1 and miR2 is calculated as

$$\mathrm{MI}_{\mathrm{miR1,miR2}} = \sum_{d \in \mathrm{miR1}} \sum_{r \in \mathrm{miR2}} p(d,r) \log \frac{p(d,r)}{p(d)p(r)}, \quad (1)$$

where $p(d, r)$ is the joint probability density function (pdf) of miR1 and miR2, and $P(d)$ and $p(r)$ are the marginal pdf's

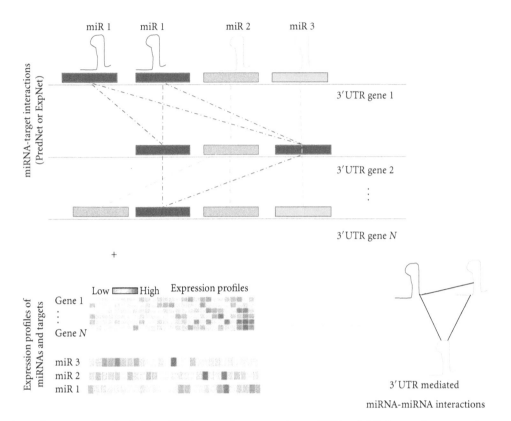

FIGURE 1: Overview of MRE-mediated miRNA-miRNA network construction. miRNA-miRNA interaction network was constructed by combing miRNA-target networks and expression profiles of both miRNAs and targets. I considered competition between miRNAs for common targets to construct miRNA-miRNA network. miRNAs that target same 3′UTR or MRE and are conditionally dependent on target are anticipated to be functionally associated.

of miR1 and miR2, respectively. The modulation effect of mRNA (m) on miR1 and miR2 is calculated as

$$\Delta MI_{miR1,miR2/m} = \left| MI(miR1, miR2) - MI\left(miR1, \frac{miR2}{m}\right) \right|. \quad (2)$$

The significance (P value (miR1, miR2/m)) for each interaction (miR1, miR2) given a mRNA (m) was calculated by permutating (shuffling) the expression values of m across the 139 samples 1000 times and then comparing the observed ΔMI value against the expected ΔMI values from the permutation distribution. Since miRNAs target multiple mRNAs, I obtained multiple P values for each miRNA-miR interaction given a mRNA and then find the final significance P value across all mRNA targets by converting individual P values p_k for each miRNA-miR to a X^2 test statistics using Fisher's method, where $X^2 = -2\sum_{k=1}^{N} \ln(p_k)$, where N is the total number of targets for miRNA. This method is very similar to the miRNA mediated mRNA interactions constructed by Sumaizin et al. [17] but the major difference is that they consider miRNAs as modulators and I consider mRNAs as modulators.

Computing the mutual information between all miRNAs pairs given all possible mRNAs is very time consuming.

Thus I used prior knowledge from miRNA-target interactions as a base to predict mRNA mediated miRNA-miRNA interactions. For each miRNA from miRNA-target interaction in PredNet or ExpNet and its targets, I calculated $\Delta MI_{miRNA,miR/target}$ across all miRNAs (miR) in Taylor dataset and obtained a P value by shuffling the expression of target across the 139 samples. As a result I obtained a P value for each miRNA-miR interaction given a target. The final step was to generate one P value for the miRNA-miR interactions that depend on different targets. The P values were converted using Fisher's method. Only significant ($P < e^{-5}$) were considered to build the miRNA-miRNA interactions network.

3. Results

3.1. MRE-Mediated miRNA-miRNA Interactions. Genome-wide inference of MRE modulators identified a miRNA-miRNA posttranscriptional regulatory network. I modelled the network graphically, with miRNAs represented as nodes and their MRE-mediated interactions as undirected edges. This network represents an indirect regulatory effect between miRNAs. A miRNA can influence the expression of its miRNA partners by regulating their common target and thus modulate the partner's miRNA activity. I first used ExpNet data to construct the miRNA-miRNA network. Figure 2

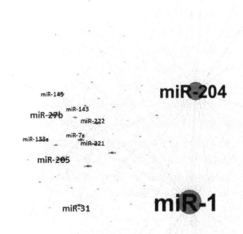

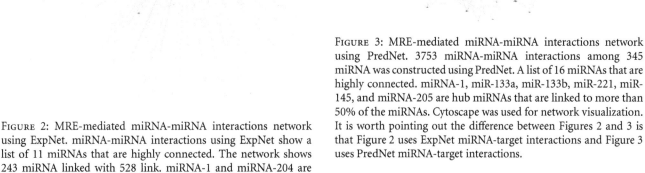

FIGURE 2: MRE-mediated miRNA-miRNA interactions network using ExpNet. miRNA-miRNA interactions using ExpNet show a list of 11 miRNAs that are highly connected. The network shows 243 miRNA linked with 528 link. miRNA-1 and miRNA-204 are hub miRNAs that are linked to more than 50% of the miRNAs. The size of the miRNA node is proportional to the miRNA connectivity. Cytoscape was used for network visualization [18].

FIGURE 3: MRE-mediated miRNA-miRNA interactions network using PredNet. 3753 miRNA-miRNA interactions among 345 miRNA was constructed using PredNet. A list of 16 miRNAs that are highly connected. miRNA-1, miR-133a, miR-133b, miR-221, miR-145, and miRNA-205 are hub miRNAs that are linked to more than 50% of the miRNAs. Cytoscape was used for network visualization. It is worth pointing out the difference between Figures 2 and 3 is that Figure 2 uses ExpNet miRNA-target interactions and Figure 3 uses PredNet miRNA-target interactions.

shows 528 interactions among 243 miRNAs. The miRNAs in the network have an average of 20 interactions ranging from 1 to 190. This suggests that, on average, there are 20 targets that mediate interactions between miRNA pairs.

The overall regulatory effect on a node depends on several variables, including the number of mRNAs that harbour a binding site for the node, the number of distinct binding sites on a mRNA, and the expression level of the modulator mRNA. 11 miRNAs are more connected than others. The network revealed that miNRA-1 and miRNA-204 are hub miRNAs in the network with connection to more than 70% of the miRNAs in the network. Additional miRNAs like miR-205, miR-27b, miR-31, miR-222, miR-221, miR-133a, miR-143, let-7a, and miR-145 was shown also to be highly connected to other miRNAs. I will refer to this set of miRNAs as the 11 miRNAs. I further applied the method on PredNet and showed that the 11 miRNAs are hub nodes (Figure 3). This suggests that the resulting network is not biased to the miRNA-target interactions used.

I then asked if the resulting MRE-mediated miRNA-miRNA network is biased to the number of mRNA targets that miRNAs share. So I constructed a miRNA-miRNA network (Figure S1) based only on the common mRNA targets. Interactions in this network represent how much the two partner miRNAs share common targets. Surprisingly, none of the hub miRNAs in Figure 2 showed any significance. This means that the interactions among the 11 miRNAs and the high connectivity of the 11 miRNAs is not due the large number of common binding sites between miRNAs. I then constructed another miRNA-miRNA based on expression correlation (Figure S2) and found interesting results. The identified hub miRNAs are highly correlated with each other, but not correlated with other miRNAs in the genome. Several miRNAs like miR-1224-3p and miR-937 was shown to be correlated with most of the miRNAs but not with our identified list of miRNAs. This result indicates that our hub miRNAs are correlated in subset of samples and not all of them.

Further an MRE-mediated miRNA-miRNA network was constructed using only expression data from primary prostate samples (98). The purpose of this network is to assess if the MRE-mediated miRNAs network is biased to the primary cancer samples that constitute large portion of the samples used in the study. Also it helps to reveal miRNAs that may play a role in subtyping primary cancer. Interestingly miR-1, miR-155, and miR-16 were found to be hub miRNA.

This could shed light on the role of miRNAs in different stages of prostate cancer progression.

3.2. Tumor Suppressor miRNAs Network in Prostate Cancer.

To find the robustness of the interactions between the 11 miRNAs, PredNet was used to construct the MRE-mediated miRNA-miRNA interactions of 345 miRNA nodes and 3753 edges. A more stringent cutoff was then used to reduce the network to 70 miRNA nodes connected by 128 edges. Both resulting networks support that the 11 miRNAs are significantly associated and miRNA-1 which is the master regulator of miRNA interactions. This result indicates that the 11 miRNAs are regulating each other and they have similar mode of actions. Several miRNAs among the 11 miRNA (miRNA-1, miRNA-145, miRNA-143) have been characterized as tumor suppressors in prostate cancer [3, 6]. Thus our network results suggest that the other miRNAs may act as a network of tumor suppressors.

3.3. Functional Analysis of Key 11 miRNAs.

Here I asked if the 11 key miRNAs (hub miRNAs) have any functional role in prostate cancer. I extracted the target genes of the 11 key miRNAs from experimentally verified miRNA-target interactions (ExpNet) and characterized their function using DAVID online tool (http://david.abcc.ncifcrf.gov/). 462 genes are targeted by the 11 miRNAs, 240 of them are targeted by miRNA-1. The function of the 462 genes was characterized by analyzing the biological pathways they are involved in and the biological processes they are part of in addition to biological terms associated with them. Target genes are associated with phosphoprotein $(1.1 \times e^{-21})$, proto-oncogene $(2.6 \times e^{-13})$, disease mutation $(5.2 \times e^{-8})$, acetylation $(6.7 \times e^{-7})$, actin-binding $(1.2 \times e^{-6})$, and apoptosis $(8.2 \times e^{-6})$. Analyzing the pathways revealed strong correlation between the target genes and several types of cancer including prostate, melanoma, thyroid, pancreatic cancers (Figure 4). Target genes also are involved in several biological processes like cell proliferation, cell motion, regulation of cell death, regulation of biosynthetic, and metabolic processes and kinase activity (Figure 5). All these enrichment analysis support that the 11 miRNAs play key role in prostate cancer by targeting genes from multiple biological processes. Though the enriched pathways are not prostate specific, they show that the 11 miRNAs target core pathways and mainly phosphorylation signaling pathways.

3.4. Diagnostic and Prognostic Relevance of Key miRNAs.

The diagnostic and prognostic power of the 11 miRNAs was further characterized using independent prostate expression dataset. The expression of the 11 miRNAs was extracted from GSE23022 and analyzed the power of the 11 miRNA in discriminating tumor samples from normal samples using three methods. Hierarchical clustering was used to group patients based on the expression level of the 11 miRNAs (Figure 6). The heatmap clearly shows three distinct groups: tumor, normal, and a mixed group. Principal component analysis showed that normal and tumor samples are distinguishable using the first three principal components (Figure 7). Finally,

support vector machine classified the samples (tumor versus normal) using the expression of the 11 miRNAs with 85%. To find the significance of this classification, I randomly generated 1000 lists of 11 miRNAs and calculated the average accuracy (50.7%) P value (0).

Taylor data was used to assess the power of the 11 miRNA to discriminate primary from normal samples (88% versus 77% (random)) (Figure S4). I compared this result with the 11 most downregulated genes identified using significant analysis of microarray (SAM) [23] and found that 5 (miR-221, 222, 145, 133a, 143) out of the key miRNAs are among the 11 most downregulated genes. The top 11 upregulated genes were able to classify cancer from normal samples with 90% and the 11 downregulated genes are able to classify the samples with 86%. This indicates that the 11 hub miRNAs are good diagnostic biomarkers. I then analyzed the power of the 11 miRNAs to discriminate metastatic samples from primary cancer using Taylor gene expression data. Results showed that the 11 miRNAs significantly discriminate primary from metastatic samples with 99.1% using SVM. Using random list of 11 miRNAs resulted in an average of 88.8%P value (0). Principal component analysis showed that metastatic samples are clearly separated from primary and normal (Figure 8); however, some primary samples are very close to normal samples. One reason could be because the primary samples are still in early stages of cancer and due to the heterogeneity of the primary cancer. This indicates that these 11 miRNAs are important molecules in prostate cancer initiation and progression.

To analyze the prognostic power of the 11 miRNAs, I extracted their expression from Taylor data and used cox regression model to find association between miRNAs expression and cancer recurrence. Clustering the samples using k-means based on the 11 miRNAs into two groups showed that the two groups have significant different outcome (HR: 4.9, 95%CI (2.15–11.19), P = 0.00016) (Figure 9). Using univariate cox regression revealed that all the 11 miRNAs are associated with outcome; low expression level of the 11 miRNA is associated with aggressive cancer. Using univariate regression model showed that miR-1 is the most significant miRNA associated with outcome. I then analyzed the differential expression profiles of the 11 miRNAs in aggressive cancer versus nonaggressive (based on Taylor groups) and found that all of them are significantly downregulated in aggressive cancer (P less that 1×10^{-5}). Table 1 shows the hazard ratio, multivariate regression coefficients, and the differential expression power using fold change and SAM analysis.

4. Discussion

The applications of systems biology to understand complex disease driven by the fact that complex diseases like cancer are attributed to dysregulation of multiple components of the cellular system [24]. Prostate cancer is the most widely spread cancer in male in western countries. One of the challenging in studying prostate cancer is the heterogeneity of the system. Several genes are attributed to initiate and

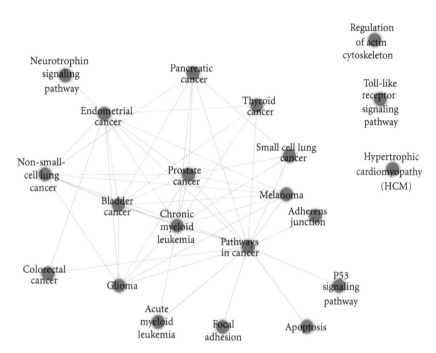

FIGURE 4: Pathway enrichment analysis of the 450 target genes of the 11 miRNA using Enrichment Map [19]. 450 genes targeted by the 11 miRNA were identified using ExpNet. I used DAVID online tool to identify enriched pathways of the 450 genes using Enrichment Map [19]. Results showed that the target genes are enriched with multiple cancer pathways including prostate, thyroid, and pancreatic cancer pathways.

TABLE 1: Diagnostic and prognostic characteristics of the 11 miRNAs from Taylor data.

	HR (95% CI)	Cox multivariate regression coefficient	Fold change (cancer/normal)	SAM q-value
hsa-let-7a	0.77 (0.18–3.26)	−0.25	0.88	2.3
hsa-miR-1	0.30 (0.09–0.9)	−1.17	0.64	0
hsa-miR-133a	1.23 (0.41–3.67)	0.20	0.43	0
hsa-miR-143	1.67 (0.53–5.19)	0.51	0.49	0
hsa-miR-145	1.72 (0.31–9.6)	0.54	0.45	0
hsa-miR-204	1.34 (0.68–2.66)	0.29	0.48	0
hsa-miR-205	1.03 (0.8–1.34)	0.03	0.22	0
hsa-miR-27b	2.85 (0.77–10.5)	1.05	0.63	0
hsa-miR-221	0.29 (0.05–1.53)	−1.22	0.42	0
hsa-miR-222	1.23 (0.23–6.4)	0.2	0.35	0
hsa-miR-31	0.63 (0.31–1.2)	−0.45	0.39	0

develop prostate cancer, in addition to role of miRNAs in initiating and progressing prostate cancer [4]. Several miRNAs profiling studies have been conducted to identify miRNAs that are differentially expressed in tumor versus normal tissues [10]. Identifying prognostic miRNAs that can help to predict patient outcome or the stage of disease is another important aspect to understand diseases progression. Identifying miRNA-mRNA function modules is another important task in miRNA genetics. One of the least studied factors affect the functionality of miRNAs is competing for target. Recent study showed that targets that compete for miRNAs pose a regulatory effect on each other by limiting the availability of miRNA [16, 17]. Using this notion, Sumazin et al. [17] generated a miRNA-mediated network among RNA molecules. Here it is worth mentioning that miRNAs mediate all RNA molecules that harbour a

binding site for the miRNA. This study motivated us to analyze the systematic function of miRNAs in prostate cancer by analyzing the influence of each miRNA on the other miRNAs through the target. miRNAs that share MRE of several targets and their expression conditionally dependent on the target are anticipated to regulate each other.

In this work I analyze the functional role of miRNAs in prostate cancer by integrating expression data of targets and miRNAs and miRNA-target networks. Several studies that integrated expression data with miRNA-target networks lead to identifying miRNA-target modules that may play a role in prostate cancer [14]. However, in this work I integrated expression data using conditional mutual information to assess the conditional dependence between pairs of miRNA and their common target(s). miRNAs modulate each other through their common targets that affect miRNA availability.

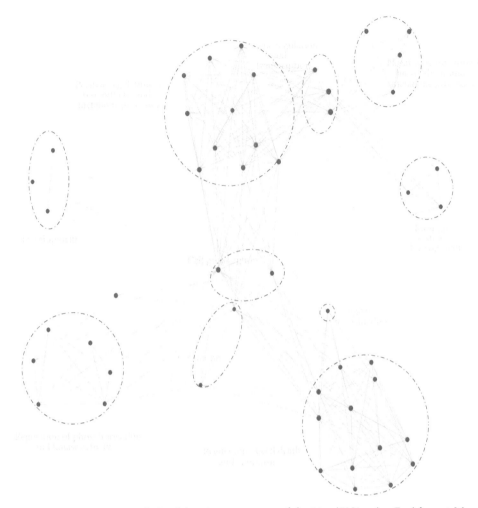

FIGURE 5: Biological processes enrichment analysis of the 450 target genes of the 11 miRNA using Enrichment Map [19]. Analyzing the biological processes enriched in the miRNA target genes using DAVID tool showed that targets are enriched with several biological processes like cell proliferation, cell death, and biosynthetic metabolism. Enrichment Map [19] was used for visualizing the network of biological processes.

The association between miRNAs depends on the number of common targets and the significance of the conditional dependence on the target.

One of the challenges I faced in this study is constructing the miRNA-miRNA interaction network using all possible targets as mediators that is computationally very expensive. To reduce computational cost, I started with the miRNA-target network and we only computed conditional dependency between one miRNA and the rest of miRNAs given the expression of the targets. I used both experimentally verified and computationally predicted miRNA-target interactions to identify the miRNA-miRNA networks. Both networks showed that miRNA-1 is a hub miRNA in both networks. This indicates that it has regulatory effect over other miRNAs through its targets. Based on the two networks (Figures 2 and 3), 11 miRNAs were identified as hub miRNAs and further analyzed their function and prognostic role. Analyzing their function showed that they play a role in several biological processes including cell proimmigration, cell death, and metabolic biosynthesis (Figure 5). Analyzing

their prognostic role revealed that the 11 miRNAs act as diagnostic and prognostic biomarkers. The low expression of the 11 miRNAs showed to be associated with cancer recurrence (Figure 9). Several miRNAs among the 11 miRNas are already in clinical trials (miR-16, miR-222, miR-221) [3]. Here it is worth mentioning that the 11 hub miRNAs are not the top differentially downregulated miRNAs but they are powerful diagnostic biomarkers.

The results in this work caught the attention to the significance of miR-1. Therefore, I further investigated its role in prostate cancer and argue that it is the guardian of the miRNA-mediated gene expression control. microRNA-1(miR-1) is reported to be one of the most consistently downregulated microRNAs in human prostate tumors [25]. Recent study showed that miR-1 is further reduced in distant metastasis tumors and is a candidate predictor of disease recurrence. miR-1 is encoded by the miR-1-133 cluster which has two copies (at 18q11 and 20q13) in the human genome producing identical mature miR sequences for miR-1 and miR-133. It was recently reported that miR-1, miR-133, and

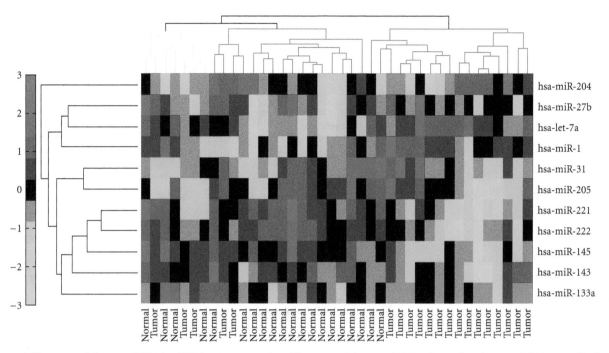

FIGURE 6: Heatmap of the 11 miRNA in GES23022 prostate data. Heatmap of the 11 miRNAs shows that the 11 miRNAs are effective to group tumor samples. Clustering the samples using k-means revealed three groups, tumor, normal, and mixed cluster.

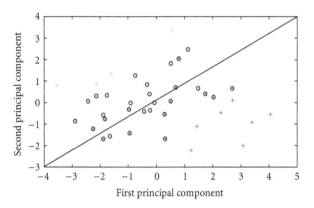

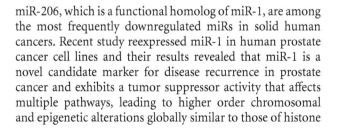

FIGURE 7: SVM classification of samples in GSE23022 across the first two PCAs. I first identified the first two principal components (PCAs) and then use SVM to classify samples based on the first two components. Results show that normal and tumors samples are separated with some misclassification at the boundary of the support vectors.

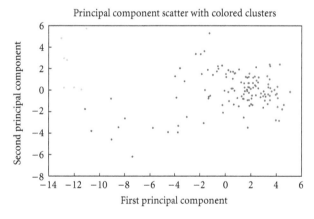

FIGURE 8: Prostate samples across the first two PCAs using Taylor miRNA expression data. I first identified the first two principal components (PCAs) using Taylor data that has normal, primary, and metastasis samples. Results show that metastasis samples are well separated from normal and primary samples across the first component.

miR-206, which is a functional homolog of miR-1, are among the most frequently downregulated miRs in solid human cancers. Recent study reexpressed miR-1 in human prostate cancer cell lines and their results revealed that miR-1 is a novel candidate marker for disease recurrence in prostate cancer and exhibits a tumor suppressor activity that affects multiple pathways, leading to higher order chromosomal and epigenetic alterations globally similar to those of histone

deacetylase inhibitors. Our results found that miRNA-1 targets 240 genes from ExpNet and 527 in PredNet. Both lists showed that they are enriched with phosphoproteins ($5.3 \times e^{-6}$) and acetylation proteins ($3.7 \times e^{-7}$). 3′UTR-mediated miRNA interactions show consistent results that miRNA-1 is a hub miRNA using different miRNA-target interactions with different cutoff values (Figures 2 and 3). I found that miRNA-1 is hub in primary prostate cancer network and

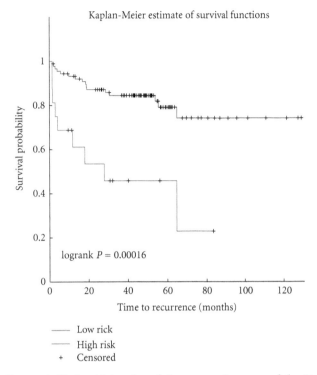

Kaplan-Meier estimate of survival functions

— Low rick
— High risk
+ Censored

FIGURE 9: Kaplan Meier plot of the prognostic power of the 11 miRNAs. We characterized the prognostic power of the 11 miRNAs by extracting their expression from Taylor data and group samples based on their expression into two groups. The two groups showed a very significant separation between high-risk and low-risk patients. This indicates that the 11 miRNA can act as therapeutic targets for prostate cancer treatment.

a hub in the other miRNA-miRNA networks revealed that miRNA-1 is a key regulator of genes and a master coordinator of other miRNAs. Epigenetic analysis showed that promoter hypermethylation may be the reason behind the reduced expression of miRNA1-133 cluster including miRNA-1 [25].

Next I asked if the miRNA interactions are biased toward other factors that may influence the association among miRNAs. First, correlation between miRNAs was shown to influence the interactions among the 11 miRNAs. I found that the 11 miRNAs are correlated but they are not correlated with other miRNAs, which indicates that these miRNAs have something common between them and not with other miRNAs. The second factor is the number of common targets that might influence the network. So I calculated the association between miRNAs based on the number of common targets between them and found that the 11 miRNAs are not significantly connected and they are not among the hub genes. This indicates that the number of common targets between miRNAs did not influence the interactions between miRNAs.

Lastly, the expression of primary prostate samples was used to identify the miRNA-miRNA interactions based on expression of primary cancer samples alone. Interestingly, I found that miR-1 is still the most connected miRNA and other miRNAs (miR-155, miR-16) are hubs. This indicates

that these miRNAs play a significant role in cancer initiation and not metastasis.

5. Conclusion

As the field of miRNA continues to grow, a deeper understanding of miRNA expression, function, and control in prostate cancer will influence the development of miRNA-based therapeutics. In this work I showed that miRNA-1 is a key player in regulating gene expression and has high influence on other miRNAs. 11 miRNAs are identified as a network of tumor suppressors that have prognostic role in cancer recurrence.

Acknowledgments

The author would like to thank NSERC for funding.

References

[1] G. Ruvkun, "Molecular biology: glimpses of a tiny RNA world," *Science*, vol. 294, no. 5543, pp. 797–799, 2001.

[2] S. Sevli, A. Uzumcu, M. Solak, M. Ittmann, and M. Ozen, "The function of microRNAs, small but potent molecules, in human prostate cancer," *Prostate Cancer and Prostatic Diseases*, vol. 13, no. 3, pp. 208–217, 2010.

[3] A. Gordanpour, R. K. Nam, L. Sugar, and A. Seth, "MicroRNAs in prostate cancer: from biomarkers to molecularly-based therapeutics," *Prostate Cancer and Prostatic Diseases*, vol. 1, p. 6, 2012.

[4] L. He and G. J. Hannon, "MicroRNAs: small RNAs with a big role in gene regulation," *Nature Reviews Genetics*, vol. 5, no. 8, p. 631, 2004.

[5] Y. Pang, C. Y. F. Young, and H. Yuan, "MicroRNAs and prostate cancer," *Acta Biochimica et Biophysica Sinica*, vol. 42, no. 6, pp. 363–369, 2010.

[6] B. Zhang, X. Pan, G. P. Cobb, and T. A. Anderson, "microRNAs as oncogenes and tumor suppressors," *Developmental Biology*, vol. 302, no. 1, pp. 1–12, 2007.

[7] G. A. Calin and C. M. Croce, "MicroRNA signatures in human cancers," *Nature Reviews Cancer*, vol. 6, no. 11, pp. 857–866, 2006.

[8] S. D. Hsu, F. M. Lin, W. Y. Wu et al., "Mirtarbase: a database curates experimentally validated microRNA-target interactions," *Nucleic Acids Research*, vol. 39, no. 1, pp. D163–D169, 2011.

[9] A. Esquela-Kerscher and F. J. Slack, "Oncomirs-microRNAs with a role in cancer," *Nature Reviews Cancer*, vol. 6, no. 4, pp. 259–269, 2006.

[10] M. Ozen, C. J. Creighton, M. Ozdemir, and M. Ittmann, "Widespread deregulation of microRNA expression in human prostate cancer," *Oncogene*, vol. 27, no. 12, pp. 1788–1793, 2008.

[11] A. Grimson, K. K. H. Farh, W. K. Johnston, P. Garrett-Engele, L. P. Lim, and D. P. Bartel, "MicroRNA targeting specificity in mammals: determinants beyond seed pairing," *Molecular Cell*, vol. 27, no. 1, pp. 91–105, 2007.

[12] A. Krek, D. Grün, M. N. Poy et al., "Combinatorial microRNA target predictions," *Nature Genetics*, vol. 37, no. 5, pp. 495–500, 2005.

[13] J. I. Satoh and H. Tabunoki, "Comprehensive analysis of human microRNA target networks," *Biodata Mining*, vol. 4, no. 1, p. 17, 2011.

[14] V. Jayaswal, M. Lutherborrow, D. D. F. Ma, and Y. H. Yang, "Identification of microRNA-mRNA modules using microarray data," *BMC Genomics*, vol. 12, p. 138, 2011.

[15] J. C. Huang, T. Babak, T. W. Corson et al., "Using expression profiling data to identify human microRNA targets," *Nature Methods*, vol. 4, no. 12, pp. 1045–1049, 2009.

[16] L. Poliseno, L. Salmena, J. Zhang, B. Carver, W. J. Haveman, and P. P. Pandolfi, "A coding-independent function of gene and pseudogene mRNAs regulates tumour biology," *Nature*, vol. 465, no. 7301, pp. 1033–1038, 2010.

[17] P. Sumazin, X. Yang, H.-S. Chiu et al., "An extensive microRNA-mediated network of RNA-RNA interactions regulates established oncogenic pathways in glioblastoma," *Cell*, vol. 147, no. 2, pp. 370–381, 2011.

[18] M. Smoot, K. Ono, J. Ruscheinski, P. Wang, and T. Ideker, "Cytoscape 2.8: new features for data integration and network visualization," *Bioinformatics*, vol. 27, no. 3, pp. 431–432, 2011.

[19] D. Merico, R. Isserlin, O. Stueker, A. Emili, and G. D. Bader, "Enrichment map: a network-based method for gene-set enrichment visualization and interpretation," *PLos one*, vol. 15, no. 11, p. e13984, 2010.

[20] F. Xiao, Z. Zuo, G. Cai, S. Kang, X. Gao, and T. Li, "Mirecords: an integrated resource for microRNA-target interactions," *Nucleic Acids Research*, vol. 37, no. 1, pp. D105–D110, 2009.

[21] B. S. Taylor, N. Schultz, H. Hieronymus et al., "Integrative genomic profiling of human prostate cancer," *Cancer Cell*, vol. 18, no. 1, pp. 11–22, 2010.

[22] S. Wach, E. Nolte, J. Szczyrba et al., "MicroRNA profiles of prostate carcinoma detected by multiplatform microRNA screening," *International Journal of Cancer*, vol. 130, pp. 611–621, 2012.

[23] V. G. Tusher, R. Tibshirani, and G. Chu, "Significance analysis of microarrays applied to the ionizing radiation response," *Proceedings of the National Academy of Sciences of the United States of America*, vol. 98, no. 9, pp. 5116–5121, 2001.

[24] J. J. Hornberg, F. J. Bruggeman, H. V. Westerhoff, and J. Lankelma, "Cancer: a systems biology disease," *Biosystems*, vol. 83, no. 2-3, pp. 81–90, 2006.

[25] R. S. Hudson, M. Yi, D. Esposito et al. et al., "MicroRNA-1 is a candidate tumor suppressor and prognostic marker in human prostate cancer," *Nucleic Acids Research*, vol. 40, no. 8, pp. 3689–3703, 2012.

9

A High-Throughput Computational Framework for Identifying Significant Copy Number Aberrations from Array Comparative Genomic Hybridisation Data

Ian Roberts,[1] Stephanie A. Carter,[1] Cinzia G. Scarpini,[1]
Konstantina Karagavriilidou,[1] Jenny C. J. Barna,[2] Mark Calleja,[3] and Nicholas Coleman[1]

[1] Department of Pathology, University of Cambridge, Tennis Court Road, Cambridge CB2 1QP, UK
[2] Department of Biochemistry, University of Cambridge, Tennis Court Road, Cambridge CB2 1QW, UK
[3] The Cavendish Laboratory, University of Cambridge, J. J. Thomson Avenue, Cambridge CB3 0HE, UK

Correspondence should be addressed to Nicholas Coleman, nc109@cam.ac.uk

Academic Editor: Yves Van de Peer

Reliable identification of copy number aberrations (CNA) from comparative genomic hybridization data would be improved by the availability of a generalised method for processing large datasets. To this end, we developed swatCGH, a data analysis framework and region detection heuristic for computational grids. swatCGH analyses sequentially displaced (sliding) windows of neighbouring probes and applies adaptive thresholds of varying stringency to identify the 10% of each chromosome that contains the most frequently occurring CNAs. We used the method to analyse a published dataset, comparing data preprocessed using four different DNA segmentation algorithms, and two methods for prioritising the detected CNAs. The consolidated list of the most commonly detected aberrations confirmed the value of swatCGH as a simplified high-throughput method for identifying biologically significant CNA regions of interest.

1. Introduction

Correlating specific genomic copy number aberrations (CNA) with disease is an important and challenging first step in biomarker discovery [1]. Detecting CNAs that define genomic regions of interest using array comparative genomic hybridisation (aCGH) requires precise integration of probe signal amplitude, size (i.e., width) of copy number imbalanced region, and frequency of imbalance across a sample set, all referenced to relevant clinico-pathologic features.

There are two broad methods of aCGH data interpretation for biomarker discovery. The first, exemplified by the R Bioconductor package cghMCR [2], identifies regions showing the most frequent CNAs within a sample set, ranked by average signal amplitude. This approach to prioritization may under-call low prevalence high-level CNAs, such as homozygous deletions or gene amplifications that occur in small subsets of the samples analysed. The second method, targeted gene identification, exemplified by the genome topography scanning (GTS) algorithm [3] and Genomic Identification of Significant Targets in Cancer (GISTIC) module [4], is designed to localize regions of copy number imbalance most likely to be of functional significance. The GTS method models CNAs using parameters of signal intensity, region width and recurrence across a sample set, moderated by gene content. While this approach is able to identify significant regions of imbalance in heterogeneous samples, it relies on prior knowledge. GISTIC calculates the background rate of random chromosomal aberrations and identifies regions that are aberrant more often than would be expected by chance, with greater weight given to high amplitude events. Although gaining favour, a recent report notes GISTIC has trouble identifying relevant minimal regions of interest within larger tracts of CNA [5].

There are currently few open source methods for consolidating aCGH data across a set of samples. In addition,

A High-Throughput Computational Framework for Identifying Significant Copy Number Aberrations from Array
Comparative Genomic Hybridisation Data

79

there are particular difficulties with handling large data sets derived from very high-density oligonucleotide-based aCGH platforms, where there may be a need to review many distinct significant regions of interest. To address these issues, we developed sliding windows adaptive thresholds CGH (swatCGH), a new computational framework for simplifying aCGH data analysis. swatCGH is a heuristic method based on strengths of the major existing approaches. It provides a robust systematic approach, which effectively automates the aCGH analysis process in order to identify CNA regions of interest and improve the reliability of candidate gene identification.

The framework is based on the analysis of average signal amplitude, region width and frequency of CNA occurrence, and enables these parameters to be identified as independent or associated events, including sample subset analysis by agglomerative hierarchical clustering. For each chromosome, swatCGH preferentially identifies regions that display the largest average signal intensity in the greatest proportion of the sample cohort.

The stages of swatCGH were designed to accommodate technical factors that may confound aCGH data analysis, particularly methods of signal intensity preprocessing, such as background correction, normalization, and classification of probe copy number states following segmentation [6, 7]. The R Bioconductor [8] based method enables application of multiple preprocessing configurations, probe segmentation algorithms, and classification strategies, in order to provide the most robust definition of significant CNA regions of interest. Uniquely, the approach also allows comparison and consolidation of analyses resulting from the various preprocessing methods used.

Here, we provide a detailed description of swatCGH. We exemplify the approach using a previously published aCGH dataset based on an analysis of 38 glioblastoma multiforme (GBM) samples using Agilent 44 K oligonucleotide arrays (GSE7602) [3]. The dataset had previously been analysed by GTS, leading to identification of functional redundancy between CDKN2A and CDKN2C tumour suppressor genes in GBM. We analysed the dataset by swatCGH, using data preprocessed with each of the four most frequently cited segmentation algorithms; circular binary segmentation from the package DNAcopy [9, 10], an adaptive weights smoothing method from the package GLAD [11], an homogeneous hidden Markov model (HomHMM) provided by the package aCGH [12], and a biologically tuned HMM (BioHMM) from the package snapCGH [13]. By consolidating data from the four analyses, we identified the most robust CNA regions of interest in the dataset. Based on our comparison of methods for prioritizing detected CNAs, we present results as a summarized list ranked by mean signal intensity, with web-style summary pages to facilitate data verification and efficient selection of candidate genes. In addition, the detailed report of all parameters analysed allows for thorough assessment of other potential regions of interest that are not recorded on the ranked list. By comparing our findings with the previous GTS study [3], we conclude that our heuristic framework offers a simplified high-throughput approach to defining novel genomic loci of potential clinical relevance.

2. Materials and Methods

2.1. Overview of Key Features of swatCGH Framework. swatCGH may be viewed as an aCGH informatics pipeline, in which the input comprises aCGH raw data files, experimental details, an array layout file, and a set of configurations describing the parameters to be used in the analysis. Because of the computational requirements of the methods, we used the high-throughput facilities of CamGrid, Cambridge University's federated computational grid, based on Condor middleware [14]. To permit automated distribution of the analysis, separate R jobs were generated, to perform discrete steps of preprocessing, segmentation, region definition, and reporting.

swatCGH has three important distinctive features. First, in order to reduce noise, we identified CNAs based on signal intensities of groups of neighbouring probes. We identified significant CNA regions of interest across a sample set, based on windows of fixed numbers of probes ranging from 3 to 20. For each window, we measured the percentage of samples within the set which showed the same aCGH copy number classification, a value referred to as the probe window score (PWS). We undertook sequential reanalysis following window displacement by one probe along the length of each chromosome, (i.e., using sliding windows). Data for all PWS across a sample set provides a measure of the overall prevalence of each CNA within the set. Second, we determined the most frequently occurring regions of interest across a sample set for each chromosome separately. Placing PWS in genome position order along a chromosome, we applied varying thresholds to the frequency of CNA occurrence across the sample set, in order to identify the most frequently occurring 10% of CNAs. Accordingly, chromosomes showing a relatively high frequency of CNAs required more stringent thresholds to identify the most commonly occurring 10% regions of interest. We refer to this process as applying adaptive thresholds (AT), an approach that enables identification of lower prevalence abnormalities that may nevertheless be highly significant in sample subgroups. Third, based on findings reported below, the identified CNA regions of interest were ranked by mean signal intensity (similar to cghMCR, [2]), ensuring that significant poorly annotated regions of the genome were not neglected.

Further details of these features of swatCGH are provided in the following sections. The published dataset used for exemplification (GSE7602) was chosen because it was derived from a relatively large number of well-characterised tumour samples, was based on a high-density oligonucleotide microarray platform, and had previously been analysed by GTS [3].

2.2. swatCGH Framework Applied to a Computational Grid. Supplementary Figure S1 presents an overview of our aCGH data processing framework, illustrating the integration of swatCGH into Condor CamGrid. Detailed descriptions of all R scripting methods are available online at doi:10.1155/2012/876976 (http://www.path.cam.ac.uk/research/investigators/coleman/swatCGH/). swatCGH is initiated on a local Condor submission node, with aCGH data being imported, compressed, and prepared for grid submission. Next, a single Condor job submits data to CamGrid for Batch mode R preprocessing using snapCGH. Essentially, this stage comprises data import, background subtraction, and normalization within arrays. Thereafter, a data interdependent Condor process is performed on a per segmentation method, per chromosome basis. This stage utilizes Condor's own directed acyclic graph manager (DAGMan) to schedule the linked jobs. The DAGMan stage is composed of three sepa rate jobs, each defined by a single R script. First, array data is partitioned into separate autosomes, then imputation, segmentation, and classification of aCGH states is perform- ed. Second, probe window scoring for a range of probe window sizes is undertaken. Third, swatCGH generates web-style reports of identified contiguous regions of interest. Following Condor DAGMan completion, a postprocessing stage finalizes the analysis by removing temporary files and consolidating the separate chromosomes into a fully linked report that describes CNA across the genome.

To ensure access to all required R Bioconductor libraries, we used a shared copy of R, served to CamGrid from a host running a chirp server. To enable the use of R batch mode on CamGrid the necessary process of generating discrete R scripts for each executed Condor job was undertaken via the use of template files. The process of turning a template file into a job specific script file was undertaken within the swatCGH shell wrapper, using *sed*, the Unix stream editor. While our implementation of the swatCGH framework utilized Condor CamGrid due to its local availability, we consider that modification of the framework for use with other distributed computational facilities and schedulers (e.g., Globus) would be a straightforward matter, due to the use of simple text configuration and template files.

2.3. Classification of Segmented Chromosomal Regions.

We apply a 5-point classification scheme to array probes within segmented regions, comprising: high level loss; loss; normal copy; gain; high-level gain/amplification. In classification score tables, these states are represented by -2, -1, 0, 1, and 2, respectively. Classification is undertaken using the nudSegmentation algorithm (snapCGH and BayesCGH Bio- conductor packages), which states that segments are copy number abnormal if their absolute computed fluorescence ratios are greater than the difference between the middle fifty of the distributions of normalised observed fluorescence ratios and the middle fifty of the predicted values, multiplied by an appropriate factor change (we used a default value of 75% factor change difference). nudSegmentation separates high-level CNA from single copy gain or loss based on region width, the upper limit of which was set at 10 probes (approximatly 700 Kb on the Agilent 44 K platform).

2.4. Algorithm for Determining CNA Prevalence.

Figure 1 illustrates the processes involved in probe window scoring, using a hypothetical array experiment (Figure 1(a)) com- prising 6 samples (A–F) hybridised to a 20 probe platform (probes numbered 1–20), where grey shaded horizontal bars indicate regions of gain. We define a continuous region of unbroken CNA, in which all probes are consensually imbalanced, as a contiguous region of interest (CRI). To identify CRIs, we first construct a classification score table (Figure 1(b)), in which probe gain is denoted by 1 and no change by 0. Had there been loss, deletion, or amplification, scores of -1, -2, or 2 would have been recorded. Figure 1(c) illustrates probe window scoring for the smallest window size of three probes. Each window receives a score that indicates the proportion of samples in which the same aCGH classification (gain or loss) is seen for all probes within the window. In this exercise, gain is combined with amplification and loss with deletion. For example, no sample shows gain of all probes in the first window (probes 1 to 3), hence 3PWS_1– 3 = 0%. The rectangle slides one probe down, and samples A, D, and E all now share consensus gain for probes 2–4, hence 3PWS_2–4 = 50%. The process repeats until all probe windows have received a score (Figure 1(d)), after which a prevalence plot (Figure 1(e)) summarises the discrete regions of gain identified. The plot (Figure 1(e)) is intersected with an AT in order to select CRIs that occur above a given frequency within the sample set. In general, AT values are set for each chromosome to identify the 5% that contains the most commonly occurring copy number gains and the 5% that contains the most commonly occurring copy number losses. Within each CRI, we define the smallest region of probes showing the most frequent concordant CNA across the sample set. Such a region is referred to as a minimum region of interest (MRI). By definition, a CRI will contain at least one MRI, although it may contain more than one MRI. For CRIs that show no variation in frequency of CNA between probes, the MRI and CRI will be the same.

We compute PWS for window sizes ranging from 3 to 20 probes, corresponding to approximately 210 Kb $\sim$ 1.4 Mb on the Agilent 44 K platform. Calculating CNA recurrence across probe windows effectively provides technical replica- tion that smoothes point fluctuations introduced by techni- cal error, non-specific binding, or copy number variations affecting discrete oligonucleotide probes. We consider that PWS from larger window sizes will more robustly reflect recurrent CNAs within a sample set, and be less susceptible to noise. swatCGH therefore requires that CNA regions of interest detected in larger window sizes are also present in internal smaller windows, at equal or higher frequencies of recurrence. This process is exemplified in Supplementary Figure S2, for the deletion mapping of the CDKN2A locus on chromosome 9, based on the published GBM dataset [3]. Here, analysis using a 20 probe size window shows a discrete region of loss on 9p. Reanalysis with 5-probe windows and 3-probe windows confirms the significance of the CNA and focuses the MRI to 21.73 Mb–22 Mb.

2.5. Chromosome-Specific Adaptive Thresholds Delimit Re- gions of Interest.

Considering each chromosome separate- ly, we apply decreasing ATs to delineate the 5% of the chro- mosome that contains most frequently occurring regions of copy number gain and the 5% that contains most freq- uent regions of copy number loss (10% overall CNA). This strategy normalizes the CNA detection process across chromosomes and for different segmentation algorithms, and allows lower chromosome specific prevalence CNA to

A High-Throughput Computational Framework for Identifying Significant Copy Number Aberrations from Array Comparative Genomic Hybridisation Data

81

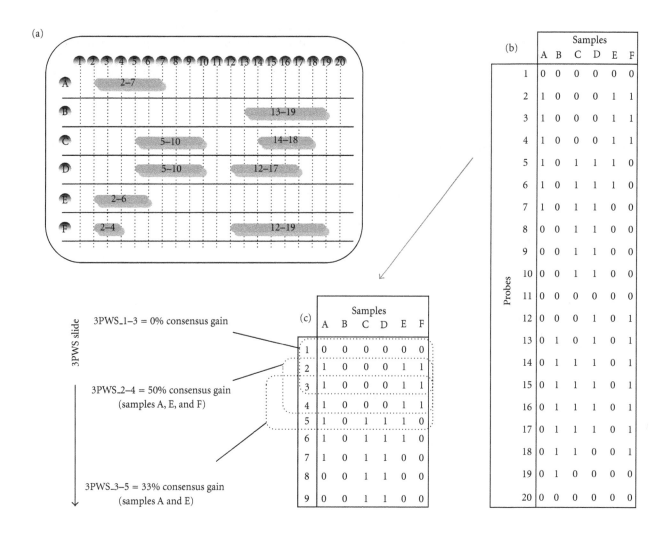

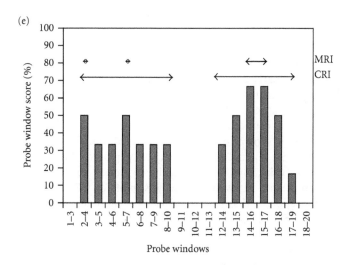

FIGURE 1: Illustration of the probe window scoring method. Panel (a) is a hypothetical aCGH experiment (samples A–F, probes 1–20). Horizontal bars are regions of copy number gain. Panel (b) is the same information in classification table format. Panel (c) shows scoring of the classification table for the first three of the 3-probe windows. Panels (d) and (e) summarise the scoring, with the graph plotting for each probe window (*x* axis) the percentage of samples showing the same aCGH classification (i.e., probe window score). This identifies two CRIs (probes 2–10 and 12–19). The MRIs within each region are shaded in panel (d).

be determined. Supplementary Figure S2D illustrates application of an 80% AT to gate CNA regions of interest on chromosome 9. We use the following rules for selecting the ATs, which are applied independently to regions of copy number gain and copy number loss on each chromosome. (1) We select the lowest threshold that results in approximately 5% CNA; (2) computing % CNA across the chromosome, ATs are selected in sequence from 80% to 20%, in decreasing 10% steps. If an AT results in 0% CNA, the next higher threshold is accepted, even if CNA > 5%; (3). Where the lowest stringency threshold (i.e., 20% frequency across the sample set) results in 0% CNA, the chromosome is deemed to be without CNA.

Figure 2 uses the GBM dataset to demonstrate the process of selecting CNA regions of gain on chromosome 7 (EGFR locus; Figures 2(a), 2(b), and 2(c)), while also illustrating aspects of swatCGH graphical output. An example of detecting CNA regions of loss is given in Supplementary Figure S3 (chromosome 9; CDKN2A). In Figure 2, panel (a) shows a chromosome overview plot, which summarises chromosome CNAs, and represents the starting point for identification of regions of interest. The overview plot is composed of three parts. The upper panel is the median aCGH profile of all arrays, where purple margins are 95% confidence intervals. The centre panel is a sample recurrence chart, which shows probe window score by chromosome position (using 3-probe windows), and indicates the frequency of CNAs across the sample set. The ideogram axis is at the centre (row c), with the frequency of CNAs for individual probe windows being shown by narrow bars above and below. Probe windows showing copy number gain are in green above the ideogram (in row b), while windows showing copy number loss are in red below the ideogram (in row d). Where adjacent 3-probe windows show the same frequency of CNA, they merge to form longer bars.

Aligning the median aCGH plot (upper panel in Figure 2(a)) with the frequency of recurrence across samples (middle panel in Figure 2(a)) provides a useful method for readily identifying CNAs most likely to be significant. In the analysis shown in Figure 2(a), an AT of 80% was required, hence the gated CRIs represent probe window spans that are gained or lost in ≥80% of the sample cohort. These gated CRIs are summarised as thick green bars for gain (row a) and thick red bars for loss (row e). All CRIs are numerically indexed, for subsequent cross referencing. For example, chromosome 7 copy number gain CRI#3 (containing the EGFR locus) is shown in detail in Figure 2(b). Finally, the lower panel in Figure 2(a) is a frequency plot of high-level CNAs (gains and losses), maximally scaled to 25% of the sample set. In swatCGH analysis, plots of CRIs by genome location, and sample-based views of all indentified MRIs are generated by default and presented as web-style reports. Supplementary Figure S4 provides a genome wide overview of CNAs in the 38 sample GBM data set following segmentation by DNAcopy.

2.6. Reviewing Significant Regions of Interest. A major difficulty in aCGH analysis is identifying CNAs that are most likely to target genes of functional importance. To assist

rapid selection of such regions, swatCGH produces web-style summary pages for each chromosome, for each method of data segmentation, at a selected range of probe window sizes. Summary pages provide links to all processed data, supporting verification of the selected regions. The reports provided comprise chromosome overview, copy number karyograms, sample clustering by regions, regional probe classifications, and supporting data in tabular format. Unsupervised hierarchical clustering is undertaken using the classified aCGH call scores within the gated CRIs for each chromosome, in order to demonstrate any sample-dependent CNA patterns. The fact that the top 10% most frequently occurring CNAs are defined for all chromosomes ensures a detailed CNA profile for each sample and prevents significant low recurrence CNAs from being missed. This approach is likely to enrich for genes or genomic regions that mediate phenotype variation across clinico-pathological subgroups. Finally, swatCGH generates a table of CRI data ordered by genome position, with each row representing a discrete region. Rows are serially indexed, and maintain the indexed order of CRIs shown in the chromosome overview plots (Figure 2(a) and Supplementary Figure S3A). Following a region hyperlink reveals the aCGH classification of all probes in the region, as illustrated for one CRI in Figure 2(b). In addition, hyperlinks to on-line genome databases are also provided (Figure 2(c)).

3. Results

3.1. Comparison of CNA Detection following Four Segmentation Algorithms. All parameters relevant to swatCGH analysis of the GSE7602 dataset are provided in a single plain text file (Supplementary Text File 1). We demonstrated the performance of swatCGH by analysing the published GBM aCGH data, following the application of the segmentation algorithms DNAcopy, GLAD, HomHMM, and BioHMM (using developer-recommended default parameters), scoring window sizes of 3–20 probes. CRIs in individual chromosomes were identified based on adaptive thresholds of 20%–80% of the samples analysed, in order to identify the 10% most frequently occurring CNAs.

Using unfiltered data for the 38 GBM samples, we observed that BioHMM and HomHMM led to detection of a greater number of discrete CRIs than DNAcopy or GLAD (Table 1, italic columns). However, while BioHMM and HomHMM led to identification of percentages of the genome showing CNA that were similar to the 10% target of adaptive thresholding (10.96% and 8.89%, resp.), the CRIs detected following DNAcopy and GLAD represented 25.17% and 31.08%, respectively. The latter methods identify relatively large CRIs and more stringent ATs led to <10% of the genome being detected as showing CNAs. Interestingly, when comparing the ratios of the sizes of the DNA regions identified as showing copy number gain to those showing copy number loss, BioHMM led to detection of a greater proportion of gain (ratio 2.03), while DNAcopy led to preferential identification of loss (0.64). GLAD and HomHMM led to detection of similar intermediate ratios of gain to loss (1.62 and 1.55, respectively).

A High-Throughput Computational Framework for Identifying Significant Copy Number Aberrations from Array Comparative Genomic Hybridisation Data

83

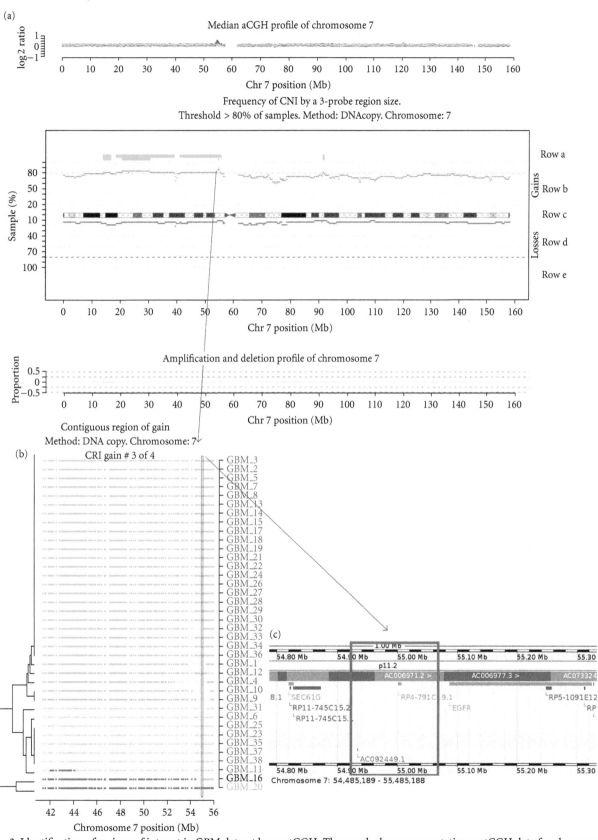

FIGURE 2: Identification of regions of interest in GBM dataset by swatCGH. The panels show representative swatCGH data for chromosome 7, showing copy number gain using data segmented by DNAcopy. Panel (a) shows the chromosome overview plot, representing the median aCGH profiles (top), sample recurrence plot (middle), and high-level CNA plot (bottom). Dashed lines in the middle panel represent 80% AT. Panel (b) is regional probe classification view of a copy number gain CRI on chromosome 7 (42–56 Mb). In panel (b) samples are clustered by probe classifications (green = gain; red = loss; grey = normal; yellow = high-level gain; cyan = high-level loss). The red box indicates the MRI identified for the region, linked by the arrow from the same region of the middle plot in panel (a). Panel (c) illustrates a hyperlink from the MRI to the ENSEMBL genome browser, provided in swatCGH output.

TABLE 1: Comparison of regions of interest identified by swatCGH following four methods of DNA segmentation. The values shown are derived from 3-probe window analysis of the GBM dataset, using adaptive thresholding to limit CNAs to 10% of the genome. For each segmentation method data is provided for regions of copy number gain, regions of copy number loss, and for the total CNA. *Italic columns* represent findings for CRIs using unfiltered data, while roman columns represent data for MRIs filtered for significance using amplitude-based prioritization ($P < 0.1$).

	All regions		Filtered regions ($P < 0.1$)	
	Number CRIs	Proportion CNA	Number CRIs	Proportion CNA
BioHMM				
Gain	*253*	**7.34%**	69	**1.33%**
Loss	*227*	**3.62%**	44	**0.56%**
Total	*480*	**10.96%**	113	**1.89%**
Gain : Loss		**2.03**		**2.40**
GLAD				
Gain	*66*	**18.91%**	11	**1.04%**
Loss	*65*	**12.17%**	7	**0.18%**
Total	**131**	**31.08%**	18	**1.22%**
Gain : Loss		**1.55**		**5.67**
DNAcopy				
Gain	*99*	**9.81%**	13	**0.81%**
Loss	*118*	**15.36%**	19	**0.99%**
Total	*217*	**25.17%**	32	**1.80%**
Gain : Loss		**0.64**		**0.82**
HomHMM				
Gain	*275*	**5.48%**	46	**0.93%**
Loss	*216*	**3.39%**	24	**0.29%**
Total	*491*	**8.87%**	70	**1.23%**
Gain : Loss		**1.62**		**3.20**

3.2. Amplitude-Dependent Prioritization of Detected CNAs. We investigated two approaches to prioritization of the regions of interest derived from swatCGH analysis. First, we filtered MRIs using a modification of the signal amplitude dependent method of Aguirre et al. [2]:

$$f(x) = \frac{e^{-(x-\mu)^2/(2\sigma^2)}}{\sigma\sqrt{2\pi}}. \tag{1}$$

Briefly, a probability density function (1) was computed using a permutation approach from mean signal intensities (μ) with scale parameter (σ) for each probe window size employed, with sampling size in the probability distribution being weighted for chromosome length. MRIs were filtered for regions demonstrating a statistically significant deviation in mean signal intensity (mean log 2 ratio across all arrays, $P < 0.1$). The number of CRIs that contained a significant MRI is shown in Table 1, roman columns. For data preprocessed by all DNA segmentation methods, we observed generally proportional reductions in the number of CRIs detected, compared to those identified from the unfiltered data. Interestingly, however, all segmentation methods now led to detection of similar percentages of the genome showing CNAs (1.22%–1.89%; Table 1 roman columns).

The regions of interest identified from 3-probe window data are shown in Supplementary Tables S1A (copy number gain) and S1B (copy number loss), ordered by significance value of MRIs. These data illustrate the value of AT setting

in identifying lower prevalence CNAs. For example, using Supplementary Table S1A DNAcopy data as reference, the 80% AT value required to achieve ~5% CNA gain on chromosome 7 (SEC61G, 89%) would entirely eliminate gains determined on chromosome 4 (CHIC2) that had a maximal prevalence of 32% and required 20% AT to achieve 5% CNA. While all segmentation methods led to identification of chromosomes 7 and 9 as the regions of most frequent copy number gain and loss respectively, there were discrepancies in the regions lower in the ranked lists. For example, BioHMM and GLAD led to identification of gain on chromosome 1, while HomHMM led to detection of gain on chromosomes 8 and 17. Similarly, only BioHMM led to identification of loss on chromosome 4, while other methods led to detection of loss on chromosome 1. Intersection of the methods suggest chromosomes 3, 4, 5, 7, and 20 are the most common sites of copy number gain, while chromosomes 1, 9, 10, 11, 13, and 14 are the most common sites of copy number loss. DNAcopy led to identification of this CNA profile most closely (summarized in Supplementary Figure S5). Figure 3 shows CNA on three of these target chromosomes using the copy number karyogram format of DNAcopy analysis. At high resolution, all segmentation methods led to mapping of the top copy number loss MRI to the CDKN2A locus (chromosome 9; 21.87 Mb). DNAcopy led to mapping the top copy number gain MRI to RP4-791C19, a clone located mid-way between SEC61G and EGFR. The remaining methods led to mapping the top region of gain precisely to SEC61G (chromosome 7; 54.9 Mb).

A High-Throughput Computational Framework for Identifying Significant Copy Number Aberrations from Array
Comparative Genomic Hybridisation Data

85

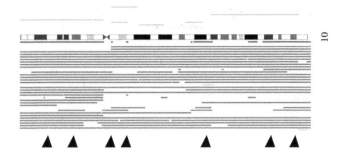

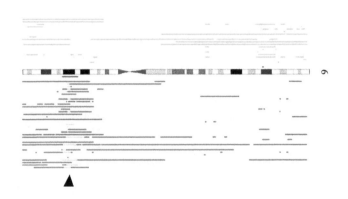

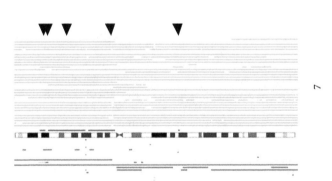

FIGURE 3: Representative swatCGH copy number karyograms. The results shown are for chromosomes 7, 9, and 10, using data segmented by DNAcopy. Red bars at the bottom of each ideogram indicate regions of copy number loss, while cyan bars signify high-level loss. Green bars at the top of each ideogram represent regions of copy number gain, while yellow bars represent high-level gain. The purple bars on either side of each ideogram denote the CRIs identified by swatCGH analysis. Arrowheads locate MRIs identified as significant using amplitude based prioritization ($P < 0.1$).

3.3. Gene-Centred Prioritization of Detected CNAs.

The second method used to prioritize the MRIs derived from swatCGH was a modified version of GTS [3], which moderates average signal intensity by frequency of occurrence across a sample set and also incorporates weighting for gene density:

$$ARI = \log 2\left(\overline{\text{MRI signal intensity}}\right) \times \text{recurrence}, \quad (2)$$

$$RIC = \frac{\text{Number of genes per MRI}}{\text{Number of probes per MRI}}, \quad (3)$$

$$AFI = \frac{(RIC \times ARI)}{ARI}, \quad (4)$$

$$GDW = AFI \times ARI. \quad (5)$$

For this approach, we generated values for average aberration recurrence index (ARI; mean aberration log 2 ratios multiplied by recurrence, (2)) and aberration focality index (AFI) as originally described [3]. To estimate regional information content for AFI calculation, we determined the regional information content (RIC), being the number of genes present within an MRI divided by the number of probes comprising the MRI (3). The product of ARI and AFI (4) gave a prioritization score, gene density weighting (GDW), which reflected not only average signal intensity but also recurrence and information content (5). This gene-centred prioritization method was applied first to the list of MRIs filtered by the amplitude-dependent prioritization method (i.e., those in Supplementary Table S1) and resulted in the reordering shown in Supplementary Table S2.

Using this modified GTS approach, BioHMM and GLAD again led to identification of SEC61G as the top gained locus, while HomHMM led to SEC61G being placed second, behind SKAP2. DNAcopy did not lead to identification of SEC61G gain, instead EGFLAM was identified as the top gained locus. In addition, the lower placed loci were reordered. The majority of the segmentation methods now led to elevation of EGFLAM (chr 5), EDN3 (chr 20), and CHIC2 (chr 4) above minor placed chromosome 7 loci, which dominated in the list ranked only by amplitude (Supplementary Table S1). Changes were also seen in the ranking of regions of copy number loss. Whereas regions on chromosomes 9 and 10 dominated, CDKN2C and FAF1 now ranked above CDKN2A after analysis following GLAD and DNAcopy segmentation.

We next applied the gene-centred prioritization method to the unfiltered MRI list, to test whether any MRIs had been excluded by the initial amplitude-based filtering step. We selected the top 10 MRIs identified from unfiltered data processed by each segmentation method, for comparison with data from the previous analysis (i.e., the data shown in Supplementary Table S2). Of the 80 MRIs so selected (Supplementary Table S3), 34 would have been excluded by amplitude-dependent filtering (i.e., $P > 0.1$). In addition to previously reported region listings, BioHMM now led to identification of copy number gain at loci on chromosomes 16 (CDH11; IRX5) and 17 (MAPT), and copy number losses at loci on chromosomes 1 (NPH4) and 15 (SPRED1). DNAcopy led to identification of gains on chromosomes 2 (Y_RNA), 16 (CDH11, CDH9, and IRF8) and 17 (MAPT), and losses on chromosomes 13 (SLITRK5; CYSLTR2), 14 (EGLN3; NPAS3), 15 (SPRED1), and 18 (TCF4; SNORA73). GLAD led to identification of gains on chromosomes 16 and 12, and losses on chromosomes 12, 13, 15, and 18, while HomHMM led to identification of additional gains on chromosomes 3 (TPRG1), 8 (EXT1), and 1 (FCRL5; NBPF15) and losses on chromosomes 12 (NAV3) and 11 (DSCAML1).

Based on these observations, we conclude that prioritization by amplitude favours the highest frequency CNAs that also display largest signal amplitude within the sample set, for example, gains on chromosome 7 and losses on chromosomes 9, and 10, regardless of whether the regions are gene-coding. In contrast, prioritization by recurrence-moderated average signal intensity, weighted for gene density, favours either gene dense regions, or large genes in smaller regions of imbalance, where the ratio of genes to probes will be disproportionately low.

3.4. Integration of Ranked Regions of Interest. Finally, we combined all previous analyses to identify the most consistently detected CNAs in the dataset. For each of the two prioritization methods, we consolidated regions detected by the four segmentation algorithms into a consensus list of MRIs, requiring at least two segmentation methods to independently flag a region (Supplementary Figure S6). The gene-centred prioritization analysis used for this exercise was performed using data previously filtered by the amplitude-based prioritization method (Supplementary Table S2). We identified regions present in both lists to produce an overall set of 35 MRIs that we consider most robustly describes CNAs in the dataset (Supplementary Table 4). We performed agglomerative hierarchical clustering based on probes in the 35 CRIs that encompassed the 35 MRIs, using data that had been segmented with DNAcopy. CRIs were required to be detected above an AT of 40%, hence the CHIC2 locus was excluded. The sample set clustered into three subgroups (Figure 4). Notable characteristics included chromosome 3 gains in Group A, gross CNA on chromosome 11 in Group B, and losses on chromosome 10 in Group C. At locus level resolution (based on the MRIs), we observed CDKN2A loss across all groups, GRID1 loss predominantly in Group C, and elevated frequency of CDKN2C loss in group A (See Figure 4 key). The region of chromosome 7 spanning MEOX2 (15.7 Mb) to EGFR (55.1 Mb) was generally gained in all groups. There was increased frequency of Claudin and SUMO1 gain in Group A, FGF10 gain in groups A and B, and striking heterogeneity of PDGFD copy number in group B.

3.5. Initial Comparison with GISTIC. In a parallel analysis, we determined the proportion of genome deemed to show CNA by GISTIC for each of the four segmentation methods. The findings are provided in Supplementary Table S5 and may be compared directly with those in Table 1. Whereas the italic columns of Table 1 report the number of CRIs and the proportion of genome in CNA by swatCGH, Supplementary Table S5 reports the number of genes and proportion of genome called in CNA as determined from "wide peak intervals". For swatCGH the average total proportion of genome in CNA was 1.5% (range 1.2–1.9%). The equivalent value by GISTIC was 2.8% (0.35–3.9%), with HomHMM generating an outlier value of 0.35%. The broader regions of CNA identified by GISTIC resulted in a list of ~400 candidate genes. In contrast, for swatCGH the prioritized CRI list was between 18 and 113 significant regions, resulting in a list of ~200 candidate genes across all segmentation methods (Supplementary Table S4).

4. Discussion

swatCGH was designed as a simplified approach to selecting CNA regions of interest from aCGH data. This open source method enables consolidation of data across a sample set and can accommodate the large information content of high-resolution analyses, where theoretical limits extend beyond millions of probes by thousands of samples as defined by R data frame properties (see R documentation at http://cran.r-project.org/). The method incorporates sliding

A High-Throughput Computational Framework for Identifying Significant Copy Number Aberrations from Array
Comparative Genomic Hybridisation Data

87

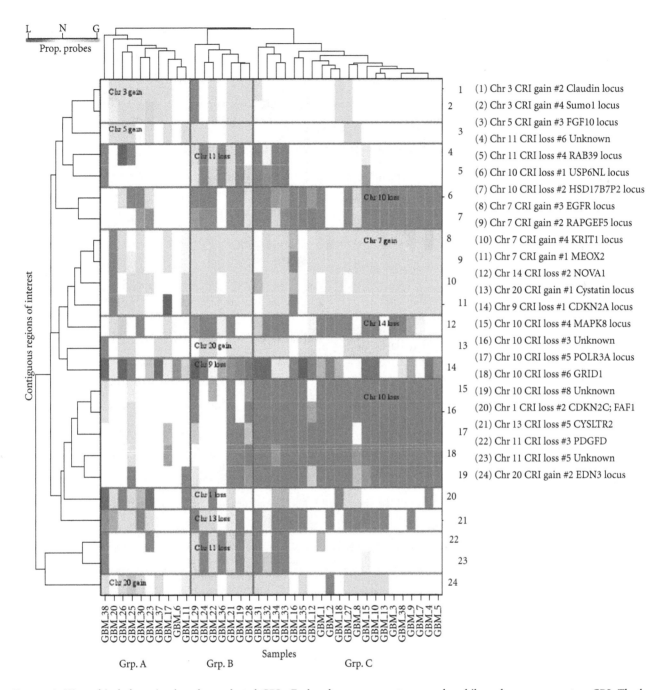

FIGURE 4: Hierarchical clustering based on selected CRIs. Each column represents a sample, while each row represents a CRI. The key provides details of each CRI, including the index number given during swatCGH processing. Shading denotes the proportion of probes in each CRI that demonstrated copy number gain (orange) or copy number loss (blue).

windows, as signal intensities estimated from groups of neighbouring probes are less likely to be subject to noise perturbation than discrete probes. Adaptive thresholds applied on a per chromosome basis increase the probability of identifying lower prevalence abnormalities that may contribute to significant patterns of disease heterogeneity, paralleling an aim of GTS, but in contrast to methods such as GISTIC, that are weighted towards oncogene detection. Selection of prioritized candidate targets is not computed by integration across probe window sizes. Instead, users are able to select

a results panel based on a window size most appropriate for the array probe density used, and review outcomes for a range of probe window sizes by navigation through the web-based CNA reports. In our approach, the process for ranking CNA regions of interest is driven by mean signal intensity, preventing omission of significant nonannotated regions of the genome, and supporting inclusion of important lower prevalence abnormalities. The overall method is robust, systematic, and customizable, with all parameters specified in a single text file. The reporting of all analysis steps undertaken enables ready evaluation of all genomic loci, not just those in the ranked lists.

In applying swatCGH to a GBM test dataset, we observed considerable differences in the CRIs detected after data was preprocessed with four different segmentation algorithms most likely reflecting differences in arithmetic approaches to segmentation used by each algorithm. Interestingly, BioHMM, HomHMM, and GLAD led to preferential detection of copy number gain compared to copy number loss. This may be related to the empirically observed technical bias that can occur following aCGH normalisation, which produces a reduction in the dynamic range of global signal intensity in regions of copy number loss, compared to regions of copy number gain [15]. Interestingly, DNAcopy led to identification of a greater amount of loss than gain, associated with detection of more loss and less gain than the other segmentation methods, consistent with observations in the original description of the method [9], and most likely reflects the approach used for change point detection.

The most significant MRIs identified following processing by all four segmentation algorithms were generally similar (Supplementary Tables S1–S4). Indeed, DNAcopy, BioHMM, and HomHMM all led to the identification of a large majority of our final list of 35 consensus MRIs (Supplementary Table S4). The two methods used to prioritize MRIs had effects on the resulting ranked gene lists. The published analysis of the dataset used GTS, augmented by prioritization of CNAs based on a combination of focality, amplitude, and recurrence across the sample set [3]. This led to the biologically important novel observation that CDKN2C is a frequently deleted tumour suppressor gene in GBM. When we analysed the data set using a prioritization method based on signal amplitude alone, CDKN2C loss was also highly ranked following data segmentation with DNAcopy (ranked 4th) and GLAD (ranked 2nd), although not following segmentation with BioHMM or HomHMM. Reordering the amplitude-prioritized data by GTS-based gene density weighting led to elevation of CDKN2C in ranked lists of data segmented by DNAcopy (new rank 2nd) and GLAD (new rank 1st), indicating that gene density weighting has the potential to add value in some settings. However, we also observed limitations of the GTS-based approach when considering copy number gain in the dataset. Using the signal amplitude method of prioritizing regions of interest, the top region of gain identified after BioHMM, HomHMM, and GLAD was SEC61G, while the top region identified after DNAcopy was RP4-791C19, which maps midway between SEC61G and EGFR. However, when the GTS-based method was applied to the ranked genes, the RP4-791C19 locus was not identified in the DNAcopy segmented dataset, as it is nongene coding. This observation illustrates how methods of interpreting CGH data that weight importance by genomic content are critically dependent on accurate probe mapping and annotation.

The agglomerative hierarchical clustering function of swatCGH detects significant relationships between regions of interest across samples. In the data set analysed, we identified a cluster (Group A) in which there was enrichment for CDKN2C deletion in association with the more widespread deletion of CDKN2A, mirroring the original published observation [3]. The relevant cluster group was also defined by gain of chromosome 3 loci in the absence of CNAs on chromosomes 10 and 11, features that may contribute further to the phenotype of tumours in the cluster.

In conclusion, swatCGH is a distributed high-throughput aCGH data analysis heuristic that facilitates identification of CNA regions of interest suitable for further genetic and functional investigations.

Funding

This work was supported by Cancer Research UK and the Medical Research Council.

Acknowledgments

The authors thank Doug Thain for modifications to Parrot, and Lorenz Wernisch for helpful comments on the paper.

References

[1] A. Kallioniemi, "CGH microarrays and cancer," *Current Opinion in Biotechnology*, vol. 19, no. 1, pp. 36–40, 2008.

[2] A. J. Aguirre, C. Brennan, G. Bailey et al., "High-resolution characterization of the pancreatic adenocarcinoma genome," *Proceedings of the National Academy of Sciences of the United States of America*, vol. 101, no. 24, pp. 9067–9072, 2004.

[3] R. Wiedemeyer, C. Brennan, T. P. Heffernan et al., "Feedback circuit among INK4 tumor suppressors constrains human glioblastoma development," *Cancer Cell*, vol. 13, no. 4, pp. 355–364, 2008.

[4] R. Beroukhim, G. Getz, L. Nghiemphu et al., "Assessing the significance of chromosomal aberrations in cancer: methodology and application to glioma," *Proceedings of the National Academy of Sciences of the United States of America*, vol. 104, no. 50, pp. 20007–20012, 2007.

[5] F. Sanchez-Garcia, U. D. Akavia, E. Mozes, and D. Pe'er, "JISTIC: identification of significant targets in cancer," *BMC Bioinformatics*, vol. 11, p. 189, 2010.

[6] R. Chari, W. W. Lockwood, and W. L. Lam, "Computational methods for the analysis of array comparative genomic hybridization," *Cancer Informatics*, vol. 2, pp. 48–58, 2006.

[7] D. Pinkel and D. G. Albertson, "Comparative genomic hybridization," *Annual Review of Genomics and Human Genetics*, vol. 6, pp. 331–354, 2005.

[8] R. C. Gentleman, V. J. Carey, D. M. Bates et al., "Bioconductor: open software development for computational biology and bioinformatics," *Genome Biology*, vol. 5, no. 10, p. R80, 2004.

[9] A. B. Olshen, E. S. Venkatraman, R. Lucito, and M. Wigler, "Circular binary segmentation for the analysis of array-based DNA copy number data," *Biostatistics*, vol. 5, no. 4, pp. 557–572, 2004.

[10] E. S. Venkatraman and A. B. Olshen, "A faster circular binary segmentation algorithm for the analysis of array CGH data," *Bioinformatics*, vol. 23, no. 6, pp. 657–663, 2007.

[11] P. Hupé, N. Stransky, J. P. Thiery, F. Radvanyi, and E. Barillot, "Analysis of array CGH data: from signal ratio to gain and loss of DNA regions," *Bioinformatics*, vol. 20, no. 18, pp. 3413–3422, 2004.

[12] J. Fridlyand, A. M. Snijders, D. Pinkel, D. G. Albertson, and A. N. Jain, "Hidden Markov models approach to the analysis of

A High-Throughput Computational Framework for Identifying Significant Copy Number Aberrations from Array
Comparative Genomic Hybridisation Data

89

array CGH data," *Journal of Multivariate Analysis*, vol. 90, no. 1, pp. 132–153, 2004.

[13] J. C. Marioni, N. P. Thorne, and S. Tavaré, "BioHMM: a heterogeneous hidden Markov model for segmenting array CGH data," *Bioinformatics*, vol. 22, no. 9, pp. 1144–1146, 2006.

[14] D. Thain, T. Tannenbaum, and M. Livny, "Distributed computing in practice: the Condor experience," *Concurrency Computation Practice and Experience*, vol. 17, no. 2–4, pp. 323–356, 2005.

[15] B. P. P. van Houte, T. W. Binsl, H. Hettling, W. Pirovano, and J. Heringa, "CGHnormaliter: an iterative strategy to enhance normalization of array CGH data with imbalanced aberrations," *BMC Genomics*, vol. 10, p. 401, 2009.

10

CMD: A Database to Store the Bonding States of Cysteine Motifs with Secondary Structures

Hamed Bostan,[1] Naomie Salim,[2] Zeti Azura Hussein,[3] Peter Klappa,[4] and Mohd Shahir Shamsir[1]

[1] *Faculty of Biosciences and Bioengineering, Universiti Teknologi Malaysia, 81310 Johor Bahru, Johor, Malaysia*
[2] *Faculty of Computer Science and Information Systems, Universiti Teknologi Malaysia, 81310 Johor Bahru, Johor, Malaysia*
[3] *School of Bioscience and Biotechnology, Faculty of Science and Technology, Universiti Kebangsaan Malaysia, 43600 Bangi, Selangor, Malaysia*
[4] *School of Biosciences, University of Kent, Canterbury, Kent CT2 7NJ, UK*

Correspondence should be addressed to Mohd Shahir Shamsir, shahir@utm.my

Academic Editor: Huixiao Hong

Computational approaches to the disulphide bonding state and its connectivity pattern prediction are based on various descriptors. One descriptor is the amino acid sequence motifs flanking the cysteine residue motifs. Despite the existence of disulphide bonding information in many databases and applications, there is no complete reference and motif query available at the moment. Cysteine motif database (CMD) is the first online resource that stores all cysteine residues, their flanking motifs with their secondary structure, and propensity values assignment derived from the laboratory data. We extracted more than 3 million cysteine motifs from PDB and UniProt data, annotated with secondary structure assignment, propensity value assignment, and frequency of occurrence and coefficiency of their bonding status. Removal of redundancies generated 15875 unique flanking motifs that are always bonded and 41577 unique patterns that are always nonbonded. Queries are based on the protein ID, FASTA sequence, sequence motif, and secondary structure individually or in batch format using the provided APIs that allow remote users to query our database via third party software and/or high throughput screening/querying. The CMD offers extensive information about the bonded, free cysteine residues, and their motifs that allows in-depth characterization of the sequence motif composition.

1. Background

Disulphide bonds are formed by oxidation of two cysteine residues in a protein and are significant to a protein's conformational stability as they confer greater thermal and chemical stability as well as stabilizing structural intermediates to ensure the correct folding pathway. However, the connectivity of the disulphide bonds in protein sequences can only be determined experimentally. Given this difficulty, the ability to evaluate or predict the disulphide bonding state and connectivity from the sequence would prove to be highly valuable in engineering proteins for biotechnological and medical applications. Computational approaches towards disulphide connectivity prediction have been based on various descriptors. One of these descriptors is the sequence motifs generated by combining the flanking residues on the either side of the the cysteine residue [1, 2]. These immediate residues flanking the cysteine have been shown to influence the cysteine's redox potential and the cysteine's steric accessibility [3]. These sequence motifs have been fed into various prediction methods [4] such as machine learning approaches (i.e., statistical methods, neural networks (NNs) [5], and support vector machine (SVM) [6–8] such as DiANNA [3], DISULFIND [9], DCON [10], and CysView [11]. Currently, all the cysteine motifs are extracted by parsing data from protein databases and feeding them into the prediction tools. Motivated by the absence of a database and usefulness of the cysteine flanking motifs in predicting the cysteine bonding state and connectivity prediction, we have developed cysteine motif database (CMD) as a tool to mine and store these motifs. The creation of CMD allows the motif extraction and facilitates the study of their secondary structures, bonding and connectivity propensities. In this paper, we present CMD as a publicly available tool that complements existing prediction tools.

2. Construction and Content

2.1. Content. The CMD data was compiled from Protein Data Bank (PDB) (http://www.rcsb.org) and UniProt (http://www.uniprot.org). For each databank, two different datasets were created; a complete protein dataset and a second 100% nonhomologous unique sequence dataset (100% similar sequences were omitted). We have featured CMD with both datasets for each PDB and UniProt, allowing researchers to utilize the database in its entirety (73656 structures for PDB and 531462 structures for UniProt) or to include only unique sequences (33874 for PDB and 140723 for UniProt). Using these datasets, we extracted 878,000 cysteine motifs based on 1st, 2nd, 3rd, 4th, and 5th flanking residues of the cysteine as these immediate residues are within proximity to exert influence on the cysteine (Table 1). The assignment of the bonding state of cysteine residues and their bonding partners is based on the SSBOND and DISULPHIDE BOND tags in each PDB and UniProt files. The motifs were clustered according to the occurrence of the bonding state, that is, always bonded, always nonbonded, and both bonded and nonbonded (nonbonded state with another cysteine or to other atoms such as metals). Each of the bonded cysteine is also mapped to each inter and intra-chain disulphide bond cysteine partner.

The motifs were categorized between inter and intradomain with the secondary structure assignments for each motif sequence (if available) determined using secondary structure reference files retrieved from PDB.

2.2. Construction. The data contained in CMD is stored in Microsoft SQL server 2005 data storage architecture. Cysteine motif pattern tables are indexed based on Protein ID, motifs, chain number, and secondary structure to enhance the efficiency of the querying performance. Table-based partitioning was used to increase the flexibility and performance on Motif data tables. In these tables, over three million motifs are stored which can be queried and processed. All preprocessing, data extraction, and injection for motif sequences and their secondary structure were carried out in Net 4.0 platform using C# programming language. The web interface of CMD is based on ASP. Net extension integrated with Ajax technology to provide a strong, simple, and user friendly environment for end users. The web application is hosted on an Internet Information Services (IIS) HTTP server version 7.5.7600.16385. CMD will be updated automatically with latest data from PDB and Uniprot.

In addition, several APIs available in CMD enable developers to query our database remotely and embed the results in their own system independently. A complete list of available APIs together with the method of inline implementation is available in the FAQ section of the CMD website.

TABLE 1

	PDB (All)	PDB (NH)	UniProt (All)	UniProt (NH)
Proteins	73656	33874	531462	140723
Patterns	535544	230213	2509611	966374
Bonded motifs	148505	64246	189238	113365
Nonbonded motifs	387039	165967	2320373	853009
Intrachain	84591	36473	—	—
Interchain	4013	1900	—	—

NH: Nonhomologous unique sequences which have been affected by 100% similarity removal.

3. Data Update

Using RCSB and UniProt API's, the software will retrieve all the Protein IDs available in the mentioned resources. A query will list all the existing Protein IDs in our local dataset. All new Protein IDs will be identified using both above references. Using RCSB and UniProt ftp services, all the newly identified protein files will be downloaded using the Protein ID's to our local server. As in our method of preprocessing and data set preparation, all SEQRESS and SSBOND tags will be extracted from the downloaded files. All cysteine motifs based on the 1st, 2nd, 3rd, 4th, and 5th number of flanking residue on each side (neighboring residues) will be captured and extracted to the records of data with cysteine at the meddle. Each record contains the motif sequence, Chain ID, cysteine residue position in the sequence, bonding status of cysteine residue and the Protein ID as the reference. Each record will be inserted into our database. A log will be generated for the successful procedure or any run time error.

4. Utility and Discussion

4.1. User Interface. The CMD website features an interactive and comprehensive cysteine Motif query engine by supporting different search keywords, such as Protein IDs and motif sequences in the FASTA format. Users can filter according to proteins which are mutated and engineered proteins. All results can be downloaded as text and CSV for further analysis (Figures 1, 2, and 3).

4.2. Utility: Example Applications. CMD facilitate studies focused on cysteine disulphide bonding status prediction and analysis by processing the data. Here we present two applications of our system that illustrate the potential of CMD in greater details.

4.2.1. Application 1: Statistical Analysis of Bonding State. To analyze the predictive power of CFMD, we investigated the cysteine bonding pattern of human protein disulphide isomerase (PDII, P07237 [UniParc]). PDI catalyses the formation (oxidation) and rearrangement (isomerisation) of disulphide bonds during the folding of secretory and

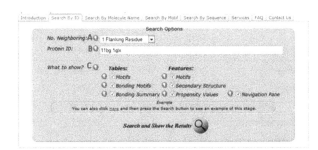

FIGURE 1: Annotated diagram describing the search options for "Search By ID" section. (A) Users can choose either PDB or SwissProt. (B) Users can enter single or multiple ProteinIDs separated by comma (,) as keyword. (C) Users can choose which of the results to appear in the output.

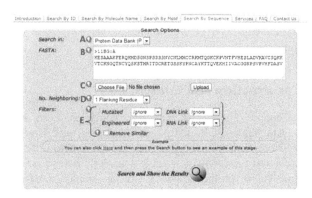

FIGURE 2: Annotated diagram of "Search By FASTA Sequence" section showing all search options and filtering criteria. (A) Users can choose either PDB or SwissProt. (B) Users can enter single or multiple FASTA sequences to be investigated for each motif inside. (C) Users can also upload a FASTA format file to be investigated. (D) Users can choose the number of amino acid residues on each side of cysteine for motif extraction process within the FASTA sequence. (E) Users can filter the proteins in which the motif will be investigated. User can specify whether the protein was engineered or mutated and choose whether the protein contains any DNA or RNA link. They can also filter out the similar proteins and keep only one identical copy of them for advanced investigations.

membrane-bound proteins (for review see [12]), thus stabilising the native structure of these proteins. PDI contains two domains with high sequence homology to thioredoxin. One of these thioredoxin motives is found at position 52–55, while the second motif is located at position 396–399. The active site cysteine residues in the thioredoxin motives are essential for the oxidase/isomerase activity of PDI. In each motif the two cysteine residues within the sequence—WCGHC—can potentially form a disulphide bond.

To investigate whether both thioredoxin motives have similar disulphide bond propensities, that is, whether both thioredoxin motives are in the same bonded form, we analysed the disulphide bonding pattern with the CFMD (Figure 4 and Table 2). Our analysis predicted that the first thioredoxin motif around residues 52–55 indeed forms an intradomain disulphide bond; the second cysteine residue in the sequence CGHCKAL has a very high propensity of forming a disulphide bond with the first cysteine residue. However, the second thioredoxin motif is not predicted to be disulphide bonded, since the second cysteine residue in the sequence CGHCKQL has zero propensity of forming a disulphide bond with the first cysteine residue in this motif. We therefore predict that the two thioredoxin motives in PDI are in different bonding states; while the first—WCGHC—motif is in the oxidized and thus disulphide bonded form, the second thioredoxin motif is in the reduced form. From this analysis we conclude that the two thioredoxin motives in PDI have different reduction potentials. This result is in excellent agreement with the findings of Chambers and coworkers [13], who showed that the two thioredoxin motives react differently to Ero1a, the *in vivo* oxidant of PDI.

4.2.2. Application 2: Protein Identification and Motif Exploration. Catalytic functionalities of some enzymatic proteins are dependant on the oxidation and reduction of state of their cysteine residues. The oxidation of cysteine residues and formation of disulphide bonds take place in a reducing environment. In prokaryotes, disulphide bonds are mainly formed in the periplasmic space outside the membrane. In contrast, the formation of disulphide bonds takes place in endoplasmic reticulum (ER) in eukaryotes. As a result, proteins with stable disulfide bonds rarely reside in the

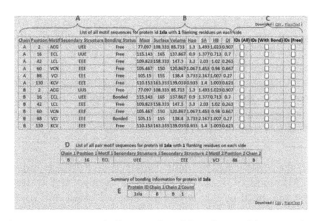

FIGURE 3: Annotated diagram describing the result's annotation for the "Search By Molecule Name" section. (A) Showing the motifs, secondary structure, cysteine position in the sequence, and the chain name. (B) Showing the propensity values of the motif sequence. (C) The navigation pane facilitating accessing ProteinIDs having common and similar features. (D) Listing the pair patterns existing in the protein in details. (E) The summary of bonding for the selected protein.

cytoplasm. This knowledge would apply on a larger scale, making the local and global profile of each protein environment, its folding localization, and classification becoming a potential contribution on the disulphide bonding prediction mechanism.

CMD offers the user a unique ability to identify and mine all known proteins using specific motif sequence, and explore their classification, motif sequences, structure, and bonding status. During the creation of the datasets, we discovered 15875 unique motifs that are always bonded

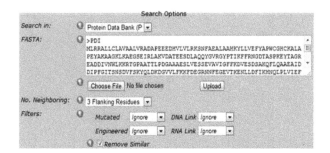

FIGURE 4: Query for full length human protein disulphide isomerase (PDII, P07237 [UniParc]). (A) Screenshot of parameters for CFMD.

TABLE 2: Edited output from (A). The bold rows indicate the second active site cysteine residues in the respective thioredoxin motif. Column 1 (Thioredoxin motif) was added for additional clarification. The cysteine residue in italics indicates the queried cysteine residue, the respective position of which is given in the second column.

Thioredoxin motif	Position	Motif	Total	Bond	Coefficient
			0	0	0
1	52	APW*C*GHC	12	5	0.417
1	**55**	**CGH*C*KAL**	**1**	**1**	**1**
			0	0	0
			0	0	0
2	396	APW*C*GHC	12	5	0.417
2	**399**	**CGH*C*KQL**	**2**	**0**	**0**

(EATLRCWALGF with the highest occurrence) and 41577 unique patterns that are always nonbonded (ALSVPCSDSKA with the highest occurrence) for the five flanking residues that can be utilized for cysteine state prediction. The number of these unique motifs is considerably higher than prior number of motifs used in cysteine bond prediction [3, 14] and not limited to specific genomes [15].

4.3. Data Availability. The CMD databases are accessible through a web portal at http://birg4.fbb.utm.my/cmd. The entire database with annotations is available for download in the SQL format, describing the relations between classes and fragments. As an additional service for programmers and third party developers, all queries available in CMD are freely accessible using available web services and web application programming interfaces (API). Also for automated high-throughput querying, all information contained in the CMD database can be downloaded using ftp services.

5. Discussion

The CMD combined data of bonded and free cysteine motifs aims to fill a gap in the knowledge query that will allow in-depth characterization of the composition propensity, and its role in determining the bonding state. Despite the bonding information regarding cysteine residues in proteins available in many databases and several applications focused on

disulphide bridge formation prediction, there is no complete reference with a proper form of representation and analysis available at the moment. This database is automatically updated from the PDB and UniProt that currently contain 878000 cysteine motifs with more than 77,000 unique cysteine motifs and cysteine pairing motifs. Compilation of these cysteine motifs together with their secondary structures and propensity value assignments, and the ability to query using Protein IDs and motif sequences is a novel and significant feature over prior prediction works which use considerably smaller datasets [3]. In addition to the novelty of the motif query tool, CMD has several novelties such as inclusion of UniProt data, the distinction between inter or intrachain disulphide bonds, inter or intradomain bonds, and an application programming interfaces (APIs) for interfacing with other bioinformatics tools.

6. Conclusion

The creation of CMD is useful when analyzing cysteine/disulfide bond formation and its motif sequence composition analysis by providing (1) a query tool for cysteine motifs based upon a comprehensive cysteine motif database curated from PDB and UniProt, (2) secondary structure and propensity values assignments of each motif sequence, and (3) datasets of detailed information of the motifs such as occurrence frequency and their amino acids propensity value. We believe that CMD's usefulness will be the query tool that will complement other protein 3D structural databases and similarly motif-based prediction tools.

Availability and Requirements

The CMD database is available to the public for free at http://birg4.fbb.utm.my/cmd/. Contact: shahir@utm.my.

Funding

Ministry of Science, Technology and Innovation (MOSTI) Grant no. 07-05-MGI-GMB007.

Conflict of Interests

The authors declare that they have no conflict of interests.

Acknowledgment

The authors would like to acknowledge Chew Teong Han for the support throughout the development of CMD.

References

[1] S. M. Muskal, S. R. Holbrook, and S. H. Kim, "Prediction of the disulfide-bonding state of cysteine in proteins," *Protein Engineering*, vol. 3, no. 8, pp. 667–672, 1990.

[2] M. H. Mucchielli-Giorgi, S. Hazout, and P. Tufféry, "Predicting the disulfide bonding state of cysteines using protein descriptors," *Proteins*, vol. 46, no. 3, pp. 243–249, 2002.

[3] F. Ferrè and P. Clote, "DiANNA 1.1: an extension of the DiANNA web server for ternary cysteine classification," *Nucleic Acids Research*, vol. 34, pp. W182–W185, 2006.

[4] R. Singh, "A review of algorithmic techniques for disulfide-bond determination," *Briefings in Functional Genomics and Proteomics*, vol. 7, no. 2, pp. 157–172, 2008.

[5] J. Song, Z. Yuan, H. Tan, T. Huber, and K. Burrage, "Predicting disulfide connectivity from protein sequence using multiple sequence feature vectors and secondary structure," *Bioinformatics*, vol. 23, no. 23, pp. 3147–3154, 2007.

[6] Y. C. Chen, Y. S. Lin, C. J. Lin, and J. K. Hwang, "Prediction of the bonding states of cysteines using the support vector machines based on multiple feature vectors and cysteine state sequences," *Proteins*, vol. 55, no. 4, pp. 1036–1042, 2004.

[7] P. L. Martelli, P. Fariselli, and R. Casadio, "Prediction of disulfide-bonded cysteines in proteomes with a hidden neural network," *Proteomics*, vol. 4, no. 6, pp. 1665–1671, 2004.

[8] C. H. Tsai, B. J. Chen, C. H. Chan, H. L. Liu, and C. Y. Kao, "Improving disulfide connectivity prediction with sequential distance between oxidized cysteines," *Bioinformatics*, vol. 21, no. 24, pp. 4416–4419, 2005.

[9] A. Ceroni, A. Passerini, A. Vullo, and P. Frasconi, "Disulfind: a disulfide bonding state and cysteine connectivity prediction server," *Nucleic Acids Research*, vol. 34, pp. W177–W181, 2006.

[10] A. Vullo and P. Frasconi, "Disulfide connectivity prediction using recursive neural networks and evolutionary information," *Bioinformatics*, vol. 20, no. 5, pp. 653–659, 2004.

[11] J. Lenffer, P. Lai, W. El Mejaber et al., "CysView: protein classification based on cysteine pairing patterns," *Nucleic Acids Research*, vol. 32, supplement, pp. W350–W355, 2004.

[12] F. Hatahet and L. W. Ruddock, "Protein disulfide isomerase: a critical evaluation of its function in disulfide bond formation," *Antioxidants and Redox Signaling*, vol. 11, no. 11, pp. 2807–2850, 2009.

[13] J. E. Chambers, T. J. Tavender, O. B. V. Oka, S. Warwood, D. Knight, and N. J. Bulleid, "The reduction potential of the active site disulfides of human protein disulfide isomerase limits oxidation of the enzyme by Ero1α," *Journal of Biological Chemistry*, vol. 285, no. 38, pp. 29200–29207, 2010.

[14] P. Baldi, J. Cheng, and A. Vullo, "Large-scale prediction of disulphide bond connectivity," *Advances in Neural Information Processing Systems*, no. 17, pp. 97–104, 2005.

[15] B. D. O'Connor and T. O. Yeates, "GDAP: a web tool for genome-wide protein disulfide bond prediction," *Nucleic Acids Research*, vol. 32, pp. W360–W364, 2004.

11

Efficient Serial and Parallel Algorithms for Selection of Unique Oligos in EST Databases

Manrique Mata-Montero,[1] **Nabil Shalaby,**[2] **and Bradley Sheppard**[1,2]

[1] *Department of Computer Science, Memorial University, Canada*
[2] *Department of Mathematics and Statistics, Memorial University, Canada*

Correspondence should be addressed to Nabil Shalaby; nshalaby@mun.ca

Academic Editor: Alexander Zelikovsky

Obtaining unique oligos from an EST database is a problem of great importance in bioinformatics, particularly in the discovery of new genes and the mapping of the human genome. Many algorithms have been developed to find unique oligos, many of which are much less time consuming than the traditional brute force approach. An algorithm was presented by Zheng et al. (2004) which finds the solution of the unique oligos search problem efficiently. We implement this algorithm as well as several new algorithms based on some theorems included in this paper. We demonstrate how, with these new algorithms, we can obtain unique oligos much faster than with previous ones. We parallelize these new algorithms to further improve the time of finding unique oligos. All algorithms are run on ESTs obtained from a Barley EST database.

1. Introduction

Expressed Sequence Tags (or ESTs) are fragments of DNA that are about 200–800 bases long generated from the sequencing of complementary DNA. ESTs have many applications. They were used in the Human Genome Project in the discovery of new genes and are often used in the mapping of genomic libraries. They can be used to infer functions of newly discovered genes based on comparison to known genes [1].

An oligonucleotide (or oligo) is a subsequence of an EST. Oligos are short, since they are typically no longer than 50 nucleotide bases. Oligos are often referred to in the context of their length by adding the suffix "mer". For example, an oligo of length 9 would be referred to as a 9-mer. The importance of oligos in relation to EST databases is quite significant. An oligo that is unique in an EST database serves as a representative of its EST sequence. The oligonucleotides (or simply oligos) contained in these EST databases have applications in many areas such as PCR primer design, microarrays, and probing genomic libraries [2–4].

In this paper we will improve on the algorithms presented in [2] to solve the *unique oligos search* problem. This problem requires us to determine all oligos that appear in one EST sequence but not in any of the others. In addition, we will consider two oligos to be virtually identical if they fall within a certain number of mismatches from each other. In the appendix we include all the algorithms used and developed in this paper.

2. The Unique Oligos Search Problem

In this paper we use the notation $HD(x, y)$ to denote the Hamming Distance between the strings x and y. Given an EST database $D = \{x_1, x_2, \ldots, x_k\}$, where x_i is a string over the alphabet $\{A, C, G, G\}$, integers d and l, and l-mer y, we say that y occurs approximately in D if there exists a substring z of some EST x_i such that $HD(y, z) \leq d$. We also say that an m-mutant list of a string s is a list of all possible strings, s^*, of length $|s|$ over the alphabet $\{A, C, G, T\}$ such that $HD(s, s^*) \leq m$. Such a string s^* is referred to as an m-mutant of s. A unique oligo of D is defined as an l-mer u such that u occurs exactly in one EST and does not occur approximately in any other EST. The unique oligos search problem is the problem of finding all unique oligos in an EST database.

Require: EST database $D = \{x_1, x_2, \ldots, x_k\}$, integer l (length of unique oligos) and integer d
       (maximum number of mismatches between non-unique oligos)
Ensure: All unique l-mers in D
(1) $q \leftarrow l/(\lfloor d/2 \rfloor + 1)$
(2) $posi \leftarrow \text{findqmers}(q)$ (hashtable of positions of all qmers in D)
(3) **for** $i \leftarrow 1$ to 4^q {split loop iterations among processors} **do**
(4) $x \leftarrow i$ as a base 4 integer of length q
(5) $mismatchlist \leftarrow$ list of base 4 integers of length q mismatching x by 1 digit
(6) $modifiedmismatchlist \leftarrow$ the numbers in $mismatchlist$ in base 10
(7) $mut \leftarrow$ list of each $hashtable[i]$ for all $i \in modifiedmismatchlist$
(8) $\text{goo2}(q, l, d, posi[i], mut)$
(9) **end for**

ALGORITHM 1: Algorithm for the unique oligos problem.

Many algorithms have been presented to solve this problem [5, 6]. The algorithm presented in [2] relies on an observation that if two l-mers agree within a specific Hamming Distance, then they must share a certain substring. These observations are presented in this paper as theorems.

Theorem 1. *Suppose one has two l-mers l_1 and l_2 such that $HD(l_1, l_2) \leq d$. If one divides them both into $\lfloor d/2 \rfloor + 1$ substrings, $l_1^1 l_1^2 \cdots l_1^{\lfloor d/2 \rfloor + 1}$ and $l_2^1 l_2^2 \cdots l_2^{\lfloor d/2 \rfloor + 1}$, and each l_j^i, except possibly $l_j^{\lfloor d/2 \rfloor + 1}$, has length $\lceil l/(\lfloor d/2 \rfloor + 1) \rceil$, then there exists at least one $i_0 \in \{1, 2, \ldots, \lfloor d/2 \rfloor + 1\}$, such that $HD(l_1^{i_0}, l_2^{i_0}) \leq 1$.*

Proof. Suppose by contradiction that for any $i \in \{1, 2, \ldots, \lfloor d/2 \rfloor + 1\}$, l_1^i and l_2^i have at least 2 mismatches. Then $HD(l_1, l_2) \geq d + 2$ which is a contradiction to the fact that $HD(l_1, l_2) \leq d$. $\qquad \square$

Using this observation, an algorithm was presented in [2] which solves the unique oligos search problem in time $O((l - q)qr^2 4^q)$. The algorithm can be thought of as a two-phase method. In the first phase we record the position of each q-mer in the database into a hash table of size 4^q. We do so in such a way that for each q-mer x over the alphabet $\{A, C, G, T\}$ we have that $hashtable[hashfunction[x]] = \{\{s_1, p_1\}, \{s_2, p_2\}, \ldots, \{s_n, p_n\}\}$ whereby s_i is an EST sequence, p_i is the position of x within that sequence, and n is the number of occurrences of x in the database. In the second phase, we extend every pair of identical q-mers into l-mers and compare these l-mers for nonuniqueness. We also do the same for pairs that have a Hamming Distance of 1. If they are nonunique, we mark them accordingly. Theorem 1 guarantees that if an l-mer is nonunique, then it must share a q-mer substring that differs by at most one character with another q-mer substring from another l-mer. Hence, if an l-mer is nonunique, it will be marked during phase two.

Assuming there are n symbols in our EST database, the filing of the q-mers into the hash table takes time $\Theta(qn)$. In phase two, we assume that the distribution of q-mers in the database is uniform; in other words, that each table contains $r \approx n/4^q$ entries. Thus we have $O(r^2)$ comparisons within each table entry. Each q-mer also has a 1-mutant list of size $3q$,

so, we have $O(qr^2)$ comparisons for each entry in the table. Also, the time required to extend each pair of q-mers to l-mers is $2(l - q + 1)$. Given that we have 4^q entries in the hash table, we have a total time complexity of

$$O\left((l - q)qr^2 4^q\right) = O\left((l - q)q\left(\frac{n}{4^q}\right)^2 4^q\right)$$
$$= O\left(\frac{(l - q)qn^2}{4^q}\right), \tag{1}$$

where

$$q = \frac{l}{\lfloor d/2 \rfloor + 1}. \tag{2}$$

In [7], several variations of Theorem 1 are presented. We can use these theorems to generate similar algorithms with slightly different time complexities.

Theorem 2. *Suppose one has two l-mers l_1 and l_2 such that $HD(l_1, l_2) \leq d$. If one divides them both into $d + 1$ substrings, $l_1^1 l_1^2 \cdots l_1^{d+1}$ and $l_2^1 l_2^2 \cdots l_2^{d+1}$, and each l_j^i, except possibly l_j^{d+1}, has length $\lceil l/(d+1) \rceil$, then there exists at least one $i_0 \in \{1, 2, \ldots, d + 1\}$, such that $l_1^{i_0} = l_2^{i_0}$.*

Proof. Suppose by contradiction that we cannot find any $i_0 \in \{1, 2, \ldots, d + 1\}$ such that $l_1^{i_0} = l_2^{i_0}$. Then there exists at least one mismatch between l_1^i and l_2^i for each $i \in \{1, 2, \ldots, d + 1\}$, and thus we have at least $d + 1$ mismatches which contradicts the fact that $HD(l_1, l_2) \leq d$. $\qquad \square$

Based on Theorem 2 we can design a second algorithm that works in a similar way to Algorithm 1. The major difference between these algorithms is that in Algorithm 2 we are not required to do comparisons with each hash table entries mutant list. This means we have $O(r^2)$ comparisons within each table entry which yields a total time complexity of

$$O\left((l - q)r^2 4^q\right) = O\left((l - q)\left(\frac{n}{4^q}\right)^2 4^q\right)$$
$$= O\left(\frac{(l - q)n^2}{4^q}\right), \tag{3}$$

Require: EST database $D = \{x_1, x_2, \ldots, x_k\}$, integer l (length of unique oligos) and integer d
        (maximum number of mismatches between non-unique oligos)
Ensure: All unique l-mers in D
(1) $q \leftarrow l/(d + 1)$
(2) $posi \leftarrow$ findqmers(q) (hashtable of positions of all qmers in D)
(3) **for** $i \leftarrow 1$ to 4^q {split loop iterations among processors} **do**
(4)   goo($q, l, d, posi[i]$)
(5) **end for**

ALGORITHM 2: Algorithm for the unique oligos problem.

Require: EST database $D = \{x_1, x_2, \ldots, x_k\}$, integer l (length of unique oligos) and integer d
        (maximum number of mismatches between non-unique oligos)
Ensure: All unique l-mers in D
(1) $q \leftarrow l/(\lfloor d/3 \rfloor + 1)$
(2) $posi \leftarrow$ findqmers(q) (hashtable of positions of all qmers in D)
(3) **for** $i \leftarrow 1$ to 4^q {split loop iterations among processors} **do**
(4) $x \leftarrow i$ as a base 4 integer of length q
(5) $mismatchlist \leftarrow$ list of base 4 integers of length q mismatching x by at most 2 digits
(6) $modifiedmismatchlist \leftarrow$ the numbers in $mismatchlist$ in base 10
(7) $mut \leftarrow$ list of each $hashtable[i]$ for all $i \in modifiedmismatchlist$
(8)   goo2($q, l, d, posi[i], mut$)
(9) **end for**

ALGORITHM 3: Algorithm for the unique oligos problem.

Require: EST database $D = \{x_1, x_2, \ldots, x_k\}$, integer q
Ensure: A hashtable of all $qmer$ positions.
(1) $hashtable \leftarrow$ a hashtable of all $qmer$ positions in D
(2) **for** $i \leftarrow 1$ to k **do**
(3)   **for** $j \leftarrow 1$ to length($D[i]$) $- q + 1$ **do**
(4) $hashedqmer \leftarrow$ map($D[i], j, j + q - 1$)
(5) $hashtable[hashedqmer] \leftarrow$ Append($hashtable[hashedqmer], \{i, j\}$)
(6)   **end for**
(7) **end for**

ALGORITHM 4: Findqmers (q).

(1) $r \leftarrow$ substring(s, i, j)
(2) $t \leftarrow r$ under the transformation $\{A, C, G, T\} \rightarrow \{0, 1, 2, 3\}$
(3) **return** t

ALGORITHM 5: Map (string s, i, j).

(1) $r \leftarrow$ substring of s from character i to character j
(2) **return** r

ALGORITHM 6: Substring (string s, i, j).

```
(1) posi ← a list of positions of a specified qmer in D
    (posi = {{x₁, y₁}, {x₂, y₂},...} where {x, y} corresponds to position y of sequence x)
(2) mut ← a list of positions of qmers in D that mismatch this qmer by either 1 or 2 characters
    (depending on the filtration algorithm using this function)
(3) for i ← 1 to length(posi) do
(4)    for j ← i + 1 to length(posi) do
(5)       if posi[i][1] ≠ posi[j][1] then
(6)          lq1 ← list of l-mers generated from the extension of the qmer in position posi[i]
(7)          lq2 ← list of l-mers generated from the extension of the qmer in position posi[j]
(8)          for x ← 1 to length(lq1) do
(9)             for y ← 1 to length(lq2) do
(10)               if HD(lq1[x], lq2[y]) ≤ d then
(11)                  mark the lmers as non-unique
(12)               end if
(13)            end for
(14)         end for
(15)      end if
(16)   end for
(17)   for k ← 1 to length(mut) do
(18)      if posi[i][1] ≠ mut[k][1] then
(19)         lq1 ← list of l-mers generated from the extension of the qmer in position posi[i]
(20)         lq2 ← list of l-mers generated from the extension of the qmer in position mut[k]
(21)         for x ← 1 to length(lq1) do
(22)            for y ← 1 to length(lq2) do
(23)               if HD(lq1[x], lq2[y]) ≤ d then
(24)                  mark the lmers as non-unique
(25)               end if
(26)            end for
(27)         end for
(28)      end if
(29)   end for
(30) end for
```

ALGORITHM 7: goo2($q, l, d, posi, mut$).

```
(1) posi ← a list of positions of qmer in D
    (posi = {{x₁, y₁}, {x₂, y₂},...} where {x, y} corresponds to position y of sequence x)
(2) for i ← 1 to length(posi) do
(3)    for j ← i + 1 to length(posi) do
(4)       if posi[i][1] ≠ posi[j][1] then
(5)          lq1 ← list of l-mers generated from the extension of the qmer in position posi[i]
(6)          lq2 ← list of l-mers generated from the extension of the qmer in position posi[j]
(7)          for x ← 1 to length(lq1) do
(8)             for y ← 1 to length(lq2) do
(9)                if HD(lq1[x], lq2[y]) ≤ d then
(10)                  mark the lmers as non-unique
(11)               end if
(12)            end for
(13)         end for
(14)      end if
(15)   end for
(16) end for
```

ALGORITHM 8: goo($q, l, d, posi$).

TABLE 1: Results of serial algorithms.

Algorithm	l	d	q	Dataset	Time taken (secs)	Non-unique oligos
Algorithm 2	28	6	4	1 (78 ESTs)	163	46,469
Algorithm 1	28	6	7	1 (78 ESTs)	131	46,469
Algorithm 3	27	6	9	1 (78 ESTs)	231	46,564
Algorithm 2	28	6	4	2 (2838 ESTs)	197, 500	1,611,241
Algorithm 1	28	6	7	2 (2838 ESTs)	117, 714	1,611,241
Algorithm 3	27	6	9	2 (2838 ESTs)	94, 317	1,614,235

TABLE 2: Results of parallel algorithms on 12 processors.

Algorithm	l	d	q	Dataset	Time taken (secs)	Non-unique oligos
Algorithm 2	28	6	4	1 (78 ESTs)	33	46,469
Algorithm 1	28	6	7	1 (78 ESTs)	29	46,469
Algorithm 3	27	6	9	1 (78 ESTs)	66	46,564
Algorithm 2	28	6	4	2 (2838 ESTs)	40, 420	1,611,241
Algorithm 1	28	6	7	2 (2838 ESTs)	22, 848	1,611,241
Algorithm 1	27	6	9	2 (2838 ESTs)	18, 375	1,614,235

where

$$q = \frac{l}{d + 1}. \tag{4}$$

A third theorem was also briefly mentioned [7]; however, it was not implemented in an algorithm. We use this theorem to create a third algorithm to solve the unique oligos search problem.

Theorem 3. *Suppose one has two l-mers l_1 and l_2 such that $HD(l_1, l_2) \leq d$. If one divides them both into $\lfloor d/3 \rfloor + 1$ substrings, $l_1^1 l_1^2 \cdots l_1^{\lfloor d/3 \rfloor + 1}$ and $l_2^1 l_2^2 \cdots l_2^{\lfloor d/3 \rfloor + 1}$, and each l_j^i, except possibly $l_j^{\lfloor d/3 \rfloor + 1}$, has length $\lceil l/(\lfloor d/3 \rfloor + 1) \rceil$, then there exists at least one $i_0 \in \{1, 2, \ldots, \lfloor d/3 \rfloor + 1\}$, such that $HD(l_1^{i_0}, l_2^{i_0}) \leq 2$.*

Proof. Suppose by contradiction that for any $i \in \{1, 2, \ldots, \lfloor d/3 \rfloor + 1\}$, l_1^i and l_2^i have at least 3 mismatches. Then $HD(l_1, l_2) \geq d + 3$ which is a contradiction to the fact that $HD(l_1, l_2) \leq 2$. $\qquad\square$

The algorithm is somewhat similar to Algorithm 1. The main difference is that we compare every q-mer to q-mers in its corresponding 2-mutant list, rather than its 1-mutant list. Each q-mer has $9 \binom{q}{2} + 3q = 9q(q-1)/2 + 3q$ 2-mutants, so we have $O(q^2 r^2)$ comparisons for each entry in the hash table yielding a total time complexity of

$$O\left((l - q) q^2 r^2 4^q\right) = O\left((l - q) q^2 \left(\frac{n}{4^q}\right)^2 4^q\right)$$
$$= O\left(\frac{(l - q) q^2 n^2}{4^q}\right), \tag{5}$$

where

$$q = \frac{l}{\lfloor d/3 \rfloor + 1}. \tag{6}$$

It is important to note the 4^q term in the denominator of our time complexity expressions. Since this term is exponential, it will have the largest impact on the time taken to run our algorithms. Based on this observation, we expect Algorithm 3 to run the fastest, followed by Algorithm 1 and then Algorithm 2.

3. Implementation

We implement these algorithms using C on a machine with 12 Intel Core i7 CPU 80 @ 3.33 GHz processors and 12 GB of memory. The datasets we use in this implementation are Barley ESTs taken from the genetic software HarvEST by Steve Wanamaker and Timothy Close of the University of California, Riverside (http://harvest.ucr.edu/). We use two different EST databases, one with 78 ESTs and another with 2838. In our experiments we search for oligos of lengths 27 and 28 since they are common lengths for oligonucleotides. As we increase the size of the database, we see that Algorithm 3 is the most efficient as anticipated (data shown in Tables 1 and 2).

One important thing to note about all of these algorithms is the fact that the main portion of them is a for loop which iterates through each index of the hash table. It is also obvious that loop iterations are independent of each other. These two factors make the algorithms perfect candidates for parallelism. Rather than process the hash table one index at a time, our parallel algorithms process groups of indices simultaneously. Ignoring the communication between processors, our algorithms optimally parallelize our three serial algorithms.

There are many APIs in different programming languages that aid in the task of parallel programming. Some examples of this in the C programming language are OpenMP and POSIX Pthreads. OpenMP allows one to easily parallelize a C program amongst multiple cores of a multicore machine [8]. OpenMP also has an extension called Cluster OpenMP which allows one to parallelize across multiple machines in a computing cluster.

A new trend in parallel programming is in the use of GPUs. GPUs are the processing units inside computers graphics card. C has several APIs which allow one to carry out GPU programming. The two such APIs are OpenCL and CUDA [9, 10].

In the second implementation of our algorithms we use OpenMP to parallelize our algorithms throughout the 12 cores of our machine. We can easily see that we achieve near optimal parallelization with our parallel algorithms; that is, the time taken by the parallel algorithms is approximately that of the serial algorithms divided by the number of processors.

4. Conclusion

In this paper we used three algorithms to solve the unique oligos search problem which are extensions of the algorithm presented in [2]. We observed that we can achieve a significant performance improvement by parallelizing our algorithms. We can also see that Algorithm 3 yields the best results for larger databases. For smaller databases, however, the time difference between each pair of algorithms is negligible, but results in Algorithm 3 being the slowest, and this is due to the time required to compute the mismatches of each q-mer. Other algorithms can be obtained by setting q to different values. See Algorithms 1, 2, 3, 4, 5, 6, 7, and 8.

References

[1] M. D. Adams, J. M. Kelley, J. D. Gocayne et al., "Complementary DNA sequencing: expressed sequence tags and human genome project," *Science*, vol. 252, no. 5013, pp. 1651–1656, 1991.

[2] J. Zheng, T. J. Close, T. Jiang, and S. Lonardi, "Efficient selection of unique and popular oligos for large EST databases," *Bioinformatics*, vol. 20, no. 13, pp. 2101–2112, 2004.

[3] S. H. Nagaraj, R. B. Gasser, and S. Ranganathan, "A hitchhiker's guide to expressed sequence tag (EST) analysis," *Briefings in Bioinformatics*, vol. 8, no. 1, pp. 6–21, 2007.

[4] W. Klug, M. Cummings, and C. Spencer, *Concepts of Genetics*, Prentice-Hall, Upper Saddle River, NJ, USA, 8th edition, 2006.

[5] F. Li and G. D. Stormo, "Selection of optimal DNA oligos for gene expression arrays," *Bioinformatics*, vol. 17, no. 11, pp. 1067–1076, 2001.

[6] S. Rahmann, "Rapid large-scale oligonucleotide selection for microarrays," in *Proceedings of the 1st IEEE Computer Society Bioinformatics Conference (CSB '02)*, pp. 54–63, IEEE Press, Stanford, Calif, USA, 2002.

[7] S. Go, *Combinatorics and its applications in DNA analysis [M.S. thesis]*, Department of Mathematics and Statistics, Memorial University of Newfoundland, 2009.

[8] OpenMP.org, 2012, http://openmp.org/wp/.

[9] Khronos Group, "OpenCL—The open standard for parallel programming of heterogeneous systems," 2012, http://www.khronos.org/opencl/.

[10] Nvidia, "Parallel Programming and Computing Platform—Cuda—Nvidia," 2012, http://www.nvidia.com/object/cuda_home_new.html.

12

In Silico Docking of HNF-1a Receptor Ligands

Gumpeny Ramachandra Sridhar,[1] **Padmanabhuni Venkata Nageswara Rao,**[2]
Dowluru SVGK Kaladhar,[3] **Tatavarthi Uma Devi,**[4] **and Sali Veeresh Kumar**[3]

[1] *Endocrine and Diabetes Centre, 15-12-15 Krishnanagar, Visakhapatnam 530 002, India*
[2] *Department of Computer Science and Engineering, GITAM University, Visakhapatnam 530045, India*
[3] *Department of Biochemistry and Bioinformatics, GITAM University, Visakhapatnam 530045, India*
[4] *Department of Computer Science, GITAM University, Visakhapatnam 530045, India*

Correspondence should be addressed to Gumpeny Ramachandra Sridhar, sridharvizag@gmail.com

Academic Editor: Ramana Davuluri

Background. HNF-1a is a transcription factor that regulates glucose metabolism by expression in various tissues. *Aim.* To dock potential ligands of HNF-1a using docking software *in silico*. *Methods.* We performed *in silico* studies using HNF-1a protein 2GYP·pdb and the following softwares: ISIS/Draw 2.5SP4, ARGUSLAB 4.0.1, and HEX5.1. *Observations.* The docking distances (in angstrom units: 1 angstrom unit (Å) = 0.1 nanometer or 1×10^{-10} metres) with ligands in decreasing order are as follows: resveratrol (3.8 Å), aspirin (4.5 Å), stearic acid (4.9 Å), retinol (6.0 Å), nitrazepam (6.8 Å), ibuprofen (7.9 Å), azulfidine (9.0 Å), simvastatin (9.0 Å), elaidic acid (10.1 Å), and oleic acid (11.6 Å). *Conclusion.* HNF-1a domain interacted most closely with resveratrol and aspirin

1. Introduction

Hepatic nuclear factor 1 alpha (HNF-1a) is a liver enriched transcription factor that was first discovered in studies aimed at identifying proteins that were responsible for tissue-specific regulation of gene expression in the human liver [1]. These transcription factors were also found in tissues other than liver, including pancreatic islets and kidneys, suggesting they could have a more widespread role in physiological processes [2]. Together, the HNF family is part of a network of transcription factors that together control gene expression during embryogenic development and during adulthood [1]. Genes regulated by HNF-1a also encode products involved in the synthesis of seroproteins, carbohydrates and in detoxification [2]. HNF encoding genes arose by duplication of an ancestral gene at the onset of vertebrate evolution, an evolutionary mechanism for the generation of novel functions [3]. Mutations of HNF transcription family are well known to cause the autosomal dominant maturity onset diabetes of young (MODY), a clinically heterogeneous form of early onset of diabetes resulting from a primary defect in pancreatic beta cell function [4]. Some consider diabetes to be "a disorder of abnormal transcription factors" [4]. However it is now established that MODY results from a dysfunction of transcription factors [5] that regulate beta cell function by controlling downstream targets [6]. Protein-ligand interactions are increasingly employed to derive three dimensional structures of protein complexes. Computational techniques have become important to understand the molecular mechanisms of biological systems, as well as in obtaining leads for therapeutic agent identification. Considering the wide ranging effects of transcription factors in beta cell physiology, and the diverse pharmacological ligands that are available to manage the metabolic disturbances characterized by premature aging of diabetes, we performed an exploratory *in silico* study using various ligands as potential docking partners for HNF-1a.

2. Methods

We performed *in silico* studies using HNF-1a protein (PDB id: 2GYP·pdb) and fatty acids (listed in the table) by using the software: ISIS/Draw 2.5 [7], ARGUSLAB4.0.1, HEX5.1 [8].

TABLE 1: Docking of ligands with HNF-1a.

Ligand drug/fatty acid	Binding distance with HNF-1a (Angstroms) Å
Resveratrol	3.8
Aspirin	4.5
Stearic acid	4.9
Retinol	6.0
Nitrazepam	6.8
Ibuprofen	7.9
Azulfidine	9.0
Simvastatin	9.0
Palmitic acid	9.8
Elaidic acid	10.1
Oleic acid	11.6
Sirtuin 6	17.6
Sirtuin 3	28.9
Sirtuin 4	43.5
Sirtuin 1	43.5
Sirtuin 2	43.9
Sirtuin 5	43.9

2.1. ISIS/Draw. ISIS/Draw is a chemical drawing GUI software, commonly employed as a chemical structure drawing software following the advent of bioinformatics explosion [7]. It is a simple and concise pure chemical drawing software, which is generally the first choice for use in 2D drawings.

2.2. ArgusLab. ArgusLab is a freely distributed software for Windows platform, commonly used as an introductory molecular modeling package especially in the academic environment [8]. It has a user-friendly interface and an intuitive calculation menus. The docking engine approximates an exhaustive search method. It requires a PDB format file for both ligand and receptor [8]. 2D depictions of prospective ligands were drawn using the ISIS/Draw 2.5 and these structures were optimized for energy using AGRUS Lab. The following ligands designed *in silico* were used: resveratrol, aspirin, stearic acid, retinol, nitrazepam, ibuprofen, azulfidine, simvastatin, elaidic acid, and oleic acid.

2.3. HEX5.1. The energy optimized ligand structures are docked with HNF-1a using HEX5.1.

3. Results

The docking distances with different ligands are presented in Table 1 and the structures are shown in Figure 1. The decreasing docking distance were as follows: resveratrol (3.8 Å), aspirin (4.5 Å), stearic acid (4.9 Å), retinol (6.0 Å), nitrazepam (6.8 Å), ibuprofen (7.9 Å), azulfidine (9.0 Å),

simvastatin (9.0 Å), elaidic acid (10.1 Å), and oleic acid (11.6 Å).

4. Discussion

A convergence of biochemical, mathematical, and computational approaches is being applied to evaluate protein-ligand interactions for identifying pharmacological targets to modulate protein activity. HNF-1a is a transcription factor that belongs to a family of proteins having "DNA binding domains that specifically recognize a short DNA sequence and of an activation or repression domain that influences gene transcription" [5]. It is a conserved protein in vertebrate evolution, composed of three functional domains, belonging to the homeodomain family [4, 5]. It has functions in multiple tissues and organs; an absence of the gene manifests after birth, showing its role in diverse metabolic networks. Recent studies have identified as yet unknown proteins such as the high mobility group protein-B1 (HMGB1) that can interact with HNF-1a [9], forming another layer of regulation in the HNF transcriptional network. Resveratrol activates HNF family of proteins, which exist in all domains of life [10]. Sirtuin resveratrol interactions have led to intense search for compounds that can enhance life-span and delay the process of senescence in tissues and organisms. Sirtuin (Sir-2) was first identified in the bacterium *Saccharomyces cerevisae* as a regulator of DNA recombination, gene silencer, and playing roles in DNA repair and chromosomal longevity. It is believed to be the critical link between caloric restriction and enhanced life span. Ligands of sirtuins, of which resveratrol is the first identified activator, [11], have gained recognition. The only non-genetic and non-pharmacological way to extend life span and prevent the metabolic changes of aging is by calorie restriction: "dietary regimen in which an organism is provided with at least 20% fewer calories than it would naturally consume *ad libitum* while maintaining adequate nutrition" [10]. The effectiveness of resveratrol has been observed *in vitro, in vivo,* and across many species [10]. Considering its effectiveness across species, the underlying mechanism is believed to be "ancient, relatively simple, and well conserved." Sirtuins, the modulators of this interaction evolved from an ancient molecule that responded to stress and to the availability of food. The family of sirtuins have multiple roles in metabolism, and are modified by dietary changes: SIRT1 promotes fat metabolism in white adipose tissue through interaction with PPAR gamma and adiponectin; it affects pancreatic beta cell in mice by affecting uncoupling protein 2 gene (UCP2) which uncouples oxygen consumption from ATP generation, and dissipates energy as heat; SIRT3 decreases the production of reactive oxygen species; and SIRT4 regulates amino-acid-stimulated insulin secretion in pancreatic beta cells. The sirtuins are versatile energy sensors that enable transcription to sense the metabolic rate of the cell. They act at various levels to repress transcription and to deacetylate non histone proteins including forkhead box type O transcription factor (FOXO) and PPAR gamma [12]. Expressed ubiquitously in human tissues, they show sequence homology and contain conserved

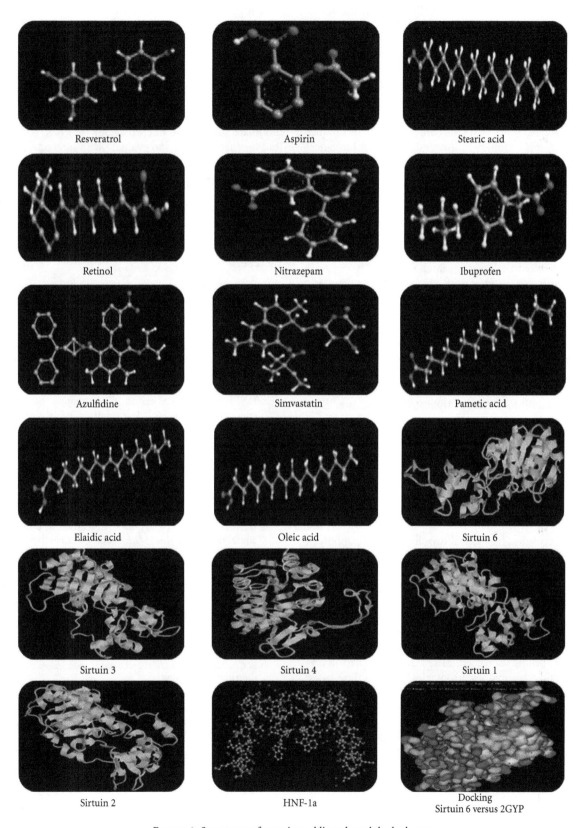

Resveratrol

Aspirin

Stearic acid

Retinol

Nitrazepam

Ibuprofen

Azulfidine

Simvastatin

Pametic acid

Elaidic acid

Oleic acid

Sirtuin 6

Sirtuin 3

Sirtuin 4

Sirtuin 1

Sirtuin 2

HNF-1a

Docking
Sirtuin 6 versus 2GYP

FIGURE 1: Structures of protein and ligands and docked area.

catalytic and NAD binding domains. They have important roles in the control of cell proliferation and in metabolic regulation. Together they could be "important determinants of whole-body metabolism and protect against many chronic diseases associated with metabolic dysfunction" [12].

Protein docking methods calculate 3D structure of a protein complex starting from its individual structural components, and give information of protein-ligand interactions. Practical difficulties with high throughput structural genomics are likely to result in computational techniques being increasingly employed for understanding biological systems. Undoubtedly protein docking problem is "easy to state but hard to solve." A number of docking algorithms now use two-step search and score procedures: *ab initio* methods generate an initial list of ligands which are then re-scored with available biophysical information and knowledge-based potentials from analyzing existing interfaces.

HEX5.1 is a commonly used molecular docking package that appropriates an exhaustive search method. The ligand is described as a torsion tree; grids are constructed overlying the binding site. Root node is placed on a search point in the binding site and a set of rotations is created. For each rotation, torsions in breadth-first order are constructed. Those that survive the torsion search are scored. Even though it may not perform as well as commercially available docking methods, HEX5.1 is a first method to narrow lead ligands, owing to its graphical user interface, and its relative speed compared to other complicated algorithms. Even though extending life span without genetic modification and without compromising nutritional status appears inviting, the need for calorie restriction requires volitional control, which is not always easily put into practice. Metabolic networks involving a common set of genes implicated in a switch from Krebs cycle and respiration to glycolysis and glycerol biosynthesis were implicated as a method to extend life span [13].

SIRT1 activation has been shown to involve a panoply of processes involving oxidative stress [14], the p53 pathways [15], FOXO [16] as well as DAF 16 [17]. Right from the report of resveratrol activating sirtuins to expand longevity without reducing fecundity [11], a number of compounds were screened for SIRT1 modulation: high-throughput screening was employed to identify compounds with SIRT1 activating and inhibiting potential [18]. Among a library of 147,000 compounds screened, SIRT1 activators had lipolytic and anti-inflammatory properties. Quinoxaline-based potent SIRT1 activators were identified in this study [18]. Similarly, a high throughput *in vitro* fluorescent polarization assay recognized a number of small molecule SIRT1 ligands that were 1,000 times more potent than resveratrol [19]. These bound to SRT1 enzyme-peptide substrate complex at an allosteric site amino terminal to the catalytic domain. In diet-induced obese and in genetically obese mice, these compounds improved insulin sensitivity, lowered plasma glucose, and improved mitochondrial capacity [19].

Recent animal studies have shown that chronic supplementation of resveratrol suppressed DNA damage and oxidative stress [20]. Similarly sirtuin 1 antisense oligonucleotide was shown to decrease plasma levels of total cholesterol,

by increased cholesterol uptake and export from the liver. This suggested that inhibition of hepatic SirT1 could be a potential method to treat type 2 diabetes mellitus [21]. Along with sirtuins, other pathways and networks may operate in extending lifespan, including forkhead transcription factors and metabolic regulators in mTOR [22]. The "potential longevity pathways are most likely not mutually exclusive."

In summary our *in silico* docking study suggests that resveratrol and aspirin are ligands that could potentially modulate the hepatic nuclear factor network. It provides a lead for further studies to evaluate such interactions.

Conflict of Interests

The authors declare that they have no conflict of interests related to this paper.

References

[1] S. S. Fajans, G. I. Bell, and K. S. Polonsky, "Molecular mechanisms and clinical pathophysiology of maturity-onset diabetes of the young," *The New England Journal of Medicine*, vol. 345, no. 13, pp. 971–980, 2001.

[2] S. Cereghini, "Liver-enriched transcription factors and hepatocyte differentiation," *The FASEB Journal*, vol. 10, no. 2, pp. 267–282, 1996.

[3] C. Haumaitre, M. Reber, and S. Cereghini, "Functions of HNF1 family members in differentiation of the visceral endoderm cell lineage," *Journal of Biological Chemistry*, vol. 278, no. 42, pp. 40933–40942, 2003.

[4] K. Yamagata, "Regulation of pancreatic β-cell function by the HNF transcription network: lessons from maturity-onset diabetes of the young (MODY)," *Endocrine Journal*, vol. 50, no. 5, pp. 491–499, 2003.

[5] G. U. Ryffel, "Mutations in the human genes encoding the transcription factors of the hepatocyte nuclear factor (HNF)1 and HNF4 families: functional and pathological consequences," *Journal of Molecular Endocrinology*, vol. 27, no. 1, pp. 11–29, 2001.

[6] S. A. Duncan, M. A. Navas, D. Dufort, J. Rossant, and M. Stoffel, "Regulation of a transcription factor network required for differentiation and metabolism," *Science*, vol. 281, no. 5377, pp. 692–695, 1998.

[7] Z. Li, H. Wan, Y. Shi, and P. Ouyang, "Personal experience with four kinds of chemical structure drawing software: review on chemdraw, chemwindow, ISIS/draw, and chemsketch," *Journal of Chemical Information and Computer Sciences*, vol. 44, no. 5, pp. 1886–1890, 2004.

[8] A. Chikhi and A. Bensegueni, "Docking efficiency comparison of Surflex, a commercial package and Arguslab, a licensable freeware," *Journal of Computer Science & Systems Biology*, vol. 1, pp. 81–86, 2008.

[9] M. Yu, J. Wang, W. Li et al., "Proteomic screen defines the hepatocyte nuclear factor 1α-binding partners and identifies HMGB1 as a new cofactor of HNF1α," *Nucleic Acids Research*, vol. 36, no. 4, pp. 1209–1219, 2008.

[10] S. Michan and D. Sinclair, "Sirtuins in mammals: insights into their biological function," *Biochemical Journal*, vol. 404, no. 1, pp. 1–13, 2007.

[11] J. G. Wood, B. Rogina, S. Lavu et al., "Sirtuin activators mimic caloric restriction and delay ageing in metazoans," *Nature*, vol. 430, no. 7000, pp. 686–689, 2004.

[12] H. Yamamoto, K. Schoonjans, and J. Auwerx, "Sirtuin functions in health and disease," *Molecular Endocrinology*, vol. 21, no. 8, pp. 1745–1755, 2007.

[13] M. Wei, P. Fabrizio, F. Madia et al., "Tor1/Sch9-regulated carbon source substitution is as effective as calorie restriction in life span extension," *PLoS Genetics*, vol. 5, no. 5, Article ID e1000467, 2009.

[14] E. M. Dioum, R. Chen, M. S. Alexander et al., "Regulation of hypoxia-inducible factor 2α signaling by the stress-responsive deacetylase sirtuin 1," *Science*, vol. 324, no. 5932, pp. 1289–1293, 2009.

[15] J. Luo, A. Y. Nikolaev, S. I. Imai et al., "Negative control of p53 by $Sir2\alpha$ promotes cell survival under stress," *Cell*, vol. 107, no. 2, pp. 137–148, 2001.

[16] A. Brunet, L. B. Sweeney, J. F. Sturgill et al., "Stress-dependent regulation of FOXO transcription factors by the SIRT1 deacetylase," *Science*, vol. 303, no. 5666, pp. 2011–2015, 2004.

[17] M. C. Motta, N. Divecha, M. Lemieux et al., "Mammalian SIRT1 represses forkhead transcription factors," *Cell*, vol. 116, no. 4, pp. 551–563, 2004.

[18] V. M. Nayagam, X. Wang, C. T. Yong et al., "SIRT1 modulating compounds from high-throughput screening as anti-inflammatory and insulin-sensitizing agents," *Journal of Biomolecular Screening*, vol. 11, no. 8, pp. 959–967, 2006.

[19] J. C. Milne, P. D. Lambert, S. Schenk et al., "Small molecule activators of SIRT1 as therapeutics for the treatment of type 2 diabetes," *Nature*, vol. 450, no. 7170, pp. 712–716, 2007.

[20] M. Sengottuvelan, K. Deeptha, and N. Nalini, "Resveratrol ameliorates DNA damage, prooxidant and antioxidant imbalance in 1,2-dimethylhydrazine induced rat colon carcinogenesis," *Chemico-Biological Interactions*, vol. 181, no. 2, pp. 193–201, 2009.

[21] D. M. Erion, S. Yonemitsu, Y. Nie et al., "SirT1 knockdown in liver decreases basal hepatic glucose production and increases hepatic insulin responsiveness in diabetic rats," *Proceedings of the National Academy of Sciences of the United States of America*, vol. 106, no. 27, pp. 11288–11293, 2009.

[22] R. M. Anderson, D. Shanmuganayagam, and R. Weindruch, "Caloric restriction and aging: studies in mice and monkeys," *Toxicologic Pathology*, vol. 37, no. 1, pp. 47–51, 2009.

Exploring Biomolecular Literature with EVEX: Connecting Genes through Events, Homology, and Indirect Associations

Sofie Van Landeghem,[1,2] **Kai Hakala,**[3] **Samuel Rönnqvist,**[3] **Tapio Salakoski,**[3,4] **Yves Van de Peer,**[1,2] **and Filip Ginter**[3]

[1] *Department of Plant Systems Biology, VIB, Technologiepark 927, 9052 Gent, Belgium*
[2] *Department of Plant Biotechnology and Bioinformatics, Ghent University, Technologiepark 927, 9052 Gent, Belgium*
[3] *Department of Information Technology, University of Turku, Joukahaisenkatu 3-5, 20520 Turku, Finland*
[4] *Turku BioNLP Group, Turku Centre for Computer Science (TUCS), Joukahaisenkatu 3-5, 20520 Turku, Finland*

Correspondence should be addressed to Filip Ginter, ginter@cs.utu.fi

Academic Editor: Jin-Dong Kim

Technological advancements in the field of genetics have led not only to an abundance of experimental data, but also caused an exponential increase of the number of published biomolecular studies. Text mining is widely accepted as a promising technique to help researchers in the life sciences deal with the amount of available literature. This paper presents a freely available web application built on top of 21.3 million detailed biomolecular events extracted from all PubMed abstracts. These text mining results were generated by a state-of-the-art event extraction system and enriched with gene family associations and abstract generalizations, accounting for lexical variants and synonymy. The EVEX resource locates relevant literature on phosphorylation, regulation targets, binding partners, and several other biomolecular events and assigns confidence values to these events. The search function accepts official gene/protein symbols as well as common names from all species. Finally, the web application is a powerful tool for generating homology-based hypotheses as well as novel, indirect associations between genes and proteins such as coregulators.

1. Introduction

The field of natural language processing for biomolecular texts (BioNLP) aims at large-scale text mining in support of life science research. Its primary motivation is the enormous amount of available scientific literature, which makes it essentially impossible to rapidly gain an overview of prior research results other than in a very narrow domain of interest. Among the typical use cases for BioNLP applications are support for database curation, linking experimental data with relevant literature, content visualization, and hypothesis generation—all of these tasks require processing and summarizing large amounts of individual research articles. Among the most heavily studied tasks in BioNLP is the extraction of information about known associations between biomolecular entities, primarily genes, and gene products, and this task has recently seen much progress in two general directions.

First, relationships between biomolecular entities are now being extracted in much greater detail. Until recently, the focus was on extracting untyped and undirected binary relations which, while stating that there is *some* relationship between two objects, gave little additional information about the nature of the relationship. Recognizing that extracting such relations may not provide sufficient detail for wider adoption of text mining in the biomedical community, the focus is currently shifting towards a more detailed analysis of the text, providing additional vital information about the detected relationships. Such information includes the type of the relationship, the specific roles of the arguments (e.g., affector or affectee), the polarity of the relationship (positive versus negative statement), and whether it was stated in a speculative or affirmative context. This more detailed text mining target was formalized as an *event extraction* task and greatly popularized in the series of BioNLP Shared Tasks on Event Extraction [1, 2]. These shared tasks mark a truly community-wide effort to develop efficient systems to extract sufficiently detailed information for real-world, practical applications, with the highest possible accuracy.

Second, text mining systems are now being applied on a large scale, recognizing the fact that, in order for a text mining service to be adopted by its target audience, that is, researchers in the life sciences, it must cover as much of the available literature as possible. While small-scale studies on well-defined and carefully constructed corpora comprising several hundred abstracts are of great utility to BioNLP research, actual applications of the resulting methods require the processing of considerably larger volumes of text, ideally including all available literature. Numerous studies have been published demonstrating that even complex and computationally intensive methods can be successfully applied on a large scale, typically processing all available abstracts in PubMed and/or all full-text articles in the open-access section of PubMed Central. For instance, the *iHOP* [3] and *Medie* [4] systems allow users to directly mine literature relevant to given genes or proteins of interest, allowing for structured queries far beyond the usual keyword search. *EBIMed* [5] offers a broad scope by also including gene ontology terms such as biological processes, as well as drugs and species names. Other systems, such as the *BioText search engine* [6] and *Yale Image Finder* [7] allow for a comprehensive search in full-text articles, including also figures and tables. Finally, the *BioNOT* system [8] focuses specifically on extracting negative evidence from scientific articles.

The first large-scale application that specifically targets the extraction of detailed events according to their definition in the BioNLP Shared Tasks is the dataset of Björne et al. [9], comprising 19 million events among 36 million gene and protein mentions. This data was obtained by processing all 18 million titles and abstracts in the 2009 PubMed distribution using the winning system of the BioNLP'09 Shared Task. In a subsequent study of Van Landeghem et al. [10], the dataset was refined, generalized, and released as a relational (SQL) database referred to as *EVEX*. Among the main contributions of this subsequent study was the generalization of the events, using publicly available gene family definitions. Although a major step forward from the original text-bound events produced by the event extraction system, the main audience for the EVEX database was still the BioNLP community. Consequently, the dataset is not easily accessible for researchers in the life sciences who are not familiar with the intricacies of the event representation. Further, as the massive relational database contains millions of events, manual querying is not an acceptable way to access the data for daily use in life science research.

In this study, we introduce a publicly available web application based on the EVEX dataset, presenting the first application that brings large-scale event-based text mining results to a broad audience of end-users including biologists, geneticists, and other researchers in the life sciences. The web application is available at http://www.evexdb.org/. The primary purpose of the application is to provide the EVEX dataset with an intuitive interface that does not presuppose familiarity with the underlying event representation.

The application presents a comprehensive and thoroughly interlinked overview of all events for a given gene or protein, or a gene/protein pair. The main novel feature of this application, as compared to other available large-scale text mining applications, is that it covers highly detailed event structures that are enriched with homology-based information and additionally extracts indirect associations by applying cross-document aggregation and combination of events.

In the following section, we provide more details on the EVEX text mining dataset, its text-bound extraction results, and the gene family-based generalizations. Further, we present several novel algorithms for event ranking, event refinement, and retrieval of indirect associations. Section 3 presents an evaluation of the EVEX dataset and the described algorithms. The features of the web application are illustrated in Section 4, presenting a real-world use case on the budding yeast gene *Mec1*, which has known mammalian and plant homologs. We conclude by summarizing the main contributions of this work and highlighting several interesting opportunities for future work.

2. Data and Methods

This section describes the original event data, as well as a ranking procedure that sorts events according to their reliability. Further, two abstract layers are defined on top of the complex event structures, enabling coarse grouping of similar events, and providing an intuitive pairwise point of view that allows fast retrieval of interesting gene/protein pairs. Finally, we describe a hypothesis generation module that finds missing links between two entities, allowing the user to retrieve proteins with common binding partners or genes that act as coregulators of a group of common target genes.

2.1. EVEX Dataset

2.1.1. Core Events. The core set of text mining results accessible through the EVEX resource has been generated by the Turku Event Extraction System, the winning system of the BioNLP'09 Shared Task (ST) on Event Extraction [1]. This extraction system was combined with the BANNER named entity recognizer [11], forming a complete event extraction pipeline that had the highest reported accuracy on the task in 2009, and still remains state-of-the-art, as shown in the recent ST'11 [12]. This event extraction pipeline was applied to all citations in the 2009 distribution of PubMed [9]. As part of the current study, citations from the period 2009–2011 have been processed, using essentially the same pipeline with several minor improvements, resulting in 40.3 million tagged gene symbols and 21.3 million extracted events. The underlying event dataset has thus been brought up to date and will be regularly updated in the future.

The dataset contains events as defined in the context of the ST'09, that is, predicates with a variable number of arguments which can be gene/protein symbols or, recursively, other events. Each argument is defined as having the role of *Cause* or *Theme* in the event. There are nine distinct event types: binding, phosphorylation, regulation

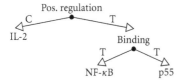

FIGURE 1: Event representation of the statement *IL-2 acts by enhancing binding activity of NF-κB to p55*, illustrating recursive nesting of events where the (T)heme of the *positive regulation* event is the *binding* event. The (C)ause argument is the gene symbol *IL-2* (figure adapted from [10]).

(positive, negative, and unspecified), protein catabolism, transcription, localization, and gene expression. Further, each event refers to a specific *trigger word* in text. For example, the word *increases* typically triggers a positive regulation event and *degradation* typically refers to protein catabolism. An example event structure is illustrated in Figure 1.

Event definitions impose several restrictions on event arguments: (1) events of the type phosphorylation, protein catabolism, transcription, localization, and gene expression must only have a single argument, a Theme, which must be a gene or a protein, (2) events of the binding type may have any number of gene/protein Theme arguments and cannot have a Cause argument, and finally (3) regulation events must have exactly one Theme argument and may have one Cause argument, with no restrictions as to whether these arguments are genes/proteins or recursively other events. In the following text, we will state events using a simple bracketed notation, where the event type is stated first, followed by a comma-separated list of arguments enclosed in parentheses. For instance, the event in Figure 1 would be stated as *Positive-Regulation(C:IL-2, T:Binding(T:NF-κB, T:p55))*, where *C:* and *T:* denote the role of the argument as (C)ause or (T)heme. For brevity, we will further refer to all biochemical entities, even proteins and mRNA, as *genes*.

2.1.2. Event Generalizations.
One of the major limitations of the original core set of events is that they are strictly text-bound and provide no facility for a more general treatment, such as being able to abstract from different name spelling variants and symbol synonymy. Further, biochemical entities were originally treated as merely text strings with no database identity referring to external resources such as UniProt [13] or Entrez Gene [14]. The EVEX dataset addresses these issues by providing event generalizations [10].

First, the identified gene symbols in the EVEX dataset are canonicalized by removing superfluous affixes (prefixes and suffixes) to obtain the core gene symbol, followed by discarding nonalphanumeric characters and lowercasing. For instance, the full string *human Esr-1 subunit* is canonicalized into *esr1*. The purpose of this canonicalization is to abstract away from minor spelling variants and to deal with the fact that the BANNER named entity recognizer often includes a wider context around the core gene symbol. The canonicalization algorithm itself cannot, however, deal with the ambiguity prevalent among the symbols. EVEX thus

further resolves these canonical gene symbols, whenever possible, into their most likely families, using two distinct resources for defining homologous genes and gene families: *HomoloGene* (eukaryots, [14]) and *Ensembl* (vertebrates, [15]). As part of this study, we extended EVEX to also include families from *Ensembl Genomes*, which provides coverage for metazoa, plants, protists, fungi, and bacteria [16]. Building on top of these definitions, the EVEX dataset now defines four *event generalizations*, whereby all events whose arguments have the same canonical form, or resolve to the same gene family, are aggregated. As a result, it becomes straightforward to retrieve all information on a specific gene symbol, abstracting away from lexical variants through the canonicalization algorithm, or to additionally apply the synonym-expansion module through the family-based generalizations. These different generalizations are all implemented on the web application (Section 4.2).

2.2. Event Ranking.
To rank the extracted events according to their reliability, we have implemented an event scoring algorithm based on the output of the Turku Event Extraction System. This machine learning system uses linear Support Vector Machines (SVMs) as the underlying classifier [17]. Every classification is given a confidence score, the distance to the decision hyperplane of the linear classifier, where higher scores are associated with more confident decisions. There is not a single master classifier to predict the events in their entirety. Rather, individual classifications are made to predict the event trigger and each of its arguments. In order to assign a single confidence score to a specific event occurrence, the predictions from these two separate classifiers must be aggregated.

The confidence scores of the two different classifiers are not directly mutually comparable, and we therefore first normalize all scores in the dataset to zero mean and unit standard deviation, separately for triggers and arguments. Subsequently, the score of a specific event occurrence is assigned to be the *minimum* of the normalized scores of its event trigger and its arguments, that is, the lowest normalized confidence among all classification decisions involved in extracting that specific event. Using minimum as the aggregation function roughly corresponds to the *fuzzy and* operator in that it requires all components of an event to be confident for it to be ranked high. Finally, the score of a generalized event is the average of the scores of all its occurrences.

To assign a meaningful interpretation to the normalized and aggregated confidence values, events within the top 20% of the confidence range are classified as "very high confidence." The other 4 categories, each representing the next 20% of all events, are respectively labeled as "high confidence," "average confidence," "low confidence" and "very low confidence." When presenting multiple possible hits for a certain query, the web application uses the original scores to rank the events from high to low reliability.

2.3. Event Refinement.
The extraction of event structures is highly dependent on the lexical and syntactic constructs

used in the sentence and may therefore contain unnecessary complexity. This is because the event extraction system is trained to closely follow the actual statements in the sentence and thus, for instance, will mark both of the words *increase* and *induces* as triggers for positive regulation events in the sentence *Ang II induces a rapid increase in MAPK activity*. Consequently, the final event structure is extracted as *Positive-Regulation(C: Ang II, T: Positive-Regulation(T: MAPK))*, that is, *Ang II* is a Cause argument of a positive regulation event, which has another positive regulation event as its Theme.

While correctly extracted, such nested single-argument regulatory events (i.e., regulations with a Theme but no Cause argument), often forming chains that are several events long, are unnecessarily complex. Clearly, the event above can be restated as *Positive-Regulation(C: Ang II, T: MAPK)*, removing the nested single-argument positive regulation event. This refinement helps to establish the event as equivalent with all other events that can be refined to the same elementary structure, enhancing the event aggregation possibilities in EVEX. However, when presenting the details of the extracted event to the user, the original structure of the event is preserved.

Table 1 lists the set of refinement rules. In this context, positive and negative regulation refer to having a general positive or negative effect, while an unspecified regulation could not be resolved to either category due to missing information in the sentence.

To simplify the single-argument regulatory events, we proceed iteratively, removing intermediary single-argument regulatory events as long as any rule matches. A particular consideration is given to the polarity of the regulations. While a nested chain of single-argument positive regulations can be safely reduced to a single positive regulation, the outcome of reducing chains of single-argument regulations of mixed polarity is less obvious. As illustrated in Table 1, application of the rules may result in a change of polarity of the outer event. For instance, a regulation of a negative regulation is interpreted as a negative regulation, changing the polarity of the outer event from unspecified to negative. To avoid excessive inferences not licensed by the text, the algorithm only allows one such change of polarity. Any subsequent removal of a nested single-argument regulatory event that results in a type change forces the new type of the outer event to be of the unspecified regulation type.

2.4. Pairwise Abstraction. The most basic query issued on the EVEX web application involves a single gene, which triggers the generation of a structured overview page, listing associated genes grouped by their type of connection with the query gene (Section 4.1). The most important underlying functionality implemented by the web application is thus the ability to identify and categorize pairs of related genes. This pairwise point of view comes natural in the life sciences and can be implemented on top of the events with ease by analyzing common event structures and defining argument pairs within. The refinements discussed in Section 2.3 substantially decrease the number of unique

event structures present in the data, restricting the required analysis to a comparatively small number of event structures. Furthermore, we only need to consider those events that involve more than one gene or that are a recursive argument in such an event, limiting the set of event occurrences from 21 M to 12 M events.

As an example, let us consider the event *Positive-Regulation(C:Thrombin, T:Positive-Regulatio(C:EGF, Phosphorylation(T:Akt)))*, extracted from the sentence *Thrombin augmented EGF-stimulated Akt phosphorylation*. The pairs of interest here are *Thrombin—Akt* and *EGF—Akt*, both associations coarsely categorized as *regulation*. Therefore, whenever a user queries for *Thrombin*, the *Akt* gene will be listed among the regulation targets, and, whenever a user queries for *Akt*, both *Thrombin* and *EGF* will be listed as regulators. Note, however, that the categorization of the association as *regulation* is only for the purpose of coarse grouping of the results on the overview page. The user will additionally be presented with the details of the original event, which is translated from the bracketed notation into the English statement *Upregulation of AKT phosphorylation by EGF is upregulated by Thrombin*.

There is a limited number of prevalent event structures which account for the vast majority of event occurrences. Table 2 lists the most common structures, together with the gene pairs extracted from them. The algorithm to extract the gene pairs from the event structures proceeds as follows.

(1) All argument pairs are considered a candidate and classified as *binding* if both participants are a Theme of one specific binding event, and *regulation* otherwise. (Note that due to the restrictions of event arguments as described in Section 2.1, only binding and regulation events can have more than one argument.)

(2) If one of the genes is a Theme argument of an event which itself is a Cause argument, for example, *G2* in *Regulation(C:Regulation(C:G1, T:G2), T:G3)*, the association type of the candidate pair *G2-G3* is reclassified as *indirect regulation*, since the direct regulator of *G3* is the Cause argument of the nested regulation (*G1*).

(3) If one of the genes is a Cause argument of an event which itself is a Theme argument, for example, *G2* in *Regulation(C:G1, T:Regulation(C:G2, T:G3))*, the candidate pair (*G1-G2*) is discarded.

While the association between *G1* and *G2* is discarded in step (3) since it in many cases cannot convincingly be classified as a regulation, it is represented as a *coregulation* when indirect associations, described in the following section, are sought.

2.5. Indirect Associations. A cell's activity is often organized into regulatory modules, that is, sets of coregulated genes that share a common function. Such modules can be found by automated analysis and clustering of genome-wide expression profiles [18]. Individual events, as defined by the BioNLP Shared Tasks, do not explicitly express

TABLE 1: Listing of the refinement rules, involving any nested combination of the three types of regulation: positive regulation (Pos), negative regulation (Neg) and unspecified regulation (Reg). Each parent event has a regulatory (T)heme argument and an optional (C)ause. The nested regulations are all regulations without a Cause and their detailed structure is omitted for brevity. In full, the first structure would read *Pos(C:geneA, T:Pos(T:geneB))* which is rewritten to *Pos(C:geneA, T:geneB)* with *geneA* and *geneB* being any two genes.

Original	Result	Example
Pos(C, T:Pos)	*Pos(C, T)*	BRs induce accumulation of BZR1 protein
Pos(C, T:Reg)	*Pos(C, T)*	PKS5 mediates PM H +- ATPase regulation
Reg(C, T:Pos)	*Pos(C, T)*	CaM regulates activation of HSFs
Neg(C, T:Neg)	*Pos(C, T)*	E2 prevented downregulation of p21
Reg(C, T:Reg)	*Reg(C, T)*	PDK1 is involved in the regulation of S6K
Neg(C, T:Reg)	*Neg(C, T)*	GW5074 prevents this effect on ENT1 mRNA
Neg(C, T:Pos)	*Neg(C, T)*	BIN2 negatively regulates BZR1 accumulation
Reg(C, T:Neg)	*Neg(C, T)*	The effect of hCG in downregulating ER beta
Pos(C, T:Neg)	*Neg(C, T)*	DtRE is required for repression of CAB2

TABLE 2: The most prevalent (refined) event patterns in the EVEX data, considering only events with more than one gene or protein symbol, and their recursively nested events. These aggregated patterns refer to any type of regulation (*Reg*), to binding events between two genes (*Bind*), and to any physical event (*Phy*) concerning a single gene such as protein-DNA binding, protein catabolism, transcription, localization, phosphorylation, and gene expression. The first two columns refer to the percentage of event occurrences covered by the given pattern and the cumulative percentage of event occurrences up to and including the pattern. The right-most column depicts the extracted gene pair and a coarse classification of its association type. *A* and *B* refer to gene symbols, and bindings are represented with ×. Further, $A > B$ means *A regulates B*, while $A \gg B$ expresses an indirect regulation.

Occ. [%]	Cum. occ. [%]	Event pattern	Gene pair
58.6	58.6	*Phy(T:A)*	—
15.0	73.6	**Reg(T:A)*	—
8.4	82.0	**Reg(T:Phy(T:A))*	—
8.0	90.0	*Bind(T:A, T:B)*	$A \times B$
4.7	94.7	**Reg(C:A, T:B)*	$A > B$
3.8	98.5	**Reg(C:A, T:Phy(T:B))*	$A > B$
0.2	98.7	**Reg(C:*Reg(T:Phy(T:A)), T:Phy(T:B))*	$A \gg B$
0.2	98.9	**Reg(C:Phy(T:A), T:B)*	$A \gg B$
0.2	99.1	**Reg(C:Phy(T:A), T:Phy(T:B))*	$A \gg B$

such associations. However, indirect regulatory associations can be identified by combining the information expressed in various events retrieved across different articles. For instance, the events *Regulation(C:geneA, T:geneZ)* and *Regulation(C:geneB, T:geneZ)* can be aggregated to present the hypothesis that *geneA* and *geneB* coregulate *geneZ*. Such hypothesis generation is greatly simplified by the fact that the events have been refined using the procedure described in Section 2.3 and the usage of a relational database, which allows efficient querying across events.

The indirect associations as implemented for the web application include coregulation and common binding partners (Table 3). These links have been precalculated and stored in the database, enabling fast retrieval of, for example, coregulators or genes that are targeted by a common regulator, facilitating the discovery of functional modules through text mining information. However, it needs to be stated that these associations are mainly hypothetical, as, for example, coregulators additionally require coexpression. Details on gene expression events can be found by browsing the sentences of specific genes as described in Section 4.1.

TABLE 3: Indirect associations between gene *A* and gene *B*, established by combining binding and regulatory events through a common interaction partner gene *Z*. Bindings are represented with × and for regulations $A > B$ means *A regulates B*.

Association	Interpretation
$A > Z < B$	*A* and *B* coregulate *Z*
$A < Z > B$	*A* and *B* are being regulated by *Z*
$A \times Z \times B$	*A* and *B* share a common binding partner *Z*

3. Results and Performance Evaluation

In this section, we present the evaluation of the EVEX resource from several points of view. First, we discuss the performance of the event extraction system used to produce the core set of events in EVEX, reviewing a number of published evaluations both within the BioNLP Shared Task and in other domains. Second, we present several evaluations of the methods and data employed specifically in the EVEX resource in addition to the core event predictions: we review existing results as well as present new evaluations of the confidence scores and their correlation with event precision, the family-based generalization algorithms, and the novel event refinement algorithms introduced above. Finally, we discuss two biologically motivated applications of EVEX, demonstrating the usability of EVEX in real-world use cases.

3.1. Core Event Predictions. The Turku Event Extraction System (TEES), the source of the core set of EVEX events, was extensively evaluated on the BioNLP Shared Tasks. It was the winning system of the ST'09, achieving 46.73% recall, 58.48% precision, and 51.95%F-score [9]. In the current study, the original set of event predictions extracted from the PubMed 2009 distribution has been brought up to date using an improved version of TEES. This updated system was recently shown to achieve state-of-the-art results in the ST'11, obtaining 50.06% recall, 59.48% precision, and 54.37%F-score on the corresponding abstract-only GENIA subchallenge [12].

To assess the generalizability of the text mining results from domain-specific datasets to the whole of PubMed, a precision rate of 64% was previously obtained by manual evaluation of 100 random events [19]. In the same study, the named entities (i.e., gene and protein symbols) as extracted by BANNER were estimated to achieve a precision of 87%. These figures indicate that the performance of the various text mining components generalize well from domain-specific training data to the entire PubMed.

3.2. Confidence Values. To investigate the correlation of the confidence values (Section 2.2) to the correctness of the extracted events, we have measured the precision and recall rates of binding events between two genes, simulating a use case that involves finding related binding partners for a certain query gene (Section 4.1). This experiment was conducted on the ST'09 development set, consisting of 150 PubMed abstracts with 94 gold-standard binding pairs. For this dataset, 67 interacting pairs were found in EVEX, with confidence values ranging between −1.7 and 1.3. When evaluated against the gold-standard data, the whole set of predictions achieves 59.7% precision and 42.6% recall.

Using the confidence values for ranking, we have subsequently applied a cut-off threshold on the results, only keeping predictions with confidence values above the threshold. A systematic screening was performed between the interval of −1.7 and 1.3, using a step-size of 0.05 (60 evaluations). The results have been aggregated and summarized in Figure 2, depicting the average precision and recall values for each aggregated interval of 0.6 length. For example, a cut-off value between 0.10 and 0.70 (fourth interval) would result in an average precision rate of 70.0% and recall of 14.4%. Only taking the top ranked predictions, with a threshold above 0.7 (fifth interval), results in extremely high precision (91.9%) but only 4.8% recall. On the scale of EVEX, however, 4.8% recall would still translate to more than a million high-precision events.

3.3. EVEX Generalizations. As described in Section 2.1, the EVEX resource provides several algorithms to generalize gene symbols and their events, providing the opportunity to identify and aggregate equivalent events across various articles, accounting for lexical variants and synonymy. In a first step, a canonical form of the gene symbols is produced, increasing the proportion of symbols that can be matched to gene databases. This algorithm has previously been evaluated on the ST'09 training set, which specifically aims at identifying entities that are likely to match gene and protein symbol databases. By canonicalizing the symbols as predicted by BANNER, an increase of 11 percentage points in F-score was obtained [10].

The family-based generalizations have also been previously evaluated for both HomoloGene and Ensembl definitions. To expand the coverage of these generalizations, in this study, we have added definitions from Ensembl Genomes. The statistics on coverage of gene symbols, brought up to date by including the 2009–2011 abstracts, are depicted in Table 4. While only a small fraction of all unique canonical symbols matches the gene families from HomoloGene or Ensembl (Genomes) (between 3 and 6%), this small fraction accounts for more than half of all occurrences (between 51 and 61%). The family disambiguation algorithm thus discards a long tail of very infrequent canonical symbols. These findings are similar to the previous statistics presented by Van Landeghem et al. [10]. Additionally, the newly introduced families of Ensembl Genomes clearly provide a higher coverage: 8-9 percentage points higher than HomoloGene or Ensembl.

3.4. Event Refinement. By removing the chains of single-argument regulatory events, the refinement process simplifies and greatly reduces the heterogeneity in event structures, facilitating semantic interpretation and search for similar events. This process reduces the number of distinct event structures by more than 60%.

The main purpose of the event refinement algorithm, in combination with the pairwise view of the events, is to increase the coverage of finding related genes for a certain input query gene. When applying the algorithm as detailed in Section 2.3, the number of events with more than one gene symbol as direct argument increases from 1471 K to 1588 K, successfully generating more than a hundred thousand simplified events that can straightforwardly be parsed for pairwise relations.

It has to be noted, however, that the results of the refinement algorithm are merely used as an abstract layer to group similar events together and to offer quick access to relevant information. The original event structures as extracted by TEES are always presented to the user when detailed information is requested, allowing the user to reject or accept the inferences made by the refinement algorithm.

3.5. Biological Applications. The EVEX dataset and the associated web application have recently been applied in a focused study targeting the regulation of NADP(H) expression in *E. coli*, demonstrating the resource in a

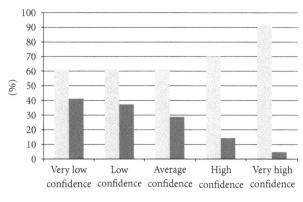

FIGURE 2: Evaluation of predicted binding events, measured against the gold-standard data of the ST'09 development set. By sorting the events according to their confidence values, a tradeoff between precision and recall is obtained.

TABLE 4: Gene symbol coverage comparison, showing the number of distinct canonical symbols as well as the number of different occurrences covered, out of the total number of 40.3 M extracted gene symbols.

	Distinct symbols		Occurrences	
Canonical	1833.1 K	100.0%	40.3 M	100.0%
HomoloGene	68.2 K	3.7%	21.1 M	52.3%
Ensembl	60.0 K	3.2%	20.9 M	51.8%
Ensembl Genomes	100.6 K	5.5%	24.3 M	60.1%

real-life biological use case, with encouraging results [20]. The Ensembl Genomes generalization was used to allow for homology-based inference, and the regulatory network extracted from EVEX was integrated with microarray coexpression data. As part of this study, 461 occurrences of two-argument events in the NADP(H) regulatory network were manually evaluated, with precision of 53%. This figure compares favorably with the BioNLP'09 Shared Task official evaluation results of 50% for binding events and 46% for regulation events, the only event types that allow more than one argument. The event occurrences that were judged to be correctly extracted were further evaluated for the correctness of the assignment of their arguments to Ensembl Genomes families: 72% of event occurrences had both of their arguments assigned to the correct family.

In a separate study, the suitability of the EVEX dataset and web application to the task of pathway curation was analyzed with a particular focus on recall [21]. When analysing three high-quality pathway models, TLR, mTOR and yeast cell cycle, 60% of all interactions could be retrieved from EVEX using the canonical generalization. A thorough manual evaluation further suggested that, surprisingly, the most common reason for a pathway interaction not being extracted is not a failure of the event extraction pipeline, but rather a lack of semantic coverage. In these cases, the interaction corresponds to an event type not defined in the ST'09 task and thus out of scope for the event extraction system. Only 11% of interactions in the evaluated pathways were not recovered due to a failure of the event extraction system. This result shows that the recall in EVEX, at least in

the pathways under evaluation by Ohta et al., is clearly above the recall value published for the event extraction system in isolation. This increase can very likely be attributed to the volume of the event data in EVEX and the ability to aggregate several event occurrences into a single generalized event, where the failure to extract an individual event occurrence does not automatically mean the failure to extract the generalized event.

4. Web Application

To illustrate the functionality and features of the web application, we present a use case on a specific budding yeast gene, *Mec1*, which is conserved in *S. pombe*, *S. cerevisiae*, *K. lactis*, *E. gossypii*, *M. grisea*, and *N. crassa*. *Mec1* is required for meiosis and plays a critical role in the maintenance of genome stability. Furthermore, it is considered to be a homolog of the mammalian *ATR/ATM*, a signal transduction protein [22].

4.1. Gene Overview. The main functionality of the EVEX resource is providing fast access to relevant information and related biomolecular entities of a gene or pair of genes of interest. (Analysis of large gene lists is currently not supported, as such a bioinformatics use case is already covered by the publicly available MySQL database.) The most straightforward way to achieve this is through the canonical generalization, searching for a gene symbol or a pair of genes separated by a comma.

When typing the first characters of a gene symbol, a list of candidate matches is proposed, guiding the user to likely gene symbols found in text. The search page then automatically generates a listing of relevant biomolecular events, grouped by event type. At the top of the page, an overview of all regulators, regulated genes, and binding partners is provided, each accompanied with an example sentence. Further, coregulators are listed together with the number of coregulated genes (Section 2.5). Figure 3 shows the results when searching for *Mec1*. This overview lists 21 regulation targets, 11 regulators, 27 binding partners, and 263 coregulators. Within each category, the events are ranked by confidence, ranging from (very) high to average and (very) low (Section 2.2). Further, example sentences are always chosen to be those associated with the highest confidence score.

Selecting the target *RAD9*, the web application visualises all event structures expressing regulation of *RAD9* by *Mec1* (Figure 4). This enables a quick overview of the mechanisms through which the regulation is established, which can have a certain polarity (positive/negative) and may involve physical events such as phosphorylation or protein-DNA binding. The different types of event structures are coarsely grouped into categories of similar events and presented from most to least reliable using the confidence scores.

Exploring the relationship between *RAD9* and *Mec1* further, EVEX enables a search of all events linking these two genes through any direct or indirect association (Figure 5). This page provides conclusive evidence for a binding event between *RAD9* and *Mec1*. Further, both a *Mec1 regulates RAD9* and a *RAD9 regulates Mec1* event are presented. However, inspecting the sentences, the first one is obviously the only correct one. This illustrates the opportunity to use the large-scale event extraction results for pruning false positives of the text mining algorithm, as the false result only has 1 piece of evidence, and with a "very low" confidence, while the correct regulation is supported by 3 different evidence excerpts, two of which are of "high" confidence, and is thus displayed first.

Apart from the regulatory and binding mechanisms, the overview page also lists potential coregulations, enumerating targets that are regulated by both genes, such as *Rad53*. When accessing the details for this hypothesis, all evidence excerpts supporting both regulations are presented. Other indirect associations, such as common regulators and binding partners, can be retrieved equally fast.

Finally, the overview page of *Mec1* (Figure 3) contains additional relevant information including links to sentences stating events of *Mec1* without a second argument, grouped by event type. While these events incorporate only a single gene or protein and may not be very informative by themselves, they are highly relevant for information retrieval purposes, finding interesting sentences and articles describing specific processes such as protein catabolism or phosphorylation.

At the bottom of the overview page, a similar and even more general set of sentences can be found, providing pointers to relevant literature while still requiring manual analysis to determine the exact type of information. Such

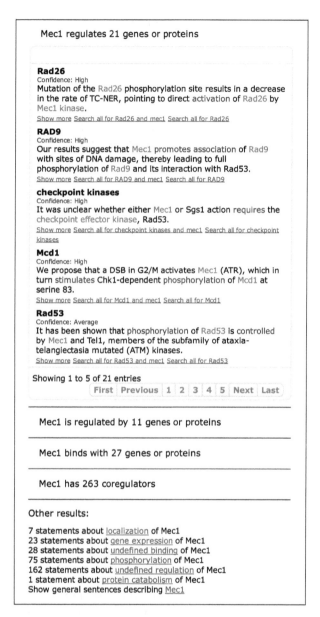

FIGURE 3: Search results for *Mec1* on the canonical generalization. An overview of directly associated genes is presented, grouped by event type. In the screenshot, only the box with regulation targets is shown, but the other event types may also be expanded. At the bottom, relevant links to additional sentences and articles are provided.

sentences, even though they contain no extracted events, may include useful background information on the gene such as relevant experimental studies, related diseases, or general functions and pathways.

4.2. Homology-Based Inference. In comparative genomics, it is common practice to transfer functional annotations between related organisms for genes sharing sequence similarity [23, 24]. The EVEX resource provides such functionality for inferring interactions and other biomolecular events based on homology, by summarizing all events pertaining

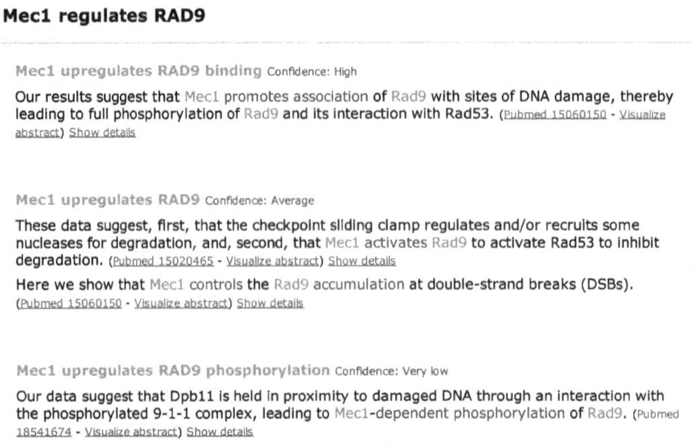

Mec1 regulates RAD9

Mec1 upregulates RAD9 binding Confidence: High

Our results suggest that Mec1 promotes association of Rad9 with sites of DNA damage, thereby leading to full phosphorylation of Rad9 and its interaction with Rad53. (Pubmed 15060150 - Visualize abstract) Show details

Mec1 upregulates RAD9 Confidence: Average

These data suggest, first, that the checkpoint sliding clamp regulates and/or recruits some nucleases for degradation, and, second, that Mec1 activates Rad9 to activate Rad53 to inhibit degradation. (Pubmed 15020465 - Visualize abstract) Show details

Here we show that Mec1 controls the Rad9 accumulation at double-strand breaks (DSBs). (Pubmed 15060150 - Visualize abstract) Show details

Mec1 upregulates RAD9 phosphorylation Confidence: Very low

Our data suggest that Dpb11 is held in proximity to damaged DNA through an interaction with the phosphorylated 9-1-1 complex, leading to Mec1-dependent phosphorylation of Rad9. (Pubmed 18541674 - Visualize abstract) Show details

FIGURE 4: Detailed representation of all evidence supporting the regulation of RAD9 by Mec1. Regulatory mechanisms can have a certain polarity (positive/negative) and may involve physical events such as phosphorylation or protein-DNA binding.

to a certain family when searching for one of its members (Section 2.1).

For example, instead of only looking at the information for one particular gene symbol as described previously, we can extend the search through Ensembl Genomes and retrieve information on homologous genes and their synonyms. The generated listings of regulators and binding partners are structured in exactly the same way as before, but this time each symbol refers to a whole gene family rather than just one gene name.

Conducting such a generalized search for *Mec1*, EVEX retrieves interaction information for *Mec1* and its homologs. The resulting page presents not only results for the symbol *Mec1*, but also for common symbols which are considered synonyms on the gene-family level, such as *ATR*. This type of synonym expansion goes well beyond a simple keyword query.

For each gene family present in the text mining data, a family profile lists all genes and synonyms for a specific family, linking to the authoritative resources such as Entrez Gene and the Taxonomy database at NCBI. While *ESR1* is a known but deprecated synonym of *Mec1* [25], it is not considered as a viable synonym of *Mec1*, considering *Esr1* generally refers to the family of estrogen receptors. The synonym disambiguation algorithm of Van Landeghem et al. [10], which is the basis of the gene family generalizations, will thus prevent *Esr1* from being used as a synonym for *Mec1*. Reliable synonyms found in text do however include *ATR* and *SCKL*.

The EVEX web application includes several distinct methods of defining gene families (Section 2.1), each accommodating for specific organisms and use cases. For example, Ensembl Genomes defines rather coarse grained families resulting in a family of 19 evolutionarily conserved genes, including the budding yeast gene *Mec1*, its mammalian *ATR* orthologs, and genes from green algae and Arabidopsis. In contrast, the corresponding family defined by HomoloGene only includes the 6 conserved *Mec1* genes in the Ascomycota.

4.3. Manual Inspection of Text Mining Results. An important aspect of the EVEX web application is the ability to retrieve the original sentences and articles for all claims extracted from literature. In the previous sections, we have described how EVEX can assist in the retrieval of directly and indirectly associated genes and proteins by generating summary overviews. However, to be applicable in real-life use cases and to be valuable to a domain expert, it is necessary to distinguish trustworthy predictions from unreliable hypotheses. For this reason, automatically generated confidence values are displayed for each extracted interaction, ranging from (very) high to average and (very) low. On top of those, the site always provides the opportunity to inspect the textual evidence in detail.

Consider, for example, the phosphorylation of *RAD9*, regulated by *Mec1* (Figure 4). To allow a detailed inspection of this event, the web application integrates the *stav* visualiser [26], which was developed as a supporting resource for the ST'11 [2] (Figure 6). This open-source tool provides a detailed and easily graspable presentation of the event structures and the associated textual spans. To any user interested in the text mining details, this visualization provides valuable insights into the automated event extraction process. Additionally, the web application provides the opportunity to visualise whole PubMed abstracts with the *stav* visualiser, allowing a fast overview of event information contained within an abstract.

4.4. Site Navigation. To easily trace back previously found results, a session-based search history at the righthand side of the screen provides links to the latest searches issued on the site. Further, a box with related searches suggests relevant queries related to the current page. Finally, the web application provides a powerful method to browse indirectly associated information, by allowing the retrieval of nested and parent interactions of a specific event. For example, when accessing the details of *Mec1*'s regulation of *RAD9* phosphorylation and selecting the phosphorylation event,

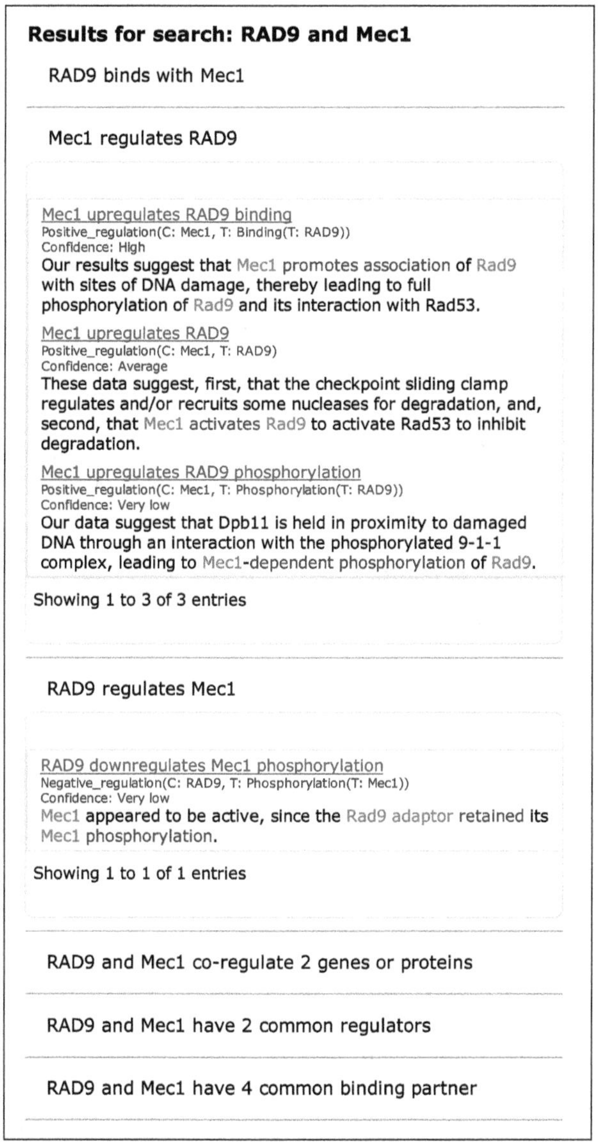

Results for search: RAD9 and Mec1

RAD9 binds with Mec1

Mec1 regulates RAD9

Mec1 upregulates RAD9 binding
Positive_regulation(C: Mec1, T: Binding(T: RAD9))
Confidence: High
Our results suggest that Mec1 promotes association of Rad9
with sites of DNA damage, thereby leading to full
phosphorylation of Rad9 and its interaction with Rad53.

Mec1 upregulates RAD9
Positive_regulation(C: Mec1, T: RAD9)
Confidence: Average
These data suggest, first, that the checkpoint sliding clamp
regulates and/or recruits some nucleases for degradation, and,
second, that Mec1 activates Rad9 to activate Rad53 to inhibit
degradation.

Mec1 upregulates RAD9 phosphorylation
Positive_regulation(C: Mec1, T: Phosphorylation(T: RAD9))
Confidence: Very low
Our data suggest that Dpb11 is held in proximity to damaged
DNA through an interaction with the phosphorylated 9-1-1
complex, leading to Mec1-dependent phosphorylation of Rad9.

Showing 1 to 3 of 3 entries

RAD9 regulates Mec1

RAD9 downregulates Mec1 phosphorylation
Negative_regulation(C: RAD9, T: Phosphorylation(T: Mec1))
Confidence: Very low
Mec1 appeared to be active, since the Rad9 adaptor retained its
Mec1 phosphorylation.

Showing 1 to 1 of 1 entries

RAD9 and Mec1 co-regulate 2 genes or proteins

RAD9 and Mec1 have 2 common regulators

RAD9 and Mec1 have 4 common binding partner

FIGURE 5: All events linking *Mec1* and *RAD9* through either direct or indirect associations. In the screenshot, only the regulation boxes are shown in detail, but the other event types may also be expanded. This page enables a quick overview of the mechanisms through which two genes interact, while at the same time highlighting false positive text mining results which can be identified by comparing confidence values and the evidence found in the sentences.

evidence is shown for many parent events involving different regulation polarities and various genes causing this specific phosphorylation. As such, we quickly learn that *RAD9* phosphorylation has many different potential regulators, such as *Ad5, Ad12,* and *C-Abl.* This sort of explorative information retrieval and cross-article discovery is exactly the type of usage aimed at by the EVEX resource.

5. Conclusions and Future Work

This paper presents a publicly available web application providing access to over 21 million detailed events among more than 40 million identified gene/protein symbols in nearly 6 million PubMed titles and abstracts. This dataset is the result of processing the entire collection of PubMed titles and abstracts through a state-of-the-art event extraction system and is regularly updated as new citations are added to PubMed. The extracted events provide a detailed representation of the textual statements, allowing for recursively nested events and different event types ranging from phosphorylation to catabolism and regulation. The EVEX web application is the first publicly released resource that provides intuitive access to these detailed event-based text mining results.

As the application mainly targets manual explorative browsing for supporting research in the life sciences, several steps are taken to allow for efficient querying of the large-scale event dataset. First, events are assigned confidence scores and ranked according to their reliability. Further, the events are refined to unify different event structures that have a nearly identical interpretation. Additionally, the events are aggregated across articles, accounting for lexical variation and generalizing gene symbols with respect to their gene family. This aggregation allows for efficient access to relevant information across articles and species. Finally, the EVEX web application groups events with respect to the involvement of pairs of genes, providing the users with a familiar gene-centric point of view, without sacrificing the expressiveness of the events. This interpretation is extended also to combinations of events, identifying indirect associations such as common coregulators and common binding partners, as a form of literature-based hypothesis generation.

There are a number of future directions that can be followed in order to extend and further improve the EVEX web application. The core set of events can be expanded by also processing all full-text articles from the open-access section of PubMed Central. Further, as BioNLP methods keep evolving towards more detailed and accurate predictions, the dataset can be enriched with new information, for example, by including epigenetics data as recently introduced by the BioNLP'11 Shared Task [2, 27] and integrating noncausal entity relations [28, 29]. Additionally, gene normalization data can be incorporated, enabling queries using specific gene or protein identifiers [30]. Finally, a web service may be developed to allow programmatic access to the EVEX web application, allowing bulk queries and result export for further postprocessing in various bioinformatics applications.

Acknowledgments

S. Van Landeghem would like to thank the Research Foundation Flanders (FWO) for funding her research and a travel grant to Turku. Y. Van de Peer wants to acknowledge support from Ghent University (Multidisciplinary Research Partnership Bioinformatics: from nucleotides to networks) and the Interuniversity Attraction Poles Programme (IUAP P6/25), initiated by the Belgian State, Science Policy Office (BioMaGNet). This work was partly funded by the Academy

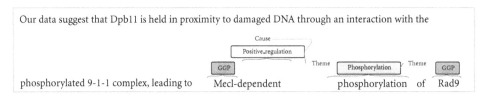

FIGURE 6: Visualization of a specific event occurrence by the stav text annotation visualiser. Genes and gene products ("GGPs") are marked, as well as the trigger words that refer to specific event types. Finally, arrows denote the roles of each argument in the event (e.g. Theme or Cause). This visualization corresponds to the formal bracketed format of the event: *Positive-regulation(C: Mec1, T:Phosphorylation(T:RAD9))*.

of Finland, and the computational resources were provided by CSC-IT Center for Science Ltd., Espoo, Finland and the Department of IT, University of Turku, Finland.

References

[1] J.-D. Kim, T. Ohta, S. Pyysalo, Y. Kano, and J. Tsujii, "Overview of BioNLP'09 shared task on event extraction," in *Proceedings of the BioNLP Workshop Companion Volume for Shared Task*, pp. 1–9, Association for Computational Linguistics, 2009.

[2] J.-D. Kim, S. Pyysalo, T. Ohta, R. Bossy, N. Nguyen, N. Nguyen, and J. Tsujii, "Overview of BioNLP shared task 2011," in *Proceedings of the BioNLP Workshop Companion Volume for Shared Task*, pp. 1–6, Association for Computational Linguistics, 2011.

[3] R. Homann and A. Valencia, "A gene network for navigating the literature," *Nature Genetics*, vol. 36, no. 7, article 664, 2004.

[4] T. Ohta, Y. Miyao, T. Ninomiya et al., "An intelligent search engine and GUI-based efficient MEDLINE search tool based on deep syntactic parsing," in *Proceedings of the COLING/ACL 2006 Interactive Presentation Sessions*, pp. 17–20, Association for Computational Linguistics, 2006.

[5] D. Rebholz-Schuhmann, H. Kirsch, M. Arregui, S. Gaudan, M. Riethoven, and P. Stoehr, "EBIMed—text crunching to gather facts for proteins from Medline," *Bioinformatics*, vol. 23, no. 2, pp. e237–e244, 2007.

[6] M. A. Hearst, A. Divoli, H. H. Guturu et al., "BioText search engine: beyond abstract search," *Bioinformatics*, vol. 23, no. 16, pp. 2196–2197, 2007.

[7] S. Xu, J. McCusker, and M. Krauthammer, "Yale Image Finder (YIF): a new search engine for retrieving biomedical images," *Bioinformatics*, vol. 24, no. 17, pp. 1968–1970, 2008.

[8] S. Agarwal, H. Yu, and I. Kohane, "BioNOT: a searchable database of biomedical negated sentences," *BMC Bioinformatics*, vol. 12, Article ID 420, 2011.

[9] J. Björne, F. Ginter, S. Pyysalo, J. Tsujii, and T. Salakoski, "Scaling up biomedical event extraction to the entire PubMed," in *Proceedings of the BioNLP Workshop Companion Volume for Shared Task*, pp. 28–36, Association for Computational Linguistics, 2010.

[10] S. Van Landeghem, F. Ginter, Y. Van de Peer, and T. Salakoski, "EVEX: a PubMed-scale resource for homology-based generalization of text mining predictions," in *Proceedings of the BioNLP Workshop Companion Volume for Shared Task*, pp. 28–37, Association for Computational Linguistics, 2011.

[11] R. Leaman and G. Gonzalez, "BANNER: an executable survey of advances in biomedical named entity recognition," *Pacific Symposium on Biocomputing. Pacific Symposium on Biocomputing*, pp. 652–663, 2011.

[12] J. Björne, F. Ginter, and T. Salakoski, "Generalizing biomedical event extraction," *BMC Bioinformatics*, vol. 13, supplement 8, article S4, 2012.

[13] The UniProt Consortium, "Ongoing and future developments at the universal protein resource," *Nucleic Acids Research*, vol. 39, supplement 1, pp. D214–D219, 2011.

[14] E. W. Sayers, T. Barrett, D. A. Benson et al., "Database resources of the National Center for Biotechnology Information," *Nucleic Acids Research*, vol. 38, supplement 1, pp. D5–D16, 2009.

[15] P. Flicek, M. R. Amode, D. Barrell et al., "Ensembl 2011," *Nucleic Acids Research*, vol. 39, no. 1, pp. D800–D806, 2011.

[16] P. J. Kersey, D. Lawson, E. Birney et al., "Ensembl genomes: extending ensembl across the taxonomic space," *Nucleic Acids Research*, vol. 38, supplement 1, pp. D563–D569, 2009.

[17] K. Crammer and Y. Singer, "Ultraconservative online algorithms for multiclass problems," *Journal of Machine Learning Research*, vol. 3, no. 4-5, pp. 951–991, 2003.

[18] E. Segal, M. Shapira, A. Regev et al., "Module networks: identifying regulatory modules and their condition-specific regulators from gene expression data," *Nature Genetics*, vol. 34, no. 2, pp. 166–176, 2003.

[19] J. Björne, F. Ginter, S. Pyysalo, J. Tsujii, and T. Salakoski, "Complex event extraction at PubMed scale," *Bioinformatics*, vol. 26, no. 12, Article ID btq180, pp. i382–i390, 2010.

[20] S. Kaewphan, S. Kreula, S. Van Landeghem, Y. Van de Peer, P. Jones, and F. Ginter, "Integrating large-scale text mining and co-expression networks: targeting NADP(H) metabolism in *E. coli* with event extraction," in *Proceedings of the 3rd Workshop on Building and Evaluating Resources for Biomedical Text Mining (BioTxtM '12)*, 2012.

[21] T. Ohta, S. Pyysalo, and J. Tsujii, "From pathways to biomolecular events: opportunities and challenges," in *Proceedings of the BioNLP Workshop Companion Volume for Shared Task*, pp. 105–113, Association for Computational Linguistics, 2011.

[22] J. A. Carballo and R. S. Cha, "Meiotic roles of Mec1, a budding yeast homolog of mammalian ATR/ATM," *Chromosome Research*, vol. 15, no. 5, pp. 539–550, 2007.

[23] Y. Loewenstein, D. Raimondo, O. C. Redfern et al., "Protein function annotation by homology-based inference," *Genome Biology*, vol. 10, no. 2, article 207, 2009.

[24] S. Proost, M. Van Bel, L. Sterck et al., "PLAZA: a comparative genomics resource to study gene and genome evolution in plants," *Plant Cell*, vol. 21, no. 12, pp. 3718–3731, 2009.

[25] R. Kato and H. Ogawa, "An essential gene, ESR1, is required for mitotic cell growth, DNA repair and meiotic recombination in Saccharomyces cerevisiae," *Nucleic Acids Research*, vol. 22, no. 15, pp. 3104–3112, 1994.

[26] P. Stenetorp, G. Topić, S. Pyysalo, T. Ohta, J.-D. Kim, and J. Tsujii, "BioNLP Shared Task 2011: supporting resources," in

Proceedings of the BioNLP Workshop Companion Volume for Shared Task, pp. 112–120, Portland, Oregon, USA, 2011.

[27] J. Björne and T. Salakoski, "Generalizing biomedical event extraction," in *Proceedings of the BioNLP Workshop Companion Volume for Shared Task*, pp. 183–191, Association for Computational Linguistics, 2011.

[28] S. Pyysalo, T. Ohta, and J. Tsujii, "Overview of the entity relations (REL) supporting task of BioNLP Shared Task 2011," in *Proceedings of the BioNLP Workshop Companion Volume for Shared Task*, pp. 83–88, Association for Computational Linguistics, 2011.

[29] S. Van Landeghem, J. Björne, T. Abeel, B. De Baets, T. Salakoski, and Y. Van de Peer, "Semantically linking molecular entities in literature through entity relationships," *BMC Bioinformatics*, vol. 13, supplement 8, article S6, 2012.

[30] Z. Lu, H. Y. Kao, C. H. Wei et al., "The gene normalization task in BioCreative III," *BMC Bioinformatics*, vol. 12, supplement 8, article S2, 2011.

14

Intervention in Biological Phenomena via Feedback Linearization

Mohamed Amine Fnaiech,[1] Hazem Nounou,[1] Mohamed Nounou,[2] and Aniruddha Datta[3]

[1] Electrical and Computer Engineering Program, Texas A&M University at Qatar, P.O. Box 23874, Doha, Qatar
[2] Chemical Engineering Program, Texas A&M University at Qatar, P.O. Box 23874, Doha, Qatar
[3] Department of Electrical and Computer Engineering, Texas A&M University, College Station, TX 77843, USA

Correspondence should be addressed to Hazem Nounou, hazem.nounou@qatar.tamu.edu

Academic Editor: Erchin Serpedin

The problems of modeling and intervention of biological phenomena have captured the interest of many researchers in the past few decades. The aim of the therapeutic intervention strategies is to move an undesirable state of a diseased network towards a more desirable one. Such an objective can be achieved by the application of drugs to act on some genes/metabolites that experience the undesirable behavior. For the purpose of design and analysis of intervention strategies, mathematical models that can capture the complex dynamics of the biological systems are needed. S-systems, which offer a good compromise between accuracy and mathematical flexibility, are a promising framework for modeling the dynamical behavior of biological phenomena. Due to the complex nonlinear dynamics of the biological phenomena represented by S-systems, nonlinear intervention schemes are needed to cope with the complexity of the nonlinear S-system models. Here, we present an intervention technique based on feedback linearization for biological phenomena modeled by S-systems. This technique is based on perfect knowledge of the S-system model. The proposed intervention technique is applied to the glycolytic-glycogenolytic pathway, and simulation results presented demonstrate the effectiveness of the proposed technique.

1. Introduction

Biological systems are complex processes with nonlinear dynamics. S-systems are proposed in [1, 2] as a canonical nonlinear model to capture the dynamical behavior of a large class of biological phenomena [3, 4]. They are characterized by a good tradeoff between accuracy and mathematical flexibility [5]. In this modeling approach, nonlinear systems are approximated by products of power-law functions which are derived from multivariate linearization in logarithmic coordinates. It has been shown that this type of representation is a valid description of biological processes in a variety of settings. S-systems have been proposed in the literature to mathematically capture the behavior of genetic regulatory networks [6–13]. Moreover, the problem of estimating the S-system model parameters, the rate coefficients and the kinetic orders, has been addressed by several researchers [12, 14–16]. In [17], the authors studied the controllability of S-systems based on feedback linearization approach.

Recently, the authors in [18] developed two different intervention strategies, namely, indirect and direct, for biological phenomena modeled by S-systems. The goal of these intervention strategies is to transfer the target variables from an initial steady-state level to a desired final one by manipulating the control variables. The complexity of the nonlinear biological models led researchers to focus on nonlinear control approaches, such as sliding mode control that was introduced in [19].

A basic problem in control theory is how to use feedback in order to modify the original internal dynamics of nonlinear systems to achieve some prescribed behavior [20]. In particular, feedback linearization can be used for the purpose of imposing, on the associated closed-loop system, a desired behavior of some prescribed autonomous linear system. When the system to be controlled is linear time-invariant system, this is known as the problem of pole placement, while in the more general case of nonlinear systems, this is known as the problem of feedback linearization [21, 22].

Significant advances have been made in the theory of non-linear state feedback control, such as feedback linearization and input-output decoupling techniques [21, 22]. The state feedback linearization technique has been widely utilized in many applications. For example, the authors in [23] have used feedback linearization in cancer therapy, where full knowledge of the state and parameter vectors is assumed to transform a multiinput multioutput nonlinear system into a linear and controllable one using nonlinear state feedback. Then, linear control techniques can be applied for the resulting system [22, 24].

Hence, in this paper we consider the problem designing a nonlinear intervention strategy based on feedback linearization for biological phenomena modeled by S-systems. In this proposed algorithm, the control variables are designed such that an integral action is added to the system. The main advantage of the integral action is in improving the steady state performance of the closed-loop system. As a case study, the proposed intervention strategy is applied to a glycolytic-glycogenolytic pathway model. The glycolytic-glycogenolytic pathway model is selected as it plays an important role in cellular energy generation when the level of glucose in the blood is low (fasting state) and glycogen has to be broken down to provide the substrate to run glycolysis. By controlling the glycogenolytic reaction, one can exert control over whether glycolysis will run or not under low-glucose conditions.

This paper is organized as follows. In Section 2, the S-system model is presented and the control problem is formulated. In Section 3, some mathematical preliminaries as well as the feedback linearizable control scheme are presented. In Section 4, the glycolytic-glycogenolytic pathway model is considered as a case study. Finally, concluding remarks and possible future research directions are outlined in Section 5.

2. S-System Presentation and Problem Formulation

Consider the following S-system model [25]:

$$\dot{x}_i = \alpha_i \prod_{j=1}^{N+m} x_j^{\theta_{ij}} - \beta_i \prod_{j=1}^{N+m} x_j^{\mu_{ij}}, \quad i = 1, 2, \ldots, N, \quad (1)$$

where $\alpha_i > 0$ and $\beta_i > 0$ are rate coefficients and θ_{ij} and μ_{ij} are kinetic orders and there exist $N + m$ variables (genes/metabolites) where the first N variables are dependent and the remaining m variables are independent variables. Assume that p out of the N dependent variables are target (or output) variables (i.e., genes/metabolites that need to be regulated to some desired final values), where these output variables are defined as

$$y_j = x_i, \quad j = 1, \ldots, p, \quad (2)$$

and $i \in \mathcal{Y} \subset \{1, \ldots, N\}$, where $\mathcal{Y}$ is the set of indices corresponding to the dependent variables that are selected as output variables. The steady-state analysis of the S-system model [1, 18] shows that when the number of dependent variables with prespecified desired values is equal to the

number of independent variables (which means that we have enough degrees of freedom), the above S-system model equations will have a unique steady-state solution under the nonsingularity assumption. Hence, in order to control the expressions/concentrations of the target variables, we consider an integral control approach where the following r equations are added to the above S-system:

$$\dot{x}_i = u_j, \quad j = 1, \ldots, p, \quad (3)$$

where $i \in \mathcal{U} \subset \{N + 1, \ldots, N + m\}$, where $\mathcal{U}$ is the set of indices corresponding to the independent variables that are used as control variables. This means that r out of the m independent variables will be used as control variables, and the overall system will have p inputs and p outputs. It should be noted that the formulation above can be easily extended to deal with systems having more inputs than outputs. Let us denote by $\mathcal{X} = \{1, \ldots, N\} + \mathcal{U}$, where $\mathcal{X}$ corresponds to the indices of all variables except the independent variables that are not used as control variables. Here, it is assumed that the values (expressions/concentrations) of the independent variables that are not used as control variables are known constants (i.e., $x_i = \delta_i$, $i \in \{N + 1, \ldots, N + m\} - \mathcal{U}$, where δ_i are known constants) [6].

Figure 1 shows the S-system (1) augmented by the integral control. The S-system with integral control (1)–(3) can be written in the form

$$\dot{x} = f(x) + g(x)u,$$
$$y = h(x), \quad (4)$$

where $x = [x_i]^T \in \mathbb{R}^{N+p}$, $i \in \mathcal{X}$, $u = [u_1, \ldots, u_p]^T \in \mathbb{R}^p$, $y = [y_1, \ldots, y_p]^T \in \mathbb{R}^p$ and

$$f(x) = \begin{bmatrix} \alpha_1 \prod_{j=1}^{N+m} x_j^{\theta_{1j}} - \beta_1 \prod_{j=1}^{N+m} x_j^{\mu_{1j}} \\ \vdots \\ \alpha_N \prod_{j=1}^{N+m} x_j^{\theta_{Nj}} - \beta_N \prod_{j=1}^{N+m} x_j^{\mu_{Nj}} \\ 0 \\ \vdots \\ 0 \end{bmatrix} \Big\} p, \quad (5)$$

$$g(x) = \begin{bmatrix} 0_{N \times p} \\ I_{p \times p} \end{bmatrix}, \quad h(x) = [x_i]^T, \quad i \in \mathcal{Y},$$

which can be expressed as

$$\dot{x} = f(x) + \sum_{i=1}^{p} g_i(x) u_i, \quad (6)$$

$$y_i = h_i(x), \quad (7)$$

where $g_i(x) = [0_1, 0_2, \ldots, 0_{N+i-1}, 1_{N+i}, 0_{N+i+1}, \ldots, 0_{N+p}]^T$, for $i = 1, \ldots, p$.

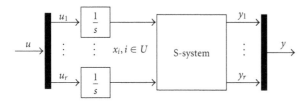

FIGURE 1: S-system with integral control architecture.

Problem Formulation. Suppose that the outputs of the S-system (1) are initially at the steady-state condition y_{0_j}, $j = 1, \ldots, p$. Let us denote by y_{d_j}, $j = 1, \ldots, p$, the desired final steady state values of the output (target) variables. Then, the main goal of the feedback linearizable controller is to determinate the control inputs u_j, $j = 1, \ldots, p$, that can guide the target variables from the initial steady-state condition to the final one [18].

3. Feedback Linearizable Intervention

Here, we show how feedback linearization can be utilized to design a nonlinear intervention strategy to control biological phenomena modeled by S-systems. Feedback linearization can be used to obtain a linear relationship between the output vector y and a new input vector v, by making a right choice of the linearizing law. Once the equivalent model becomes linear, we may design a dynamic control law-based classical linear control theory. Before starting the development of this control technique, it is important to introduce the following mathematical preliminaries [20–22].

3.1. Mathematical Preliminaries. Let the vector function $f : \Re^n \to \Re^n$ be a vector field in $\Re^n$. The vector function $f(x)$ is called a smooth vector function if it has continuous partial derivatives of any required order [26]. Given a scalar function $h(x)$ and a vector field $f(x)$, we define a new scalar function $L_f h$, called the Lie derivative of h with respect to f, as follows.

Definition 1 (see [26]). Let $h : \Re^n \to \Re$ be a smooth scalar function, and $f : \Re^n \to \Re^n$ be a smooth vector field on $\Re^n$, then the Lie derivative of h with respect to f is a scalar function defined by $L_f h = \nabla h f$.

Thus, the Lie derivative $L_f h$ is simply the directional derivative of h along the direction of the vector f. Repeated Lie derivatives can be defined recursively as follows:

$$L_f^{(0)} h = h,$$

$$L_f^{(i)} h = L_f \left(L_f^{(i-1)} h \right) = \nabla \left(L_f^{(i-1)} h \right) f, \quad \text{for } i = 1, 2, \ldots. \tag{8}$$

Similarly, if g is another vector field, then the scalar function $L_g L_f h(x)$ can be described as

$$L_g L_f h = \nabla \left(L_f h \right) g. \tag{9}$$

Definition 2 (see [26]). Let f and g be two vector fields on $\Re^n$. The Lie bracket of f and g is a third vector field defined by

$$[f, g] = \nabla g f - \nabla f g, \tag{10}$$

where the Lie bracket $[f, g]$ is commonly written as $\text{ad}_f g$ (where ad stands for "adjoint").

Repeated Lie brackets can then be defined recursively by $\text{ad}_f^{(0)} g = g, \ldots, \text{ad}_f^{(i)} g = [f, \text{ad}_f^{(i-1)} g]$.

3.2. Feedback Linearizable Controller. Consider the S-system model (6). Differentiating the jth output y_j of this system with respect to time, we get

$$\dot{y}_j = L_f h_j(x) + \sum_{i=1}^{p} \left(L_{g_i} h_j(x) \right) u_i, \tag{11}$$

for $j = 1, 2, 3, \ldots p$. Note in (7) that if each of the $L_{g_i} h_j(x) = 0$, then the inputs do not appear in the equation. Define y_j to be the smallest integer such that at least one of the inputs appears in $y_j^{(\gamma_j)}$, that is

$$y_i^{(\gamma_j)} = L_f^{(\gamma_j)} h_j(x) + \sum_{i=1}^{p} L_{g_i} \left(L_f^{(\gamma_j - 1)} h_j(x) \right) u_i, \tag{12}$$

with at least one of the $L_{g_i}(L_f^{(\gamma_j-1)} h_j) \neq 0$, for some x. Let the $p \times p$ matrix $D(x)$ be defined as

$$D(x) = \begin{pmatrix} L_{g_1} L_f^{(\gamma_1-1)} h_1 & L_{g_2} L_f^{(\gamma_1-1)} h_1 & \cdots & L_{g_p} L_f^{(\gamma_1-1)} h_1 \\ L_{g_1} L_f^{(\gamma_2-1)} h_2 & L_{g_2} L_f^{(\gamma_2-1)} h_2 & \cdots & L_{g_p} L_f^{(\gamma_2-1)} h_2 \\ \vdots & \vdots & & \vdots \\ L_{g_1} L_f^{(\gamma_p-1)} h_p & L_{g_2} L_f^{(\gamma_p-1)} h_p & \cdots & L_{g_p} L_f^{(\gamma_p-1)} h_p \end{pmatrix}. \tag{13}$$

Based on the above definitions, the relative degree for multi-input multioutput (MIMO) systems is defined next.

Definition 3 (see [27]). The system (6)-(7) is said to have vector relative degree $\gamma_1, \gamma_2, \ldots, \gamma_p$ at x_0 if $L_{g_i} L_f^{(k)} h_i(x) \equiv 0$, $0 \leq k \leq \gamma_i - 2$, for $i = 1, \ldots, p$ and the matrix $D(x_0)$ is nonsingular.

If a system has well-defined vector relative degree, then (12) can be expressed as

$$\left[y_1^{(\gamma_1)}, y_2^{(\gamma_2)}, \ldots, y_p^{(\gamma_p)} \right]^T = \xi(x) + D(x)u, \tag{14}$$

where

$$\xi(x) = \left[L_f^{(\gamma_1)} h_1(x), L_f^{(\gamma_2)} h_2(x), \ldots, L_f^{(\gamma_p)} h_p(x) \right]^T. \tag{15}$$

Since $D(x_0)$ is nonsingular, it follows that $D(x) \in \Re^{p \times p}$ is bounded away from nonsingularity for $x \in U$, a neighborhood U of x_0. Then, the state feedback control law

$$u = D(x)^{-1}(-\xi(x) + v) \tag{16}$$

yields the linear closed-loop system

$$y_i^{(\gamma_j)} = v_i. \tag{17}$$

The block diagram of the linearized system is shown in Figure 2.

Feedback linearization transforms the system into a linear system where linear control approaches can be applied. Here, v represents the new input vector of the linearized system.

In the case the system has vector relative degree, where $\gamma_1 + \cdots + \gamma_p = n$, the nonlinear system can be converted into a controllable linear system, where the feedback control law is defined in (16) and the coordinate transformation is $\xi(x) = [L_f^{(j)} h_i(x)]^T$, $0 \le j \le \gamma_i - 1$, $0 \le i \le p$. Let the following distributions be defined as [27]

$$G_0(x) = \text{span}\{g_1(x), \ldots, g_p(x)\},$$

$$G_1(x) = \text{span}\{g_1(x), \ldots, g_p(x), \text{ad}_f g_1, \ldots, \text{ad}_f g_p(x)\},$$

$$\vdots$$

$$G_i(x) = \text{span}\{\text{ad}_f^{(k)} g_i(x) : 0 \le k \le i, 0 \le j \le p\}, \tag{18}$$

for $i = 1, \ldots, n - 1$, then we have the following result.

Proposition 4 (see [27]). *Suppose that the matrix $g(x_0)$ has rank p. Then, there exist p functions $\lambda_1, \ldots, \lambda_p$, such that the system*

$$\dot{x} = f(x) + g(x)u,$$
$$y = \lambda(x), \tag{19}$$

has vector relative degree $(\gamma_1, \ldots, \gamma_p)$ with $\gamma_1 + \gamma_2 + \cdots + \gamma_p = n$ if

(i) *for each $0 \le i \le n - 1$ the distribution G_i has constant dimension in the neighborhood U of x_0;*

(ii) *the dimension G_{n-1} has dimension n;*

(iii) *for each $0 \le i \le n - 2$ the dimension G_i is involutive.*

The proof of this proposition can be found in [27].

The new control vector $v = [v_1, \ldots, v_p]^T$ is designed based on the desired closed-loop response, which can be written as

$$v_j = y_{d_j}^{(\gamma_j)} + k_{\gamma_j - 1}\left(y_{d_j}^{(\gamma_j - 1)} - y_j^{(\gamma_j - 1)}\right) + \cdots + k_1\left(y_{d_j} - y_j\right) \tag{20}$$

for $j = 1, \ldots, p$, where $\{y_{d_j}, y_{d_j}^{(1)}, \ldots, y_{d_j}^{(\gamma_j - 1)}, y_{d_j}^{(\gamma_j)}\}$ denotes the desired reference trajectories for the outputs. The proportional gains are chosen such that the following polynomial is a Hurwitz polynomial [28]:

$$s^{\gamma_j} + k_{\gamma_j - 1}s^{\gamma_j - 1} + \cdots + k_2 s + k_1 = 0. \tag{21}$$

The block diagram of the closed-loop system in the feedback linearizable form is shown in Figure 3.

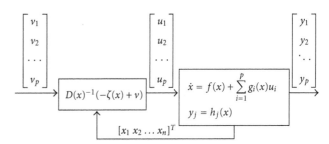

FIGURE 2: Diagram block of the linearizable system.

4. Case Study

In this section, we demonstrate the efficacy of the feedback linearizable intervention approach described in this paper by applying it to a well-studied biological pathway model representing the glycolytic-glycogenolytic pathway shown in Figure 4 [17, 29]. Glycolysis is the process of breaking up a six-carbon glucose molecule into two molecules of a three-carbon compound, and glycogenolysis is the process by which the stored glycogen in the body is broken up to meet the needs for glucose. In glycogenolysis, the phosphorylase enzyme acts on the polysaccharide glycogen to reduce its length by one glucose unit. The glucose unit is released as a glucose-1 phosphate. The glycolytic-glycogenolytic pathway can be mathematically represented by the following S-system model:

$$\dot{x}_1 = \alpha_1 x_4^{\theta_{14}} x_6^{\theta_{16}} - \beta_1 x_1^{\mu_{11}} x_2^{\mu_{12}} x_7^{\mu_{17}},$$

$$\dot{x}_2 = \alpha_2 x_1^{\theta_{21}} x_2^{\theta_{22}} x_5^{\theta_{25}} x_7^{\theta_{27}} x_{10}^{\theta_{210}} - \beta_2 x_2^{\mu_{22}} x_3^{\mu_{23}} x_8^{\mu_{28}}, \tag{22}$$

$$\dot{x}_3 = \alpha_3 x_2^{\theta_{32}} x_3^{\theta_{33}} x_8^{\theta_{38}} - \beta_3 x_3^{\mu_{33}} x_9^{\mu_{39}}.$$

In this case, $N = 3$, $m = 7$ and the parameter are defined as $\alpha_1 = 0.077884314$, $\theta_{14} = 0.66$, $\theta_{16} = 1$, $\beta_1 = 1.06270825$, $\mu_{11} = 1.53$, $\mu_{12} = -0.59$, $\mu_{17} = 1$, $\alpha_2 = 0.585012402$, $\theta_{21} = 0.95$, $\theta_{22} = -0.41$, $\theta_{25} = 0.32$, $\theta_{27} = 0.62$, $\theta_{210} = 0.38$, $\beta_2 = \alpha_3 = 0.0007934561$, $\mu_{22} = \theta_{32} = 3.97$, $\mu_{23} = \theta_{33} = -3.06$, $\mu_{28} = \theta_{38} = 1$, $\beta_3 = 1.05880847$, $\mu_{33} = 0.3$, and $\mu_{39} = 1$. Here, the model variables are defined as follows: x_1 is glucose-1-P, x_2 is glucose-6-P, x_3 is fructose-6-P, x_4 is inorganic phosphate ion, x_5 is glucose, x_6 is phosphorylase a, x_7 is phosphoglucomutase, x_8 is phosphoglucose isomerase, x_9 is phosphofructokinase, and x_{10} is glucokinase.

For this model, the metabolites x_4 through x_{10} are defined as independent variables, which are the variables that are not affected by other variables, and the metabolites x_1 through x_3 are defined as the dependent variables, which are the primary variables of interest that we wish to control. Here, we choose the independent variables x_4, x_5, and x_8 as manipulated or control variables, as shown in Figure 4, as they can affect the production of the dependent variables x_1, x_2, and x_3. Also, we choose to keep the independent variables x_6, x_7, x_9, and x_{10} fixed ignoring their effect on the controlled variables, and assuming that the controller only uses the independent variables x_4, x_5, and x_8 to control the dependent variables x_1, x_2, and x_3. The independent variables have the following values $x_4 = 10$, $x_5 = 5$, $x_6 = 3$, $x_7 = 40$, $x_8 = 136$,

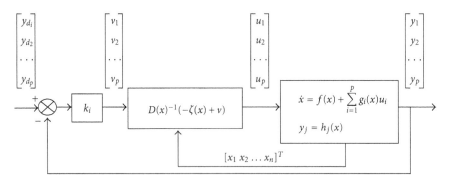

FIGURE 3: Closed loop of the linearizable system.

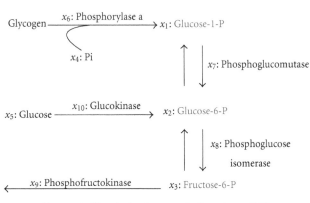

FIGURE 4: Glycolytic-glycogenolytic pathway [29].

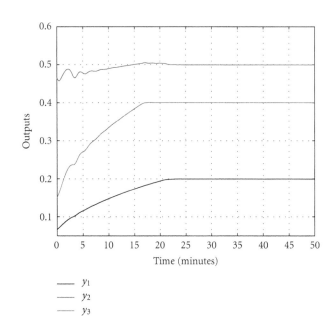

FIGURE 5: Closed-loop outputs for constant reference signals.

$x_9 = 2.86$, and $x_{10} = 4$. Here, we try to control x_1, x_2, and x_3 by manipulating x_4, x_5, and x_8, so we have

$$
\begin{aligned}
y_1 &= x_1, \\
y_2 &= x_2, \\
y_3 &= x_3, \\
\dot{x}_4 &= u_1, \\
\dot{x}_5 &= u_2, \\
\dot{x}_8 &= u_3,
\end{aligned}
\tag{23}
$$

and all other $x_i's$ for $i = 6, 7, 9$, and 10 are kept fixed. The initial values of the outputs y_1, y_2, and y_3 are selected as 0.067, 0.465, and 0.150, respectively, and the desired reference outputs are selected as $y_{d1} = 0.2$, $y_{d2} = 0.5$, and $y_{d3} = 0.4$.

Hence, the overall system can be expressed in the form of (6), where

$$
f(x) = \begin{bmatrix}
a_1 x_4^{\theta_{14}} - b_1 x_1^{\mu_{11}} x_2^{\mu_{12}} \\
a_2 x_1^{\theta_{21}} x_2^{\theta_{22}} x_5^{\theta_{25}} - b_2 x_2^{\mu_{22}} x_3^{\mu_{23}} x_8^{\mu_{28}} \\
a_3 x_2^{\theta_{32}} x_3^{\theta_{33}} x_8^{\theta_{38}} - b_3 x_3^{\mu_{33}} \\
0 \\
0 \\
0
\end{bmatrix},
$$

$$
g(x) = \left[g_1(x), g_2(x), g_3(x) \right]
$$

$$
= \begin{bmatrix}
0 & 0 & 0 & 1 & 0 & 0 \\
0 & 0 & 0 & 0 & 1 & 0 \\
0 & 0 & 0 & 0 & 0 & 1
\end{bmatrix}^T,
$$

$$
h(x) = \begin{bmatrix} h_1(x) \\ h_2(x) \\ h_3(x) \end{bmatrix} = \begin{bmatrix}
1 & 0 & 0 & 0 & 0 & 0 \\
0 & 1 & 0 & 0 & 0 & 0 \\
0 & 0 & 1 & 0 & 0 & 0
\end{bmatrix},
\tag{24}
$$

where $a_1 = \alpha_1 x_6^{\theta_{16}}$, $a_2 = \alpha_2 x_7^{\theta_{27}} x_{10}^{\theta_{210}}$, $a_3 = \alpha_3$, $b_1 = \beta_1 x_7^{\mu_{17}}$, $b_2 = \beta_2$, and $b_3 = \beta_3 x_9^{\mu_{39}}$.

Based on the S-system model describing the glycolytic-glycogenolytic pathway, it can be verified that the outputs need to be differentiated twice with respect to time so that the input variables (u_1, u_2, or u_3) appear in the expressions of differentiated outputs, as follows:

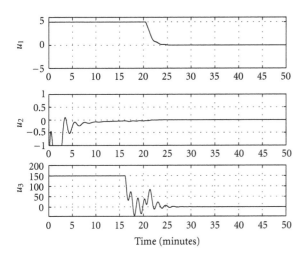

FIGURE 6: Control signals for constant reference signals.

$$y_1^{(2)} = L_f^{(2)} h_1(x) + L_{g_1}\left(L_f h_1(x)\right) u_1,$$

$$y_2^{(2)} = L_f^{(2)} h_2(x) + L_{g_2}\left(L_f h_2(x)\right) u_2 + L_{g_3}\left(L_f h_2(x)\right) u_3,$$

$$y_3^{(2)} = L_f^{(2)} h_3(x) + L_{g_3}\left(L_f h_3(x)\right) u_3,$$

$$\tag{25}$$

where

$$L_f^{(2)} h_1(x) = b_1^2 \mu_{11} x_1^{2\mu_{11}-1} x_2^{2\mu_{12}}$$
$$- b_1 a_1 \mu_{11} x_1^{\mu_{11}-1} x_2^{\mu_{12}} x_4^{\theta_{14}}$$
$$+ b_1 b_2 \mu_{12} x_2^{\mu_{12}+\mu_{22}-1} x_1^{\mu_{11}} x_3^{\mu_{23}} x_8^{\mu_{28}}$$
$$- b_1 a_2 \mu_{12} x_2^{\mu_{12}+\theta_{21}-1} x_1^{\mu_{11}+\theta_{21}} x_5^{\theta_{25}},$$

$$L_f^{(2)} \mu_2(x) = a_1 a_2 \theta_{21} x_1^{\theta_{21}-1} x_2^{\theta_{22}} x_4^{\theta_{14}} x_5^{\theta_{25}}$$
$$- a_2 b_1 x_1^{\theta_{21}+\mu_{11}-1} x_2^{\theta_{22}+\mu_{12}} x_5^{\theta_{25}}$$
$$+ a_2^2 \theta_{22} x_2^{2\theta_{22}-1} x_1^{2\theta_{21}} x_5^{\theta_{25}}$$
$$- a_2 b_2 x_2^{\theta_{22}+\mu_{22}-1} x_1^{\theta_{21}} x_3^{\mu_{23}} x_5^{\theta_{25}} x_8^{\mu_{28}}$$
$$- b_2 a_2 \mu_{22} x_2^{\theta_{12}} x_2^{\mu_{22}+\theta_{22}-1} x_3^{\mu_{23}} x_5^{\theta_{25}} x_8^{\mu_{28}}$$
$$+ b_2^2 \mu_{22} x_2^{2\mu_{22}-1} x_3^{2\mu_{23}} x_8^{2\mu_{28}}$$
$$- b_2 a_3 \mu_{23} x_2^{\mu_{22}+\theta_{32}} x_3^{\mu_{23}+\theta_{33}-1} x_8^{\mu_{28}+\theta_{38}}$$
$$+ b_2 b_3 \mu_{23} x_2^{\mu_{22}} x_3^{\mu_{23}+\mu_{33}-1} x_8^{\mu_{28}},$$

$$L_f^{(2)} \mu_3(x) = a_3 a_2 \theta_{32} x_1^{\theta_{21}} x_2^{\theta_{32}+\theta_{22}-1} x_3^{\theta_{33}} x_5^{\theta_{25}} x_8^{\theta_{38}}$$
$$- a_3 b_2 \theta_{32} x_2^{\theta_{32}+\mu_{22}-1} x_3^{\theta_{33}+\mu_{23}} x_8^{\theta_{38}+\mu_{28}}$$
$$+ a_3^2 \theta_{33} x_2^{2\theta_{32}} x_3^{2\theta_{33}-1} x_8^{2\theta_{38}}$$
$$- a_3 b_3 \theta_{33} x_2^{\theta_{32}} x_3^{\theta_{33}+\mu_{33}-1} x_8^{\theta_{38}}$$
$$- b_3 a_3 \mu_{33} x_2^{\theta_{32}} x_3^{\mu_{33}+\theta_{33}-1} x_8^{\theta_{38}}$$
$$+ b_3^2 \mu_{33} x_3^{2\mu_{33}-1},$$

$$L_{g_1}\left(L_f h_1(x)\right) = a_1 x_4^{\theta_{14}-1},$$

$$L_{g_2}\left(L_f h_2(x)\right) = a_2 \theta_{25} x_1^{\theta_{21}} x_2^{\theta_{22}} x_5^{\theta_{25}-1},$$

$$L_{g_3}\left(L_f h_2(x)\right) = - b_2 \mu_{28} x_2^{\mu_{22}} x_3^{\mu_{23}} x_8^{\mu_{28}-1},$$

$$L_{g_3}\left(L_f h_3(x)\right) = a_3 \theta_{38} x_2^{\theta_{32}} x_3^{\theta_{33}} x_8^{\theta_{38}-1}.$$

$$\tag{26}$$

Hence, in this case the system has vector relative degree $\gamma = [\gamma_1, \gamma_2, \gamma_3]^T = [2, 2, 2]^T$, and hence we have $\gamma_1 + \gamma_2 + \gamma_3 = 6$.

The matrix form of the system of differential equations presented in (25) can be written in the form of (14), where

$$\xi(x) = \left[L_f^{(2)} h_1(x), L_f^{(2)} h_2(x), L_f^{(2)} h_3(x)\right]^T,$$

$$D(x) = \begin{pmatrix} L_{g_1}\left(L_f h_1(x)\right) & 0 & 0 \\ 0 & L_{g_2}\left(L_f h_2(x)\right) & L_{g_3}\left(L_f h_2(x)\right) \\ 0 & 0 & L_{g_3}\left(L_f h_3(x)\right) \end{pmatrix}.$$

$$\tag{27}$$

The matrix $D(x)$ is invertible if the following condition is satisfied:

$$L_{g_1}\left(L_f h_1(x)\right) \times L_{g_2}\left(L_f h_2(x)\right) \times L_{g_3}\left(L_f h_3(x)\right) \neq 0. \tag{28}$$

Based on (25), it can be seen that the control variables u_1 and u_2 appear only in the expressions of $y_1^{(2)}$ and $y_2^{(2)}$, respectively. However, u_3 appears in the expressions of $y_2^{(2)}$ and $y_3^{(2)}$. Hence, u_1 and u_3 need to be used to control y_1 and y_3, respectively, and both u_2 and u_3 are needed to control y_2.

Hence, the control laws based on (16) can be expressed as

$$u_1 = \frac{\left(-L_f^{(2)} h_1(x) + v_1\right)}{L_{g_1}\left(L_f h_1(x)\right)},$$

$$u_2 = \frac{\left(-L_f^{(2)} h_2(x) - L_{g_3}\left(L_f h_3(x)\right) u_3 + v_2\right)}{L_{g_2}\left(L_f h_2(x)\right)}, \tag{29}$$

$$u_3 = \frac{\left(-L_f^{(2)} h_3(x) + v_3\right)}{L_{g_3}\left(L_f h_3(x)\right)}.$$

Substituting the expressions of the control variables (29) in (25), we obtain the following decoupled linear system:

$$y_1^{(2)} = v_1,$$

$$y_2^{(2)} = v_2, \tag{30}$$

$$y_3^{(2)} = v_3.$$

The new control variables v_j, for $j = 1, 2, 3$, need to be designed so that the target variables y_j track some desired reference trajectories, y_{d_j}.

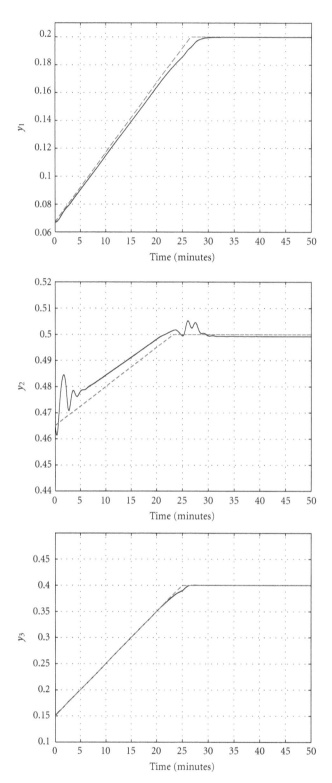

FIGURE 7: Output response for closed-loop tracking.

Using (20), the new control variables v_j, for $j = 1, 2, 3$, are found to be

$$v_1 = \ddot{y}_{d_1} + k_1(\dot{y}_{d_1} - \dot{y}_1) + k_{11}(y_{d_1} - y_1),$$
$$v_2 = \ddot{y}_{d_2} + k_2(\dot{y}_{d_2} - \dot{y}_2) + k_{21}(y_{d_2} - y_2), \qquad (31)$$
$$v_3 = \ddot{y}_{d_3} + k_3(\dot{y}_{d_3} - \dot{y}_3) + k_{31}(y_{d_3} - y_3).$$

The new control components, v_1, v_2, and v_3, are defined in (31), where the parameters are selected as $k_1 = 1$, $k_{11} = 5$, $k_2 = 10^{-3}$, $k_{21} = 20$, $k_3 = 3$, and $k_{31} = 5$.

Figures 5 and 6 show the output response and the control input signals when the feedback linearizable controller is applied. It is clear from Figure 5 that the system outputs

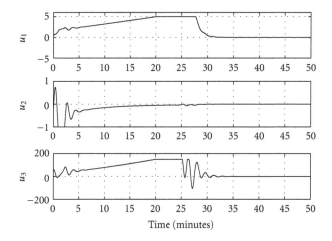

FIGURE 8: Control signals for closed-loop tracking.

converge to their desired values. Another simulation study is implemented for a different reference trajectory, where the value of the reference signal increases linearly before saturating at the desired final value. The closed-loop output response in this case is shown in Figure 7 and the control signals are shown in Figure 8. It is clear from Figure 7 that the feedback linearizable controller is driving the target variables to track the desired reference trajectories.

To study the robustness properties of the feedback linearizable controller, similar simulation studies have been conducted when the parameters μ_{22} and β_2 are varied within 10% of their nominal values. It has been found that the closed-loop system is stable only for parameter variations within 1% and with unacceptable performance. This agrees with our earlier assumption that full system knowledge is needed for proper operation of the feedback linearizable controller.

5. Conclusion

In this paper, feedback linearizable control has been applied for intervention of biological phenomena modeled in the S-system framework. As a case study, the glycogenolytic-glycolytic pathway model has been used to demonstrate the efficacy of feedback linearization in controlling biological phenomena modeled by S-system. One main drawback of this approach is that it assumes full knowledge of the biological system model. Usually, the S-system model does not perfectly represent the actual dynamics of the biological phenomena. Hence, one future research direction is to develop an adaptive intervention strategy that is capable of controlling the biological system even in the presence of model uncertainties. Another future research direction is to develop intervention techniques that take into account additional constraints due to the nature of the drug injection process. Definitely, incorporating such knowledge from medical practitioners would require imposing constraints on the magnitude, duration, and possibly the rate of change of the injected drug into the design of intervention technique.

Acknowledgments

This work was made possible by NPRP Grant NPRP08-148-3-051 from the Qatar National Research Fund (a Member of Qatar Foundation). The statements made herein are solely the responsibility of the authors.

References

[1] M. A. Savageau, "Biochemical systems analysis. I. Some mathematical properties of the rate law for the component enzymatic reactions," *Journal of Theoretical Biology*, vol. 25, no. 3, pp. 365–369, 1969.

[2] E. O. Voit, *Canonical Nonlinear Modeling: S-System Approach to Understanding Complexity*, Van Nostrand/Reinhold, New York, NY, USA, 1991.

[3] E. O. Voit, "A systems-theoretical framework for health and disease: inflammation and preconditioning from an abstract modeling point of view," *Mathematical Biosciences*, vol. 217, no. 1, pp. 11–18, 2009.

[4] E. O. Voit, F. Alvarez-Vasquez, and Y. A. Hannun, "Computational analysis of sphingolipid pathway systems," *Advances in Experimental Medicine and Biology*, vol. 688, pp. 264–275, 2010.

[5] R. Gentilini, "Toward integration of systems biology formalism: the gene regulatory networks case," *Genome informatics. International Conference on Genome Informatics.*, vol. 16, no. 2, pp. 215–224, 2005.

[6] E. O. Voit and J. Almeida, "Decoupling dynamical systems for pathway identification from metabolic profiles," *Bioinformatics*, vol. 20, no. 11, pp. 1670–1681, 2004.

[7] I. C. Chou, H. Martens, and E. O. Voit, "Parameter estimation in biochemical systems models with alternating regression," *Theoretical Biology and Medical Modelling*, vol. 3, article 25, 2006.

[8] T. Kitayama, A. Kinoshita, M. Sugimoto, Y. Nakayama, and M. Tomita, "A simplified method for power-law modelling of metabolic pathways from time-course data and steady-state flux profiles," *Theoretical Biology and Medical Modelling*, vol. 3, article 24, 2006.

[9] L. Qian and H. Wang, "Inference of genetic regulatory networks by evolutionary algorithm and H_∞ filtering," in *Proceedings of the IEEE/SP 14th WorkShoP on Statistical Signal Processing (SSP '07)*, pp. 21–25, August 2007.

[10] J. Vera, R. Curto, M. Cascante, and N. V. Torres, "Detection of potential enzyme targets by metabolic modelling and optimization: application to a simple enzymopathy," *Bioinformatics*, vol. 23, no. 17, pp. 2281–2289, 2007.

[11] H. Wang, L. Qian, and E. R. Dougherty, "Steady-state analysis of genetic regulatory networks modeled by nonlinear ordinary differential equations," in *Proceedings of the IEEE Symposium on Computational Intelligence in Bioinformatics and Computational Biology (CIBCB '09)*, pp. 182–185, April 2009.

[12] H. Wang, L. Qian, and E. Dougherty, "Inference of gene regulatory networks using S-system: a unified approach," *IET Systems Biology*, vol. 4, no. 2, pp. 145–156, 2010.

[13] A. Marin-Sanguino, S. K. Gupta, E. O. Voit, and J. Vera, "Biochemical pathway modeling tools for drug target detection in cancer and other complex diseases," *Methods in Enzymology*, vol. 487, pp. 319–369, 2011.

[14] O. R. Gonzalez, C. Küper, K. Jung, P. C. Naval, and E. Mendoza, "Parameter estimation using simulated annealing

for S-system models of biochemical networks," *Bioinformatics*, vol. 23, no. 4, pp. 480–486, 2007.

[15] Z. Kutalik, W. Tucker, and V. Moulton, "S-system parameter estimation for noisy metabolic profiles using Newton-flow analysis," *IET Systems Biology*, vol. 1, no. 3, pp. 174–180, 2007.

[16] I. C. Chou and E. O. Voit, "Recent developments in parameter estimation and structure identification of biochemical and genomic systems," *Mathematical Biosciences*, vol. 219, no. 2, pp. 57–83, 2009.

[17] A. Ervadi-Radhakrishnan and E. O. Voit, "Controllability of non-linear biochemical systems," *Mathematical Biosciences*, vol. 196, no. 1, pp. 99–123, 2005.

[18] N. Meskin, H. N. Nounou, M. Nounou, A. Datta, and E. R. Dougherty, "Intervention in biological phenomena modeled by S-systems," *IEEE Transactions on Biomedical Engineering*, vol. 58, no. 5, pp. 1260–1267, 2011.

[19] A. G. Hernández, L. Fridman, A. Levant, Y. Shtessel, S. I. Andrade, and C. R. Monsalve, "High order sliding mode controller for blood glucose in type 1 diabetes, with relative degree fluctuations," in *Proceedings of the 11th International Workshop on Variable Structure Systems (VSS '10)*, pp. 416–421, June 2010.

[20] A. Isidori, A. J. Krener, C. Gori-Giorgi, and S. Monaco, "Nonlinear decoupling via feedback: a differential geometric approach," *IEEE Transactions on Automatic Control*, vol. 26, no. 2, pp. 331–345, 1981.

[21] A. Isidori, *Nonlinear Control Systems*, Springer, 1989.

[22] A. Isidori and M. D. Benedetto, *Feedback Linearization of Nonlinear Systems*, Taylor Francis Group-CRC Press, 2010.

[23] T. L. Chien, C. C. Chen, and C. J. Huang, "Feedback linearization control and its application to MIMO cancer immunotherapy," *IEEE Transactions on Control Systems Technology*, vol. 18, no. 4, pp. 953–961, 2010.

[24] B. Jakubczyk and W. Respondek, "On linearization of control systems," *Bulletin de l'Académie Polonaise des Sciences, Série des Sciences Mathématiques*, vol. 28, pp. 517–522, 1980.

[25] E. O. Voit, *Computational Analysis of Biochemical Systems. A Practical Guide for Biochemists and Molecular Biologists*, Cambridge University Press, 2000.

[26] J. J. E. Slotine and W. Li, *Applied Nonlinear Control*, Pearson Education, 1991.

[27] S. Sastry, *Nonlinear Systems: Analysis, Stability and Control*, Springer, 1999.

[28] R. Marino and P. Tomei, "Global adaptive output-feedback control of nonlinear systems, part II. Nonlinear parameterization," *IEEE Transactions on Automatic Control*, vol. 38, no. 1, pp. 33–48, 1993.

[29] N. V. Torres, "Modelization and experimental studies on the control of the glycolytic- glycogenolytic pathway in rat liver," *Molecular and Cellular Biochemistry*, vol. 132, no. 2, pp. 117–126, 1994.

15

BioEve Search: A Novel Framework to Facilitate Interactive Literature Search

Syed Toufeeq Ahmed,[1] Hasan Davulcu,[2] Sukru Tikves,[2] Radhika Nair,[2] and Zhongming Zhao[1,3]

[1] *Department of Biomedical Informatics, Vanderbilt University, Nashville, TN 37232, USA*
[2] *Department of Computer Science and Engineering, Arizona State University, Tempe, AZ 85281, USA*
[3] *Department of Cancer Biology, Vanderbilt University School of Medicine, Nashville, TN 37232, USA*

Correspondence should be addressed to Syed Toufeeq Ahmed, syed.t.ahmed@vanderbilt.edu

Academic Editor: Jin-Dong Kim

Background. Recent advances in computational and biological methods in last two decades have remarkably changed the scale of biomedical research and with it began the unprecedented growth in both the production of biomedical data and amount of published literature discussing it. An automated extraction system coupled with a cognitive search and navigation service over these document collections would not only save time and effort, but also pave the way to discover hitherto unknown information implicitly conveyed in the texts. *Results.* We developed a novel framework (named "BioEve") that seamlessly integrates Faceted Search (Information Retrieval) with Information Extraction module to provide an interactive search experience for the researchers in life sciences. It enables guided step-by-step search query refinement, by suggesting concepts and entities (like genes, drugs, and diseases) to quickly filter and modify search direction, and thereby facilitating an enriched paradigm where user can discover related concepts and keywords to search while information seeking. *Conclusions.* The BioEve Search framework makes it easier to enable scalable interactive search over large collection of textual articles and to discover knowledge hidden in thousands of biomedical literature articles with ease.

1. Background

Human genome sequencing marked the beginning of the era of large-scale genomics and proteomics, leading to large quantities of information on sequences, genes, interactions, and their annotations. In the same way that the capability to analyze data increases, the output by high-throughput techniques generates more information available for testing hypotheses and stimulating novel ones. Many experimental findings are reported in the -omics literature, where researchers have access to more than 20 million publications, with up to 4,500 new ones per day, available through to the widely used PubMed citation index and Google Scholar. This vast increase in available information demands novel strategies to help researchers to keep up to date with recent developments, as *ad hoc* querying with Boolean queries is tedious and often misses important information.

Even though PubMed provides an advanced keyword search and offers useful query expansion, it returns hundreds or thousands of articles as result; these are sorted by publication date, without providing much help in selecting or drilling down to those few articles that are most relevant regarding the user's actual question. As an example of both the amount of available information and the insufficiency of naïve keyword search, the name of the protein *p53* occurs in 53,528 PubMed articles, and while a researcher interested specifically in its role in *cancer* and its interacting partners might try the search "*p53 cancer interaction*" to narrow down the results, this query still yields 1,777 publications, enough for months of full-time reading [1]. Nonetheless, PubMed is a very widely used free service and is providing an invaluable service to the researchers around the world. In March 2007, PubMed served 82 million (statistics of Medline searches: http://www.nlm.nih.gov/bsd/medline_growth.html) query searches and the usage is ever increasing. A few commercial products are currently available that provide additional services, but they also rely on basic keyword search, with no real discovery or dynamic faceted search. Examples are OvidSP and Ingenuity Answers, both of which support bookmarking as one means of keeping track of visited citations. Research tools such as EBIMed (EBIMed: http://www.ebi.ac .uk/Rebholz-srv/ebimed/index.jsp) [2] and AliBaba (AliBaba: http://alibaba.informatik.hu-berlin.de) [3] provide additional cross-referencing of entities to databases such as UniProt or to the GeneOntology. They also try to identify relations between entities, such as protein-protein interactions, functional protein annotations, or gene-disease associations.

Search tools should provide dedicated and intuitive strategies that help to find relevant literature, starting with initial keyword searches and drilling down results via overviews enriched with autogenerated suggestions to refine queries. One of the first steps in biomedical text mining is to recognize named entities occurring in a text, such as genes and diseases. Named entity recognition (NER) is helpful to identify relevant documents, index a document collection, and facilitate information retrieval (IR) and semantic searches [4]. A step on top of NER is to normalize each entity to a base form (also called grounding and identification); the base form often is an identifier from an existing, relevant database; for instance, protein names could be mapped to UniProt IDs [5, 6]. Entity normalization (EN) is required to get rid of ambiguities such as homonyms, and map synonyms to one and the same concept. This further alleviates the tasks of indexing, IR, and search. Once named entities have been identified, systems aim to extract relationships between them from textual evidences; in the biomedical domain, these include gene-disease associations and protein-protein interactions. Such relations can then be made available for subsequent search in relational databases or used for constructing particular pathways and entire networks [7].

Information extraction (IE) [8–11] is the extraction of salient facts about prespecified types of events, entities [12], or relationships from free text. Information extraction from free text utilizes shallow-parsing techniques [13], part-of-speech tagging [14], noun and verb phrase chunking [15], predicate-subject and object relationships [13], and learned [8, 16, 17] or hand-build patterns [18] to automate the creation of specialized databases. Manual pattern engineering approaches employ shallow parsing with patterns to extract the interactions. In the system presented in [19], sentences are first tagged using a dictionary-based protein name identifier and then processed by a module which extracts interactions directly from complex and compound sentences using regular expressions based on part of speech tags. IE systems look for entities, relationships among those entities, or other specific facts within text documents. The success of information extraction depends on the performance of the various subtasks involved.

The Suiseki system of Blaschke et al. [20] also uses regular expressions, with probabilities that reflect the experimental accuracy of each pattern to extract interactions into predefined frame structures. Genies [21] utilizes a grammar-based

natural language processing (NLP) engine for information extraction. Recently, it has been extended as GeneWays [22], which also provides a Web interface that allows users to search and submit papers of interest for analysis. The BioRAT system [23] uses manually engineered templates that combine lexical and semantic information to identify protein interactions. The GeneScene system [24] extracts interactions using frequent preposition-based templates.

Over the last years, a focus has been on the extraction of protein-protein interactions in general, recently including extraction from full text articles, relevance ranking of extracted information, and other related aspects (see, for instance, the BioCreative community challenge [25]). The BioNLP'09 Shared Task concentrated on recognition of more fine-grained molecular events involving proteins and genes [26]. Both papers give overviews over the specific tasks and reference articles by participants.

One of the first efforts to extract information on biomolecular events was proposed by Yakushiji et al. [27]. They implemented an argument structure extractor based on full sentence parses. A list of target verbs have specific argument structures assigned to each. Frame-based extraction then searches for filler of each slot required according to the particular arguments. On an small in-house corpus, they found that 75% of the errors can be attributed to erroneous parsing and another 7% to insufficient memory; both causes might have less impact on recent systems due to more accurate parsers and larger memory.

Ding et al. [28] studied the extraction of protein-protein interactions using the Link Grammar parser. After some manual sentence simplification to increase parsing efficiency, their system assumed an interaction whenever two proteins were connected via a link path; an adjustable threshold allowed to cut off too long paths. As they used the original version of Link Grammar, Ding et al. [28] argued that adaptations to the biomedical domain would enhance the performance.

An information extraction application analyzes texts and presents only the specific information from them that the user is interested in [29]. IE systems are knowledge intensive to build and are to varying degrees tied to particular domains and scenarios such as target schema. Almost all IE applications start with fixed target schema as a goal and are tuned to extract information from unstructured text that will fit the schema. In scenarios where target schema is unknown, open information extraction systems [30] like KnowItNow [31] and TextRunner [32] allow rules to be defined easily based on the extraction need. An hybrid application (IR + IE) that leverages the best of information retrieval (ability to relevant texts) and information extraction (analyze text and present only specific information user is interested in) would be ideal in cases when the target extraction schema is unknown. An iterative loop of IR and IE with user's feedback will be potentially useful. For this application, we will need main components of IE system (like parts-of-speech tagger, named entity taggers, shallow parsers) preprocesses the text before being indexed by a custom-built augmented index that helps retrieve queries of the type "Cities such as ProperNoun(Head(NounPhrase))." Cafarella and Etzioni

[33] have done work in this direction to build a search engine for natural language and information extraction applications.

Exploratory search [34] is a topic that has grown from the fields of information retrieval and information seeking but has become more concerned with alternatives to the kind of search that has received the majority of focus (returning the most relevant documents to a Google-like keyword search). The research is motivated by questions like "what if the user does not know which keywords to use?" or "what if the user is not looking for a single answer?". Consequently, research began to focus on defining the broader set of information behaviors in order to learn about situations when a user is—or feels—limited by having only the ability to perform a keyword search (source: http://en.wikipedia.org/wiki/Exploratory_search). Exploratory search can be defined as specialization of information exploration which represents the activities carried out by searchers who are either [35]:

(1) unfamiliar with the domain of their goal (i.e., need to learn about the topic in order to understand how to achieve their goal);

(2) unsure about the ways to achieve their goals (either the technology or the process); or even

(3) unsure about their goals in the first place.

A faceted search system (or parametric search system) presents users with key value metadata that is used for query refinement [36]. By using facets (which are metadata or class labels for entities such as genes or diseases), users can easily combine the hierarchies in various ways to refine and drill down the results for a given query; they do not have to learn custom query syntax or to restart their search from scratch after each refinement. Studies have shown that users prefer faceted search interfaces because of their intuitiveness and ease of use [37]. Hearst [38] shares her experience, best practices, and design guidelines for faceted search interfaces, focusing on supporting flexible navigation, seamless integration with directed search, fluid alternation between refining and expanding, avoidance of empty results sets, and most importantly making users at ease by retaining a feeling of control and understanding of the entire search and navigation process. To improve web search for queries containing named entities [39], automatically identify the subject classes to which a named entity might refer to and select a set of appropriate facets for denoting the query.

Faceted search interfaces have made online shopping experiences richer and increased the accessibility of products by allowing users to search with general keywords and browse and refine the results until the desired sub-set is obtained (SIGIR'2006 Workshop on Faceted Search (CFP): http://sites.google.com/site/facetedsearch/). Faceted navigation delivers an experience of progressive query refinement or elaboration. Furthermore, it allows users to see the impact of each incremental choice in one facet on the choices in other facets. Faceted search combines faceted navigation with text search, allowing users to access (semi) structured content, thereby providing support for discovery

and exploratory search, areas where conventional search falls short [40].

2. Approach

In an age of ever increasing published research documents (available in search-able textual form) containing amounts of valuable information and knowledge that are vital to further research and understanding, it becomes imperative to build tools and systems that enable easier and quick access to right information the user is seeking for, and this has already become an information overload problem in different domains. Information Extraction (IE) systems provide an structured output by extracting nuggets of information from these text document collections, for a defined schema. The output schema can vary from simple pairwise relations to a complex, nested multiple events.

Faceted search and navigation is an efficient way to browse and search over a structured data/document collection, where the user is concerned about the completeness of the search, not just top ranked results. Faceted search system needs structured input documents, and IE systems extract structured information from text documents. By combining these two paradigms, we are able to provide faceted search and navigation over unstructured text documents, and, with this fusion, we are also able to leverage real utility of information extraction, that is, finding hidden relationships as the user goes through a search process, and to help refine the query to more satisfying and relevant level, all while keeping user feel incontrol of the whole search process.

We developed BioEve Search (http://www.bioeve.org/) framework to provide fast and scalable search service, where users can quickly refine their queries and drill down to the articles they are looking for in a matter of seconds, corresponding to a few number of clicks. The system helps identify hidden relationships between entities (like drugs, diseases, and genes), by highlighting them using a tag cloud to give a quick visualization for efficient navigation. In order to have sufficient abstraction between various modules (and technologies used) in this system, we have divided this framework into four different layers (refer to Figure 1) and they are (a) Data Store layer, (b) Information Extraction layer, (c) Faceting layer, and (d) Web Interface layer. Next sections explain each layer of this framework in more details.

2.1. Data Store Layer. The Data Store layer preprocesses and stores the documents in an indexed data store to make them efficiently accessible to the modules of upper layer (information extraction layer). Format conversion is needed sometimes (from ASCII to UTF-8 or vice versa), or XML documents need to be converted to text documents before being passed to next module. After the documents are in the required format and cleansed, they are stored in a indexed data store for efficient and fast access to either individual documents or the whole collections. The data store can be implemented using an Indexer service like (Apache Lucene (Lucene: http://lucene.apache.org/) or any database like MySQL). The Medline dataset is available as zipped XML

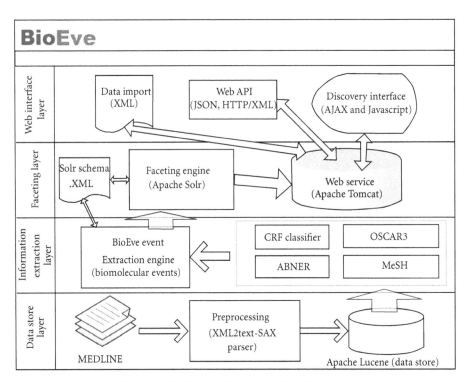

FIGURE 1: BioEve search framework architecture.

files that needed XML2 text conversion, after which we could ingest them into an indexer, Apache Lucene in our case. Such an indexer allows for faster access and keyword-based text search to select a particular subset of abstracts for further processing.

2.2. Information Extraction Layer. For recognizing different gene/protein names, DNA, RNA, cell line, and cell types, we leveraged ABNER [41], A Biomedical Named Entity Recognizer. We used OSCAR3 (Oscar3: http://sourceforge .net/projects/oscar3-chem/) (Open Source Chemistry Analysis Routines) to identify chemical names and chemical structures. To annotate disease names, symptoms, and causes, we used a subset of the Medical Subject Heading (MeSH) dataset (MeSH: http://www.nlm.nih.gov/mesh/).

2.2.1. Annotating Biomolecular Events in the Text. A first step towards bio-event extraction is to identify phrases in biomedical text which indicate the presence of an event. The labeled phrases are classified further into nine event types (based on the Genia corpus (BioNLP'09 Shared Task 1: http://www.nactem.ac.uk/tsujii/GENIA/SharedTask/)). The aim of marking such interesting phrases is to avoid looking at the entire text to find participants, as deep parsing of sentences can be a computationally expensive process, especially for the large volumes of text. We intend to mark phrases in biomedical text, which could contain a potential event, to serve as a starting point for extraction of event participants. Section 6.1 gives more details about our experimentations with classification and annotation of biomedical entities.

All the classification and annotation were done *offline* before the annotated articles are indexed for the search as

once an article is classified and annotated with different entity types, it does not need to be processed again for each search query. This step can be done preindexing and as a batch process.

2.3. Faceting Layer

2.3.1. Faceting Engine. To provide faceted classification and navigation over these categories (facets), many off-the-shelf systems are available such as in academia; Flamenco project (Flamenco: http://flamenco.berkeley.edu/) (from University of California Berkeley) and mspace (mspace: http://mspace .fm/) (University of Southampton) and in enterprise area; Apache Solr (Apache Solr: http://lucene.apache.org/solr/) and Endeca (Endeca: http://www.endeca.com/). We used the Apache Solr library for faceted search, which also provides an enterprise quality full-text search.

2.3.2. Shared Schema between IE Layer and Faceting Layer. In order to facilitate indexing and faceting over the extracted semi-structured text articles, both IE layer and faceting layer needs to share a common schema. A sample of shared schema used for enabling interaction between these layers is shown in Scheme 1.

2.4. Web Interface Layer. With the advent of Web 2.0 technologies, web-based interfaces have undergone delightful improvements and now provide rich dynamic experiences. Key component in this layer is a user interface that connects the user with the web service from the faceting layer and provides features that allow search, selection of facet/values, refinement, query restart, and dynamic display of a result

```
<field name="pmid" type="string" indexed="true" stored="true" required="true"/>
<field name="text" type="text" indexed="true" stored="true" multiValued="true"/>
<field name="title" type="text" indexed="true" stored="true"/>
<field name="gene" type="string" indexed="true" stored="true" multiValued="true"/>
<field name="drug" type="string" indexed="true" stored="true" multiValued="true"/>
<field name="disease" type="string" indexed="true" stored="true" multiValued="true"/>
```

SCHEME 1

set as user interacts and navigates. It also provides the bulk import of data for further analysis of the faceting/extraction.

The web interface provides following features for interactive search and navigation. The interface presents a number of entities types (on the left panel) along with the specific instances/values, from previous search results, and the current query. Users can choose any of the highlighted values of these entity types to interactively refine the query (add new values/remove any value from the list with just one click) and thereby drill down to the relevant articles quickly without actually reading the entire abstracts. Users can easily remove any of the previous search terms, thus widening the current search. We implemented the BioEve user interface using AJAX (AJAX: http://evolvingweb.github.com/ajax-solr/), Javascript, and JSON to provide rich dynamic experience. The web interface runs on an Apache Tomcat server. Next section explains about navigation aspect of the user interface.

3. User Interface: A Navigation Guide

Search interface is divided into left and right panels, see Figure 2, basically displaying enriched keywords and results, respectively.

Left panel: it offers suggestions and insights (based on cooccurrence frequency with the query terms) for different entities types, such as genes, diseases, and drugs/chemicals.

(i) Left panel shows navigation/refinement categories (genes, diseases, and drugs); users can click on any of the entity names (in light blue) to refine the search. By clicking on an entity, the user adds that entity to the search and the results on the right panel are refreshed on the y to reflect the refined results.

(ii) Users can add or remove any number of refinements to the current search query until they reach the desired results set (shown in the right panel).

Right panel: it shows the user's current search results and is automatically refreshed based on user's refinement and navigation choices on the left panel.

(i) The top of the panel shows users current query terms and navigation so far. Here, users can also deselect any of the previously selected entities or even all of them by single click on "remove all." By deselecting any entities, user is essentially expanding the search and the results in the right panel are refreshed *on the fly* to remaining query entities to offer a dynamic navigation experience.

(ii) Abstracts results on this panel show "title" of the abstract (in light red), full abstract text (in black, if abstract text is available).

(iii) Below the full abstract text, the list of entities mentioned in that abstracts (in light blue) is shown. These entities names are clickable and will start a new search for that entity name, with a single click.

(iv) A direct URL is also provided to the abstract page on http://pubmed.gov in case the user wants to access additional information such as authors, publication type, or links to a full-text article.

4. Interactive Search and Navigation: A Walk through and behind the Scenes

Let us start an example search process, say with the query "cholesterol" and the paragraph titled "behind-the-scenes" gives details of the computational process behind the action.

(1) The autocomplete feature helps in completion of the name while typing if the word is previously mentioned in the literature, which is the case here with "cholesterol."

Behind-the-scenes: as user starts typing, the query is tokenized (in case of multiple words) and search is made to retrieve word matches (and not the result rows yet) using the beginning with the characters user has already typed, and this loop continues. Technologies at play are jQuery, AJAX, and faceting feature of Apache Solr. Once the query is submitted by the user, the results rows also contain the annotated entity names and these are used to generate tag clouds, using the faceting classification entity frequency count.

The search results in 27177 articles hits (Figure 3). Those are a lot of articles to read. How about narrowing down these results with some insights given by BioEve Search?

(2) In left panel, "hepatic lipase" is highlighted; let us click on that as it shows some important relationship between "cholesterol" and "hepatic lipase." The search results are now narrowed down to 195 articles from 27177 (Figure 4). That is still a lot of articles to read this afternoon, how about some insights on diseases.

Behind-the-scenes: once user click on a highlighted entity name in tag cloud, this term (*gene: "hepatic lipase"*) is added to the search filter and the whole search process and tag could be generated again for the new query.

You can see disease "hyperthyroidism" highlighted in Figure 5.

(3) Selecting "hyperthyroidism" drills results down to 3, as can be seen in Figure 6.

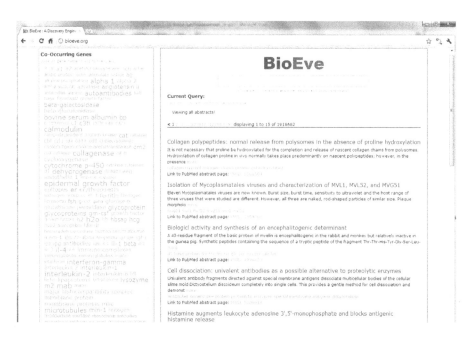

FIGURE 2: A sample screen shot of the main search screen. Left panel shows clickable top relevant entities, which if selected refines the query and results dynamically. User can deselect any of the previously selected entities to refine query more, and the results are updated dynamically to reflect the current selected list of entities.

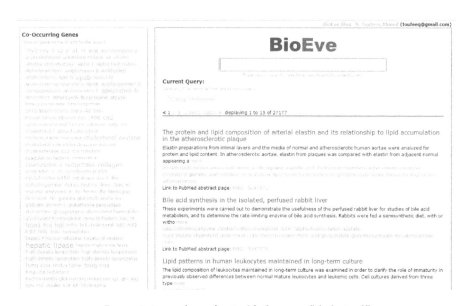

FIGURE 3: A sample result set with the query "cholesterol."

The top result is about "Treatment of hyperthyroidism: effects on hepatic lipase, lipoprotein lipase, LCAT and plasma lipoproteins". With few clicks user can refine search results to more relevant articles.

5. Initial User Reviews and Feedback

We asked three life science researchers to review and provide feedback on ease of search and novelty of the system, and

shown below is their feedback (paraphrased). Their names and other details are removed for privacy purposes.

5.1. Researcher One, P.h.D, Research Fellow, Microbiology, University of California, Berkeley

" I am impressed by ease of its use." "When I have the confidence that BioEve is indexing all the data without missing any critical article, *I*

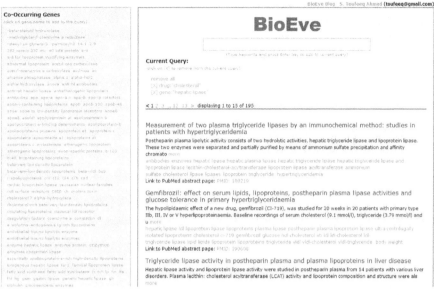

FIGURE 4: "Hepatic-lipase" selected.

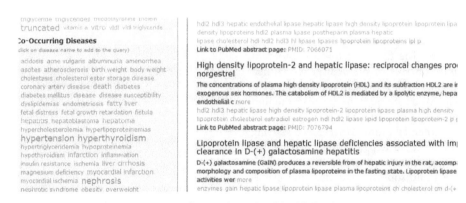

FIGURE 5: "Hyperthyroidism" highlighted.

FIGURE 6: Final refined search results.

will be compelled to use this search tool. I believe a finished product will be immensely useful and could become a popular tool for life science researchers."

5.2. Researcher Two, P.h.D, Investigator and Head, Molecular Genetics Laboratory

"*You have a powerful search.* Synchronize this with MEDLINE. Connect with more databases, OMIM, Entrez Gene .... You can get cell line database from ATCC.org."

5.3. Researcher Three, P.h.D, Postdoc Researcher, Faculty of Kinesiology, University of Calgary

"I particularly like the idea of having larger fonts for the more relevant terms highlighting what is researched more often."

6. Methods

6.1. Information Extraction: Annotating Sentences with Biomolecular Event Types. The first step towards bioevent extraction is to identify phrases in biomedical text which indicate the presence of an event. The aim of marking such interesting phrases is to avoid looking at the entire text to find participants. We intend to mark phrases in biomedical text, which could contain a potential event, to serve as a starting point for extraction of event participants. We experimented with well-known classification approaches, from a naïve Bayes classifier to the more sophisticated machine classification algorithms Expectation Maximization, Maximum Entropy, and Conditional Random Fields. Overview of different classifiers applied at different levels of granularity and the features used by these classifiers is shown in Table 1.

For naïve Bayes classifier implementation, we utilized WEKA (WEKA: http://www.cs.waikato.ac.nz/ml/weka/) library, a collection of machine learning algorithms for data mining tasks, for identifying single label per sentence approach. WEKA does not support multiple labels for the same instance. Hence, we had to include a tradeoff here by including the first encountered label in the case where the instance had multiple labels. For Expectation Maximization (EM) and Maximum Entropy (MaxEnt) algorithms, we used classification algorithms from MALLET library (MALLET: http://mallet.cs.umass.edu/index.php). Biomedical abstracts are split into sentences. For training purposes, plain text sentences are transformed into training instances as required by MALLET.

6.1.1. Feature Selection for Naïve Bayes, EM, and MaxEnt Classifiers. For the feature sets mentioned below, we used the TF-IDF representation. Each vector was normalized based on vector length. Also, to avoid variations, words/phrases were converted to lowercase. Based on WEKA library token delimiters, features were filtered to include those which had an alphabet as a prefix, using regular expressions.

TABLE 1: Classification approaches used: Naïve Bayes classifier (NBC), NBC + Expectation Maximization (EM), Maximum Entropy (MaxEnt), Conditional Random Fields (CRFs).

Granularity	Features	Classifier
Single label, Sentence level	Bag-of-words (BOW)	NBC
	BOW + gene names boosted	
	BOW + trigger words boosted	
	BOW + gene names and trigger words boosted	
Multiple labels Sentence level	BOW	NBC + EM MaxEnt
Event trigger phrase labeling	BOW + 3-gram and 4-gram prefixes and suffixes + orthographic features + trigger phrase dictionary	CRFs

For example, features like −300 bp were filtered out, but features like $p55$, which is a protein name, were retained. We experimented with the list of features described below, to understand how well each feature suits the corpus under consideration.

(i) Bag-of-words model: this model classified sentences based on word distribution.

(ii) Bag-of-words with gene names boosted: the idea was to give more importance to words, which clearly demarcate event types. To start with, we included gene names provided in the training data. Next, we used the ABNER (ABNER: http://pages.cs.wisc.edu/~bsettles/abner/), a gene name tagger, to tag gene names, apart from the ones already provided to us. We boosted weights for renamed feature "protein", by 2.0.

(iii) Bag-of-words with event trigger words boosted: we separately tried boosting event trigger words. The list of trigger words was obtained from training data. This list was cleaned to remove stop words. Trigger words were ordered in terms of their frequency of occurrence with respect to an event type, to capture trigger words which are most discriminative.

(iv) Bag-of-words with gene names and event trigger words boosted: the final approach was to boost both gene names and trigger words together. Theoretically, this approach was expected to do better than previous two feature sets discussed. Combination of discriminative approach of trigger words and gene name boosting was expected to train the classifier better.

6.1.2. Evaluation of Sentence Level Classification Using Naïve Bayes Classifier. This approach assigns a single label to

TABLE 2: Single label, sentence level results.

Classifier	Feature set	Precision
NBC	Bag-of-words	62.39%
	Bag-of-words + gene name boosting	50.00%
	Bag-of-words + trigger word boosting	49.92%
	Bag-of-words + trigger word boosting + Gene name boosting	49.77%
	Bag-of-POS tagged words	43.30%

each sentence. For evaluation purposes, the classifier is tested against GENIA development data. For every sentence, evaluator process checks if the event type predicted is the most likely event in that sentence. In case a sentence has more than one event with equal occurrence frequency, classifier predicted label is compared with all these candidate event types. The intent of this approach was to just understand the features suitable for this corpus. Classifier evaluated was NaiveBayesMultinomial classifier from Weka (http://www.cs .waikato.ac.nz/ml/weka/) library, which is a collection of machine learning algorithms for data mining tasks. Table 2 shows precision results for NBC classifier with different feature sets for single label per sentence classification.

6.2. Conditional Random Fields Based Classifier. Conditional Random fields (CRFs) are undirected statistical graphical models, a special case of which is a linear chain that corresponds to a conditionally trained finite-state machine [41]. CRFs in particular have been shown to be useful in parts-of-speech tagging [42] and shallow parsing [42]. We customized ABNER which is based on MALLET, to suit our needs. ABNER employs a set of orthographic and semantic features.

6.2.1. Feature Selection for CRF Classifier. The default model included the training vocabulary (provided as part of the BIONLP-NLPBA 2004 shared task) in the form of 17 orthographic features based on regular expressions [41]. These include upper case letters (initial upper case letter, all upper case letters, mix of upper and lower case letters), digits (special expressions for single and double digits, natural numbers, and real numbers), hyphen (special expressions for hyphens appearing at the beginning and end of a phrase), other punctuation marks, Roman and Greek words, and 3-gram and 4-gram suffixes and prefixes. ABNER uses semantic features that are provided in the form of hand-prepared (Greek letters, amino acids, chemical elements, known viruses, abbreviations of all these) and database-referenced lexicons (genes, chromosome locations, proteins, and cell lines).

6.3. Evaluation of Sentence Classification Approaches. The framework is designed for large-scale extraction of molecular events from biomedical texts. To assess its performance, we evaluated the underlying components on the GENIA event dataset made available as part of BioNLP'09 Shared Task

[26]. This data consists of three different sets: the training set consists of 800 PubMed abstracts (with 7,499 sentences), the development set has 150 abstracts (1,450 sentences), and the test set has 260 abstracts (2,447 sentences). We used the development set for parameter optimization and fine tuning and evaluated the final system on the test set. Employed classifiers were evaluated based on precision and recall. Precision indicates the correctness of the system, by measuring number of samples correctly classified in comparison to the total number of classified sentences. Recall indicates the completeness of the system, by calculating the number of results which actually belong to the expected set of results. Sentence level single label classification and sentence level multilabel classification approaches were evaluated based on how well the classifier labels a given sentence from a test set with one of the nine class labels. Phrase level classification using CRF model was evaluated based on how well the model tags trigger phrases. Evaluating this approach involved measuring the extent to which the model identifies that a phrase is a trigger phrase and how well it classifies a tagged trigger phrase under one of the nine predefined event types. Retrieved trigger phrases refer to the ones which are identified and classified by the CRF sequence tagger. Relevant trigger phrases are the ones which are expected to be tagged by the model. Retrieved and relevant trigger words refer to the tags which are expected to be classified and which are actually classified by the CRF model. All the classifiers are trained using BioNLP shared task training data and tested against BioNLP shared task development abstracts.

We compare the above three approaches for classification in Table 3. CRF has a good tradeoff as compared to Maximum Entropy classifier results. As compared to multiple labels, sentence level classifiers, it performs better in terms of having a considerably good accuracy for most of the event types with a good recall. It not only predicts the event types present in the sentence, but also localizes the trigger phrases. There are some entries where ME seems to perform better than CRF; for example, in case of *positive regulation*, where the precision is as high as 75%. However, in this case, the recall is very low (25%). The reason noticed (in training examples) was that, most of the true example sentences of positive regulation or negative regulation class type were misclassified as either phosphorylation or gene expression. The F1-score for CRF indicates that, as compared to the other approaches, CRF predicts 80% of the relevant tags, and, among these predicted tags, 68% of them are correct.

6.3.1. Evaluation of Phrase Level Labeling. Evaluation of this approach was focused more on the overlap of phrases between the GENIA annotated development and CRF tagged labels. The reason being for each abstract in the GENIA corpus, there is generally a set of biomedical entities present in it. For the shared task, only a subset of these entities was considered in the annotations, and accordingly only events concerning these annotated entities were extracted. However, based on the observation of the corpus, there was a probable chance of other events involving entities not selected for the annotations. So we focused on the coverage, where both the GENIA annotations and CRF annotations agree upon. CRF

TABLE 3: Summary of classification approaches: test instances (marked events) for each class type in test dataset. Precision, recall, and F1-score in percentage. Compared to NB + EM and CRF, Maximum Entropy based classifier had better average precision, but CRF has best recall and good precision, giving it best F-Measure of the three well-known classifiers.

Event type	Test instances	NB + EM			MaxEnt			CRF		
	Total: 942	P	R	F1	P	R	F1	P	R	F1
Phosphorylation	38	62	42	50	97	73	83	80	83	81
Protein catabolism	17	60	47	53	97	73	83	85	86	85
Gene expression	200	60	41	49	88	58	70	75	81	78
Localization	39	39	47	43	61	69	65	67	79	72
Transcription	60	24	52	33	49	80	61	57	78	66
Binding	153	56	63	59	65	62	63	65	81	72
Regulation	90	47	69	55	52	67	58	62	73	67
Positive regulation	220	70	27	39	75	25	38	55	74	63
Negative regulation	125	42	46	44	54	38	45	68	82	74
Average		51	48	47	**71**	61	63	68	**80**	73

TABLE 4: CRF sequence labeling results.

Type of evaluation	Coverage %
Exact boundary matching	79%
Soft boundary matching	82%

performance was evaluated on two fronts in terms of this overlap.

(i) *Exact boundary matching*: this involves exact label matching and exact trigger phrase match.

(ii) *Soft boundary matching*: this involves exact label matching and partial trigger phrase match, allowing 1-word window on either side of the actual trigger phrase.

Checking of the above constraints was a combination of template matching and manually filtering of abstracts. Table 4 gives an estimate of the coverage. Soft boundary matching increases the coverage by around 3%. Table 3 gives the overall evaluation of CRF with respect to GENIA corpus. With regards to the CRF results, accuracy for *positive regulation* is comparatively low. Also, the test instances for *positive regulation* were more than any other event type. So this reduced average precision to some extent.

A detailed analysis of the results showed that around 3% tags were labeled incorrectly in terms of the event type. There were some cases where it was not certain whether an event should be marked as *regulation* or *positive regulation*. Some examples include "the expression of LAL-mRNA," where "LAL-mRNA" refers to a gene. As per examples seen in the training data, the template of the form "expression of <gene name>" generally indicates presence of a *Gene expression* event. Hence, more analysis may be need to exactly filter out such annotations as true negatives or deliberately induced false positives.

7. Discussion and Conclusions

PubMed is one of the most well known and used citation indexes for the Life Sciences. It provides basic keyword searches and benefits largely from a hierarchically organized set of indexing terms, MeSH, that are semi-automatically assigned to each article. PubMed also enables quick searches for related publications given one or more articles deemed relevant by the user. Some research tools provide additional cross-referencing of entities to databases such as UniProt or to the GeneOntology. They also try to identify relations between entities of the same or different types, such as protein-protein interactions, functional protein annotations, or gene-disease associations. GoPubMed [43] guides users in their everyday searches by mapping articles to concept hierarchies, such as the Gene Ontology and MeSH. For each concept found in abstracts returned by the initial user query, GoPubMed computes a rank based on occurrences of that concept. Thus, users can quickly grasp which terms occur frequently, providing clues for relevant topics and relations, and refine subsequent queries by focusing on particular concepts, discarding others.

In this paper, we presented BioEve Search framework, which can help identify important relationships between entities such as drugs, diseases, and genes by highlights them during the search process. Thereby, allowing the researcher not only to navigate the literature, but also to see entities and the relations they are involved in immediately, without having to fully read the article. Nonetheless, we envision future extensions to provide a more complete and mainstream service and here are few of these next steps.

Keeping the search index up-to-date and complete: we are adding a synchronization module that will frequently check with Medline for supplement articles as they are published; these will typically be in the range of 2500–4500 new articles per day. Frequent synchronization is necessary to keep BioEve abreast with Medline collection and give users the access to the most recent articles.

Normalizing and grounding of entity names: as the same gene/protein can be referred by various names and symbols (e.g., the TRK-fused gene is also known as TF6; TRKT3; FLJ36137; TFG), a user searching for any of these names should find results mentioning any of the others. Removal of duplicates and cleanup of nonbiomedical vocabulary that occurs in the entity tag clouds will further improve navigation and search results.

Cross-referencing with biomedical databases: we want to cross-reference terms indexed with biological databases. For example, each occurrence of a gene could be linked to EntrezGene and OMIM; cell lines can be linked and enriched with ATCC.org's cell line database; we want to cross-reference disease names with UMLS and MeSH to provide access to ontological information. To perform this task of entity normalization, we have previously developed Gnat [6], which handles gene names. Further entity classes that exhibit relatively high term ambiguity with other classes or within themselves are diseases, drugs, species, and GeneOntology terms ("Neurofibromatosis 2" can refer to the disease or gene).

Conflict of Interests

To the authors knowledge, there is no conflict of interest with name "BioEve" or with any trademarks.

Acknowledgments

The authors like to thank Jeorg Hakenberg, Chintan Patel, and Sheela P. Kanwar for valuable discussions, ideas, and help with writing this paper. They also wish to thank the researchers who provided an initial user review and gave them valuable feedback.

References

[1] S. Pyysalo, *A dependency parsing approach to biomedical text mining*, Ph.D. thesis, 2008.

[2] D. Rebholz-Schuhmann, H. Kirsch, M. Arregui, S. Gaudan, M. Riethoven, and P. Stoehr, "EBIMed—text crunching to gather facts for proteins from Medline," *Bioinformatics*, vol. 23, no. 2, pp. e237–e244, 2007.

[3] C. Plake, T. Schiemann, M. Pankalla, J. Hakenberg, and U. Leser, "ALIBABA: pubMed as a graph," *Bioinformatics*, vol. 22, no. 19, pp. 2444–2445, 2006.

[4] U. Leser and J. Hakenberg, "What makes a gene name? Named entity recognition in the biomedical literature," *Briefings in Bioinformatics*, vol. 6, no. 4, pp. 357–369, 2005.

[5] H. Xu, J. W. Fan, G. Hripcsak, E. A. Mendonça, M. Markatou, and C. Friedman, "Gene symbol disambiguation using knowledge-based profiles," *Bioinformatics*, vol. 23, no. 8, pp. 1015–1022, 2007.

[6] J. Hakenberg, C. Plake, R. Leaman, M. Schroeder, and G. Gonzalez, "Inter-species normalization of gene mentions with GNAT," *Bioinformatics*, vol. 24, no. 16, pp. i126–i132, 2008.

[7] K. Oda, J. D. Kim, T. Ohta et al., "New challenges for text mining: mapping between text and manually curated pathways," *BMC Bioinformatics*, vol. 9, supplement 3, article S5, 2008.

[8] M. E. Califf and R. J. Mooney, "Relational learning of pattern-match rules for information extraction," in *Working Notes of AAAI Spring Symposium on Applying Machine Learning to Discourse Processing*, pp. 6–11, AAAI Press, Menlo Park, Calif, USA, 1998.

[9] N. Kushmerick, D. S. Weld, and R. B. Doorenbos, "Wrapper induction for information extraction," in *Proceedings of the International Joint Conference on Artificial Intelligence (IJCAI '97)*, pp. 729–737, 1997.

[10] L. Schubert, "Can we derive general world knowledge from texts?" in *Proceedings of the 2nd International Conference on Human Language Technology Research*, pp. 94–97, Morgan Kaufmann, San Francisco, Calif, USA, 2002.

[11] M. Friedman and D. S. Weld, "Efficiently executing information-gathering plans," in *Proceedings of the 15th International Joint Conference on Artificial Intelligence (IJCAI '97)*, pp. 785–791, Nagoya, Japan, 1997.

[12] R. Bunescu, R. Ge, R. J. Kate et al., "Comparative experiments on learning information extractors for proteins and their interactions," *Artificial Intelligence in Medicine*, vol. 33, no. 2, pp. 139–155, 2005.

[13] W. Daelemans, S. Buchholz, and J. Veenstra, "Memory-based shallow parsing," in *Proceedings of the Conference on Natural Language Learning (CoNLL '99)*, vol. 99, pp. 53–60, 1999.

[14] E. Brill, "A simple rule-based part-of-speech tagger. In Proceedings of ANLP-92," in *Proceedings of the 3rd Conference on Applied Natural Language Processing*, pp. 152–155, Trento, Italy, 1992.

[15] A. Mikheev and S. Finch, "A workbench for finding structure in texts," in *Proceedings of the Applied Natural Language Processing (ANLP '97)*, Washington, DC, USA, 1997.

[16] M. Craven and J. Kumlien, "Constructing biological knowledge bases by extracting information from text sources," in *Proceedings of the 7th International Conference on Intelligent Systems for Molecular Biology*, pp. 77–86, AAAI Press, 1999.

[17] K. Seymore, A. McCallum, and R. Rosenfeld, "Learning hidden markov model structure for information extraction," in *Proceedings of the AAAI Workshop on Machine Learning for Information Extraction*, 1999.

[18] L. Hunter, Z. Lu, J. Firby et al., "OpenDMAP: an open source, ontology-driven concept analysis engine, with applications to capturing knowledge regarding protein transport, protein interactions and cell-type-specific gene expression," *BMC Bioinformatics*, vol. 9, article 78, 2008.

[19] T. Ono, H. Hishigaki, A. Tanigami, and T. Takagi, "Automated extraction of information on protein-protein interactions from the biological literature," *Bioinformatics*, vol. 17, no. 2, pp. 155–161, 2001.

[20] C. Blaschke, M. A. Andrade, C. Ouzounis, and A. Valencia, "Automatic extraction of biological information from scientific text: protein-protein interactions," AAAI, pp. 60–67.

[21] C. Friedman, P. Kra, H. Yu, M. Krauthammer, and A. Rzhetsky, "GENIES: a natural-language processing system for the extraction of molecular pathways from journal articles," *Bioinformatics*, vol. 17, no. 1, pp. S74–S82, 2001.

[22] A. Rzhetsky, I. Iossifov, T. Koike et al., "GeneWays: a system for extracting, analyzing, visualizing, and integrating molecular pathway data," *Journal of Biomedical Informatics*, vol. 37, no. 1, pp. 43–53, 2004.

[23] D. P. A. Corney, B. F. Buxton, W. B. Langdon, and D. T. Jones, "BioRAT: extracting biological information from full-length papers," *Bioinformatics*, vol. 20, no. 17, pp. 3206–3213, 2004.

[24] G. Leroy, H. Chen, and J. D. Martinez, "A shallow parser based on closed-class words to capture relations in biomedical text," *Journal of Biomedical Informatics*, vol. 36, no. 3, pp. 145–158, 2003.

[25] M. Krallinger, F. Leitner, C. Rodriguez-Penagos, and A. Valencia, "Overview of the protein-protein interaction annotation extraction task of BioCreative II," *Genome Biology*, vol. 9, no. 2, article S4, 2008.

[26] J. D. Kim, T. Ohta, S. Pyysalo, Y. Kano, and J. Tsujii, "Overview of BioNLP'09 shared task on event extraction," in *Proceedings of the Workshop Companion Volume for Shared Task (BioNLP '09)*, pp. 1–9, Association for Computational Linguistics, Boulder, Colo, USA, 2009.

[27] A. Yakushiji, Y. Tateisi, Y. Miyao, and J. Tsujii, "Event extraction from biomedical papers using a full parser," *Pacific Symposium on Biocomputing. Pacific Symposium on Biocomputing*, pp. 408–419, 2001.

[28] J. Ding, D. Berleant, J. Xu, and A. W. Fulmer, "Extracting Biochemical Interactions from MEDLINE Using a Link Grammar Parser," in *Proceedings of the 15th IEEE International Conference on Tools with Artificial Intelligence*, pp. 467–471, November 2003.

[29] H. Cunningham, *Information Extraction, Automatic*, Encyclopedia of Language and Linguistics, 2nd edition, 2005.

[30] O. Etzioni, M. Cafarella, D. Downey et al., "Methods for domain-independent information extraction from the web: an experimental comparison," in *Proceedings of the 19th National Conference on Artificial Intelligence (AAAI '04)*, pp. 391–398, AAAI Press, Menlo Park, Calif, USA, July 2004.

[31] M. Cafarella, D. Downey, S. Soderland, and O. Etzioni, "KnowItNow: fast, scalable information extraction from the web," in *Proceedings of the Conference on Empirical Methods in Natural Language Processing*, pp. 563–570, Association for Computational Linguistics, Morristown, NJ, USA, 2005.

[32] O. Etzioni, M. Banko, S. Soderland, and D. S. Weld, "Open information extraction from the web," *Communications of the ACM*, vol. 51, no. 12, pp. 68–74, 2008.

[33] M. Cafarella and O. Etzioni, "A search engine for natural language applications," in *Proceedings of the International Conference on World Wide Web (WWW '05)*, pp. 442–452, ACM, New York, NY, USA, 2005.

[34] R. White, B. Kules, and S. Drucker, "Supporting exploratory search, introduction, special issue, communications of the ACM," *Communications of the ACM*, vol. 49, no. 4, pp. 36–39, 2006.

[35] W. T. Fu, T. G. Kannampallil, and R. Kang, "Facilitating exploratory search by model-based navigational cues," in *Proceedings of the 14th ACM International Conference on Intelligent User Interfaces (IUI '10)*, pp. 199–208, ACM, New York, NY, USA, February 2010.

[36] J. Koren, Y. Zhang, and X. Liu, "Personalized interactive faceted search," in *Proceedings of the 17th International Conference on World Wide Web (WWW '08)*, pp. 477–485, ACM, April 2008.

[37] V. Sinha and D. R. Karger, "Magnet: supporting navigation in semistructured data environments," in *Proceedings of the ACM SIGMOD International Conference on Management of Data (SIGMOD '05)*, pp. 97–106, ACM, June 2005.

[38] M. Hearst, "Design recommendations for hierarchical faceted search interfaces," in *Proceedings of the ACM Workshop on Faceted Search (SIGIR '06)*, 2006.

[39] S. Stamou and L. Kozanidis, "Towards faceted search for named entity queries," *Advances in Web and Network Technologies, and Information Management*, vol. 5731, pp. 100–112, 2009.

[40] D. Tunkelang, *Faceted Search*, Morgan & Claypool, 2009.

[41] B. Settles, "ABNER: an open source tool for automatically tagging genes, proteins and other entity names in text," *Bioinformatics*, vol. 21, no. 14, pp. 3191–3192, 2005.

[42] J. Lafferty and F. Pereira, "Conditional random fields: probabilistic models for segmenting and labeling sequence data," in *Proceedings of the 18th International Conference on Machine Learning (ICML '01)*, 2001.

[43] A. Doms and M. Schroeder, "GoPubMed: exploring PubMed with the gene ontology," *Nucleic Acids Research*, vol. 33, no. 2, pp. W783–W786, 2005.

16

Applications of Natural Language Processing in Biodiversity Science

Anne E. Thessen,[1] Hong Cui,[2] and Dmitry Mozzherin[1]

[1] Center for Library and Informatics, Marine Biological Laboratory, 7 MBL Street, Woods Hole, MA 02543, USA
[2] School of Information Resources and Library Science, University of Arizona, Tucson, AZ 85719, USA

Correspondence should be addressed to Anne E. Thessen, athessen@mbl.edu

Academic Editor: Jörg Hakenberg

Centuries of biological knowledge are contained in the massive body of scientific literature, written for human-readability but too big for any one person to consume. Large-scale mining of information from the literature is necessary if biology is to transform into a data-driven science. A computer can handle the volume but cannot make sense of the language. This paper reviews and discusses the use of natural language processing (NLP) and machine-learning algorithms to extract information from systematic literature. NLP algorithms have been used for decades, but require special development for application in the biological realm due to the special nature of the language. Many tools exist for biological information extraction (cellular processes, taxonomic names, and morphological characters), but none have been applied life wide and most still require testing and development. Progress has been made in developing algorithms for automated annotation of taxonomic text, identification of taxonomic names in text, and extraction of morphological character information from taxonomic descriptions. This manuscript will briefly discuss the key steps in applying information extraction tools to enhance biodiversity science.

1. Introduction

Biologists are expected to answer large-scale questions that address processes occurring across broad spatial and temporal scales, such as the effects of climate change on species [1, 2]. This motivates the development of a new type of data-driven discovery focusing on scientific insights and hypothesis generation through the novel management and analysis of preexisting data [3, 4]. Data-driven discovery presumes that a large, virtual pool of data will emerge across a wide spectrum of the life sciences, matching that already in place for the molecular sciences. It is argued that the availability of such a pool will allow biodiversity science to join the other "Big" (i.e., data-centric) sciences such as astronomy and high-energy particle physics [5]. Managing large amounts of heterogeneous data for this Big New Biology will require a cyberinfrastructure that organizes an open pool of biological data [6].

To assess the resources needed to establish the cyberinfrastructure for biology, it is necessary to understand the nature of biological data [4]. To become a part of the cyberinfrastructure, data must be ready to enter a digital data pool. This means data must be digital, normalized, and standardized [4]. Biological data sets are heterogeneous in format, size, degree of digitization, and openness [4, 7, 8]. The distribution of data packages in biology can be represented as a hollow curve [7] (Figure 1). To the left of the curve are the few providers producing large amounts of data, often derived from instruments and born digital such as in molecular biology. To the right of the curve are the many providers producing small amounts of data. It is estimated that 80% of scientific output comes from these small providers [7]. Generally called "small science," these data are rarely preserved [9, 10]. Scientific publication, a narrative explanation derived from primary data, is often the only lasting record of this work.

The complete body of research literature is a major container for much of our knowledge about the natural world and represents centuries of investment. The value of this information is high as it reflects observations that are difficult to replace if they are replaceable at all [7]. Much of the information has high relevance today, such as records on

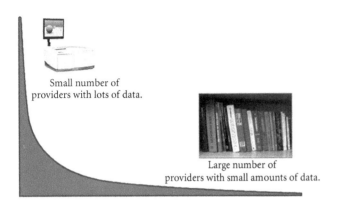

FIGURE 1: The long tail of biology. Data quantity, digitization, and openness can be described using a hyperbolic (hollow) curve with a small number of providers providing large quantities of data, and a large number of individuals providing small quantities of data.

TABLE 1: From Tang and Heidorn [13]. An example template for morphological character extraction.

Template slots	Extracted information
Genus	Pellaea
Species	mucronata
Distribution	Nev. Calif.
Leaf shape	ovate-deltate
Leaf margin	dentate
Leaf apex	mucronate
Leaf base	
Leaf arrangement	clustered
Blade dimension	
Leaf color	
Fruit/nut shape	

TABLE 2: Information extraction tasks outlined by the MUCs and their descriptions.

Task	Description
Named entity	Extracts names of entities
Coreference	Links references to the same entity
Template element	Extracts descriptors of entities
Template rotation	Extracts relationships between entities
Scenario template	Extracts events

the historical occurrence of species that will help us better understand shifting abundances and distributions. Similarly, taxonomy, with its need to respect all nomenclatural acts back to the 1750s, needs to have access to information contained exclusively within this body of literature. Unfortunately, this knowledge has been presented in the narrative prose such that careful reading and annotation are required to make use of any information [11] and only a subset has been migrated into digital form.

The number of pages of the historical biodiversity literature is estimated to be approximately hundreds of millions [12]. Currently, over 33 million pages of legacy biology text are scanned and made available online through the Biodiversity Heritage Library (http://www .biodiversitylibrary.org/) and thousands of new digital pages are published every month in open-access biology journals (estimated based on 216 journals publishing approx 10 articles per month of less than 10 pages; http://www.doaj.org/ doaj?cpid=67&func=subject). Additional biologically focused digital literature repositories can be found here (http:// www.library.illinois.edu/nhx/resources/digitalresourcecatalogs.html).

The information is in human-readable form but is too much for a person to transform into a digital data pool. Machines can better handle the volume, but cannot determine which elements of the text have value. In order to mobilize the valuable content in the literature, we need innovative algorithms to translate the entirety of the biological literature into a machine-readable form, extract the information with value, and feed it in a standards-compliant form into an open data pool. This paper discusses the application of natural language processing algorithms to biodiversity science to enable data-driven discovery.

2. Overview

2.1. Information Extraction. Research addressing the transformation of natural language text into a digital data pool

is generally labeled as "information extraction" (IE). An IE task typically involves a corpus of source text documents to be acted upon by the IE algorithm and an extraction template that describes what will be extracted. For a plant character IE task, (e.g., [13]), a template may consist of taxon name, leaf shape, leaf size, leaf arrangement, and so forth (Table 1). The characteristics of the source documents and the complexity of the template determine the difficulty level of an IE task. More complex IE tasks are often broken down to a series (stacks) of sub tasks, with a later subtask often relying on the success of an earlier one. Table 2 illustrates typical subtasks involved in an IE task. Note, not all IE tasks involve all of these subtasks. Examples of information extraction tools for biology (not including biodiversity science) can be found in Table 3.

The IE field has made rapid progress since the 1980s with the Message Understanding Conferences (MUCs) and has become very active since the 1990s due largely to the development of the World Wide Web. This has made available huge amounts of textual documents and human-prepared datasets (e.g., categorized web pages, databases) in an electronic format. Both can readily be used to evaluate the performance of an IE system. The massive production of digital information demands more efficient, computer-aided approaches to process, organize, and access the information. The urgent need to extract interesting information from large amounts of text to support knowledge discovery was recognized as an application for IE tools (e.g., identifying possible terrorists or terrorism attacks by extracting information from a large amount of email messages). For this reason,

TABLE 3: Existing IE systems for biology [17–26].

System	Approach	Structure of Text	Knowledge in	Application domain	Reference
AkanePPI	shallow parsing	sentence-split, tokenized, and annotated		protein interactions	[17]
EMPathIE	pattern matching	text	EMP database	enzymes	[18]
PASTA	pattern matching	text	biological lexicons	protein structure	[19]
BioIE	pattern matching	xml	dictionary of terms	biomedicine	[20]
BioRAT	pattern matching, sub-language driven	could be xml, html, text or asn.1, can do full-length pdf papers (converts to text)	dictionary for protein and gene names, dictionary for interactions, and synonyms; text pattern template	biomedicine	[21]
Chilibot	shallow parsing	not sure what was used in paper, but could be xml, html, text or asn.1	nomenclature dictionary	biomedicine	[22]
Dragon Toolkit	mixed syntactic semantic	text	domain ontologies	genomics	[23]
EBIMed	pattern matching	xml	dictionary of terms	biomedicine	[24]
iProLINK	shallow parsing	text	protein name dictionary, ontology, and annotated corpora	proteins	[25]
LitMiner	mixed syntactic semantic	web documents		Drosophila research	[26]

IE and other related research have acquired another, more general label "text data mining" (or simply "text mining").

Information extraction algorithms are regularly evaluated based on three metrics: recall, precision, and the F score. Consider an algorithm trained to extract names of species from documents being run against a document containing the words: cat, dog, chicken, horse, goat, and cow. The recall would be the ratio of the number of "species words" extracted to the number in the document (6). So, an algorithm that only recognized cat and dog would have low recall (33%). Precision is the percentage of what the algorithm extracts that is correct. Since both cat and dog are species words, the precision of our algorithm would be 100% despite having a low recall. If the algorithm extracted all of the species words from the document, it would have both high precision and recall, but if it also extracts other words that are not species, then it would have low precision and high recall. The F score is an overall metric calculated from precision and recall when precision and recall are considered equally important:

$$F \text{ score} = 2\left(\frac{(\text{precision} * \text{recall})}{(\text{precision} + \text{recall})}\right). \quad (1)$$

Before we review current IE systems for biodiversity science, we will first present a reference system architecture for a model IE system that covers the entire process of an IE application (Figure 2). In reviewing variant systems, we will refer to this reference architecture.

The blue-shaded areas in Figure 2 illustrate an IE system. The inputs to the IE system include source documents in a digital format (element number 1 in Figure 2), an IE template which describes the IE task (2) and knowledge entities to perform the task (3). If documents are not in a digital format, OCR technologies can be used to make the transition (4; see below section on digitization), but then it is necessary to correct OCR errors before use (5). In this model system, we use "IE template" to refer not only to those that are well defined such as the leaf character template example in Table 1, but also those more loosely defined. For example, we also consider lists of names and characters to be IE templates so the reference system can cover Named Entity Recognition systems (see below for examples) and character annotation systems (see below for examples). Knowledge entities include, for example, dictionaries, glossaries, gazetteers, or ontologies (3). The output of an IE system is often data in a structured format, illustrated as a database in the diagram (6). Ideally the structured format conforms to one of many data standards (7), which can range from relational database schemas to RDF. The arrow from Knowledge Entities to Extracted Data illustrates that, in some cases, the extracted data can be better interpreted with the support of knowledge entities (like annotation projects such as phenoscape, http://phenoscape.org/wiki/Main_Page). The arrow from Data Standards to Extracted Data suggests the same.

NLP techniques are often used in combination with extraction methods (including hand-crafted rules and/or

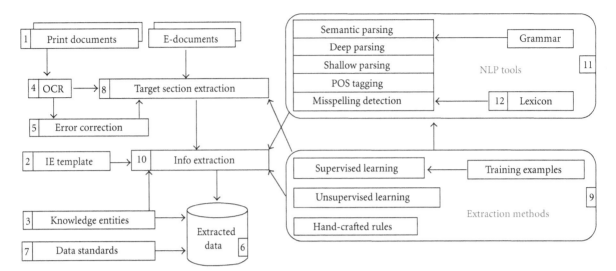

FIGURE 2: A reference system architecture for an example IE system. Numbers correspond to the text.

machine learning methods). Often the input documents contain text that are not relevant to an IE task [14]. In these cases, the blocks of text that contain extraction targets need to be identified and extracted first to avoid the waste of computational resources (8). An IE method is often used for this purpose (9). From the selected text, a series of tasks may be performed to extract target information (10) and produce final output (6; see also IE subtasks in Table 2). This is often accomplished by first applying NLP techniques (11) and then using one or a combination of extraction methods (9). The arrow from extraction methods to NLP tools in Figure 2 indicates that machine learning and hand-crafted rules can be used to adapt/improve NLP tools for an IE task by, for example, extracting domain terms to extend the lexicon (12) used by a syntactic parser or even create a special purpose parser [15]. One important element that is not included in the model (Figure 2) is the human curation component. This is important for expert confirmation that extraction results are correct.

2.2. Natural Language Processing. IE is an area of application of natural language processing (NLP). NLP enables a computer to read (and possibly "understand") information from natural language texts such as publications. NLP consists of a stack of techniques of increasing sophistication to progressively interpret language, starting with words, progressing to sentence structure (syntax or syntactic parsing), and ending at sentence meaning (semantics or semantic parsing) and meaning within sequences of sentences (discourse analysis). Typically an NLP technique higher in the stack (discourse analysis) utilizes the techniques below it (syntactic parsing). A variety of NLP techniques have been used in IE applications, but most only progress to syntactic parsing (some special IE applications specifically mentioned in this paper may not use any of the techniques). More sophisticated techniques higher in the stack (semantic parsing and discourse analysis) are rarely used in IE applications because they are highly specialized that is,

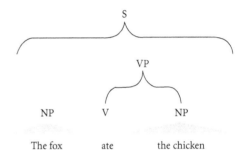

FIGURE 3: An example of shallow parsing. Words and a sentence (S) are recognized. Then, the sentence is parsed into noun phrases (NP), verbs (V), and verb phrases (VP).

cannot be reliably applied in general applications and are more computationally expensive.

Syntactic parsing can be shallow or deep. Shallow syntactic parsing (also called "chunking") typically identifies noun, verb, preposition phrases, and so forth in a sentence (Figure 3), while deep syntactic parsing produces full parse trees, in which the syntactic function (e.g., Part of Speech, or POS) of each word or phrase is tagged with a short label (Figure 4). The most commonly used set of POS tags used is the Penn Treebank Tag Set (http://bulba.sdsu.edu/jeanette/thesis/PennTags.html), which has labels for different parts of speech such as adjective phrases (ADJP), plural nouns (NNP), and so forth. Not all shallow parsers identify the same set of phrases. GENIA Tagger, for example, identifies adjective phrases (ADJP), adverb phrases (ADVP), conjunctive phrases (CONJP), interjections (INTJ), list markers (LST), noun phrases (NP), prepositional phrases (PP), participles (PRT), subordinate clauses (SBAR), and verb phrases (VP). Some shallow parsing tools are the Illinois Shallow Parser (http://cogcomp.cs.illinois.edu/page/software_view/13) the Apache OpenNLP (http://incubator.apache.org/opennlp/index.html), and GENIA Tagger

Original text:

leaf blade obovate to nearly orbiculate, 3–9 × 3–8 cm, leathery, base obtuse.

Shallow parsing result :

[NP leaf blade] [VP obovate] [VP to nearly orbiculate], [NP 3–9 × 3–8 cm], [NP leathery], [NP base obtuse].

Deep parsing result:

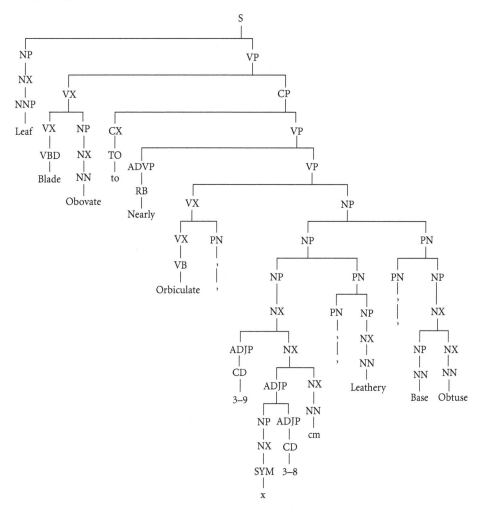

FIGURE 4: Shallow-vs-Deep-Parsing. The shallow parsing result produced by GENIA Tagger (http://text0.mib.man.ac.uk/software/geniatagger/). The deep parsing result produced by Enju Parser for Biomedical Domain (http://www-tsujii.is.s.u-tokyo.ac.jp/enju/demo.html). GENIA Tagger and Enju Parser are products of the Tsujii Laboratory of the University of Tokyo and optimized for biomedical domain. Both Parsing results contain errors, for example "obovate" should be an ADJP (adjective phrase), but GENIA Tagger chunked it as a VP (verb phrase). "blade" is a noun, but Enju parser parsed it as a verb (VBD). This is not to criticize the tools, but to point out language differences in different domains could have a significant impact on the performance of NLP tools. Parsers trained for a general domain produce erroneous results on morphological descriptions [16].

(http://www.tsujii.is.s.u-tokyo.ac.jp/GENIA/tagger/). Deep parsing tools include Stanford Parser (http://nlp.stanford.edu/software/lex-parser.shtml), Link Parser (http://www.link.cs.cmu.edu/link/) and Enju Parser (http://www-tsujii.is.s.u-tokyo.ac.jp/enju/). A majority of IE applications use the shallow parsing technique, but the use of deep parsing techniques is on the rise in biology applications. This is driven in part because shallow parsing is not adequate to extract information from biology text [27–29].

Several NLP approaches are available for IE applications in biology that go beyond shallow parsing and are not mutually exclusive.

(1) *Pattern matching* approaches exploit basic patterns in text to extract information. An example pattern is "enzyme activates protein" or X activates Y. The computer would look for the specific text pattern and assume that all X are enzymes or all Y are

proteins. Dictionary-based IE is a variant of pattern matching that focuses on finding words in text that are contained in a dictionary previously given to the computer. For example, the computer might be given a list of enzyme names (such as the UM-BBD list of enzyme names, http://umbbd.msi.umn.edu/servlets/pageservlet?ptype; X in previous example). Once the enzyme name is located, the computer can infer the pattern that it "activates Y." Another variant of pattern matching is the preposition-based parsing which focuses on finding prepositions like "by" and "of" and filling a basic template with information surrounding that preposition. An example of this would be "Y is activated by X." Pattern matching suffers from the difficulty in accounting for the wide array of linguistic patterns used in text (X activates Y, Y is activated by X, Y was activated by X, X activated Y, Y is activated via X, X, which activates Y, etc.). Many of these systems extract phrases or sentences instead of structured facts, which limits their usefulness for further informatics. An example system that uses pattern matching is given in Krauthammer et al. [37].

(2) *Full parsing* approaches expand on shallow parsing to include an analysis of sentence structure (i.e., syntax, see Figure 3). The biggest challenge with this approach is the special language of biology-specific texts. Most existing full-parsing systems are designed to handle general language texts, like news articles. The approach is also limited by grammar mistakes in the literature, which are often due to nonnative English speakers. Full parsing often runs into ambiguity due to the many ways a sentence (even moderately complex) can be interpreted by a machine. Sentence fragments, such as titles or captions, can also cause problems. UniGene Tabulator is an example of a full parser for biology [38].

(3) *Probability-based* approaches offer a solution to the linguistic variability that confounds full parsing. These approaches use weighted grammar rules to decrease sensitivity to variation. The weights are assigned through processing of a large body of manually annotated text. Probabilistic grammars are used to estimate the probability that a particular parse tree will be correct or the probability that a sentence or sentence fragment has been recognized correctly. Results can be ranked according to the probabilities. Nasr and Rambow give an example of a probability-based parser [39].

(4) *Mixed syntactic-semantic* approaches take advantage of syntactic and semantic knowledge together. This essentially combines part-of-speech taggers with named-entity recognition, such as in the BANNER system [40]. This removes reliance on lexicons and templates. This approach will be discussed further below.

(5) *Sub language-driven* approaches use the specialized language of a specific community. A specialized sub language typically has a set of constraints that determine vocabulary, composition, and syntax that can be translated into a set of rules for an algorithm. Algorithms for use in processing biology text must cope with specialized language and the telegraphic sentence structure found in many taxonomic works. Being unaware of a sub language will often lead to incorrect assumptions about use of the language. Metexa is an example of a tool that uses a specialized sub language in the radiology domain [41].

NLP techniques are often used as a (standard) initial text processing procedure in an IE application. Once a computer has an understanding of the syntactic and/or semantic meaning of the text, other methods, such as manually derived rules or machine learning based methods, are then often used for further information extraction.

2.3. Machine Learning. Machine learning has been used in IE applications since 1990s. It is a process by which a machine (i.e., computer algorithm) improves its performance automatically with experience [42]. Creating extraction rules automatically by machine learning are favored over creating them manually because the hand-crafted rules take longer to create and this time accumulates for each new document collection [43]. As a generic method, machine-learning applications may be found in all aspects of an IE system, ranging from learning lexicons for a syntactic parser, classifying and relating potential extraction targets, to fitting extracted entities into an extraction template.

Learning can take various forms including rule sets, decision trees, clustering algorithms, linear models, Bayesian networks, artificial neural networks, and genetic algorithms (which are capable of mimicking chromosome mutations). Some machine-learning algorithms (e.g., most classification algorithms such as decision trees, naïve Baysian, Support Vector Machines) rely on substantial "training" before they can perform a task independently. These algorithms fall in the category of "supervised machine learning." Some other algorithms (e.g., most clustering algorithms) require little or no training at all, so they belong to the "unsupervised machine learning" category. Due to the considerable cost associated with preparing training examples, one research theme in machine learning is to investigate innovative ways to reduce the amount of training examples required by supervised learning algorithms to achieve the desired level of performance. This gave rise to a third category of machine learning algorithms, "semisupervised." Co-training is one of the learning approaches that falls into this category. Co-training refers to two algorithms that are applied to the same task, but learn about that task in two different ways. For example, an algorithm can learn about the contents of a web site by (1) reading the text of the web site or (2) reading the text of the links to the web site. The two bodies of text are different, but refer to the same thing (i.e., the web site). Two different algorithms can be used to learn about the web site, feed each other machine-made training examples

ORIGINAL TEXT
Leaf blade orbiculate, 3–9 × 3–8 cm, leathery, base obtuse
EXPECTED EXTRACTION RESULT
leaf {leafShape: orbiculate}
leaf {bladeDimension: 3–9 × 3–8 cm}

Box 1

(which reduces the requirements of human-made training examples), and often make each other better. However, co-training requires two independent views of the same learning task and two independent learners. Not all learning tasks fulfill these requirements. One line of research in NLP that uses co-training is word sense disambiguation [44]. We are not aware of the use of this learning approach in biodiversity information extraction. The best learning algorithm for a certain task is determined by the nature of the task and characteristics of source data/document collection, so it is not always possible to design an unsupervised or semisupervised algorithm for a learning task (i.e., an unsupervised algorithm to recognize human handwriting may not be possible).

The form of training examples required by a supervised algorithm is determined largely by the learning task and the algorithm used. For example, in Tang and Heidorn [13], the algorithm was to learn (automatically generate) rules to extract leaf properties from plant descriptions. A training example used in their research as well as the manually derived, correct extraction is in Box 1 (examples slightly modified for human readability).

By comparing original text (italics) and the text in bold, the algorithm can derive a set of candidate extraction rules based on context. The algorithm would also decide the order that the extraction rules may be applied according to the rules' reliability as measured with training examples. The more reliable rules would be utilized first. Two extraction rules generated by the Tang and Heidorn [13] algorithm are shown in Box 2. Rule 1 extracts from the original text any leaf shape term (represented by <leafShape>) following a term describing leaf blade (represented by <PartBlade>) and followed by a comma (,) as the leafShape (represented by the placeholder $1). Rule 2 extracts any expression consisting of a range and length unit (represented by <Range><LengUnit>) that follows a comma (,) and is followed by another comma (,) and a leaf base term (represented by <PartBase>) as the bladeDimension.

These rules can then be used to extract information from new sentences not included in the original training example. Box 3 shows how the rules match a new statement, and are applied to extract new leafShape and bladeDimension values.

This example illustrates a case where words are the basic unit of processing and the task is to classify words by using the context where they appear (*obovate* is identified as a leaf shape because it follows the phrase "leaf blade").

In some applications, for example, named entity recognition (e.g., recognizing a word/phrase as a taxon name), an extraction target may appear in any context (e.g., a taxon name may be mentioned anywhere in a document). In these applications, the contextual information is less helpful in classifying a word/phrase than the letter combinations within the names. In NetiNeti, for example, a Naïve Baysian algorithm (a supervised learning algorithm based on Bayes conditional probability theorem) uses letter combinations to identify candidate taxon names [32]. When several training examples indicate names like *Turdus migratorius* are taxon names, NetiNeti may learn that a two-word phrase with the first letter capitalized and the last word ending with "*us*" (e.g., *Felis catus*) is probably a taxon name, even though *Felis catus* has never appeared in training examples.

Supervised learning algorithms can be more difficult to use in biology largely because compiling large training datasets can be labor intensive, which decreases the adaptability and scalability of an algorithm to new document collections. Hundreds of controlled vocabularies exist for biological sciences, which can provide some training information to an algorithm but are often not comprehensive [16].

Unsupervised learning algorithms do not use training examples. These algorithms try to find hidden structure in unlabeled data using characteristics of the text itself. Well-known unsupervised learning algorithms include clustering algorithms, dimensionality reduction, and self-organization maps, to name a few. Cui et al. Boufford [14] designed an unsupervised algorithm to identify organ names and organ properties from morphological description sentences. The algorithm took advantage of a recurring pattern in which plural nouns that start a sentence are organs and a descriptive sentence starts with an organ name followed by a series of property descriptors. These characteristics of descriptive sentences allow an unsupervised algorithm to discover organ names and properties.

The procedure may be illustrated by using a set of five descriptive statements taken from Flora of North America (Box 4).

Because *roots* is a plural noun and starts statement 1 (in addition, the words *rooting* or *rooted* are not seen in the entire document collection, so *roots* is unlikely a verb) the algorithm infers *roots* is an organ name. Then, what follows it (i.e., *yellow*) must be a property. The algorithm remembers *yellow* is a property when it encounters statement 2 and it then infers that *petals* is an organ. Similarly, when it reads statement 3, because *petals* is an organ, the algorithm infers *absent* is a property, which enables the algorithm to further infer *subtending bracts* and *abaxial hastular* in statements 4 and 5 are organs. This example shows that by utilizing the description characteristics, the algorithm is able to learn that *roots, petals, subtending bracts,* and *abaxial hastular* are organ names and *yellow* and *absent* are properties, without using any training examples, dictionaries, or ontologies.

Because not all text possesses the characteristics required by the algorithm developed by Cui et al. [14], it cannot be directly applied to all taxon descriptions. However, because descriptions with those characteristics do exist in large numbers and because of the low overhead (in terms of preparing training examples) of the unsupervised learning algorithm, it is argued that unsupervised learning should be

Rule 1: Pattern:: ∗ <PartBlade> (<leafShape>), ∗
Output:: leaf{leafShape: $1}
Rule 2: Pattern:: ∗ <PartBlade> ∗, (<Range><LengUnit>), <PartBase>
Output:: leaf{bladeDimension: $1}

Box 2

NEW TEXT
Leaf blade obovate, 1–3 × 1-2 cm, base rounded
Rule 1: Output:: leaf{leafShape: obovate}
Rule 2: Output:: leaf{bladeDimension: 1–3 × 1-2 cm}

Box 3

1. **roots** *yellow* to medium brown or black, thin.
2. **petals** *yellow* or white
3. **petals** *absent*
4. **subtendingbracts** *absent*
5. **abaxialhastular** *absent*

Box 4

exploited when possible, such as when preparing text for a supervised learning task [16].

3. Review of Biodiversity Information Extraction Systems

Our review describes the features of each system existing at the time of this writing. Many of the systems are being constantly developed with new features and enhanced capabilities. We encourage the readers to keep track of the development of these systems.

3.1. Digitization. The first step to making older biological literature machine readable is digitization (number 4 in Figure 2). Book pages can be scanned as images of text and made into pdf files, but cannot be submitted to NLP processing in this form. To make the text accessible, it must be OCRed (Optical Character Recognition) to translate the image of text (such as .pdf) into actual text (such as .txt). The Biodiversity Heritage Library is in the process of digitizing 600,000 pages of legacy text a month, making them available as pdf image files and OCR text files [45]. Most modern publications are available as pdf and html files from the publisher (and thus do not need to be scanned or OCRed). Images of text can be run through software designed to OCR files on desktop computers or as a web service (i.e., http://www.onlineocr.net/). OCR of handwriting is very different from that of text and can be quite difficult as there are as many handwriting styles as there are people. However, this type of OCR can be very important because significant portions of biodiversity data are only available as handwriting, such as museum specimen labels and laboratory notebooks. Algorithms do exist and are used for OCR of handwritten cities, states, and zip codes on envelopes and handwritten checks [46, 47].

OCR is not a perfect technology. It is estimated that >35% of taxon names in BHL OCR files contain an error [45, 48, 49]. This is skewed, however, as older documents that use nonstandard fonts carry the majority of the errors [49]. Biodiversity literature can be especially difficult to OCR as they often have multiple languages on the same page (such as Latin descriptions), an expansive historical record going back to the 15th Century (print quality and consistency issues), and an irregular typeface or typesetting [48]. OCR is poor at distinguishing indentation patterns, bold, and italicized text, which can be important in biodiversity literature [50, 51]. The current rate of digitization prohibits manual correction of these errors. Proposed solutions include components of crowd-sourcing manual corrections and machine-learning for automated corrections [48].

OCR errors may be overcome by using "fuzzy" matching algorithms that can recognize the correct term from the misspelled version. TAXAMATCH is a fuzzy matching algorithm for use in taxonomy [52]. The need for a "fuzzy matching" algorithm for detection of similar names is apparent for functions such as search, federation of content, and correction of misspellings or OCR errors. TAXAMATCH is a tool that uses phonetic- and nonphonetic-based near-match algorithms that calculate the distance of the given letter combination to a target name included in a reference database [52]. A letter combination with a close proximity to a target name is proposed as a fuzzy match. This system is being successfully used to increase hits in species databases [52] and is optimized for human typos rather than OCR errors. The php version of this code is available through Google code (http://code.google.com/p/taxamatch-webservice/) and a Ruby version is available through git hub (https://github.com/GlobalNamesArchitecture/taxamatch_rb).

3.2. Annotation. Once text has been digitized, it can be annotated in preparation for an IE task or for use as training data for algorithms (Figure 2 number 8). Both aims require different levels of annotation granularity, which can be accomplished manually or automatically using annotation software. A low level of granularity (coarse) is helpful for identifying blocks of text useful for IE. As mentioned before, not all text is useful for every IE task. In the practice of systematics, taxonomists need text containing nomenclatural acts which may be discovered and annotated automatically through terms such as "sp. nov." and "nov. comb." Annotation of these text blocks is helpful for algorithms designed to extract information about species. A finer granularity is needed for training data annotation. Words or phrases within a taxonomic work may be annotated as a name, description, location, and so forth. High granularity is more helpful for training a machine-learning algorithm but imposes a larger cost in time needed to do the manual annotation. There must be a balance between level of granularity and amount of manual investment which is determined by the specific goals at hand.

Manual annotation is very time consuming but can be assisted with annotation software. Several software packages aid with this.

taXMLit. TaXMLit is an interface to allow annotation of taxonomic literature [51]. It was developed using botanical and zoological text, but also works well on paleontological text. This system is designed for annotation of text elements such as "description" and "locality." This system requires a fairly large amount of human intervention and is not widely accepted.

GoldenGATE. GoldenGATE is an annotation tool for marking up taxonomic text in XML according to taxonX schema (http://plazi.org/files/GoldenGATE_V2_end_user_manual.pdf, [53]. Most of the annotation is done semi-automatically, with users checking the correctness of the annotations in the GoldenGATE editor that facilitates manual XML mark up. There are several plugins available for GoldenGATE, including modules for annotation specific to ZooTaxa and new plugins can be relatively easily added. The system is implemented in JAVA. This system performs best with text marked up with basic html tags (such as paragraph and header) and high-quality OCR.

ABNER. ABNER is an entity recognition algorithm designed specifically for the biomedical literature [54]. It uses a conditional random fields (CRF) model. This is a type of Bayesian statistics, wherein the computer uses characteristics of the text to determine the probability that a given term should be annotated as a given class. In this case, the available classes are: protein, DNA, RNA, Cell line, and Cell type. A human uses a point-and-click interface to confirm the algorithm results and add the annotation.

OnTheFly. OnTheFly is a text annotator that automatically finds and labels names of proteins, genes, and other small molecules in Microsoft Office, pdf, and text documents [55]. A user submits a file through the interface and it converts the file of interest into html and sends it to the Reflect tool. This tool looks for names and synonyms of proteins and small molecules to annotate as such [56]. It uses a list of 5.8 million molecule names from 373 organisms and returns matching terms. Clicking on an annotated term returns a pop-up window with additional information. In addition, this tool can create a graphical representation of the relationships between these entities using the STITCH database [57].

Phenex. Phenex was designed for use in the phenotypic literature [58]. It is a user interface that aids in manual annotation of biological text using terms from existing ontologies. Phenex allows users to annotate free text or NEXUS files. A core function of this software is to allow users to construct EQ (Entity:Quality) statements representing phenotypes. An EQ statement consists of two parts, a character (entity) and state (quality). The character is described using a term from an anatomy ontology and the state of that character is described using a term from a quality ontology (see, e.g., [59]). An example would be supraorbital bone:sigmoid. The fact that sigmoid is a shape is inferred from the PATO ontology and thus does not have to be specifically mentioned in the EQ statement (within [59] see Figure 1). Users can load the ontology containing the terms they want to use for annotation into Phenex which has an auto-complete function to facilitate work. The Phenex GUI provides components for editing, searching, and graphical displays of terms. This software is open source, released under the MIT license (http://phenoscape.org/wiki/Phenex).

3.3. Names Recognition and Discovery. A taxonomic name is connected to almost every piece of information about an organism, making names near universal metadata in biology (see Rod Page's iphylo blog entry http://iphylo.blogspot.com/2011/04/dark-taxa-genbank-in-post-taxonomic.html for an exception). This can be exploited to find and manage nearly all biological data. No life-wide, comprehensive list of taxonomic names exists, but the Global Names Index (GNI) holds 20 million names and NameBank (http://www.ubio.org/index.php?pagename=namebank) holds 10 million names. There are also exclusive lists of taxonomically creditable names such as the Catalogue of Life (CoLP) and the Interim Register of Marine and Non-marine Genera (IRMNG). These lists hold 1.3 million and 1.6 million names, respectively.

Taxonomic names discovery (or Named Entity Recognition in computer science parlance) can be achieved through several approaches. *Dictionary-based approaches* rely on an existing list of names. These systems try to find names on the list directly in the text. The major drawback of this approach in biology is that there is no comprehensive list of names and terms including all misspellings, variants, and abbreviations. Dictionary-based approaches can also miss synonyms and ambiguous names. Some algorithms have been developed to aid dictionary-based approaches with recognizing variants of names in the list (e.g., see algorithms described below). *Rule-based approaches* work by applying a fixed set of rules to a text. This approach is capable of dealing with variations in word order and sentence structure in addition to word morphology. The major drawback is that the rule sets are handmade (and, therefore, labor intensive) and are rarely applicable to multiple domains. *Machine-learning approaches* use rule sets generated by the machine using statistical procedures (such as Hidden Markov Models). In this approach, algorithms are trained on an annotated body of text in which names are tagged by hand. The algorithms can be applied to text in any discipline as long as appropriate training data are available. All of these approaches have strengths and weaknesses, so they are often combined in final products.

TABLE 4: Performance metrics for the names recognition and morphological character extraction algorithms reviewed. Recall and precision values may not be directly comparable between the different algorithms. NA: not available [30].

Tool	Recall	Precision	Test Corpora	Reference
TaxonGrab	>94%	>96%	Vol. 1 Birds of the Belgian Congo by Chapin	[31]
FAT	40.2%	84.0%	American Seashells by Abbott	[32]
Taxon Finder	54.3%	97.5%	American Seashells by Abbott	[32]
Neti Neti	70.5%	98.9%	American Seashells by Abbott	[32]
LINNAEUS	94.3%	97.1%	LINNAEUS gold standard data set	[33]
Organism Tagger	94.0%	95.0%	LINNAEUS gold standard data set	[34]
X-tract	NA	NA	Flora of North America	[35]
Worldwide Botanical Knowledge Base	NA	NA	Flora of China	http://wwbota.free.fr/
Terminator	NA	NA	16 nematode descriptions	http://www.math.ucdavis.edu/ ~milton/genisys/terminator.html
MultiFlora	mid 60%	mid 70%	Descriptions of Ranunculus spp. from six Floras	http://intranet.cs.man.ac.uk/ai/public/ MultiFlora/MF1.html
MARTT	98.0%	58.0%	Flora of North America and Flora of China	[30]
WHISK	33.33% to 79.65%	72.52% to 100%	Flora of North America	[13]
CharaParser	90.0%	91.0%	Flora of North America	[36]

Several algorithms have been developed that are capable of identifying and discovering known and unknown (to the algorithm) taxon names in free text. These are discussed below and their performance metrics are given in Table 4.

TaxonGrab. TaxonGrab identifies names by using a combination of nomenclatural rules and a list (dictionary) of non-taxonomic English terms [31]. As most taxonomic names do not match words in common parlance, the dictionary can be used as a "black list" to exclude terms. This is not always the case because some Latin names match vernacular names, such as bison and *Bison bison*. The algorithm scans text for terms that are not found in the black list. It treats these as candidate names. These terms are then compared to the capitalization rules of Linnaean nomenclature. Algorithms of this type have low precision because misspelled, non-English words, medical, or legal terms would be flagged as a candidate name. However, these terms can be iteratively added to the black list, improving future precision. This method does have the advantage of not requiring a complete list of species names, but can only be used on English texts. Later, several additional rules were added to create a new product, FAT [60]. FAT employs "fuzzy" matching and structural rules sequentially so that each rule can use

the results of the last. The TaxonGrab code is available at SourceForge, but the FAT code is not. FAT is a part of the plazi.org toolset for markup of taxonomic text.

TaxonFinder. TaxonFinder identifies scientific names in free text by comparing the name to several lists embedded into the source code ([61], Leary personal comments). These lists are derived from a manually curated version of NameBank (http://www.ubio.org/index.php?pagename=namebank). A list of ambiguous names was compiled from words that are names, but are more often used in common parlance, like pluto or tumor. TaxonFinder breaks documents into words and compares them to the lists individually. When it encounters a capitalized word, it checks the "genus" and "above-genus" name lists. If the word is in the above-genus list, but not in the ambiguous name list, it is returned as a name. If it is in the genus list, the next word is checked to see if it is in lower case or all caps and to see if it is in the "species-or-below" name list. If it is, then the process is repeated with the next word until a complete polynomial is returned. If the next word is not in the list, then the previous name is returned as a genus. TaxonFinder is limited to dictionaries and thus will not find new names or misspellings but can discover new combinations of known names. This system can have both high precision and recall with a higher score in precision (more false negatives than false positives). A previous version of TaxonFinder, FindIT (http://www.ubio.org/tools/recognize.php), had the ability to identify authorship by recognizing the reference (usually a taxonomist's name), which TaxonFinder does not do (http://code.google.com/p/taxon-name-processing/wiki/nameRecognition). A new, Apache Lucene-based name indexer is now available from GBIF which is based on TaxonFinder (http://tools.gbif.org/namefinder/). The source code for TaxonFinder is available at Google code (http://code.google.com/p/taxon-finder/).

NetiNeti. NetiNeti takes a more unsupervised approach to names extraction [32]. The system uses natural language processing techniques involving probabilistic classifiers (Naive Bayes classifier by default) to recognize scientific names in an arbitrary document. The classifier is trained to recognize characteristics of scientific names as well as the context. The algorithm uses "white list" and "black list" detection techniques in a secondary role. As a result, scientific names not mentioned in a white list or names with OCR errors or misspellings are found with great accuracy. Some of the limitations of NetiNeti include an inability to identify genus names less than four letters long, the assumption of one letter abbreviations of genera, and limitation of contextual information available to one word on either side of a candidate name. The code of this tool is written in Python and is going to be released under GPL2 license at https://github.com/mbl-cli/NetiNeti.

Linnaeus. This is a list-based system designed specifically for identifying taxonomic names in biomedical literature and linking those names to database identifiers [33]. The system recognizes names contained in a white list (based on the NCBI classification and a custom set of synonyms) and resolves them to an unambiguous NCBI taxonomy identifier within the NCBI taxonomy database (http://www.ncbi.nlm.nih.gov/books/NBK21100/). In this way, multiple names for one species are normalized to a single identifier. This system is capable of recognizing and normalizing ambiguous mentions, such as abbreviations (*C. elegans*, which refers to 41 species) and acronyms (CMV, which refers to 2 species). Acronyms that are not listed within the NCBI classification are discovered using the Acromine service [62] and a novel acronym detector built into LINNAEUS that can detect acronym definitions within text (in the form of "species (acronym)"). Ambiguous mentions that are not resolvable are assigned a probability of how likely the mention refers to a species based on the relative frequency of nonambiguous mentions across all of MEDLINE. Applying a black list of species names that occur commonly in the English language when not referring to species (such as the common name spot) greatly reduces false positives. LINNAEUS can process files in XML and txt formats and give output in tab-separated files, XML, HTML and MySQL database tables. This code is available at SourceForge (http://sourceforge.net/projects/linnaeus/).

OrganismTagger. This system uses the NCBI taxonomy database (http://www.ncbi.nlm.nih.gov/books/NBK21100/) to generate semantically enabled lists and ontology components for organism name extraction from free text [34]. These components are connected to form a work flow pipeline using GATE (the General Architecture for Text Engineering; [63, 64]). These components are a combination of rule-based and machine-learning approaches to discover and extract names from text, including strain designations. To identify strains not in the NCBI taxonomy database, OrganismTagger uses a "strain classifier," a machine-learning (SVM model) approach trained on manually annotated documents. After the strain classifier is applied, organism names are first detected, then normalized to a single canonical name and grounded to a specific NCBI database ID. The semantic nature of this tool allows it to output data in many different formats (XML, OWL, etc.). This code along with supporting materials is available under an open source license at http://www.semanticsoftware.info/organism-tagger.

3.4. Morphological Character Extraction. Morphological characters of organisms are of interest to systematists, evolutionary biologists, ecologists, and the general public. The examples used in Figure 4 are typical of morphological descriptions. The kinds of language used in biodiversity science has the following characteristics that make it difficult for general-purpose parsers to process [15, 65, 66].

(1) Specialized Language. Most scientific terms are not in the lexicons of existing parsers. Even if they were, biological terms are more ambiguous than general English [67]. General English has 0.57% ambiguous terms while gene names have 14.2% ambiguity. Taxonomic homonyms are 15% at the genus level (http://www.obis.org.au/irmng/irmng_faq/). Life Science literature also relies heavily on abbreviations [68]. There were over 64,000 new abbreviations introduced in 2004 in the biomedical literature alone and an average of one new abbreviation every 5–10 abstracts [69]. Dictionaries, such as the Dictionary of Medical Acronyms and Abbreviations can help, but most dictionaries contain 4,000 to 32,000 terms, which is only a fraction of the estimated 800,000 believed to exist [69, 70]. This means that dictionary-based approaches will not scale to work in biology.

(2) Diversity. Descriptions are very diverse across taxon groups. Even in one group, for example, plants, variations are large. Lydon et al. [71] compared and contrasted the descriptions of five common species in six different English language Floras and found the same information in all sources only 9% of the time. They also noted differences in terminology usage across Floras.

(3) Syntax differences. Many species descriptions are in telegraphic sublanguage (that lacks of verbs) but there are also many descriptions conforming to more standard English syntax. Parsers expecting standard English syntax often mistake other groups of words

for verbs when parsing telegraphic sublanguage because they expect to see verbs in a sentence. There is not typically standardized syntax across different taxon groups or even within the same group.

Taylor [15, 72] manually constructed a grammar and a lexicon of 2000 characters, and character states (1500 from Radford [73] and 500 from descriptive text) to parse the Flora of New South Wales (4 volumes) and volume 19 of the Flora of Australia. The goal of parsing these Floras was to create sets of organism part, character, and character state from each description. These statements can be extracted from morphological taxon descriptions using the hand-crafted parser to get a machine-readable set of facts about organism characteristics. While the sublanguage nature of the plant descriptions used by Taylor [15, 72] made it easier to construct the grammar and lexicon manually, the author acknowledged the limited coverage they could be expected to achieve (60–80% recall was estimated based on manual examination of output). Algorithms for machine-aided expansion of the lexicon were suggested; however, at the time automated creation of rules was believed to be too difficult.

Since Taylor [15, 72], a variety of methods have been used to extract morphological traits from morphological descriptions. Their performance metrics are given in Table 4.

X-Tract. X-tract [35] was an interactive tool to extract morphological information from Flora of North America (FNA) descriptions available as a print and HTML version. X-tract used HTML tags embedded in the FNA pages to identify the morphological description sections. It used a glossary to classify each word in a description as structure (i.e., organs or part of organs) or character states. If a word was a character state, its corresponding characters were looked up in the glossary. Then, X-tract created a form to display the structures, substructures, characters, and character states extracted from a document for a user to review, modify, and save to a database. Evaluation of the extraction accuracy or the extent of user intervention was not provided.

Worldwide Botanical Knowledge Base. Jean-Marc Vanel initiated a project called Worldwide Botanical Knowledge Base, which also takes the approach of parsing plus glossary/lexicon. It marks up morphological descriptions at sentence level (e.g., leaf blade obovate is marked as "leaf blade") without extracting detailed character information. It stores extracted information in XML files instead of a relational database as Taylor [15, 72] and Abascal and Sánchez [35]. The project aims to support queries on species descriptions in botanical databases. The database search seems to have stopped working (http://jmvanel.free.fr/protea.html). The parser was reported to work on Flora of China and it can be downloaded from the website (http://wwbota.free.fr/). However, as of the time of this publication, the authors were unable to use the parser.

Terminator. Diederich, Fortuner and Milton [74] developed a system called Terminator, which used a hand-crafted plant glossary that amounts to an ontology including structure names, characters and character states to support character extraction. The extraction process was a combination of fuzzy keyword match and heuristic extraction rules. Because Terminator was an interactive system (i.e., a human operator selects correct extractions), the evaluation was done on 16 descriptions to report the time taken to process them. Extraction performance was evaluated only on 1 random sample: for non-numerical characters, 55% of the time a perfect structure/character/value combination was among the first 5 candidates suggested by the system.

MultiFlora. Similar to previous works, Wood, Lydon, and colleagues' MultiFlora project (http://intranet.cs.man.ac.uk/ai/public/MultiFlora/MF1.html) started with manual analysis of description documents. They created an ontology manually, which included classes of organs (i.e., petal) and features (i.e., yellow) linked by properties (i.e., hasColor). They also manually created a gazetteer, which included terms referring to the organs and features that served as a lookup list. The prototype MultiFlora system used a combination of keyword matching, internal and contextual pattern matching, and shallow parsing techniques provided by GATE to extract organ and feature information from a small collection of morphological descriptions (18 species descriptions, recall, and precision were in the range of mid 60% to mid 70%; [66, 75]). While the work of Wood, Lydon, and colleagues shows that using descriptions from different sources can be used to improve recall, the authors acknowledged that organs not included in the manually-created gazetteer/ontology have to be marked as "unknown." The extraction results were output in RDF triples and used to build a knowledgebase about plants, which is not related to Worldwide Botanical Knowledge Base reviewed earlier. RDF is a type of programming language that allows a user to make machine readable assertions in the form of an RDF triple. The EQ format mentioned earlier is a similar format used in biology. The advantage to using ontology-supported RDF/EQ is that multiple data providers can use the same ontological identifier for the same term. In this way, statements become machine-readable and can be linked regardless of the source. With ontological support, machine-based logic reasoning has become possible. An immediate application of this type of reasoning and a pool of RDF triples describing species morphology is a specimen identification key. RDF is supported by more recent biodiversity IE systems as an output format.

MARTT. MARTT [76] is an automated description markup system employing a supervised machine-learning algorithm. The system marks up a description sentence-by-sentence with tags that indicate the subject, for example, "stem" is tagged in the text statement "stem solitary." MARTT along with a test collection is downloadable from http://sites.google.com/site/biosemanticsproject/project-progress-wiki. Wei [77] conducted an exploratory study of the application of information fusion techniques to taxonomic descriptions. It confirmed Wood et al. [75] finding that combining multiple descriptions of the same species from different sources and different taxonomic ranks can provide the researchers more complete information than any single description. Wei used MARTT [76] and a set of heuristic rules to extract character information from descriptions of taxa published in both FNA and Flora of China (FoC) and categorized the extracted information between the two sources as either identical, equivalent, subsumption, complementary, overlap, or conflict. Non-conflict information from both sources was then merged together. The evaluation was conducted involving 13 human curators verifying results generated from 153 leaf descriptions. The results show that the precisions for genus level fusion, species level fusion, FNA genus-species fusion, and FoC genus-species fusion were 77%, 63%, 66%, and 71%, respectively. The research also identified the key factors that contribute to the performance of the system: the quality of the dictionary (or the domain knowledge), the variance of the vocabulary, and the quality of prior IE steps.

WHISK. Tang and Heidorn [13] adapted WHISK [78] to extract morphological character and other information from several volumes of FNA to show that IE helps the information retrieval system SEARFA (e.g., retrieval of relevant documents). The "pattern matching" learning method used by WHISK is described in Section 2. The pattern matching algorithm was assisted by a knowledge base created by manually collecting structure and character terms from training examples. The IE system was evaluated on a relatively small subset of FNA documents and it was evaluated on different template slots (see Table 1 for examples of template slots) separately. Different numbers of training and/or test examples were used for different slots (training examples ranged from 7 to 206, test examples ranged from 6 to 192) and the performance scores were obtained from one run (as opposed to using the typical protocol for supervised learning algorithms). The system performed perfectly on nonmorphological character slots (Genus, Species, and Distribution). The recall on morphological character slots (Leaf shape, Leaf margin, Leaf apex, Leaf base, Leaf arrangement, Blade dimension, Leaf color, and Fruit/nut shape) ranged from 33.33% to 79.65%. The precision ranged from 75.52% to 100%. Investigation of human user performance on plant identification using internet-based information retrieval systems showed that even with imperfect extraction performance, users were able to make significantly more identifications using the information retrieval system supported by the extracted character information than using a keyword-based full-text search system.

CharaParser. All IE systems reviewed above relied on manually created vocabulary resources, whether they are called lexicons, gazetteers, or knowledge bases. Vocabularies are a fundamental resource on which more advanced syntactic and semantic analyses are built. While manually collecting terms for a proof-of-concept system is feasible, the manual approach cannot be scaled to the problem of extracting morphological traits of all taxa. Cui, Seldon & Boufford [14] proposed an unsupervised bootstrapping based algorithm

(described in Section 2) that can extract 93% of anatomical terms and over 50% character terms from text descriptions without any training examples. This efficient tool may be used to build vocabulary resources that are required to use various IE systems on new document collections.

This unsupervised algorithm has been used in two IE systems [36, 79]. One of the systems used intuitive heuristic rules to associate extracted character information with appropriate anatomical structures. The other system (called CharaParser) adapted a general-purpose syntactic parser (Stanford Parser) to guide the extraction. In addition to structures and character extraction, both systems extract constraints, modifiers, and relations among anatomical structures (e.g., head *subtended by* distal leaves; pappi *consist of* bristles) as stated in a description. Both systems were tested on two sets of descriptions from volume 19 of FNA and Part H of Treatise on Invertebrate Paleontology (TIP); each set consisted of over 400 descriptions. The heuristic rule-based system achieved precision/recall of 63%/60% on the FNA evaluation set and 52%/43% on the TIP evaluation set on character extraction. CharaParser performed significantly better and achieved precision/recall of 91%/90% on the FNA set and 80%/87% on the TIP set. Similar to Wood et al. [66], Cui and team found the information structure of morphological descriptions was too complicated to be represented in a typical IE template (such as Table 1). Wood et al. [66] designed an ontology to hold the extracted information, while Cui and team used XML to store extracted information (Figure 5). CharaParser is expected to be released as an open-source software in Fall 2012. Interested readers may contact the team to obtain a trial version before its release.

3.5. Integrated IE Systems. Tang and Heidorn [13] supervised learning IE system, MutiFlora, and the CharaParser system, all reviewed before, can be described using the reference model depicted in Figure 2. Here, we describe another system that integrates formal ontologies. This is the text mining system that is currently under development by the Phenoscape project (http://www.phenoscape.org/). The goal of Phenoscape is to turn text phenotype descriptions to EQ expressions [80] to support machine reasoning of scientific knowledge as a transforming way of conducting biological research. In this application, EQ expressions may be considered both the IE template and a data standard. The input to the Phenoscape text mining system is digital or OCRed phylogenetic publications. The character descriptions are targeted (1 character description = 1 character statement + multiple character state statements) and used to form the taxon-character matrix. The target sections are extracted by student assistants using Phenex and put into NeXML (http://www.nexml.org/) format. NeXML is an exchange standard for representing phyloinformatic data. It is inspired by the commonly used NEXUS format, but more robust and easier to process. There is one NeXML file for a source text. NeXML files are the input to CharaParser, which performs bootstrapping-based learning (i.e., unsupervised learning) and deep parsing to extract information and output candidate EQ expressions. CharaParser learns lexicons of anatomy terms and character terms from description

```
(a) Original sentence:
    principal cauline well distributed, gradually reduced distally, bases of proximal cauline winged-petiolate or
    sessile, based of distal cauline expanded and clasping margins sometimes spinier than those of proximal;
(b) Extraction Result in XML:
    <?xml version="1.0" encoding="utf-8"?>
    <statmentn id="83.txt-6">
    <structure id="o1" name="leaf" constraint="principal cauline">
      <character name="arrengement" value="distributed" modifier="well" />
      <character name="size" value="reduced" modifier="gradually;distally" />
    </structure>
    <structure id="o2" name="base">
      <character name="architecture" value="winged-potiolate" />
      <character name="architecture" value="sessile" />
    </structure>
    <structure id="o3" name="leaf" constraint="proximal cauline">
    <relation id="r1" name="part_of" from="o2" to="o3" negation="false" />
    <structure id="o4" name="base">
      <character name="size" value="expanded" />
      <character name="architecture" value="clasping" />
    </structure>
    <structure id="o5" name="leaf" constraint="distal cauline" />
    <relation id="r2" name="part_of" from="o4" to="o5" negation="false" />
    <structure id="o6" name="margin">
      <character name="architecture" value="spinier" modifier="sometimes" constraint="thanmargins"
      constraintid="o7" />
    </structure>
    <structure id="o7" name="margin" />
    <structure id="o8" name="leaf" constraint="proximal" />
    <relation id="r3" name="part_of" from="o7" to="o8" negation="false" />
    </statment>
```

FIGURE 5: Extraction result from a descriptive sentence.

collections. Learned terms are reviewed by biologist curators (many OCR errors are detected during this step). Terms that are not in existing anatomy ontologies are proposed to the ontologies for addition. The lexicons and ontologies are the knowledge entities that the text mining system iteratively uses and enhances. With new terms added to the ontologies, the system replaces the terms in candidate EQ statements with term IDs from the ontologies. For example, [E]tooth [Q]large is turned into [E]TAO: 0001625 [Q]PATO: 0001202. The candidate EQ expressions are reviewed and accepted by biologist curators using Phenex. Final EQ expressions are loaded into the Phenoscape Knowledge base at http://kb.phenoscape.org/. This EQ populated knowledge base supports formal logical reasoning. At the time of writing, the developing work is ongoing to integrate CharaParser with Phenex to produce an integrated text-mining system for Phenoscape. It is important to notice that the applicability of Phenex and CharaParser is not taxon specific.

4. Conclusion

NLP approaches are capable of extracting large amounts of information from free text. However, biology text presents a unique challenge (compared to news articles) to machine-learning algorithms due to its ambiguity, diversity, and specialized language. Successful IE strategies in biodiversity science take advantage of the Linnaean binomial structure of names and the structured nature of taxon descriptions. Multiple tools currently exist for fuzzy matching of terms, automated annotation, named-entity recognition, and morphological character extraction that use a variety of approaches. None have yet been used on a large scale to extract information about all life, but several, such as CharaParser, show potential to be used in this way. Further improvement of biodiversity IE tools could be achieved through increased participation in the annual BioCreative competitions (http://www.biocreative.org/) and assessing tool performance on publicly available document sets so

that comparison between systems (and thus identification of methods that have real potential to address biodiversity IE problems) becomes easier.

A long-term vision for the purpose of making biodiversity data machine readable is the compilation of semantic species descriptions that can be linked into a semantic web for biology. An example of semantic species information can be found at TaxonConcept.org. This concept raises many questions concerning semantics which are outside the scope of this paper, such as what makes a "good" semantic description of a species. Many of these issues are technical and are being addressed within the computer science community. There are two data pathways that need to be developed to achieve the semantic web for biology. One is a path going forward, in which new data are made machine-readable from the beginning of a research project. The model of mobilizing data many years after collection with little to no data management planning during collection is not sustainable or desirable going into the future. Research is being applied to this area and publishers, such as Pensoft, are working to capture machine-readable data about species at the point of publication. The other is a path for mobilizing data that have already been collected. NLP holds much promise in helping with the second path.

Mobilizing the entirety of biodiversity knowledge collected over the past 250 years is an ambitious goal that requires meeting several challenges from both the taxonomic and technological fronts. Considering the constantly changing nature of biodiversity science and the constraints of NLP algorithms, best results may be achieved by drawing information from high quality modern reviews of taxonomic groups rather than repositories of original descriptions. However, such works can be rare or nonexistent for some taxa. Thus, issues such as proper aggregation of information extracted from multiple sources on a single subject (as mentioned above) still need to be addressed. In addition, demanding that a modern review be available somewhat defeats the purpose of applying NLP to biodiversity science.

While using a modern review may be ideal when available, it should not be required for information extraction.

Biodiversity science, as a discipline, is being asked to address numerous challenges related to climate change, biodiversity loss, and invasive species. Solutions to these problems require discovery and aggregation of data from the entire pool of biological knowledge including what is contained exclusively in print holdings. Digitization and IE on this scale is unprecedented. Unsupervised algorithms hold the greatest promise for achieving the scalability required because they do not require manually generated training data. However, most successful IE algorithms use combinations of supervised and unsupervised strategies and multiple NLP approaches because not all problems can be solved with an unsupervised algorithm. If the challenge is not met, irreplaceable data from centuries of research funded by billions of dollars may be lost. The annotation and extraction algorithms mentioned in this manuscript are key steps toward liberating existing biological data and even serve as preliminary evidence that this goal can be achieved.

Acknowledgments

The authors would like to thank Dr. David J. Patterson, Dr. Holly Bowers, and Mr. Nathan Wilson for thoughtful comments on an early version of this manuscript and productive discussion. This work was funded in part by the MacArthur Foundation Grant to the Encyclopedia of Life, the National Science Foundation Data Net Program Grant no. 0830976, and the National Science Foundation Emerging Front Grant no. 0849982.

References

[1] B. Wuethrich, "How climate change alters rhythms of the wild," *Science*, vol. 287, no. 5454, pp. 793–795, 2000.

[2] W. E. Bradshaw and C. M. Holzapfel, "Genetic shift in photoperiodic response correlated with global warming," *Proceedings of the National Academy of Sciences of the United States of America*, vol. 98, no. 25, pp. 14509–14511, 2001.

[3] National Academy of Sciences, "New biology for the 21st Century," *Frontiers in Ecology and the Environment*, vol. 7, no. 9, article 455, 2009.

[4] A. E. Thessen and D. J. Patterson, "Data issues in life science," *ZooKeys*, vol. 150, pp. 15–51, 2011.

[5] A. Hey, *The Fourth Paradigm: Data-Intensive Scientific Discovery*, 2009, http://iw.fh-potsdam.de/fileadmin/FB5/Dokumente/forschung/tagungen/i-science/TonyHey_-_eScience_Potsdam_Mar2010___complete_pdf.

[6] L. D. Stein, "Towards a cyberinfrastructure for the biological sciences: progress, visions and challenges," *Nature Reviews Genetics*, vol. 9, pp. 678–688, 2008.

[7] P. B. Heidorn, "Shedding light on the dark data in the long tail of science," *Library Trends*, vol. 57, no. 2, pp. 280–299, 2008.

[8] Key Perspectives Ltd, "Data dimensions: disciplinary differences in research data sharing, reuse and long term viability," Digital Curation Centre, 2010, http://scholar.google.com/scholar?hl=en&q=Data+Dimensions:+disciplinary+differences+in+research+data-sharing,+reuse+and+long+term+viability.++&btnG=Search&as_sdt=0,22&as_ylo=&as_vis=0#0.

[9] A. Vollmar, J. A. Macklin, and L. Ford, "Natural history specimen digitization: challenges and concerns," *Biodiversity Informatics*, vol. 7, no. 2, 2010.

[10] P. N. Schofield, J. Eppig, E. Huala et al., "Sustaining the data and bioresource commons," *Research Funding*, vol. 330, no. 6004, pp. 592–593, 2010.

[11] P. Groth, A. Gibson, and J. Velterop, "Anatomy of a Nanopublication," *Information Services & Use*, vol. 30, no. 1-2, pp. 51–56, 2010.

[12] M. Kalfatovic, "Building a global library of taxonomic literature," in *28th Congresso Brasileiro de Zoologia Biodiversidade e Sustentabilidade*, 2010, http://www.slideshare.net/Kalfatovic/building-a-global-library-of-taxonomic-literature.

[13] X. Tang and P. Heidorn, "Using automatically extracted information in species page retrieval," 2007, http://scholar.google.com/scholar?hl=en&q=Tang+Heidorn+2007+using+automatically+extracted&btnG=Search&as_sdt=0,22&as_ylo=&as_vis=0#0.

[14] H. Cui, P. Selden, and D. Boufford, "Semantic annotation of biosystematics literature without training examples," *Journal of the American Society for Information Science and Technology*, vol. 61, pp. 522–542, 2010.

[15] A. Taylor, "Extracting knowledge from biological descriptions," in *Proceedings of 2nd International Conference on Building and Sharing Very Large-Scale Knowledge Bases*, pp. 114–119, 1995.

[16] H. Cui, "Competency evaluation of plant character ontologies against domain literature," *Journal of the American Society for Information Science and Technology*, vol. 61, no. 6, pp. 1144–1165, 2010.

[17] Y. Miyao, K. Sagae, R. Sætre, T. Matsuzaki, and J. Tsujii, "Evaluating contributions of natural language parsers to protein-protein interaction extraction," *Bioinformatics*, vol. 25, no. 3, pp. 394–400, 2009.

[18] K. Humphreys, G. Demetriou, and R. Gaizauskas, "Two applications of information extraction to biological science journal articles: enzyme interactions and protein structures," in *Proceedings of the Pacific Symposium on Biocomputing (PSB '00)*, vol. 513, pp. 505–513, 2000.

[19] R. Gaizauskas, G. Demetriou, P. J. Artymiuk, and P. Willett, "Protien structures and information extraction from biological texts: the pasta system," *Bioinformatics*, vol. 19, no. 1, pp. 135–143, 2003.

[20] A. Divoli and T. K. Attwood, "BioIE: extracting informative sentences from the biomedical literature," *Bioinformatics*, vol. 21, no. 9, pp. 2138–2139, 2005.

[21] D. P. A. Corney, B. F. Buxton, W. B. Langdon, and D. T. Jones, "BioRAT: extracting biological information from full-length papers," *Bioinformatics*, vol. 20, no. 17, pp. 3206–3213, 2004.

[22] H. Chen and B. M. Sharp, "Content-rich biological network constructed by mining PubMed abstracts," *Bmc Bioinformatics*, vol. 5, article 147, 2004.

[23] X. Zhou, X. Zhang, and X. Hu, "Dragon toolkit: incorporating auto-learned semantic knowledge into large-scale text retrieval and mining," in *Proceedings of the19th IEEE International Conference on Tools with Artificial Intelligence (ICTAI '07)*, pp. 197–201, October 2007.

[24] D. Rebholz-Schuhmann, H. Kirsch, M. Arregui, S. Gaudan, M. Riethoven, and P. Stoehr, "EBIMed—text crunching to gather facts for proteins from Medline," *Bioinformatics*, vol. 23, no. 2, pp. e237–e244, 2007.

[25] Z. Z. Hu, I. Mani, V. Hermoso, H. Liu, and C. H. Wu, "iProLINK: an integrated protein resource for literature

mining," *Computational Biology and Chemistry*, vol. 28, no. 5-6, pp. 409–416, 2004.

[26] J. Demaine, J. Martin, L. Wei, and B. De Bruijn, "LitMiner: integration of library services within a bio-informatics application," *Biomedical Digital Libraries*, vol. 3, article 11, 2006.

[27] M. Lease and E. Charniak, "Parsing biomedical literature," in *Proceedings of the 2nd International Joint Conference on Natural Language Processing (IJCNLP '05)*, Jeju Island, Korea, 2005.

[28] S. Pyysalo and T. Salakoski, "Lexical adaptation of link grammar to the biomedical sublanguage: a comparative evaluation of three approaches," *BMC Bioinformatics*, vol. 7, supplement 3, article S2, 2006.

[29] L. Rimell and S. Clark, "Porting a lexicalized-grammar parser to the biomedical domain," *Journal of Biomedical Informatics*, vol. 42, no. 5, pp. 852–8865, 2009.

[30] H. Cui, "Converting taxonomic descriptions to new digital formats," *Biodiversity Informatics*, vol. 5, pp. 20–40, 2008.

[31] D. Koning, I. N. Sarkar, and T. Moritz, "TaxonGrab: extracting taxonomic names from text," *Biodiversity Informatics*, vol. 2, pp. 79–82, 2005.

[32] L. M. Akella, C. N. Norton, and H. Miller, "NetiNeti: discovery of scientific names from text using machine learning methods," 2011.

[33] M. Gerner, G. Nenadic, and C. M. Bergman, "LINNAEUS: a species name identification system for biomedical literature," *BMC Bioinformatics*, vol. 11, article 85, 2010.

[34] N. Naderi and T. Kappler, "OrganismTagger: detection, normalization and grounding of organism entities in biomedical documents," *Bioinformatics*, vol. 27, no. 19, pp. 2721–2729, 2011.

[35] R. Abascal and J. A. Sánchez, "X-tract: structure extraction from botanical textual descriptions," in *Proceeding of the String Processing & Information Retrieval Symposium & International Workshop on Groupware*, pp. 2–7, IEEE Computer Society, Cancun , Mexico, September 1999.

[36] H. Cui, "CharaParser for fine-grained semantic annotation of organism morphological descriptions," *Journal of the American Society for Information Science and Technology*, vol. 63, no. 4, pp. 738–754, 2012.

[37] M. Krauthammer, A. Rzhetsky, P. Morozov, and C. Friedman, "Using BLAST for identifying gene and protein names in journal articles," *Gene*, vol. 259, no. 1-2, pp. 245–252, 2000.

[38] L. Lenzi, F. Frabetti, F. Facchin et al., "UniGene tabulator: a full parser for the UniGene format," *Bioinformatics*, vol. 22, no. 20, pp. 2570–2571, 2006.

[39] A. Nasr and O. Rambow, "Supertagging and full parsing," in *Proceedings of the 7th International Workshop on Tree Adjoining Grammar and Related Formalisms (TAG '04)*, 2004.

[40] R. Leaman and G. Gonzalez, "BANNER: an executable survey of advances in biomedical named entity recognition," in *Proceedings of the Pacific Symposium on Biocomputing (PSB '08)*, pp. 652–663, Kona, Hawaii, USA, January 2008.

[41] M. Schröder, "Knowledge-based processing of medical language: a language engineering approach," in *Proceedings of the16th German Conference on Artificial Intelligence (GWAI '92)*, vol. 671, pp. 221–234, Bonn, Germany, August-September 1992.

[42] I. H. Witten and E. Frank, *Data Mining: Practical Machine Learning Tools and Techniques*, Morgan Kaufmann Series in Data Management Systems, Morgan Kaufmann, 2nd edition, 2005.

[43] C. Blaschke, L. Hirschman, and A. Valencia, "Information extraction in molecular biology," *Briefings in Bioinformatics*, vol. 3, no. 2, pp. 154–165, 2002.

[44] A. Jimeno-Yepes and A. R. Aronson, "Self-training and co-training in biomedical word sense disambiguation," pp. 182–183.

[45] C. Freeland, "An evaluation of taxonomic name finding & next steps in Biodiversity Heritage Library (BHL) developments," *Nature Precedings*, 2009, http://precedings.nature.com/documents/3372/version/1.

[46] A. Kornai, "Experimental hmm-based postal ocr system," in *Proceedings of the IEEE International Conference on Acoustics, Speech, and Signal Processing (ICASSP '97)*, vol. 4, pp. 3177–3180, April 1997.

[47] A. Kornai, K. Mohiuddin, and S. D. Connell, "Recognition of cursive writing on personal checks," in *Proceedings of the 5th International Workshop on Frontiers in Handwriting Recognition*, pp. 373–378, Citeseer, Essex, UK, 1996.

[48] C. Freeland, "Digitization and enhancement of biodiversity literature through OCR, scientific names mapping and crowdsourcing.," in *BioSystematics Berlin*, 2011, http://www.slideshare.net/chrisfreeland/digitization-and-enhancement-of-biodiversity-literature-through-ocr-scientific-names-mapping-and-crowdsourcing.

[49] A. Willis, D. King, D. Morse, A. Dil, C. Lyal, and D. Roberts, "From XML to XML: the why and how of making the biodiversity literature accessible to researchers," in *Proceedings of the 7th International Conference on Language Resources and Evaluation (LREC '10)*, pp. 1237–1244, European Language Resources Association (ELRA), Valletta, Malta, May 2010.

[50] F. Bapst and R. Ingold, "Using typography in document image analysis," in *Proceedings of Raster Imaging and Digital Typography (RIDT '98)*, pp. 240–251, Saint-Malo, France, March-April 1998.

[51] A. L. Weitzman and C. H. C. Lyal, *An XML Schema for Taxonomic Literature—TaXMLit*, 2004, http://www.sil.si.edu/digitalcollections/bca/documentation/taXMLitv1-3Intro.pdf.

[52] T. Rees, "TAXAMATCH, a "fuzzy" matching algorithm for taxon names, and potential applications in taxonomic databases," in *Proceedings of TDWG*, 2008, pp. 35, http://www.tdwg.org/fileadmin/2008conference/documents/Proceedings2008.pdf#page=35.

[53] G. Sautter, K. Böhm, and D. Agosti, "Semi-automated xml markup of biosystematic legacy literature with the goldengate editor," in *Proceedings of the Pacific Symposium on Biocomputing (PSB '07)*, pp. 391–402, World Scientific, 2007.

[54] B. Settles, "ABNER: an open source tool for automatically tagging genes, proteins and other entity names in text," *Bioinformatics*, vol. 21, no. 14, pp. 3191–3192, 2005.

[55] G. A. Pavlopoulos, E. Pafilis, M. Kuhn, S. D. Hooper, and R. Schneider, "OnTheFly: a tool for automated document-based text annotation, data linking and network generation," *Bioinformatics*, vol. 25, no. 7, pp. 977–978, 2009.

[56] E. Pafilis, S. I. O'Donoghue, L. J. Jensen et al., "Reflect: augmented browsing for the life scientist," *Nature Biotechnology*, vol. 27, no. 6, pp. 508–510, 2009.

[57] M. Kuhn, C. von Mering, M. Campillos, L. J. Jensen, and P. Bork, "STITCH: interaction networks of chemicals and proteins," *Nucleic Acids Research*, vol. 36, no. 1, pp. D684–D688, 2008.

[58] J. P. Balhoff, W. M. Dahdul, C. R. Kothari et al., "Phenex: ontological annotation of phenotypic diversity," *Plos ONE*, vol. 5, no. 5, article e10500, 2010.

[59] W. M. Dahdul, J. P. Balhoff, J. Engeman et al., "Evolutionary characters, phenotypes and ontologies: curating data from the systematic biology literature," *Plos ONE*, vol. 5, no. 5, Article ID e10708, 2010.

[60] G. Sautter, K. Bohm, and D. Agosti, "A combining approach to find all taxon names (FAT) in legacy biosystematics literature," *Biodiversity Informatics*, vol. 3, pp. 46–58, 2007.

[61] P. R. Leary, D. P. Remsen, C. N. Norton, D. J. Patterson, and I. N. Sarkar, "UbioRSS: tracking taxonomic literature using RSS," *Bioinformatics*, vol. 23, no. 11, pp. 1434–1436, 2007.

[62] N. Okazaki and S. Ananiadou, "Building an abbreviation dictionary using a term recognition approach," *Bioinformatics*, vol. 22, no. 24, pp. 3089–3095, 2006.

[63] K. Bontcheva, V. Tablan, D. Maynard, and H. Cunningham, "Evolving gate to meet new challenges in language engineering," *Natural Language Engineering*, vol. 10, no. 3-4, pp. 349–373, 2004.

[64] H. Cunningham, D. Maynard, K. Bontcheva, V. Tablan, C. Ursu et al., *Developing Language Processing Components with GATE (A User Guide)*, University of Sheffield, 2006.

[65] E. Fitzpatrick, J. Bachenko, and D. Hindle, "The status of telegraphic sublanguages," in *Analyzing Language in Restricted Domains: Sublanguage Description and Processing*, pp. 39–51, 1986.

[66] M. Wood, S. Lydon, V. Tablan, D. Maynard, and H. Cunningham, "Populating a database from parallel texts using ontology-based information extraction," in *Natural Language Processing and Information Systems*, vol. 3136, pp. 357–365, 2004.

[67] L. Chen, H. Liu, and C. Friedman, "Gene name ambiguity of eukaryotic nomenclatures," *Bioinformatics*, vol. 21, no. 2, pp. 248–256, 2005.

[68] H. Yu, W. Kim, V. Hatzivassiloglou, and W. J. Wilbur, "Using MEDLINE as a knowledge source for disambiguating abbreviations and acronyms in full-text biomedical journal articles," *Journal of Biomedical Informatics*, vol. 40, no. 2, pp. 150–159, 2007.

[69] J. T. Chang and H. Schutze, "Abbreviations in biomedical text," in *Text Mining for Biology and Biomedicine*, pp. 99–119, 2006.

[70] J. D. Wren and H. R. Garner, "Heuristics for identification of acronym-definition patterns within text: towards an automated construction of comprehensive acronym-definition dictionaries," *Methods of Information in Medicine*, vol. 41, no. 5, pp. 426–434, 2002.

[71] S. Lydon and M. Wood, "Data patterns in multiple botanical descriptions: implications for automatic processing of legacy data," *Systematics and Biodiversity*, vol. 1, no. 2, pp. 151–157, 2003.

[72] A. Taylor, "Using prolog for biological descriptions," in *Proceedings of The 3rd international Conference on the Practical Application of Prolog*, pp. 587–597, 1995.

[73] A. E. Radford, *Fundamentals of Plant Systematics*, Harper & Row, New York, NY, USA, 1986.

[74] J. Diederich, R. Fortuner, and J. Milton, "Computer-assisted data extraction from the taxonomical literature," 1999, http://math.ucdavis.edu/~milton/genisys.html.

[75] M. Wood, S. Lydon, V. Tablan, D. Maynard, and H. Cunningham, "Using parallel texts to improve recall in IE," in *Proceedings of Recent Advances in Natural Language Processing (RANLP '03)*, pp. 505–512, Borovetz, Bulgaria, 2003.

[76] H. Cui and P. B. Heidorn, "The reusability of induced knowledge for the automatic semantic markup of taxonomic descriptions," *Journal of the American Society for Information Science and Technology*, vol. 58, no. 1, pp. 133–149, 2007.

[77] Q. Wei, *Information fusion in taxonomic descriptions*, Ph.D. thesis, University of Illinois at Urbana-Champaign, Champaign, Ill, USA, 2011.

[78] S. Soderland, "Learning information extraction rules for semi-structured and free text," *Machine Learning*, vol. 34, no. 1, pp. 233–272, 1999.

[79] H. Cui, S. Singaram, and A. Janning, "Combine unsupervised learning and heuristic rules to annotate morphological characters," *Proceedings of the American Society for Information Science and Technology*, vol. 48, no. 1, pp. 1–9, 2011.

[80] P. M. Mabee, M. Ashburner, Q. Cronk et al., "Phenotype ontologies: the bridge between genomics and evolution," *Trends in Ecology and Evolution*, vol. 22, no. 7, pp. 345–350, 2007.

17

Gene Regulation, Modulation, and Their Applications in Gene Expression Data Analysis

Mario Flores,[1] Tzu-Hung Hsiao,[2] Yu-Chiao Chiu,[3] Eric Y. Chuang,[3] Yufei Huang,[1] and Yidong Chen[2,4]

[1] Department of Electrical and Computer Engineering, University of Texas at San Antonio, San Antonio, TX 78249, USA
[2] Greehey Children's Cancer Research Institute, University of Texas Health Science Center at San Antonio, San Antonio, TX 78229, USA
[3] Graduate Institute of Biomedical Electronics and Bioinformatics, National Taiwan University, Taipei, Taiwan
[4] Department of Epidemiology and Biostatistics, University of Texas Health Science Center at San Antonio, San Antonio, TX 78229, USA

Correspondence should be addressed to Yufei Huang; yufei.huang@utsa.edu and Yidong Chen; cheny8@uthscsa.edu

Academic Editor: Mohamed Nounou

Common microarray and next-generation sequencing data analysis concentrate on tumor subtype classification, marker detection, and transcriptional regulation discovery during biological processes by exploring the correlated gene expression patterns and their shared functions. Genetic regulatory network (GRN) based approaches have been employed in many large studies in order to scrutinize for dysregulation and potential treatment controls. In addition to gene regulation and network construction, the concept of the network modulator that has significant systemic impact has been proposed, and detection algorithms have been developed in past years. Here we provide a unified mathematic description of these methods, followed with a brief survey of these modulator identification algorithms. As an early attempt to extend the concept to new RNA regulation mechanism, competitive endogenous RNA (ceRNA), into a modulator framework, we provide two applications to illustrate the network construction, modulation effect, and the preliminary finding from these networks. Those methods we surveyed and developed are used to dissect the regulated network under different modulators. Not limit to these, the concept of "modulation" can adapt to various biological mechanisms to discover the novel gene regulation mechanisms.

1. Introduction

With the development of microarray [1] and lately the next generation sequencing techniques [2], transcriptional profiling of biological samples, such as tumor samples [3–5] and samples from other model organisms, have been carried out in order to study sample subtypes at molecular level or transcriptional regulation during the biological processes [6–8]. While common data analysis methods employ hierarchical clustering algorithms or pattern classification to explore correlated genes and their functions, the genetic regulatory network (GRN) approaches were employed to scrutinize for dysregulation between different tumor groups or biological processes (see reviews [9–12]).

To construct the network, most of research is focused on methods based on gene expression data derived from high-throughput technologies by using metrics such as Pearson or Spearman correlation [13], mutual information [14], co-determination method [15, 16], Bayesian methods [17, 18], and probabilistic Boolean networks [19]. Recently, new transcriptional regulation via competitive endogenous RNA (ceRNAs) has been proposed [20, 21], introducing additional dimension in modeling gene regulation. This type of regulation requires the knowledge of microRNA (miRNA) binding targets [22, 23] and the hypothesis of RNA regulations via competition of miRNA binding. Common GRN construction tries to confine regulators to be transcription factor (TF) proteins, a primary transcription programming machine, which relies

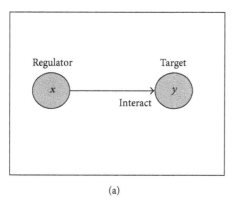
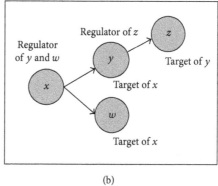

(a) (b)

FIGURE 1: Regulator-target pair in genetic regulatory network model: (a) basic regulator-target pair and (b) regulator-target complex.

on sequence-specific binding sites at target genes' promoter regions. In contrast, ceRNAs mediate gene regulation via competing miRNAs binding sites in target $3'$UTR region, which exist in >50% of mRNAs [22, 24]. In this study, we will extend the current network construction methods by incorporating regulation via ceRNAs.

In tumorigenesis, gene mutation is the main cause of the cancer [25]. The mutation may not directly reflect in the change at the gene expression level; however, it will disrupt gene regulation [26–28]. In Hudson et al., they found that mutated myostatin and MYL2 showed different coexpressions when comparing to wild-type myostatin. Chun et al. also showed that oncogenic KRAS modulates HIF-1α and HIF-2α target genes and in turn modulates cancer metabolism. Stelniec-Klotz et al. presented a complex hierarchical model of KRAS modulated network followed by double perturbation experiments. Shen et al. [29] showed a temporal change of GRNs modulated after the estradiol stimulation, indicating important role of estrogen in modulating GRNs. Functionally, modulation effect of high expression of *ESR1* was also reported by Wilson and Dering [30] where they studied previously published microarray data with cells treated with hormone receptor agonists and antagonists [31–33]. In this study, a comprehensive review of existing algorithms to uncover the modulators was provided. Given either mutation or protein expression status was unknown under many of reported studies, the problem of how to partition the diverse samples with different conditions, such as active or inactive oncogene status (and perhaps a combination of multiple mutations), and the prediction of a putative modulator of gene regulation remains a difficult task.

By combining gene regulation obtained from coexpression data and ceRNAs, we report here an early attempt to unify two systems mathematically while assuming a known modulator, estrogen receptor (ER). By employing the TCGA [3] breast tumor gene expressions data and their clinical test result (ER status), we demonstrate the approach of obtaining GRN via ceRNAs and a new presentation of ER modulation effects. By integrating breast cancer data into our unique ceRNAs discovery website, we are uniquely positioned to further explore the ceRNA regulation network and further

develop the discovery algorithms in order to detect potential modulators of regulatory interactions.

2. Models of Gene Regulation and Modulation

2.1. Regulation of Gene Expression. The complex relationships among genes and their products in a cellular system can be studied using genetic regulatory networks (GRNs). The networks model the different states or phenotypes of a cellular system. In this model, the interactions are commonly modeled as regulator-target pairs with edges between regulator and target pair representing their interaction direction, as shown in Figure 1(a). In this model a target gene is a gene whose expression can be altered (activated or suppressed) by a regulator gene. This definition of a target gene implies that any gene can be at some point a target gene or a direct or indirect regulator depending on its position in the genetic regulatory network. The regulator gene is a gene that controls (activates or suppresses) its target genes' expression. The consequences of these activated (or suppressed) genes sometimes are involved in specific biological functions, such as cell proliferation in cancer. Examples of regulator-target pair in biology are common. For example, a target gene CDCA7 (cell division cycle-associated protein 7) is a c-Myc (regulator) responsive gene, and it is part of c-Myc-mediated transformation of lymphoblastoid cells. Furthermore, as shown in Figure 1(b), a regulator gene can also act as a target gene if there exists an upstream regulator.

If the interaction is modeled after Boolean network (BN) model [34], then

$$ y_i(t+1) = f_i\left(x_{j_1}(t), \ldots, x_{j_k}(t), y_i(t)\right), \qquad (1) $$

where each regulator $x_j \in \{0, 1\}$ is a binary variable, as well as it is target y_i. As described by (1), the target y_i at time $t+1$ is completely determined by the values of its regulators at time t by means of a Boolean function $f_i \in F$, where F is a collection of Boolean functions. Thus, the Boolean network $G(V, F)$ is defined as a set of nodes (genes) $V = \{x_1, x_2, \ldots, x_n\}$ and a list of functions (edges or interactions) $F = \{f_1, f_2, \ldots, f_n\}$. Similarly such relationship can be defined in the framework of Bayesian network where the

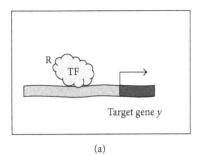 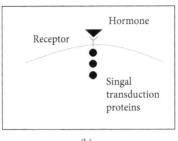 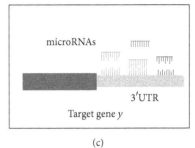

| (a) | (b) | (c) |

FIGURE 2: Three different cases of regulation of gene expression that share the network representation of a regulator target interaction.

similar regulators-target relationship as defined in (1) can be modeled by the distribution

$$P\left(y_i(t+1), x_{j_1}(t), \ldots, x_{j_k}(t), y_i(t)\right)$$
$$= P\left(y_i(t+1) \mid \mathrm{Parents}\left(y_i(t+1)\right)\right) \quad (2)$$
$$\times P\left(\mathrm{Parents}\left(y_i(t+1)\right)\right),$$

where $\mathrm{Parents}(y_i(t+1)) = \{x_{j_1}(t), \ldots, x_{j_k}(t), y_i(t)\}$ is the set of regulators, or parents, of y_i, $P(y_i(t+1) \mid \mathrm{Parents}(y_i(t+1)))$ is the conditional distribution defining the regulator-target relationship, and $P(\mathrm{Parents}(y_i(t+1)))$ models the prior distribution of regulators. Unlike in (1), the target and regulators in (2) are modeled as random variables. Despite of this difference, in both (1) and (2), the target is always a function (or conditional distribution) of the regulator (or parents). When the relationship is defined by a Boolean function as in (1), the conditional distribution in (2) take the form of a binomial distribution (or a multinomial distribution when both regulators and target take more than two states). Other distributions such as the Gaussian and Poisson can be introduced to model more complex relationships than the Boolean. The network construction, inference, and control, however, are beyond the scope of this paper, and we leave the topics to the literatures [9, 35, 36].

The interactions among genes and their products in a complex cellular process of gene expression are diverse, governed by the central dogma of molecular biology [37]. There are different regulation mechanisms that can actuate during different stages. Figure 2 shows three different cases of regulation of gene expression. Figure 2(a) shows the case of regulation of expression in which a transcription factor (TF) regulates the expression of a protein-coding gene (in dark grey) by binding to the promoter region of target gene y. Figure 2(b) is the case of regulation at the protein level in which a ligand protein interacts with a receptor to activate relay molecules to transduce outside signals directly into cell behavior. Figure 2(c) is the case of regulation at the RNA level in which one or more miRNAs regulate target mRNA y by translational repression or target transcript degradation via binding to sequence-specific binding sites (called miRNA response elements or MREs) in $3'$UTR region. As illustrated in Figure 2(c), the target genes/proteins all contain a domain of binding or docking site, enabling specific interactions

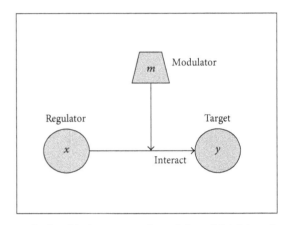

FIGURE 3: Graphical representation of the triplet interaction of regulator x, target y, and modulator m.

between regulator-target pairs, a common element in network structure.

2.2. Modulation of Gene Regulation.
Different from the concept of a coregulator commonly referred in the regulatory biology, a modulator denotes a gene or protein that is capable of altering the endogenous gene expression at one stage or time. In the context of this paper, we specifically define a modulator to be a gene that can systemically influence the interaction of regulator-target pair, either to activate or suppress the interaction in the presence/absence of the modulator. One example of modulator is the widely studied estrogen receptor (ER) in breast cancer studies [38–40]; the ER status determines not only the tumor progression, but also the chemotherapy treatment outcomes. It is well known that binding of estrogen to receptor facilitates the ER activities to activate or repress gene expression [41], thus effectively modulating the GRN. Figure 3 illustrates the model of the interaction between a modulator (m) and a regulator (x) target (y) pair that it modulates.

Following the convention used in (1) and (2), the modulation interaction in Figure 3 can be modeled by

$$y = \mathscr{F}^{(m)}(x), \quad (3)$$

where y represents target expression, x represents the parents (regulators) of target y, and $\mathscr{F}^{(m)}(\cdot)$ is the regulation function modulated by m. When $\mathcal{F}^{(m)}(\cdot)$ is stochastic, the relationship is modeled by the conditional distribution as

$$p(y, x \mid m) = p(y \mid x, m) \, p(x \mid m), \qquad (4)$$

where $p(y|x, m)$ models the regulator-target relationship modulated by m and $p(x|m)$ defines the prior distribution of regulators (parents) expression modulated by m. Different distribution models can be used to model different mechanisms for modulation. At the biological level, there are different mechanisms for modulation of the interaction x-y, and currently several algorithms for prediction of the modulators has been developed. This survey presents the latest formulations and algorithms for prediction of modulators.

3. Survey of Algorithms of Gene Regulation and Modulation Discovery

During the past years, many computational tools have been developed for regulation network construction, and then depending on the hypothesis, modulator concept can be tested and extracted. Here we will focus on modulator detection algorithms (MINDy, Mimosa, GEM, and Hermes). To introduce gene-gene interaction concept, we will also briefly discuss algorithms for regulation network construction (ARACNE) and ceRNA identification algorithm (MuTaMe).

3.1. ARACNE (Algorithm for the Reconstruction of Accurate Cellular Networks). ARACNE [14, 42] is an algorithm that extracts transcriptional networks from microarray data by using an information-theoretic method to reduce the indirect interactions. ARACNE assumes that it is sufficient to estimate 2-way marginal distributions, when sample size $M > 100$, in genomics problems, such that

$$p\left(x_i\right) = \frac{1}{z} e^{-\left[\sum_{i=1}^{N} \phi_i(x_i) + \sum_{i,j}^{N} \phi_{ij}(x_i, y_j)\right]}. \qquad (5)$$

Or a candidate interaction can be identified using estimation of mutual information MI of genes x and y, $\mathrm{MI}(x, y) = \mathrm{MI}_{xy}$, where $\mathrm{MI}_{xy} = 1$ if genes x and y are identical, and MI_{xy} is zero if $p(x, y) = p(x)p(y)$, or x and y are statistically independent. Specifically, the estimation of mutual information of gene expressions x and y of regulator and target genes is done by using the Gaussian kernel estimator. The ARACNE takes additional two steps to clean the network: (1) removing MI if its P value is less than that derived from two independent genes via random permutation and (2) data processing inequality (DPI). The algorithm further assumes that for a triplet gene (g_x, g_y, g_z), where g_x regulates g_z, through g_y, then

$$\mathrm{MI}_{x,z} < \min\left(\mathrm{MI}_{x,y}, \mathrm{MI}_{y,z}\right), \quad \text{if } x \longrightarrow y \longrightarrow z, \qquad (6)$$
$$\text{with no alternative path,}$$

where $\rightarrow$ represents regulation relationship. In other words, the lowest mutual information $\mathrm{MI}_{x,z}$ is from an indirect interaction and thus shall be removed from the GRN by

ARACNE in the DPI step. A similar algorithm was proposed [43] to utilize conditional mutual information to explore more than 2 regulators.

3.2. MINDy (Modulator Inference by Network Dynamics). Similar to ARACNE, MINDy is also an information-theoretic algorithm [44]. However, MINDy aims to identify potential transcription factor-(TF-target) gene pairs that can be modulated by a candidate modulator. MINDy assumes that the expressions of the modulated TF-target pairs are of different correlations under different expression state of the modulator. For simplicity and computational consideration, MINDy considers only two modulator expression states, that is, up- ($m = 1$) or down-expression ($m = 0$). Then, it tests if the expression correlations of potential TF-target pairs are significantly different for modulator up-expression versus down-expression. The modulator dependent correlation is assessed by the conditional mutual information (CMI) or $I(x, y \mid m = 0)$ and $I(x, y \mid m = 1)$. Similar to ARACNE, the CMI is calculated using the Gaussian kernel estimator. To test if a pair of TF (y) and target (x) is modulated by m, the CMI difference can be calculated as

$$\Delta I = I\left(x, y \mid m = 1\right) - I\left(x, y \mid m = 0\right). \qquad (7)$$

The pair is determined to be modulated if $\Delta I \neq 0$. The significance P values for $\Delta I \neq 0$ is computed using permutation tests.

3.3. Mimosa. Similarly to MINDy, Mimosa [45] was proposed to identify modulated TF-target pairs. However, it does not preselect a set of modulators of interest but rather aims to also search for the modulators. Mimosa also assumes that a modulator takes only two states, that is, absence and presence or 0 and 1. The modulated regulator-target pair is further assumed to be correlated when a modulator is present but uncorrelated when it is absent. Therefore, the distribution of a modulated TF-target pair, x and y, naturally follows a mixture distribution

$$p(x, y) = \pi p(x, y \mid m = 0) + (1 - \pi) p(x, ym = 1), \qquad (8)$$

where π is the probability of the modulator being absent. Particularly, an uncorrelated and correlated bivariant Gaussian distributions were introduced to model different modulated regulator-target relationship, such that

$$p(x, y \mid m = 0) = \frac{1}{2\pi} e^{-(1/2)(x^2 + y^2)}, \qquad (9a)$$

$$p(x, y \mid m = 1)$$
$$= \frac{1}{2\pi\sqrt{1 - \alpha^2}} e^{-(1/2)(x^2 + y^2 + 2\alpha xy)/(1 - \alpha^2)}, \qquad (9b)$$

where α models the correlation between x and y when the modulator is present. With this model, Mimosa sets out to fit the samples of every pair of potential regulator target with the mixture model (7). This is equivalent to finding

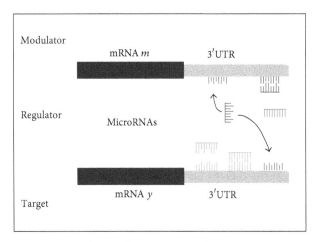

FIGURE 4: Modulation of gene regulation by competing mRNAs.

a partition of the paired expression samples into the correlated and uncorrelated samples. The paired expression samples that possess such correlated-uncorrelated partition ($0.3 < \pi < 0.7$ and $|\alpha| > 0.8$) are determined to be modulated. To identify the modulator of a (or a group of) modulated pair(s), a weighted t-test was developed to search for the genes whose expressions are differentially expressed in the correlated partition versus the uncorrelated partition.

3.4. GEM (Gene Expression Modulator). GEM [46] improves over MINDy by predicting how a modulator-TF interaction affects the expression of the target gene. It can detect new types of interactions that result in stronger correlation but low ΔI, which therefore would be missed by MINDy. GEM hypothesizes that the correlation between the expression of a modulator m and a target x must change, as that of the TF x changes. Unlike the previous surveyed algorithms, GEM first transforms the continuous expression levels to binary states (up- (1) or down-expression (0)) and then works only with discrete expression states. To model the hypothesized relationship, the following model is proposed:

$$P\left(x = 1 \mid y, m\right) = \alpha_c + \alpha_m m + \alpha_y y + \gamma m y, \qquad (10)$$

where α_c is a constant, α_m and α_y model the effect of modulator and TF on the target genes, and γ represents the effect of modulator-TF interaction on the target gene. If the modulator-TF interaction has an effect on x, then γ will be nonzero. For a given (x, y, m) triplets GEM devised an algorithm to estimate the model coefficients in (10) and a test to determine if γ is nonzero, or m is a modulator of x and y.

3.5. MuTaMe (Mutually Targeted MRE Enrichment). The goal of MuTaMe [21] is to identify ceRNA networks of a gene of interest (GoI) or mRNA that share miRNA response elements (MREs) of same miRNAs. Figure 4 shows two mRNAs, where one is the GoI y and the other is a candidate ceRNA or modulator m. In the figure, the miRNA represented in color red has MREs in both mRNA y and mRNA m; in this case the presence of mRNA m will start the competition with y for miRNA represented in color red.

The hypothesis of MuTaMe is that mRNAs that have many of the same MREs can regulate each other by competing for miRNAs binding. The input of this algorithm is a GoI, which is targeted by a group of miRNAs known to the user. Then, from a database of predicted MREs for the entire transcriptome, it is possible to obtain the binding sites and its predicted locations in the $3'$UTR for all mRNAs. This data is used to generate scores for each mRNA based on several features:

(a) the number of miRNAs that an mRNA m shares with the GoI y;

(b) the density of the predicted MREs for the miRNA; it favors the cases in which more MREs are located in shorter distances;

(c) the distribution of the MREs for every miRNA; it favors situations in which the MREs tend to be evenly distributed;

(d) the number of MREs predicted to target m; it favors situations where each miRNA contains more MREs in m.

Then each candidate transcript m will be assigned a score that results from multiplying the scores in (a) to (d). This score indicates the likelihood of the candidates to be ceRNAs and will be used to predict ceRNAs.

3.6. Hermes. Hermes [20] is an extension of MINDy that infers candidate modulators of miRNA activity from expression profiles of genes and miRNAs of the same samples. Hermes makes inferences by estimating the MI and CMI. However, different from MINDy (7), Hermes extracts the dependences of this triplet by studying the difference between the CMI of x expression and y expression conditional on the expression of m and the MI of x and y expressions as follows:

$$I = I\left(x; y \mid m\right) - I\left(x; y\right). \qquad (11)$$

These quantities and their associated statistical significance can be computed from collections of expression of genes with number of samples 250 or greater. Hermes expands MINDy by providing the capacity to identify candidate modulator genes of miRNAs activity. The presence of these modulators (m) will affect the relation between the expression of the miRNAs targeting a gene (x) and the expression level of this gene (x).

In summary, we surveyed some of the most popular algorithms for the inference of modulator. Additional modulator identification algorithms are summarized in Table 1. It is worth noting that the concept of modulator applies to cases beyond discussed in this paper. Such example includes the multilayer integrated regulatory model proposed in Yan et al. [49], where the top layer of regulators could be also considered as "modulators."

4. Applications to Breast Cancer Gene Expression Data

Algorithms of utilizing modulator concept have been implemented in various software packages. Here we will discuss

TABLE 1: Gene regulation network and modulator identification methods.

Algorithm	Features	References
ARACNE	Interaction network constructed via mutual information (MI).	[14, 42]
Network profiler	A varying-coefficient structural equation model (SEM) to represent the modulator-dependent conditional independence between genes.	[47]
MINDy	Gene-pair interaction dependency on modulator candidates by using the conditional mutual information (CMI).	[44]
Mimosa	Search for modulator by partition samples with a Gaussian mixture model.	[45]
GEM	A probabilistic method for detecting modulators of TFs that affect the expression of target gene by using a priori knowledge and gene expression profiles.	[46]
MuTaMe	Based on the hypothesis that shared MREs can regulate mRNAs by competing for microRNAs binding.	[21]
Hermes	Extension of MINDy to include microRNAs as candidate modulators by using CMI and MI from expression profiles of genes and miRNAs of the same samples.	[20]
ERα modulator	Analyzes the interaction between TF and target gene conditioned on a group of specific modulator genes via a multiple linear regression.	[48]

two new applications, MEGRA and TraceRNA, implemented in-house specifically to utilize the concept of differential correlation coefficients and ceRNAs to construct a modulated GRN with a predetermined modulator. In the case of MGERA, we chose estrogen receptor, *ESR1*, as the initial starting point, since it is one of the dominant and systemic factor in breast cancer; in the case of TraceRNA, we also chose gene *ESR1* and its modulated gene network. Preliminary results of applications to TCGA breast cancer data are reported in the following 2 sections.

4.1. MGERA. The Modulated Gene Regulation Analysis algorithm (MGERA) was designed to explore gene regulation pairs modulated by the modulator m. The regulation pairs can be identified by examining the coexpression of two genes based on Pearson correlation (similar to (7) in the context of correlation coefficient). Fisher transformation is adopted to normalize the correlation coefficients biased by sample sizes to obtain equivalent statistical power among data with different sample sizes. Statistical significance of difference in the absolute correlation coefficients between two genes is tested by the student t-test following Fisher transformation. For the gene pairs with significantly different coefficients between two genes, active and deactive statuses are identified by examining the modulated gene expression pairs (MGEPs). The MGEPs are further combined to construct the m modulated gene regulation network for a systematic and comprehensive view of interaction under modulation.

To demonstrate the ability of MGERA, we set estrogen receptor (ER) as the modulator and applied the algorithm to TCGA breast cancer expression data [3] which contains 588 expression profiles (461 ER+ and 127 ER−). By using P value <0.01 and the difference in the absolute Pearson correlation coefficients >0.6 as criteria, we identified 2,324 putative ER+ MGEPs, and a highly connected ER+ modulated gene regulation network was constructed (Figure 5). The top ten genes with highest connectivity was show in Table 2. The cysteine/tyrosine-rich 1 gene (*CYYR1*), connected to 142 genes, was identified as the top hub gene in the network and thus may serve as a key regulator under ER+ modulation.

TABLE 2: Hub genes derived from modulated gene regulation network (Figure 5).

Gene	Number of ER+ MGEPs
CYYR1	142
MRAS	109
C9orf19	95
LOC339524	93
PLEKHG1	92
FBLN5	91
BOC	91
ANKRD35	89
FAM107A	83
C16orf77	73

Gene Ontology analysis of *CYYR1* and its connected neighbor genes revealed significant association with extracellular matrix, epithelial tube formation, and angiogenesis.

4.2. TraceRNA. To identify the regulation network of ceRNAs for a GoI, we developed a web-based application TraceRNA presented earlier in [50] with extension to regulation network construction. The analysis flow chart of TraceRNA was shown in Figure 6. For a selected GoI, the GoI binding miRNAs (GBmiRs) were derived either validated miRNAs from miR-TarBase [51] or predicted miRNAs from SVMicrO [52]. Then mRNAs (other than the given GoI) also targeted by GBmiRs were identified as the candidates of ceRNAs. The relevant (or tumor-specific) gene expression data were used to further strengthen relationship between the ceRNA candidates and GoI. The candidate ceRNAs which coexpressed with GoI were reported as putative ceRNAs. To construct the gene regulation network via GBmiRs, we set each ceRNA as the secondary GoI, and the ceRNAs of these secondary GoIs were identified by applying the algorithm recursively. Upon identifying all the ceRNAs, the regulation network of ceRNAs of a given GoI was constructed.

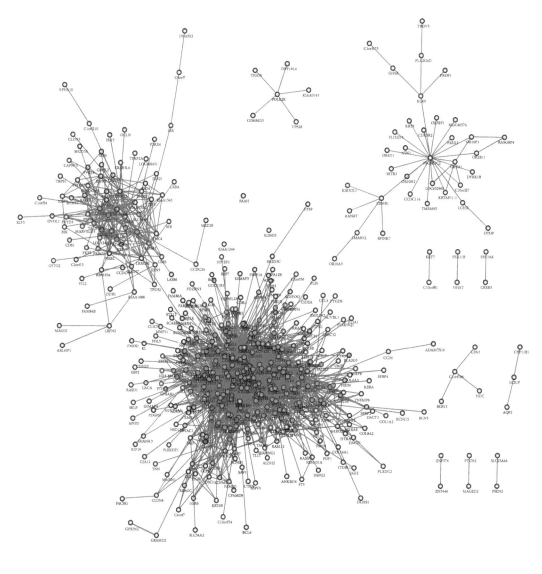

— Positive correlation under ER+ modulation

Negative correlation under ER+ modulation

○   Gene

FIGURE 5: ER+ modulated gene regulation network.

To identify ceRNA candidates, three miRNAs binding prediction algorithms, SiteTest, SVMicrO, and BCMicrO, were used in TracRNA. SiteTest is an algorithm similar to MuTaMe and uses UTR features for target prediction. SVMi-crO [52] is an algorithm that uses a large number of sequence-level site as well as UTR features including binding secondary structure, energy, and conservation, whereas BCMicrO [53] employs a Bayesian approach that integrates predictions from 6 popular algorithms including TargetScan, miRanda, PicTar, mirTarget, PITA, and DIANA-microT. Pearson correlation coefficient was used to test the coexpression between the GoI and the candidate ceRNAs. We utilized TCGA breast cancer cohort [3] as the expression data, by using 60% of GBmiRs as common miRNAs and Pearson correlation coefficient >0.9 as criteria. The final scores of putative ceRNAs (see Table 3, last column) were generated by using Borda merging method which rerank the sum of ranks from both GBmiR binding and coexpression P values [54]. To illustrate the utility of the TraceRNA algorithm for breast cancer study, we also focus on the genes interacted with the estrogen receptor alpha, *ESR1*, with GBmiRs including *miR-18a, miR-18b, miR-193b, miR-19a, miR-19b, miR-206, miR-20b, miR-22, miR-221, miR-222, miR-29b, and miR-302c*. The regulation network generated by *ESR1* as the initial GoI is shown in Figure 7, and the top 18 ceRNAs are provided in Table 3. The TraceRNA algorithm can be accessed http://compgenomics.utsa.edu/cerna/.

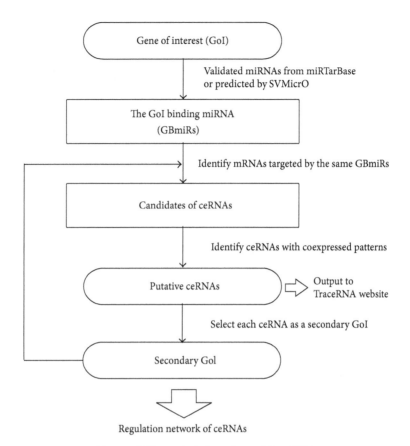

FIGURE 6: The analysis flow chart of TraceRNA.

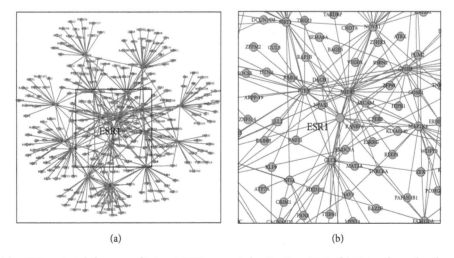

(a)   (b)

FIGURE 7: (a) ceRNA network for gene of interest ESR1 generated using TraceRNA. (b) Network graph enlarged at ESR1.

5. Conclusions

In this report, we attempt to provide a unified concept of modulation of gene regulation, encompassing earlier mRNA expression based methods and lately the ceRNA method. We expect the integration of ceRNA concept into the gene-gene interactions, and their modulator identification will further enhance our understanding in gene interaction and their systemic influence. Applications provided here also represent examples of our earlier attempt to construct modulated networks specific to breast cancer studies. Further investigation will be carried out to extend our modeling to provide a unified understanding of genetic regulation in an altered environment.

TABLE 3: Top 18 candidate ceRNAs for *ESR1* as GOI obtained from TraceRNA. *ESR1* is at rank of 174 (not listed in this table).

Gene symbol	SVMicrO-based prediction		Expression correlation		Final score
	Score	*P* value	Score	*P* value	
FOXP1	1.066	0.0043	0.508	0.016	1212
VEZF1	0.942	0.0060	0.4868	0.020	1179
NOVA1	0.896	0.0067	0.479	0.023	1160
CPEB3	0.858	0.0074	0.484	0.022	1149
MAP2K4	0.919	0.0064	0.322	0.097	1139
FAM120A	0.885	0.0069	0.341	0.082	1130
PCDHA3	0.983	0.0054	0.170	0.215	1125
SIRT1	0.927	0.0062	0.230	0.162	1117
PCDHA5	0.983	0.0054	0.148	0.233	1113
PTEN	0.898	0.0067	0.221	0.168	1104
PCDHA1	0.983	0.0054	0.140	0.239	1103
NBEA	0.752	0.0098	0.491	0.020	1102
ZFHX4	0.970	0.0056	0.154	0.229	1097
GLCE	0.798	0.0087	0.3231	0.096	1096
MAGI2	0.777	0.0092	0.321	0.097	1086
SATB2	0.801	0.0086	0.243	0.151	1078
LEF1	0.753	0.0098	0.291	0.112	1065
ATPBD4	0.819	0.0082	0.170	0.215	1060

Authors' Contribution

M. Flores and T.-H Hsiao are contributed equally to this work.

Acknowledgments

The authors would like to thank the funding support of this work by Qatar National Research Foundation (NPRP 09 -874-3-235) to Y. Chen and Y. Huang, National Science Foundation (CCF-1246073) to Y. Huang. The authors also thank the computational support provided by the UTSA Computational Systems Biology Core Facility (NIH RCMI 5G12RR013646-12).

References

[1] M. Schena, D. Shalon, R. W. Davis, and P. O. Brown, "Quantitative monitoring of gene expression patterns with a complementary DNA microarray," *Science*, vol. 270, no. 5235, pp. 467–470, 1995.

[2] E. R. Mardis, "Next-generation DNA sequencing methods," *Annual Review of Genomics and Human Genetics*, vol. 9, pp. 387–402, 2008.

[3] Cancer Genome Atlas Network, "Comprehensive molecular portraits of human breast tumours," *Nature*, vol. 490, pp. 61–70, 2012.

[4] D. Bell, A. Berchuck, M. Birrer et al., "Integrated genomic analyses of ovarian carcinoma," *Nature*, vol. 474, no. 7353, pp. 609–615, 2011.

[5] R. McLendon, A. Friedman, D. Bigner et al., "Comprehensive genomic characterization defines human glioblastoma genes and core pathways," *Nature*, vol. 455, no. 7216, pp. 1061–1068, 2008.

[6] C. M. Perou, T. Sørile, M. B. Eisen et al., "Molecular portraits of human breast tumours," *Nature*, vol. 406, no. 6797, pp. 747–752, 2000.

[7] J. Lapointe, C. Li, J. P. Higgins et al., "Gene expression profiling identifies clinically relevant subtypes of prostate cancer," *Proceedings of the National Academy of Sciences of the United States of America*, vol. 101, no. 3, pp. 811–816, 2004.

[8] M. B. Eisen, P. T. Spellman, P. O. Brown, and D. Botstein, "Cluster analysis and display of genome-wide expression patterns," *Proceedings of the National Academy of Sciences of the United States of America*, vol. 95, no. 25, pp. 14863–14868, 1998.

[9] T. Schlitt and A. Brazma, "Current approaches to gene regulatory network modelling," *BMC Bioinformatics*, vol. 8, supplement 6, article S9, 2007.

[10] H. Hache, H. Lehrach, and R. Herwig, "Reverse engineering of gene regulatory networks: a comparative study," *Eurasip Journal on Bioinformatics and Systems Biology*, vol. 2009, Article ID 617281, 2009.

[11] W. P. Lee and W. S. Tzou, "Computational methods for discovering gene networks from expression data," *Briefings in Bioinformatics*, vol. 10, no. 4, pp. 408–423, 2009.

[12] C. Sima, J. Hua, and S. Jung, "Inference of gene regulatory networks using time-series data: a survey," *Current Genomics*, vol. 10, no. 6, pp. 416–429, 2009.

[13] J. M. Stuart, E. Segal, D. Koller, and S. K. Kim, "A gene-coexpression network for global discovery of conserved genetic modules," *Science*, vol. 302, no. 5643, pp. 249–255, 2003.

[14] A. A. Margolin, I. Nemenman, K. Basso et al., "ARACNE: an algorithm for the reconstruction of gene regulatory networks in a mammalian cellular context," *BMC Bioinformatics*, vol. 7, supplement 1, article S7, 2006.

[15] E. R. Dougherty, S. Kim, and Y. Chen, "Coefficient of determination in nonlinear signal processing," *Signal Processing*, vol. 80, no. 10, pp. 2219–2235, 2000.

[16] S. Kim, E. R. Dougherty, Y. Chen et al., "Multivariate measurement of gene expression relationships," *Genomics*, vol. 67, no. 2, pp. 201–209, 2000.

[17] X. Chen, M. Chen, and K. Ning, "BNArray: an R package for constructing gene regulatory networks from microarray data by using Bayesian network," *Bioinformatics*, vol. 22, no. 23, pp. 2952–2954, 2006.

[18] A. V. Werhli, M. Grzegorczyk, and D. Husmeier, "Comparative evaluation of reverse engineering gene regulatory networks with relevance networks, graphical gaussian models and bayesian networks," *Bioinformatics*, vol. 22, no. 20, pp. 2523–2531, 2006.

[19] I. Shmulevich, E. R. Dougherty, S. Kim, and W. Zhang, "Probabilistic Boolean networks: a rule-based uncertainty model for gene regulatory networks," *Bioinformatics*, vol. 18, no. 2, pp. 261–274, 2002.

[20] P. Sumazin, X. Yang, H.-S. Chiu et al., "An extensive MicroRNA-mediated network of RNA-RNA interactions regulates established oncogenic pathways in glioblastoma," *Cell*, vol. 147, no. 2, pp. 370–381, 2011.

[21] Y. Tay, L. Kats, L. Salmena et al., "Coding-independent regulation of the tumor suppressor PTEN by competing endogenous mRNAs," *Cell*, vol. 147, no. 2, pp. 344–357, 2011.

[22] D. P. Bartel, "MicroRNAs: target recognition and regulatory functions," *Cell*, vol. 136, no. 2, pp. 215–233, 2009.

[23] D. Yue, J. Meng, M. Lu, C. L. P. Chen, M. Guo, and Y. Huang, "Understanding MicroRNA regulation: a computational perspective," *IEEE Signal Processing Magazine*, vol. 29, no. 1, Article ID 6105465, pp. 77–88, 2012.

[24] M. W. Jones-Rhoades and D. P. Bartel, "Computational identification of plant MicroRNAs and their targets, including a stress-induced miRNA," *Molecular Cell*, vol. 14, no. 6, pp. 787–799, 2004.

[25] D. Hanahan and R. A. Weinberg, "The hallmarks of cancer," *Cell*, vol. 100, no. 1, pp. 57–70, 2000.

[26] S. Y. Chun, C. Johnson, J. G. Washburn, M. R. Cruz-Correa, D. T. Dang, and L. H. Dang, "Oncogenic KRAS modulates mitochondrial metabolism in human colon cancer cells by inducing HIF-1α and HIF-2α target genes," *Molecular Cancer*, vol. 9, article 293, 2010.

[27] N. J. Hudson, A. Reverter, and B. P. Dalrymple, "A differential wiring analysis of expression data correctly identifies the gene containing the causal mutation," *PLoS Computational Biology*, vol. 5, no. 5, Article ID e1000382, 2009.

[28] I. Stelniec-Klotz, S. Legewie, O. Tchernitsa et al., "Reverse engineering a hierarchical regulatory network downstream of oncogenic KRAS," *Molecular Systems Biology*, vol. 8, Article ID 601, 2012.

[29] C. Shen, Y. Huang, Y. Liu et al., "A modulated empirical Bayes model for identifying topological and temporal estrogen receptor α regulatory networks in breast cancer," *BMC Systems Biology*, vol. 5, article 67, 2011.

[30] C. A. Wilson and J. Dering, "Recent translational research: microarray expression profiling of breast cancer. Beyond classification and prognostic markers?" *Breast Cancer Research*, vol. 6, no. 5, pp. 192–200, 2004.

[31] H. E. Cunliffe, M. Ringnér, S. Bilke et al., "The gene expression response of breast cancer to growth regulators: patterns and correlation with tumor expression profiles," *Cancer Research*, vol. 63, no. 21, pp. 7158–7166, 2003.

[32] J. Frasor, F. Stossi, J. M. Danes, B. Komm, C. R. Lyttle, and B. S. Katzenellenbogen, "Selective estrogen receptor modulators: discrimination of agonistic versus antagonistic activities by gene expression profiling in breast cancer cells," *Cancer Research*, vol. 64, no. 4, pp. 1522–1533, 2004.

[33] L. J. van't Veer, H. Dai, M. J. van de Vijver et al., "Gene expression profiling predicts clinical outcome of breast cancer," *Nature*, vol. 415, no. 6871, pp. 530–536, 2002.

[34] S. A. Kauffman, *The Origins of Order : Self-Organization and Selection in Evolution*, Oxford University Press, New York, NY, USA, 1993.

[35] J. D. Allen, Y. Xie, M. Chen, L. Girard, and G. Xiao, "Comparing statistical methods for constructing large scale gene networks," *PLoS ONE*, vol. 7, no. 1, Article ID e29348, 2012.

[36] Y. Huang, I. M. Tienda-Luna, and Y. Wang, "Reverse engineering gene regulatory networks: a survey of statistical models," *IEEE Signal Processing Magazine*, vol. 26, no. 1, pp. 76–97, 2009.

[37] F. Crick, "Central dogma of molecular biology," *Nature*, vol. 227, no. 5258, pp. 561–563, 1970.

[38] A. Hamilton and M. Piccart, "The contribution of molecular markers to the prediction of response in the treatment of breast cancer: a review of the literature on HER-2, p53 and BCL-2," *Annals of Oncology*, vol. 11, no. 6, pp. 647–663, 2000.

[39] C. Sotiriou, S. Y. Neo, L. M. McShane et al., "Breast cancer classification and prognosis based on gene expression profiles from a population-based study," *Proceedings of the National Academy of Sciences of the United States of America*, vol. 100, no. 18, pp. 10393–10398, 2003.

[40] T. Sørlie, C. M. Perou, R. Tibshirani et al., "Gene expression patterns of breast carcinomas distinguish tumor subclasses with clinical implications," *Proceedings of the National Academy of Sciences of the United States of America*, vol. 98, no. 19, pp. 10869–10874, 2001.

[41] J. S. Carroll, C. A. Meyer, J. Song et al., "Genome-wide analysis of estrogen receptor binding sites," *Nature Genetics*, vol. 38, no. 11, pp. 1289–1297, 2006.

[42] K. Basso, A. A. Margolin, G. Stolovitzky, U. Klein, R. Dalla-Favera, and A. Califano, "Reverse engineering of regulatory networks in human B cells," *Nature Genetics*, vol. 37, no. 4, pp. 382–390, 2005.

[43] K. C. Liang and X. Wang, "Gene regulatory network reconstruction using conditional mutual information," *Eurasip Journal on Bioinformatics and Systems Biology*, vol. 2008, Article ID 253894, 2008.

[44] K. Wang, B. C. Bisikirska, M. J. Alvarez et al., "Genome-wide identification of post-translational modulators of transcription factor activity in human B cells," *Nature Biotechnology*, vol. 27, no. 9, pp. 829–837, 2009.

[45] M. Hansen, L. Everett, L. Singh, and S. Hannenhalli, "Mimosa: mixture model of co-expression to detect modulators of regulatory interaction," *Algorithms for Molecular Biology*, vol. 5, no. 1, article 4, 2010.

[46] O. Babur, E. Demir, M. Gönen, C. Sander, and U. Dogrusoz, "Discovering modulators of gene expression," *Nucleic Acids Research*, vol. 38, no. 17, Article ID gkq287, pp. 5648–5656, 2010.

[47] T. Shimamura, S. Imoto, Y. Shimada et al., "A novel network profiling analysis reveals system changes in epithelial-mesenchymal transition," *PLoS ONE*, vol. 6, no. 6, Article ID e20804, 2011.

[48] H. Y. Wu et al., "A modulator based regulatory network for ERalpha signaling pathway," *BMC Genomics*, vol. 13, Supplement 6, article S6, 2012.

[49] K.-K. Yan, W. Hwang, J. Qian et al., "Construction and analysis of an integrated regulatory network derived from High-Throughput sequencing data," *PLoS Computational Biology*, vol. 7, no. 11, Article ID e1002190, 2011.

[50] M. Flores and Y. Huang, "TraceRNA: a web based application for ceRNAs prediction," in *Proceedings of the IEEE Genomic Signal Processing and Statistics Workshop (GENSIPS '12)*, 2012.

[51] S. D. Hsu, F. M. Lin, W. Y. Wu et al., "MiRTarBase: a database curates experimentally validated microRNA-target interactions," *Nucleic Acids Research*, vol. 39, no. 1, pp. D163–D169, 2011.

[52] H. Liu, D. Yue, Y. Chen, S. J. Gao, and Y. Huang, "Improving performance of mammalian microRNA target prediction," *BMC Bioinformatics*, vol. 11, article 476, 2010.

[53] Y. Dong et al., "A Bayesian decision fusion approach for microRNA target prediction," *BMC Genomics*, vol. 13, 2012.

[54] J. A. Asm and M. Montague, "Models for Metasearch," in *Proceedings of the 24th annual international ACM SIGIR conference on Research and development in information retrieval*, pp. 276–284, la, New Orleans, La, USA, 2001.

18

On the Meaning of Affinity Limits in B-Cell Epitope Prediction for Antipeptide Antibody-Mediated Immunity

Salvador Eugenio C. Caoili

Department of Biochemistry and Molecular Biology, College of Medicine, University of the Philippines Manila, Room 101, Medical Annex Building, 547 Pedro Gil Street, Ermita, Manila 1000, Philippines

Correspondence should be addressed to Salvador Eugenio C. Caoili, badong@post.upm.edu.ph

Academic Editor: Tatsuya Akutsu

B-cell epitope prediction aims to aid the design of peptide-based immunogens (e.g., vaccines) for eliciting antipeptide antibodies that protect against disease, but such antibodies fail to confer protection and even promote disease if they bind with low affinity. Hence, the Immune Epitope Database (IEDB) was searched to obtain published thermodynamic and kinetic data on binding interactions of antipeptide antibodies. The data suggest that the affinity of the antibodies for their immunizing peptides appears to be limited in a manner consistent with previously proposed kinetic constraints on affinity maturation in vivo and that cross-reaction of the antibodies with proteins tends to occur with lower affinity than the corresponding reaction of the antibodies with their immunizing peptides. These observations better inform B-cell epitope prediction to avoid overestimating the affinity for both active and passive immunization; whereas active immunization is subject to limitations of affinity maturation in vivo and of the capacity to accumulate endogenous antibodies, passive immunization may transcend such limitations, possibly with the aid of artificial affinity-selection processes and of protein engineering. Additionally, protein disorder warrants further investigation as a possible supplementary criterion for B-cell epitope prediction, where such disorder obviates thermodynamically unfavorable protein structural adjustments in cross-reactions between antipeptide antibodies and proteins.

1. Introduction

Antibody-mediated immunity is the basis of most conventional approaches to immunization, which protect against or treat disease by means of antibodies that are either endogenous (i.e., produced via active immunization, notably through the administration of vaccines that elicit antibody responses) or exogenous (i.e., acquired via passive immunization through the administration of preformed antibodies from some external source, such as a human or animal donor). Historically, these approaches have been developed and pursued mainly for the prevention and control of communicable infectious diseases viewed as public-health problems, which is ever more crucial to adequately address current and anticipated global-health challenges posed by emerging and reemerging pathogens that cause pandemics and panzootics (both of which may be inextricably linked in cases of zoonoses such as avian and swine influenza) [1]. Yet, the envisioned practical applications of antibody-mediated immunity increasingly include therapy for and prophylaxis against diseases such as cancer and hypertension that have traditionally been regarded as lifestyle related rather than infectious [2, 3] although some of these diseases may be at least partly due to infectious agents (e.g., oncogenic viruses) that are thus important targets of antibody-mediated immunity. In a very general sense, possible targets of antibody-mediated immunity include virtually all biomolecules regardless of origin and are often dichotomously categorized as being either self (i.e., autologous, or host associated) or nonself (e.g., pathogen associated), but the distinction is potentially misleading in that a typical vertebrate host normally becomes colonized by microbes acquired from its environment early in life to form a complex biological system (i.e., an ecosystem-like superorganism) comprising both the host and its symbiotically associated microbes [4], such that the concept of self arguably encompasses the host and microbial components of the system.

Antibody-mediated immunity targets a biomolecule as an antigen (i.e., substance recognized by the immune system) through a molecular-recognition process whereby a paratope (i.e., antigen-binding site on an antibody) binds an epitope (i.e., submolecular structural feature actually recognized on the antigen). In this context, the epitope is recognized as a B-cell epitope (rather than a T-cell epitope, for which the overall recognition process is much more elaborate and involves a T-cell receptor instead of antibody) [5]. Accordingly, B-cell epitope prediction is the computational identification of putative B-cell epitopes on antigen structures [6]; in practice, this is usually performed for peptidic (i.e., protein or peptide) antigens on the basis of structural information ranging from amino-acid sequences (as deduced from nucleic-acid sequences) to atomic coordinates (obtained experimentally or in turn from computational analyses of amino-acid sequences) [7]. From the perspective of generating protective antibody-mediated immunity while also avoiding adverse antibody-mediated reactions, B-cell epitope prediction is potentially useful if it correctly anticipates biological effects of paratope-epitope binding interactions, so as to guide the pursuit of beneficial rather than harmful clinical outcomes. Ideally, this would enable the design of safe and efficacious vaccines, which presupposes the ability to accurately model the in vivo kinetics of both antibody buildup and affinity maturation (i.e., the microevolutionary process by which antibody affinity can be increased through somatic hypermutation among competing B-cell clones in the course of an antibody response) insofar as clinical outcomes (e.g., protection against or enhancement of infection) reflect the interplay of antibody concentration and antibody affinity. A more computationally tractable task is the design of immunogens (e.g., peptide-based constructs) to produce antibodies or derivatives thereof (e.g., Fab fragments) that protect against disease via passive immunization, which circumvents the complexities and limitations of endogenous antibody production. Antibodies may bind antigens and thereby exert biological effects, which may occur directly due to binding per se (e.g., via direct neutralization of biological activity, as in the inhibition of enzymes or the blocking of pathogen adhesion molecules) or indirectly due to the activation of downstream immune effector mechanisms such as complement pathways and opsonization-facilitated phagocytosis [8]. These mechanisms are typically protective, but they may paradoxically promote pathogenesis under certain circumstances.

Biological outcomes of immunization are contingent upon thermodynamic and kinetic constraints on antibody-antigen interactions, as exemplified by context-dependent roles of antibodies in mediating either protection against or enhancement of infection. The latter phenomenon has been observed among infections due to a wide variety of pathogens including taxonomically diverse viruses [9, 10], notably enveloped viruses such as HIV [11, 12] and flaviviruses (e.g., dengue and West Nile viruses [13, 14]), and even bacteria and protozoa [15, 16]. Among enveloped viruses, this often occurs when virions are incompletely coated by IgG-class antibodies, which favors enhanced infection by promoting viral adsorption onto host cells via capture of virion-bound IgG by Fc-γ receptors while still permitting fusion between viral and cellular membranes [17]. HIV infection of monocytes has thus been mathematically modeled [17], thereby recapitulating the empirical observation that the enhancement of infection is favored at low antibody concentrations and by low-affinity antibody binding; hence, even high-affinity antibody binding may enhance infection below a certain threshold antibody concentration that increases as affinity decreases.

Protective antibody-mediated immunity is favored over antibody-mediated enhancement of infection by increasing either or both antibody concentration and affinity, yet this is practically feasible only up to certain limits. Even below the solubility limit of antibodies in aqueous solution, buildup of supraphysiologic antibody concentrations in vivo may produce hyperviscosity syndrome [18]. Moreover, high antibody concentrations may be difficult to attain via active immunization although this limitation might be overcome by passive immunization (e.g., with purified monoclonal antibodies). The practically feasible maximum antibody concentration, as dictated either by safety considerations or by actual outcomes of immunization, thus defines a minimum affinity below which protective antibody-mediated immunity is an unrealistic prospect. At the same time, affinity itself is subject to physicochemical and physiological constraints that limit its magnitude [19, 20]. These considerations motivate the present work, which aims to clarify their implications for B-cell epitope prediction as applied to the generation of antipeptide antibodies that protect against disease.

2. Theory and Methods

2.1. Upper Bounds for Affinity. The affinity of antibodies for antigens is often quantitatively expressed as the association constant K_A (i.e., affinity constant) or equivalent dissociation constant K_D, such that

$$K_A = \frac{1}{K_D}$$
$$K_A = \exp\left(-\frac{\Delta G}{RT}\right), \tag{1}$$

where ΔG is the free energy change of association, R the gas constant, and T the temperature. As ΔG is ultimately a function of biomolecular structure, K_A may, in principle, be estimated from structural information. Where only antigen structure is known, this may be partitioned into B-cell epitopes for which ΔG may be approximated from their solvent-accessible surface area (ASA) within the framework of structural energetics [21, 22] under certain simplifying assumptions (e.g., that the epitope is completely buried upon binding by the paratope, which loses approximately the same amounts of apolar and polar ASA as the epitope in the process [23, 24]). The value of ΔG thus obtained corresponds to a theoretical upper bound for affinity where the structural complementarity between epitope and paratope approaches that between close-packed internal surfaces of a natively folded protein. However, this may greatly exceed the affinity realized during B-cell development [19].

Naive B cells express surface immunoglobulins for receptor-mediated endocytosis of antigens as an initial step towards recruiting T-cell help for activation, which in turn prompts B-cell proliferation with mutation of immunoglobulin-coding genes to diversify the paratopic repertoire. This entails competition among B cells for T-cell help, with B-cell survival favored by rapid endocytosis of antigens for presentation to helper T cells. The endocytic antigen-uptake rate may be increased either by increasing the on-rate constant k_{on} for antigen capture or by decreasing the off-rate constant k_{off} for antigen escape. As both rate constants are related by

$$K_A = \frac{k_{on}}{k_{off}}, \tag{2}$$

mutations that increase the antigen-uptake rate also increase the affinity for antigen according to (1), for which reason the mutation phase of B-cell development is known as affinity maturation. Hence, increases in affinity for antigen tend to favor B-cell clonal selection, but only up to a certain ceiling level as may be explained in terms of limits on both k_{on} and k_{off} during affinity maturation [19], considering that the upper bound for K_A is defined by the upper bound for k_{on} and the lower bound for k_{off} according to (2).

For binding of interaction partners A and B, the upper bound for k_{on} is the on-rate constant for diffusion-limited collisional encounters, as given by

$$k_{on}^{max} = 4\pi a(D_A + D_B)\left(\frac{N}{1000}\right), \tag{3}$$

where a is the encounter distance, D_A and D_B are the diffusion constants, and N is Avogadro's number (i.e., $6.02 \times 10^{23}\,\mathrm{mol}^{-1}$). Using (3), k_{on}^{max} is obtained in $M^{-1}\,s^{-1}$ for a in cm and for D_A and D_B in $cm^2\,s^{-1}$ [25]. For binding of small protein antigens by antibodies in solution, k_{on}^{max} is estimated to be in the range of 10^5 to $10^6\,M^{-1}\,s^{-1}$ [26, 27], and antibodies in general are thus unlikely to have much higher values of k_{on}^{max} [19]. For capture of IgG-class antibodies from solution by immobilized antigens in surface plasmon resonance (SPR) studies, where the antigen diffusion constant is practically zero, k_{on}^{max} may be estimated from (3) using an encounter distance of 1.57×10^{-8} cm and an antibody diffusion constant of $4 \times 10^{-7}\,cm^2\,s^{-1}$, yielding a value of $4.75 \times 10^7\,M^{-1}\,s^{-1}$ [25].

To estimate the lower bound for k_{off} during affinity maturation, endocytic antigen uptake may be modeled to a first approximation with classical Michaelis-Menten kinetics applied to transmembrane transport, in which case the Michaelis-Menten constant is given by

$$K_M = \frac{(k_{off} + k_{in})}{k_{on}}, \tag{4}$$

where k_{in} is the rate constant for endocytic internalization of surface immunoglobulin-bound antigen. As K_M is numerically equivalent to the antigen concentration at which the steady-state rate of antigen internalization is half-maximal, a decrease in K_M confers a competitive advantage upon B cells to the extent that they are thus enabled to internalize antigen more rapidly than other B cells. Consequently, k_{on} may approach k_{on}^{max} (from (3)) in the course of affinity maturation. However, k_{off} is unlikely to decrease much further below k_{in} as the gain in competitive advantage would then be negligible [19]; according to (4), K_M approaches the lower limit of k_{in}/k_{on} for values of k_{off} much lower than k_{in}, in which case the values of K_M are approximately uniform such that none is distinctly advantageous over the others. Considering the reported half-life of 8.5 min for surface immunoglobulins prior to their endocytosis on Epstein Barr virus-transformed B-lymphoblastoid cells [28], the lower bound for k_{off} during affinity maturation is estimated to be in the range of 10^{-4} to $10^{-3}\,s^{-1}$ under the assumption that two to three surface-immunoglobulin half-lives is the upper limit beyond which increased immune-complex stability confers no competitive advantage [19].

Competition among B cells for endocytic uptake of antigens is thus a plausible mechanism that limits the emergence of antibodies with low k_{off} during affinity maturation. A related mechanism has been proposed that may likewise limit the emergence of antibodies with low k_{off}, namely, sequestration of antigens by antibodies in highly stable immune complexes that limits the availability of antigens for endocytic uptake by B cells [29]. Notwithstanding the operation of these mechanisms, the theoretical upper bound for affinity might still be closely approached where optimal complementarity between epitopes and paratopes arises fortuitously (e.g., by initial rearrangement of germline immunoglobulin-gene sequences) prior to any affinity maturation [19], and artificial selection processes (e.g., with yeast display) may transcend the limits of in vivo affinity maturation [20].

Apart from the upper bound for affinity per se and the kinetic constraints imposed during affinity maturation, an additional consideration arises in relation to cross-reaction of antipeptide antibodies with protein antigens. Typically, this involves a peptide whose sequence forms part of a cognate protein; as an immunogen, the peptide may elicit antipeptide antibodies, but these may cross-react with the protein with very low affinity. Such problems are the concern of B-cell epitope prediction for generating antipeptide antibodies that exert biological effects by cross-reacting with proteins. A major challenge therein is the difficulty of predicting the affinity with which antipeptide antibodies cross-react with proteins. If such cross-reaction is to result in biological effects, it must occur with sufficiently high affinity with the proteins in biologically relevant molecular contexts (e.g., in native conformational and oligomerization states, possibly as integral components of supramolecular complexes such as biological membranes). Relevant experimental results reported thus far have mostly been limited to qualitative assessment of the binding per se without biological correlates [30]; yet these data nonetheless suggest that cross-reaction of antipeptide antibodies with proteins tends to occur with lower affinity than the corresponding reaction of the antibodies with the immunizing peptides. This would be consistent with thermodynamically unfavorable structural adjustments (e.g., unfolding of proteins to conformationally mimic their peptide counterparts) during cross-reactions; and if this is actually the case for antipeptide antibodies, their affinity in reactions with immunizing peptides represents a plausible practical upper bound for their affinity in cross-reactions with proteins.

With regard to antipeptide antibodies that cross-react with protein antigens, three upper bounds for affinity may thus be discerned: the first pertains to binding per se in the reaction of antipeptide antibodies with their immunizing peptides, the second, to binding realized during affinity maturation, and the third, to cross-reaction of the antipeptide antibodies with protein antigens. Among these three, the first is necessarily an upper bound for the second (as the first is never exceeded during affinity maturation) but not for the third (as cross-reaction with the protein may be thermodynamically more favorable than reaction with the immunizing peptide, e.g., due to lower conformational entropy of the protein relative to the peptide); however, the third is unlikely to exceed the second where cross-reaction entails thermodynamically unfavorable structural adjustment (e.g., protein unfolding to conformationally mimic the immunizing peptide). Hence, physicochemical constraints on both affinity maturation and cross-reaction are expected to limit the affinity of antipeptide antibodies for protein antigens and, consequently, the capacity of such antibodies to mediate protective immunity (e.g., to protect against rather than enhance infection). Knowledge of such constraints is therefore potentially useful for B-cell epitope prediction in order to avoid overestimating the affinity of cross-reaction.

2.2. Retrieval and Processing of Epitope Data. To further investigate the limits on affinity of antipeptide antibodies for immunizing peptides and for cognate protein antigens, published thermodynamic and kinetic data were retrieved on binding interactions of antipeptide antibodies, using the Immune Epitope Database and Analysis Resource (IEDB; http://www.immuneepitope.org/) [31]. Relevant curated data were retrieved from IEDB by means of searches conducted with its B Cell Search facility (Figure 1), which returns records that each pertain to a B-cell assay for a particular epitope. Each record thus returned contains multiple data fields, several of which are defined in relation to the concepts of "1st Immunogen" (i.e., immunogen administered to produce antibodies) and "Antigen" (i.e., antigen used in the B-cell assay).

Searches were restricted by the data fields named "1st Immunogen Epitope Relation" and "Antigen Epitope Relation" (hereafter referred to as the immunogen and antigen fields, resp.). For both thermodynamic and kinetic data, primary and secondary searches were conducted, which respectively retrieved data on reactions of antipeptide antibodies with peptides and on cross-reactions of the same antibodies with proteins. The primary searches retrieved records for which the epitope comprised both immunogen and antigen, such that both immunogen and antigen fields had the value "Epitope". The secondary searches retrieved records

for which the epitope also comprised the immunogen but formed only a part of the antigen, such that the immunogen field had the value "Epitope" while the antigen field had the value "Source antigen". Additionally, each search was further restricted to return only those records containing either thermodynamic or kinetic data by filtering with respect to B-cell assay type (represented by the data field named "Assay"). Such filtering was performed using the Assay Finder feature of the B Cell Search facility.

Within the Assay Finder pop-up window, the B-cell assay tree was navigated to view the available assay-type categories under the subheading of "binding constant determination assay" (itself under the subheading of "antibody binding to epitope"), and appropriate selections of the said assay-type categories were defined for filtering in order to retrieve only those records matching one of the selected assay types. For thermodynamic data, the selected assay-type categories were "equilibrium association constant (KA)" and "equilibrium dissociation constant (KD)"; each of these categories comprised assay types of calorimetry, enzyme-linked immunosorbent assay (ELISA), fluorescence immunoassay (FIA), radioimmunoassay (RIA), and surface plasmon resonance (SPR), all of which were further qualified as having measurements expressed in units of either "[1/nM]" (for "KA") or "[nM]" (for "KD"). For kinetic data, the selected assay-type categories were "binding on rate measurement datum (kon)" and "binding off rate measurement datum (koff)"; each of these categories comprised assay types of FIA and SPR, both of which were further qualified as having measurements expressed in units of either "[M^{-1} s^{-1}]" (for "k_{on}") or "[s^{-1}]" (for "k_{off}").

A total of four searches (i.e., a primary and a secondary search each for thermodynamic and kinetic data) were conducted between 16 and 18 July 2012, and the search results were downloaded as IEDB full-format comma-separated value (CSV) files comprising B-cell epitope records. Subsequent processing of records focused mainly on the data field named "Quantitative measurement" whose numeric value was a thermodynamic or kinetic measurement. Records were excluded from further consideration in cases wherein the data field named "Measurement Inequality" contained an inequality symbol (either "<" or ">", indicating that the numeric value was a lower or upper bound rather than a point estimate) or for which the epitope was nonpeptidic (i.e., wherein the data field named "Epitope Object Type" had a value of "Non-peptidic" instead of "Linear peptide").

Records retrieved through each primary search were processed before those of the corresponding secondary search in order to facilitate pairing of counterpart records that essentially differed from one another only in the antigen field (whose value was "Epitope" for the primary search and "Source antigen" for the secondary search); records retrieved through a secondary search were processed only where they were thus found to be counterparts of retained records from the corresponding primary search. For kinetic data, records were retained only where data were available on both the on- and off-rate constants for a particular binding interaction. For each record that was ultimately retained, the numeric value was compared with

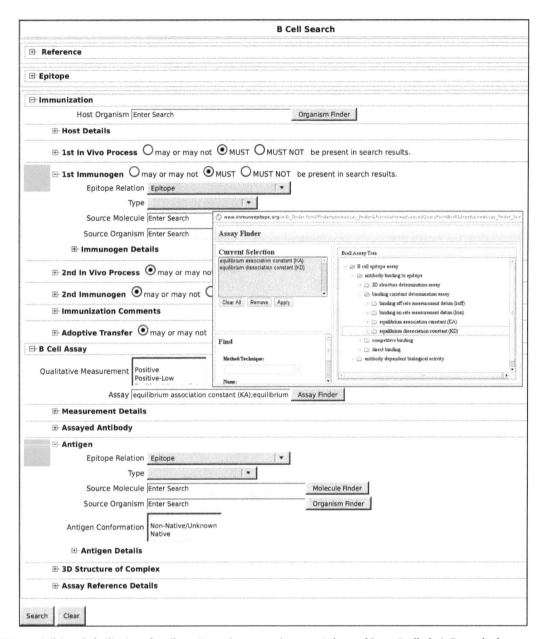

FIGURE 1: IEDB B Cell Search facility interface (http://www.immuneepitope.org/advancedQueryBcell.php). Example shown corresponds to primary search for thermodynamic data (see main text for full explanation). Green squares along left margin mark user options selected from pull-down menus, for restricting searches by data fields of the type "Epitope Relation;" upper and lower green squares, respectively, mark options for "1st Immunogen Epitope Relation" (set to "Epitope" for both primary and secondary searches) and "Antigen Epitope Relation" (set to either "Epitope" for primary searches or "Source antigen" for secondary searches). Inset with red border contains screenshot of Assay Finder pop-up window (activated by clicking the Assay Finder button, located along bottom edge of inset), which facilitates the selection of search-appropriate assay-type categories using the B-cell Assay Tree (shown in right panel of inset).

that originally reported in the underlying literature reference; where discrepancies were found, the values from literature were used for subsequent analysis, and the discrepancies were reported to the maintainers of IEDB.

Records containing thermodynamic data were segregated by units of measurement into two categories, each comprising data on either association constants or dissociation constants in units of 1/nM or nM, respectively. Corresponding association constants were calculated from dissociation constants according to (1), and all association constants were expressed in units of 1/M. Records on both association and dissociation constants were ranked in order of decreasing affinity. The ranked records were inspected for equal or nearly equal association-constant values, for which the underlying records and literature references were reviewed to explore the possibility of data redundancy; where a pair of such values was found to represent equivalent association and dissociation constants, the record for the dissociation constant was deemed redundant and was thus excluded from further analysis. The underlying literature references were also reviewed to confirm that all data included in the final analysis described antibody-antigen binding interactions themselves rather than conditions (e.g., concentrations of chaotropic agents) under which the interactions were studied.

Records containing kinetic data were segregated by units of measurement into two categories, comprising data on either on- or off-rate constants in units of $M^{-1}s^{-1}$ or s^{-1}, respectively. Records pertaining to on- and off-rate constants from a common literature reference were reviewed in conjunction with the literature reference to identify pairs of corresponding on- and off-rate constants pertaining to the same binding interaction. For each pair of rate constants thus identified, the records on thermodynamic data were searched for a corresponding record on an association constant (or equivalent dissociation constant) also pertaining to the same binding interaction and related to the rate constants according to (2).

3. Results and Discussion

3.1. Affinity. For reactions of antipeptide antibodies with peptides, a dataset of 120 records on affinities of antipeptide antibodies for their peptidic epitopes was assembled (Figure 2), comprising 56 records on polyclonal antibodies and 64 records on monoclonal antibodies. (Two records, with IEDB B-Cell IDs 1603957 and 1603959 and both containing quantitative measurements with IEDB assay type units of "KD [nM]," were excluded from the dataset because their data pertained to concentrations of the chaotropic agent ammonium thiocyanate required to dissociate 50% of bound antibody from immobilized peptide antigen in an ELISA [32], as a measure of avidity rather than an actual dissociation constant.) Reference data on these records are presented in Tables 1 and 2 for association constants above and below the median value, respectively. The lowest and highest association constants were 1.15×10^5 and $4.30 \times 10^{10} M^{-1}$, respectively, with a median of $8.57 \times 10^7 M^{-1}$. The highest association constant was thus lower than the ceiling value of $4.75 \times 10^{11} M^{-1}$ expected for affinity maturation, as calculated using (2) from values of $4.75 \times 10^7 M^{-1}s^{-1}$ for k_{on} [25] and $10^{-4}s^{-1}$ for k_{off} [19] (noting that the k_{on} value thus cited is appropriate for solid-phase immunoassays wherein immobilized antigens capture IgG-class antibodies from solution, which is the case for most data in Figure 2 including the highest association constant). These data are compatible with an affinity ceiling during affinity maturation in vivo as previously suggested on kinetic grounds [19]. However, only the monoclonal-antibody data correspond to homogeneous antibody-molecule populations; the polyclonal-antibody data represent averages for heterogeneous antibody-molecule populations, each of which may thus exhibit variation in affinity for antigen among its constituent antibody molecules such that a subset thereof might actually exceed the proposed affinity ceiling. Furthermore, although the artificial-selection processes of

monoclonal-antibody production are deliberately biased towards obtaining high-affinity clones, this fails to guarantee that the highest-affinity clones are indeed ultimately isolated (e.g., because hybridoma survival may be poorly correlated with affinity), which cautions against assuming that the monoclonal-antibody data provide stronger support than the polyclonal-antibody data for the proposed affinity limit, especially in view of the presently observed overlap between monoclonal and polyclonal antibodies in their affinity-value ranges.

For cross-reactions of antipeptide antibodies with proteins, seven additional records were found on affinities of antipeptide antibodies for protein source antigens containing the epitope sequences of the immunizing peptides, such that each additional record had a counterpart pertaining to the same antibody in the dataset for reactions of antipeptide antibodies with peptides (Figure 2). Association constants were typically more than an order of magnitude lower for cross-reactions with proteins than for the corresponding reactions with peptides, except in the case of a monoclonal antibody (rank 43 in Figure 2 and Table 1) whose association constant was actually higher for cross-reaction with protein than for reaction with peptide. This monoclonal antibody was produced by immunization with an epitope consisting of two cross-linked peptides corresponding to residues 395–402 and 402–411 (cross-linked at Gln 398 and Lys 406) of the C-terminal region on human fibrin γ-chain [53], in which case lower conformational entropy of the epitope as part of the cognate protein rather than the immunizing peptide may at least partly account for higher affinity of cross-reaction with protein relative to reaction with immunizing peptide. Overall, these results are consistent with a trend towards thermodynamically unfavorable structural adjustments upon cross-reaction with protein that lead to lower binding affinity relative to reaction with immunizing peptides, but the exceptional case of the human fibrin epitope demonstrates the possibility of higher affinity with cross-reaction.

3.2. Kinetics. For reactions of antipeptide antibodies with peptides, a dataset of 31 rate-constant record pairs containing data on corresponding on- and off-rate constants from surface plasmon resonance (SPR) studies was assembled (Figure 3; Table 3), comprising four record pairs on polyclonal antibodies and 27 record pairs on monoclonal antibodies. On the basis of underlying literature references and (2), corresponding records on affinity data (Figure 2; Tables 1 and 2) were found for most of the rate-constant record pairs, except in the cases of 11 record pairs on monoclonal antibodies (Figure 3, labels A through K); where the affinity data were published, they had been computed directly from their corresponding rate constants according to (2) rather than obtained directly (i.e., by another independent experimental means). The lowest and highest on-rate constants were 5.1×10^1 and $2.49 \times 10^6 M^{-1}s^{-1}$, respectively, with the latter below the upper bound of $4.75 \times 10^7 M^{-1}s^{-1}$ for diffusion-limited reaction as calculated in Section 3.1. The lowest and highest off-rate constants were 8.00×10^{-5} and $6.65 \times 10^{-2}s^{-1}$, respectively. Most of

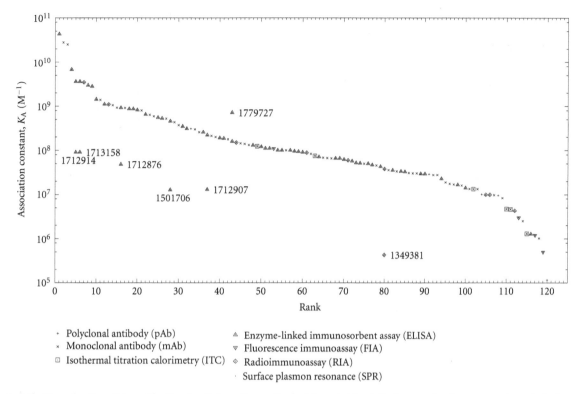

FIGURE 2: Affinities of antipeptide antibodies for their epitopes. Each data point is plotted as a pair of superposed symbols for antibody type (polyclonal or monoclonal) and B-cell assay type (as indicated in the legend). Unlabeled data points are affinity ranked and represent reactions of antipeptide antibodies with peptides (Tables 1 and 2). Other data points are labeled by IEDB B-Cell ID number and represent cross-reactions of antipeptide antibodies with proteins. Data points sharing the same abscissa value pertain to the same antibody and other B-cell assay conditions except the antigen.

the data were on immobilized antigens capturing IgG-class antibodies from solution, except for the data points labeled 86 (with the lowest off-rate) and 120 (with the lowest on-rate) in Figure 3, in which cases the data were on immobilized antibodies capturing antigens from solution. If these exceptions are excluded from consideration, the lowest on- and off-rate constants are $3.44 \times 10^3 \, M^{-1} \, s^{-1}$ and $1.46 \times 10^{-4} \, s^{-1}$, respectively (for the data points labeled 104 and 23 in Figure 3). These data are compatible with a lower bound of $1 \times 10^{-4} \, s^{-1}$ for off-rate during affinity maturation in vivo as previously suggested [19].

For cross-reactions of antipeptide antibodies with proteins, two additional rate-constant record pairs were found on antipeptide antibodies cross-reacting with a protein source antigen (tobacco mosaic virus protein) containing the peptidic epitope (source antigen residues 110–135; IEDB Epitope ID 94786) of the antibodies [76], such that each additional record had a counterpart pertaining to the same antibody in the dataset for reactions of antipeptide antibodies with peptides (Figure 3). On-rate constants were more than an order of magnitude lower for cross-reactions with protein than for the corresponding reactions with peptide; off-rate constants were either higher or lower for cross-reactions with protein than for the corresponding reactions with peptide. The lower on-rate constants for cross-reaction are consistent with thermodynamically unfavorable

structural adjustment to attain complementarity between epitope and paratope.

3.3. Data Representativeness and Redundancy. Despite the attempt to exhaustively retrieve relevant data from IEDB, the datasets thus assembled herein are small, with this problem being worse for the kinetic data. The problem is further compounded by interrelated issues of data representativeness and redundancy. The paucity of data points immediately suggests that the datasets are of limited representativeness in the sense of capturing various combinations of experimental conditions, especially in view of the myriad variables (immunogen structure, immunized species, immunization conditions, cognate antigen structure, assay conditions, etc.) likely to be correlated with immunologic outcomes. Moreover, redundancy is apparent on inspecting for similarities among the IEDB records, each of which represents a B-cell assay that may be unique only with respect to a single variable. For instance, the entire subset of kinetic data labeled with uppercase letters in Figure 3 and Table 3 is on a panel of monoclonal antibodies elicited by a single peptide and assayed for binding the same peptide (having a 26-mer sequence derived from tobacco mosaic virus protein [76]), such that each underlying B-cell assay is unique only with respect to its particular monoclonal antibody. Here, data redundancy might be approached by reducing all the data

Table 1: IEDB affinity data, above median.

Rank	B cell ID	Epitope ID	$K_A(\mathrm{M}^{-1})$	Ref. number
1	1713243	123283	4.30×10^{10}	[33]
2	1694121	119943	2.80×10^{10}	[34]
3	1377940	54911	2.50×10^{10}	[35]
4	1502913	22303	6.72×10^{9}	[36]
5	1712919	123282	3.60×10^{9}	[37]
6	1713155	123282	3.60×10^{9}	[33]
7	1662870	111856	3.47×10^{9}	[38]
8	1710417	123058	2.96×10^{9}	[37]
9	1710420	123221	2.80×10^{9}	[37]
10	1772326	131658	1.43×10^{9}	[39]
11	1313016	4701	1.39×10^{9}	[40]
12	1349361	11821	1.11×10^{9}	[41]
13	1636267	104452	1.10×10^{9}	[42]
14	1313012	4701	1.05×10^{9}	[40]
15	1313005	4701	9.26×10^{8}	[40]
16	1712874	125323	9.20×10^{8}	[37]
17	1313015	4701	9.17×10^{8}	[40]
18	1349366	7766	8.70×10^{8}	[41]
19	1244111	18084	8.70×10^{8}	[43]
20	1349364	11821	8.20×10^{8}	[41]
21	1313011	4701	8.00×10^{8}	[40]
22	1487415	7766	6.54×10^{8}	[44]
23	1789780	105769	6.41×10^{8}	[45]
24	1278023	54666	5.92×10^{8}	[46]
25	1244119	15938	5.56×10^{8}	[43]
26	1349365	7766	5.29×10^{8}	[41]
27	1313010	4701	5.24×10^{8}	[40]
28	1502914	22303	4.57×10^{8}	[36]
29	1803541	7493	4.35×10^{8}	[47]
30	1313014	4701	3.76×10^{8}	[40]
31	1487413	11821	3.48×10^{8}	[44]
32	1487416	7766	3.12×10^{8}	[44]
33	16285	59318	3.08×10^{8}	[48]
34	1587464	36959	3.00×10^{8}	[49]
35	1278024	54666	2.56×10^{8}	[46]
36	1487414	11821	2.56×10^{8}	[44]
37	1712912	124998	2.20×10^{8}	[37]
38	1329743	58132	2.13×10^{8}	[50]
39	1329922	58132	2.00×10^{8}	[50]
40	1705153	120407	1.90×10^{8}	[51]
41	1313385	33796	1.85×10^{8}	[52]
42	1329915	31002	1.79×10^{8}	[50]
43	1779729	134133	1.59×10^{8}	[53]
44	1930562	164463	1.49×10^{8}	[54]
45	1329916	31002	1.43×10^{8}	[50]
46	1329731	31002	1.39×10^{8}	[50]
47	1329918	31002	1.32×10^{8}	[50]
48	1710412	123058	1.30×10^{8}	[55]
49	1335178	75791	1.23×10^{8}	[56]
50	1244124	66382	1.20×10^{8}	[43]

Table 1: Continued.

Rank	B cell ID	Epitope ID	$K_A(\mathrm{M}^{-1})$	Ref. number
51	1865651	70070	1.10×10^{8}	[57]
52	1865652	63967	1.10×10^{8}	[57]
53	1483242	64541	1.10×10^{8}	[58]
54	1865649	15938	1.00×10^{8}	[57]
55	1883894	63967	1.00×10^{8}	[57]
56	1329744	45673	1.00×10^{8}	[50]
57	1479672	27725	1.00×10^{8}	[59]
58	1865628	18084	9.52×10^{7}	[57]
59	1244126	8267	9.36×10^{7}	[43]
60	1244234	28937	8.99×10^{7}	[43]

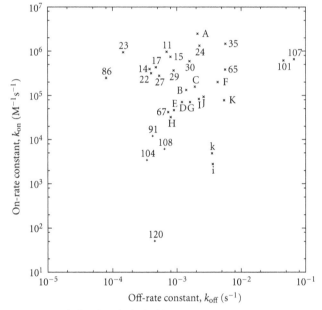

· Polyclonal antibody (pAb)

× Monoclonal antibody (mAb)

Figure 3: On- and off-rates of antipeptide antibodies binding their epitopes, obtained by surface plasmon resonance (SPR). For reactions of antipeptide antibodies with peptides, data points are labeled either by affinity rank in Figure 2 for corresponding IEDB records on affinity data or, where such records were not found, alphabetically with uppercase letters in order of decreasing affinity [76]. For cross-reactions of antipeptide antibodies with protein [76], data points are labeled with lower-case letters (i and k) matching the uppercase letter labels (I and K) of data points for the corresponding reactions of the antibodies with peptide.

for the entire panel to some representative (e.g., average) value for each rate constant (i.e., placing the entire panel on par with a single polyclonal-antibody data point), but this would entail loss of information (e.g., obscuring the observation that data point A corresponds to the highest on-rate constant). Furthermore, each member of a monoclonal-antibody panel (and for that matter each distinct idiotype of a polyclonal antibody sample) might bind a unique site on a peptide that has been operationally defined as a single B-cell epitope according to IEDB curation guidelines for lack

TABLE 2: IEDB affinity data, below median.

Rank	B cell ID	Epitope ID	$K_A(\mathrm{M}^{-1})$	Ref. number
61	1681389	113966	8.80×10^7	[60]
62	1329745	56122	8.33×10^7	[50]
63	1338803	8067	7.50×10^7	[61]
64	1883893	70070	7.09×10^7	[57]
65	1811868	7491	6.83×10^7	[62]
66	1329928	56122	6.67×10^7	[50]
67	1649813	107849	6.58×10^7	[63]
68	1883884	18084	6.58×10^7	[57]
69	1883887	15938	6.58×10^7	[57]
70	1336690	14958	6.21×10^7	[64]
71	1664695	113966	5.97×10^7	[38]
72	1883888	15938	5.71×10^7	[57]
73	1883895	63967	5.21×10^7	[57]
74	1883892	70070	5.13×10^7	[57]
75	1329924	58132	5.00×10^7	[50]
76	1652921	108291	5.00×10^7	[65]
77	1865650	66382	4.67×10^7	[57]
78	1329930	267	4.55×10^7	[50]
79	1883886	18084	4.31×10^7	[57]
80	1349380	49305	3.80×10^7	[66]
81	1329747	266	3.57×10^7	[50]
82	1883890	66382	3.55×10^7	[57]
83	1329927	56122	3.33×10^7	[50]
84	1772218	131654	3.33×10^7	[39]
85	1336692	19093	3.27×10^7	[64]
86	1697081	103097	3.08×10^7	[67]
87	1329923	58132	3.03×10^7	[50]
88	1329933	266	3.03×10^7	[50]
89	1784467	134492	2.94×10^7	[68]
90	1883891	66382	2.92×10^7	[57]
91	1464180	571	2.88×10^7	[69]
92	1329746	267	2.78×10^7	[50]
93	1329936	45673	2.78×10^7	[50]
94	1336693	3290	2.28×10^7	[64]
95	1329934	266	1.89×10^7	[50]
96	1329932	267	1.75×10^7	[50]
97	1329935	266	1.69×10^7	[50]
98	1336694	19097	1.65×10^7	[64]
99	1329929	56122	1.61×10^7	[50]
100	1652922	108482	1.41×10^7	[65]
101	1922426	162870	1.35×10^7	[70]
102	1335279	75789	1.34×10^7	[56]
103	1329937	45673	1.33×10^7	[50]
104	1464193	30063	1.01×10^7	[69]
105	1636270	104452	1.00×10^7	[42]
106	1484082	7005	9.95×10^6	[71]
107	1922425	162870	9.80×10^6	[70]
108	1464140	30093	9.58×10^6	[69]
109	1329938	45673	8.33×10^6	[50]

TABLE 2: Continued.

Rank	B cell ID	Epitope ID	$K_A(\mathrm{M}^{-1})$	Ref. number
110	1335193	74035	4.70×10^6	[56]
111	1335182	75791	4.60×10^6	[56]
112	1459804	6078	4.30×10^6	[72]
113	1245815	68401	3.00×10^6	[73]
114	1352617	24591	2.50×10^6	[74]
115	1335197	74036	1.30×10^6	[56]
116	1705155	120403	1.27×10^6	[51]
117	1245814	68401	1.20×10^6	[73]
118	1352618	24591	1.02×10^6	[74]
119	1245813	68401	5.00×10^5	[73]
120	21742	4467	1.15×10^5	[75]

of data on antigenic fine structure (in the sense of high-resolution epitope mapping) [77]; even if the unique sites overlapped to some extent, each could itself still be regarded as a B-cell epitope [5]. This underscores the difficulty of accounting for redundancy in B-cell epitope datasets. Simply reasoning by analogy, for example, to the management of redundancy in general-purpose protein-structure datasets [78–80], data might be inappropriately conflated for B-cell assay records sharing identical or otherwise similar peptide sequences, thus ignoring the possibility of yet unresolved antigenic fine structure and of radically divergent antigenic properties arising from seemingly minor sequence differences (e.g., even in a single chemical group [81]).

Undoubtedly, the problems of data representativeness and redundancy in B-cell epitope datasets must be rigorously formulated and resolved accordingly to facilitate further development of B-cell epitope prediction tools, but such a task is well beyond the scope of the present study. If at all the datasets herein are somehow representative of antibody-antigen interactions in general, this may be by virtue of thermodynamic and kinetic constraints (e.g., during affinity maturation) that immunization processes are typically subject to, which nonetheless calls for further validation on the basis of more numerous and diverse prospectively acquired experimental data as these become available.

3.4. Implications. Considering the thermodynamic and kinetic data included in the present work, two key observations emerge. First, affinity of antipeptide antibodies for proteins is likely to be overestimated if computed as a theoretical upper bound for binding per se without regard for affinity maturation. Second, affinity of antipeptide antibodies for proteins tends to be lower than for the immunizing peptides used to elicit the antibodies. These observations serve to clarify crucial problems encountered in B-cell epitope prediction that seeks to quantitatively estimate affinity of antipeptide antibodies for proteins. One problem thus clarified is the difficulty of estimating the maximum affinity of antipeptide antibodies for immunizing peptides which is realized during immunization; although this maximum affinity may be estimated from antigen structure by means of structural energetics [23, 24], the

TABLE 3: IEDB rate-constant data.

Label in Figure 3	B cell ID for on-rate constant	B cell ID for off-rate constant
11	1312987	1313002
14	1312984	1312997
15	1312948	1312990
17	1312986	1313001
21	1312983	1312996
23	1789783	1789790
24	1278965	1278971
27	1312982	1312993
29	1803539	1803540
30	1312985	1313000
35	1278972	1278973
65	1811862	1811867
67	1650289	1650291
86	1697079	1697080
91	1464226	1464233
101	1922428	1922430
104	1464248	1464255
107	1922427	1922429
108	1464204	1464211
120	22186	22187
A	1581476	1581498
B	1581474	1581496
C	1581475	1581497
D	1581473	1581494
E	1581467	1581488
F	1581471	1581492
G	1581473	1581495
H	1581472	1581493
I	1581469	1581490
J	1581470	1581491
K	1581468	1581489
i	1581939	1581944
k	1581940	1581945

highest affinity that is actually realized may be much lower due to kinetic constraints on affinity maturation [19, 20] and also to suboptimal immunization conditions such as choice of adjuvant [41, 43, 44, 57, 59, 64, 69, 75, 82]. A related problem is the difficulty of estimating affinity of the antipeptide antibodies for proteins in view of the structural differences between the immunizing peptides and the proteins [30, 83]; even if the affinity of the antibodies for the immunizing peptides is known, it may differ markedly from the affinity for cognate proteins of the peptides, which may be much lower due to thermodynamically unfavorable structural adjustments of cross-reaction.

The abovementioned problems could be addressed in several ways. In particular, affinity maturation could be accounted for in B-cell epitope prediction by an appropriate

ceiling on predicted affinity values. Furthermore, immunization conditions (e.g., adjuvants) could be optimized so as to maximize the affinity of elicited antipeptide antibodies. In certain cases, however, the ceiling on predicted affinity values may be lower than previously suggested on the basis of endocytic uptake of univalent antigen [19], particularly for multivalent antigens that can cross-link surface immunoglobulins on B cells. Immunoglobulin cross-linking by multivalent antigens entails multiple simultaneous epitope-paratope binding interactions, in which case high avidity (i.e., overall strength of binding) may result even where the individual epitope-paratope binding interactions are each of low affinity. Surface-immunoglobulin cross-linking may thus enable efficient endocytic uptake of multivalent antigens by B cells even in the setting of low-affinity epitope-paratope interactions, and it may also favor B-cell activation more directly via transmembrane signal-transduction pathways [84, 85]. In view of this added complexity posed by multivalent antigens, which include immunogens that comprise typical peptide-carrier protein conjugates and multiple antigenic peptides, the outcome of higher affinity might be favored by avoiding surface-immunoglobulin cross-linking during affinity maturation (e.g., by immunizing with a construct containing only one copy of the B-cell epitope that is the intended target of the antibody response). More generally, limitations of natural affinity maturation in vivo might be overcome by artificial selection methods (e.g., based on yeast display [20]) or by protein engineering of paratopes for improved complementarity to target epitopes. As to the problem of predicting affinities of cross-reactions between antipeptide antibodies and their envisioned protein targets, this might be at least partly addressed by basing predictions on similarities between each immunizing peptide and its corresponding region on the protein target, with emphasis on conformation and on overall physical accessibility to antibodies. This approach may be readily feasible in cases where the immunizing peptide and its corresponding protein region share the same sequence and are intrinsically disordered (i.e., unfolded and behaving as dynamic random coils with rapidly fluctuating backbone conformations [86]) while the protein region is located on an antibody-accessible site (e.g., exposed on the surface of an extracellular protein domain), such that the antipeptide antibodies may bind the protein with essentially the same affinity as for the peptide insofar as thermodynamically unfavorable structural adjustments would be unnecessary for the protein to mimic the peptide. Although the classical concept of completely folded native protein structures identifies dynamic disorder with denatured states, intrinsic protein disorder has more recently been observed in native states of an increasingly diverse repertoire of proteins among all domains of life, with the extent of disorder ranging from short protein segments to full-length proteins [86]. An antibody-accessible natively disordered protein region may thus be structurally mimicked by a similarly disordered peptide of identical sequence, and if the peptide bears a B-cell epitope that is bound by a complementary paratope with sufficient affinity, the peptide may elicit antipeptide antibodies that bind the peptide and the protein region with similar affinities via a process of paratope-induced epitope folding whereby the epitope becomes immobilized in a conformation that is readily adopted in both the peptide and the cognate protein. Existing B-cell epitope prediction methods may actually account for this possibility to some extent (e.g., using flexibility parameters, or implicitly via machine learning). Thus utilizing information on dynamic disorder broadens the scope of B-cell epitope prediction based on structural similarity between peptides and their cognate proteins, as exemplified by prior work on identifying β-turns as markers of epitope structure [87] considering that they may be present in both peptide and protein structure [88] particularly where they form early in the course of the folding process [89].

The preceding considerations are applicable to B-cell epitope prediction for generating antipeptide antibodies that exert biological effects by cross-reacting with proteins, both for active immunization (e.g., with peptide-based vaccines) and for passive immunization (e.g., with antipeptide antibodies from exogenous sources). For each candidate protein target of antipeptide antibodies, the target structure (i.e., the target protein as it occurs in its biologically relevant conformational state and higher-order structural context [30]) may be partitioned into candidate B-cell epitopes for which antibody affinity could be estimated [23, 24], either with or without the assumption of a ceiling on affinity during affinity maturation [19, 20]. This affinity-ceiling assumption would be made only where affinity maturation would actually be relevant to the envisioned practical application (e.g., active immunization with peptide-based vaccines, but not passive immunization with monoclonal antipeptide antibodies), and the exact value of the affinity ceiling would depend on factors such as host characteristics (especially those pertaining to B-cell development) and details of the immunization process (including adjuvants and the nature of the immunogen, e.g., univalent versus multivalent). To evaluate each candidate B-cell epitope for potential utility, an affinity cutoff value could be established for cross-reaction of antipeptide antibodies with the epitope as part of the target structure, such that the epitope would be deemed potentially useful only if the estimated antibody affinity were to exceed the cutoff value. The cutoff value itself might be determined in relation to some estimated maximum antibody concentration (e.g., based on projected postvaccination outcomes) necessary to achieve a certain biological outcome (e.g., protection against rather than enhancement of viral infection, as mathematically modeled for enveloped viruses [17]). If a sufficient number of potentially useful candidate epitopes is thus found even with an affinity-ceiling assumption for affinity maturation in vivo, the epitopes could be incorporated into a peptide-based vaccine for active immunization; otherwise, the affinity cutoff value could be adjusted downwards (e.g., by raising the maximum antibody concentration to a physically realistic yet reasonably safe level), and potentially useful epitopes that might then be found could be incorporated into a peptide-based immunogen for generating antibodies to mediate passive immunization (e.g., by the administration of antipeptide monoclonal antibodies). In cases where the affinity-ceiling assumption

were to preclude the identification of suitable candidate epitopes, this assumption could be dropped with the proviso that artificial affinity selection (e.g., based on yeast display) or antibody engineering would enable realization of the predicted affinities. Additionally, protein disorder might yet serve as a supplementary predictive criterion (e.g., by focusing exclusively on candidate epitopes that are predicted to be intrinsically disordered in the target structure), so as to avoid uncertainties of modeling thermodynamically unfavorable structural adjustment among the target proteins as they mimic the immunizing peptides. Bearing in mind this theoretical consideration, protein disorder warrants further investigation on the basis of additional data as these become available.

The practical significance of affinity limits in B-cell epitope prediction is thus clearly evident in relation to the problem of antibody-mediated enhancement of infection. At a host-population level, mass immunization (e.g., by natural infection, vaccination, or passive acquisition of antibodies) may initially confer protective antibody-mediated immunity to infection by attaining sufficiently high antibody concentrations among many hosts, but subsequent shifts from protective to infection-enhancing effects may occur as antibody concentrations decrease over time. In light of the preceding considerations, B-cell epitope prediction is meaningful if it quantitatively captures pertinent antibody-mediated biological effects in a context-dependent manner that informs clinical and public-health decisions, possibly by demonstrating the inadequacy of antibody-based approaches in particular situations (e.g., where antibody affinity falls below some critical threshold for practical utility).

More generally, biological effects of antibody-mediated immunity can be analyzed in relation to both antibody affinity and antibody concentration in order to appreciate the practical implications of B-cell epitope prediction. To clarify this approach, an instructive example is that of a nonreplicating toxin bound by an antibody, such that binding of the toxin by the antibody neutralizes the toxin while both the affinity and the concentration of the antibody in vivo (e.g., in plasma) are independent variables. Toxin biological activity can be expressed within a toxicologic dose-response framework as the killed fraction of a host population following the administration of a standardized toxin dose (possibly normalized per unit body mass) to each member of the population, for a given affinity-concentration pair (i.e., combination of antibody-affinity and antibody-concentration values, both held to be uniform over the entire population). For each affinity-concentration pair, a dose-response curve can be constructed by plotting the killed fraction (as the ordinate) against the toxin dose (as the abscissa). Granted that each dose-response curve is a strictly monotonically increasing function of typical sigmoidal form extending from the origin (i.e., zero killed fraction at zero toxin dose) and having a unique point at 50% (i.e., half-maximal) killed fraction, the toxin dose corresponding to the latter point is the median lethal dose LD_{50} for the particular affinity-concentration pair. The LD_{50} may be expressed as the median lethal concentration LC_{50} (e.g., in a body fluid or in-vitro culture medium), which facilitates analysis in relation to antibody concentration. Without loss of generality, this can be illustrated using a simple model featuring rapid-equilibrium reversible binding of toxin by antibody, toxicity due only to free (i.e., unbound) toxin, and a sigmoidal dose-response curve in the absence of antibody, such that the curve is shifted towards increased survival by either or both increased antibody concentration and increased antibody affinity for toxin. The toxin-antibody dissociation constant K_D (cf. (1)) may thus be written in terms of the concentrations of toxin Tx, antibody Ab, and toxin-antibody complex TxAb, either as

$$K_D = \frac{[\text{Tx}][\text{Ab}]}{[\text{TxAb}]} \tag{5}$$

or equivalently as

$$K_D = \frac{([\text{Tx}]_{\text{tot}} - [\text{TxAb}])([\text{Ab}]_{\text{tot}} - [\text{TxAb}])}{[\text{TxAb}]}, \tag{6}$$

where each symbol with enclosing square brackets ([]) denotes the molar concentration of the corresponding species and the subscript (tot) denotes the total for free and bound forms of a species. Likewise, the probability P of toxin-induced death may be written either as

$$P = \frac{1}{1 + \text{LC}_{50}/[\text{Tx}]} \tag{7}$$

or equivalently as:

$$P = \frac{1}{1 + \text{LC}_{50}/([\text{Tx}]_{\text{tot}} - [\text{TxAb}])} \tag{8}$$

such that the dose-response relationship for toxin lethality may thus be represented by plotting P against total toxin concentration expressed relative to LC_{50} (Figure 4). Increasing either or both affinity and concentration consequently increases the LC_{50} (as more toxin is required to kill half the population). The protective benefit attributed to a particular affinity-concentration pair can be quantitatively expressed relative to zero antibody concentration (e.g., as the difference between the LC_{50} with and without antibody), and a plot of concentration against affinity can be constructed for affinity-concentration pairs that confer equal protective benefit (Figure 5). From a biomedical perspective, critical points on the plot would include those corresponding to physical and physiologic upper bounds on affinity and concentration; the physical upper bounds are the theoretical maximum affinity for paratope-epitope binding and the solubility limit of antibody in plasma while the physiologic upper bounds are the expected maximum affinity realized through affinity maturation and the normal endogenous-antibody concentration. Between the normal endogenous-antibody concentration and the solubility limit of antibody in plasma, additional thresholds can be defined (e.g., for pathologic conditions due to plasma hyperviscosity resulting from excessively high antibody concentrations). If B-cell epitope prediction is performed to estimate antibody affinities for putative neutralization epitopes of the toxin [23], the estimated affinities can in turn be used to calculate

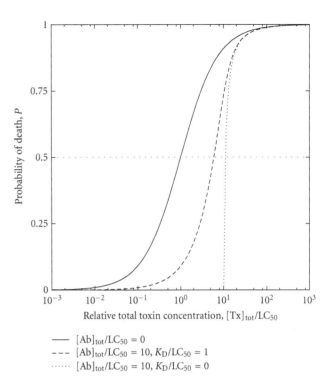

FIGURE 4: Representative theoretical dose-response curves for toxin of median lethal concentration LC_{50} and antitoxin antibody of dissociation constant K_D, based on (5) through (8). Toxin and antibody concentrations are expressed in terms of respective total values $[\text{Tx}]_{\text{tot}}$ and $[\text{Ab}]_{\text{tot}}$ comprising free and bound species in binding equilibrium.

the antibody concentrations required to achieve predefined levels of protective benefit (i.e., increase in LD_{50} relative to zero antibody concentration), and the concentrations can be assessed in terms of feasibility (from a purely technical standpoint) and acceptability (with attention to health risks, costs, and other nontechnical considerations). Where continuous long-term protection might be sought, the assessment would entail the calculation of dosing intervals for the administration of either exogenous antibody for passive immunization (e.g., as schematically depicted in Figure 6) or booster doses of vaccine for active immunization. If active immunization were thus deemed unrealistic or impractical as a means to attain adequate affinity or concentration, passive immunization might be considered as an alternative (possibly with artificial selection methods that circumvent the physiologic affinity limit); if even passive immunization were deemed unrealistic or impractical, yet other alternatives (e.g., pharmacologic) might be explored.

Similar analyses can be conducted for more complicated cases, notably communicable infectious diseases (in which case ID_{50}, the median infectious dose of a pathogen, can replace or supplement LD_{50} as a parameter of interest). For these diseases, a key epidemiologic consideration is the emergent property of herd immunity (i.e., overall resistance of a host population to the spread of an infectious disease, even where a fraction of hosts lacks protective immunity as

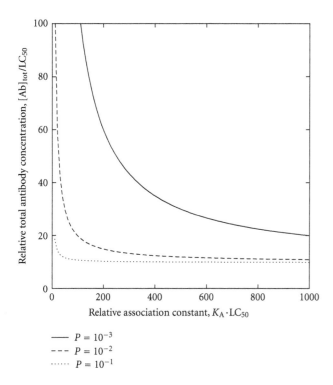

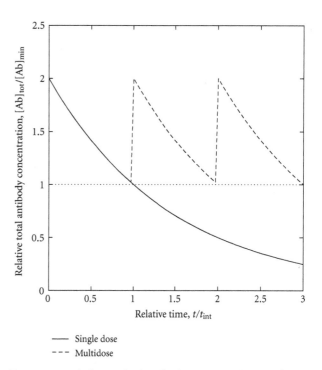

FIGURE 5: Contour map based on dose-response relationships of Figure 4 for $[Tx]_{tot}/LC_{50} = 10$ (i.e., total toxin concentration tenfold greater than LC_{50}), depicting P as a function of both antibody affinity (expressed in terms of the association constant K_A; cf. (1)) and antibody concentration (i.e., minimum required antibody concentration of Figure 6).

FIGURE 6: Passively-acquired antibody concentration as a function of time. After administering a dose of antibody to raise the total antibody concentration $[Ab]_{tot}$ above the minimum required antibody concentration $[Ab]_{min}$, $[Ab]_{tot}$ eventually falls below $[Ab]_{min}$ unless more antibody is administered within the maximum dosing interval t_{int}.

individuals), which allows for some degree of fault tolerance (e.g., for incomplete population coverage by immunization programs and for variability in the protection afforded by individual host immune responses). In cases where antibody-dependent enhancement of infection occurs, the prospect of realizing benefit must be weighed against the risk of causing harm; depending on exactly how this is accomplished, the possibility of harm may argue against antibody-mediated immunity attained through active rather than passive immunization (considering that the effects of active immunization are much more difficult to reverse) or even against antibody-mediated immunity altogether (considering that entirely cell-mediated immunity may be a viable alternative in certain instances, as suggested by the observation that hosts unable to mount antibody responses can nonetheless successfully resist viral infection by means of T-cell responses [90]). In the last case, B-cell epitope prediction might thus serve to identify putative epitopes that ought to be excluded from, rather than included in, immunogens designed as vaccines. This may be especially relevant where the rational design of vaccine immunogens to elicit protective antibodies is of questionable feasibility, as exemplified by the open problem of HIV vaccine design [91].

In all such analyses, the casting of antibody-mediated immunity in terms of benefit, harm, risk, cost, and allied concepts inevitably introduces a normative dimension into the discussion of B-cell epitope prediction, the meaning of which is then understood as contingent upon interrelated issues of ethics, economics, and society at large. Hence, antibody affinity for binding putative epitopes ultimately enters into moral calculations under forms of aggregative consequentialism such as utilitarianism (which seeks to maximize aggregate utility in the sense of overall wellbeing) and prioritarianism (which is similar to utilitarianism but employs weighting schemes to prioritize those who are relatively worse-off in terms of individual wellbeing). This is conditioned by the application of ethical principles such as nonmaleficence (i.e., avoidance of causing harm), which derives from the medical precept of *primum non nocere* (first do no harm) and is conceptually related to the precautionary principle (i.e., assigning the burden of proof, in the interest of sustainability, to proponents of activities that may threaten health and environment) [92]. Comprehension of these issues is necessary to rationally approach major global-health challenges such as the efficient implementation of vaccination programs, especially with regard to timely allocation of limited vaccine supplies [93, 94].

4. Conclusions

Affinity of antipeptide antibodies for their immunizing peptides appears to be limited in a manner consistent with kinetic constraints on affinity maturation, and cross-reaction of these antibodies with proteins tends to occur with even lower affinity. These observations serve to better inform B-cell epitope prediction for generating antipeptide antibodies that cross-react with proteins, particularly to avoid overestimation of affinity for both active and passive immunization. Whereas active immunization is subject to limitations of affinity maturation in vivo and of the capacity to accumulate endogenous antibodies, passive immunization may transcend such limitations, possibly via artificial affinity-selection processes and protein engineering. In addition to affinity, protein disorder warrants further investigation as a possible supplementary criterion for B-cell epitope prediction where such disorder obviates thermodynamically unfavorable structural adjustments in cross-reactions of antipeptide antibodies with proteins. These considerations could guide the further development of B-cell epitope prediction that is meaningful in relation to biomedical applications insofar as it addresses the biological impact of antibody-mediated immunity in ways that facilitate quantitative evaluation of both benefit and harm, from clinical and public-health perspectives; this is conceivably feasible if based on accurate estimation of antibody affinities for putative epitopes that in turn enables calculation of antibody concentrations required for various biological effects of antibody-mediated immunity, thereby supporting informed decisions to adopt particular strategies (e.g., induction versus avoidance of antibody-mediated immunity, and active versus passive immunization) in the context of a comprehensive theoretical framework that encompasses interrelated technical, ethical, economic, and societal concerns.

Acknowledgments

This work was supported in part by a grant (PGMA-SEGS) from the Commission on Higher Education of the Philippine Government.

References

[1] S. E. Caoili, "B-cell epitope prediction for peptide-based vaccine design: towards a paradigm of biological outcomes for global health," *Immunome Research*, vol. 7, no. 2, article 2, 2011.

[2] T. A. Röhn and M. F. Bachmann, "Vaccines against noncommunicable diseases," *Current Opinion in Immunology*, vol. 22, no. 3, pp. 391–396, 2010.

[3] J. Söllner, "Beyond epitopes: future and application of computational vaccinology," *Human Vaccines*, vol. 7, no. 7, pp. 795–797, 2011.

[4] G. Eberl, "A new vision of immunity: homeostasis of the superorganism," *Mucosal Immunology*, vol. 3, no. 5, pp. 450–460, 2010.

[5] M. H. Van Regenmortel, "What is a B-cell epitope?" *Methods in Molecular Biology*, vol. 524, pp. 3–20, 2009.

[6] Y. El-Manzalawy and V. Honavar, "Recent advances in B-cell epitope prediction methods," *Immunome Research*, vol. 6, no. 2, article S2, 2010.

[7] J. Söllner, A. Heinzel, G. Summer et al., "Concept and application of a computational vaccinology workflow," *Immunome Research*, vol. 6, no. supplement 2, article S7, 2010.

[8] J. Söllner, R. Grohmann, R. Rapberger, P. Perco, A. Lukas, and B. Mayer, "Analysis and prediction of protective continuous B-cell epitopes on pathogen proteins," *Immunome Research*, vol. 4, article 1, 2008.

[9] S. M. C. Tirado and K. J. Yoon, "Antibody-dependent enhancement of virus infection and disease," *Viral Immunology*, vol. 16, no. 1, pp. 69–86, 2003.

[10] A. Takada and Y. Kawaoka, "Antibody-dependent enhancement of viral infection: molecular mechanisms and in vivo implications," *Reviews in Medical Virology*, vol. 13, no. 6, pp. 387–398, 2003.

[11] Z. Beck, Z. Prohászka, and G. Füst, "Traitors of the immune system-Enhancing antibodies in HIV infection: their possible implication in HIV vaccine development," *Vaccine*, vol. 26, no. 24, pp. 3078–3085, 2008.

[12] H. Stoiber, "Complement, Fc receptors and antibodies: a Trojan horse in HIV infection?" *Current Opinion in HIV and AIDS*, vol. 4, no. 5, pp. 394–399, 2009.

[13] T. C. Pierson and M. S. Diamond, "Molecular mechanisms of antibody-mediated neutralisation of flavivirus infection," *Expert Reviews in Molecular Medicine*, vol. 10, article e12, 2008.

[14] M. S. Diamond, T. C. Pierson, and D. H. Fremont, "The structural immunology of antibody protection against West Nile virus," *Immunological Reviews*, vol. 225, no. 1, pp. 212–225, 2008.

[15] S. Mahalingam and B. A. Lidbury, "Antibody-dependent enhancement of infection: bacteria do it too," *Trends in Immunology*, vol. 24, no. 9, pp. 465–467, 2003.

[16] S. B. Halstead, S. Mahalingam, M. A. Marovich, S. Ubol, and D. M. Mosser, "Intrinsic antibody-dependent enhancement of microbial infection in macrophages: disease regulation by immune complexes," *The Lancet Infectious Diseases*, vol. 10, no. 10, pp. 712–722, 2010.

[17] O. Lund, J. Hansen, E. Mosekilde, J. O. Nielsen, and J. E. S. Hansen, "A model of enhancement and inhibition of HIV infection of monocytes by antibodies against HIV," *Journal of Biological Physics*, vol. 19, no. 2, pp. 133–145, 1993.

[18] M. A. Gertz and R. A. Kyle, "Hyperviscosity syndrome," *Journal of Intensive Care Medicine*, vol. 10, no. 3, pp. 128–141, 1995.

[19] J. Foote and H. N. Eisen, "Kinetic and affinity limits on antibodies produced during immune responses," *Proceedings of the National Academy of Sciences of the United States of America*, vol. 92, no. 5, pp. 1254–1256, 1995.

[20] J. Foote and H. N. Eisen, "Breaking the affinity ceiling for antibodies and T cell receptors," *Proceedings of the National Academy of Sciences of the United States of America*, vol. 97, no. 20, pp. 10679–10681, 2000.

[21] K. P. Murphy, "Predicting binding energetics from structure: looking beyond $\Delta G°$," *Medicinal Research Reviews*, vol. 19, no. 4, pp. 333–339, 1999.

[22] S. P. Edgcomb and K. P. Murphy, "Structural energetics of protein folding and binding," *Current Opinion in Biotechnology*, vol. 11, no. 1, pp. 62–66, 2000.

[23] S. E. C. Caoili, "A structural-energetic basis for B-cell epitope prediction," *Protein and Peptide Letters*, vol. 13, no. 7, pp. 743–751, 2006.

[24] S. E. C. Caoili, "Immunization with peptide-protein conjugates: impact on benchmarking B-cell epitope prediction for vaccine design," *Protein and Peptide Letters*, vol. 17, no. 3, pp. 386–398, 2010.

[25] C. J. van Oss, "Kinetics and energetics of specific intermolecular interactions," *Journal of Molecular Recognition*, vol. 10, no. 5, pp. 203–216, 1997.

[26] S. H. Northrup and H. P. Erickson, "Kinetics of protein-protein association explained by Brownian dynamics computer simulation," *Proceedings of the National Academy of Sciences of the United States of America*, vol. 89, no. 8, pp. 3338–3342, 1992.

[27] C. S. Raman, R. Jemmerson, B. T. Nall, and M. J. Allen, "Diffusion-limited rates for monoclonal antibody binding to cytochrome c," *Biochemistry*, vol. 31, no. 42, pp. 10370–10379, 1992.

[28] C. Watts and H. W. Davidson, "Endocytosis and recycling of specific antigen by human B cell lines," *EMBO Journal*, vol. 7, no. 7, pp. 1937–1945, 1988.

[29] K. V. S. Rao, "Selection in a T-dependent primary humoral response: new insights from polypeptide models," *Acta Pathologica, Microbiologica et Immunologica*, vol. 107, no. 9, pp. 807–818, 1999.

[30] S. E. C. Caoili, "Benchmarking B-cell epitope prediction for the design of peptide-based vaccines: problems and prospects," *Journal of Biomedicine and Biotechnology*, vol. 2010, Article ID 910524, 14 pages, 2010.

[31] Q. Zhang, P. Wang, Y. Kim et al., "Immune epitope database analysis resource (IEDB-AR)," *Nucleic Acids Research*, vol. 36, pp. W513–518, 2008.

[32] L. M. Silva-Flannery, M. Cabrera-Mora, J. Jiang, and A. Moreno, "Recombinant peptide replicates immunogenicity of synthetic linear peptide chimera for use as pre-erythrocytic stage malaria vaccine," *Microbes and Infection*, vol. 11, no. 1, pp. 83–91, 2009.

[33] S. Subramanian, A. A. Karande, and P. R. Adiga, "Helix stabilization in the C-terminal peptide of chicken riboflavin carrier protein enhances immunogenicity and prolongs contraceptive potential as an epitope-based vaccine in female rats," *Biochemical and Biophysical Research Communications*, vol. 287, no. 1, pp. 236–243, 2001.

[34] N. A. Verwey, R. Veerhuis, H. A. M. Twaalfhoven et al., "Quantification of amyloid-beta 40 in cerebrospinal fluid," *Journal of Immunological Methods*, vol. 348, no. 1-2, pp. 57–66, 2009.

[35] C. Zahnd, S. Spinelli, B. Luginbühl, P. Amstutz, C. Cambillau, and A. Plückthun, "Directed in vitro evolution and crystallographic analysis of a peptide-binding single chain antibody fragment (scFv) with low picomolar affinity," *Journal of Biological Chemistry*, vol. 279, no. 18, pp. 18870–18877, 2004.

[36] H. Cordes, A. L. Bergström, J. Ohm, H. Laursen, and P. M. H. Heegaard, "Characterisation of new monoclonal antibodies reacting with prions from both human and animal brain tissues," *Journal of Immunological Methods*, vol. 337, no. 2, pp. 106–120, 2008.

[37] S. Subramanian, A. A. Karande, and P. R. Adiga, "Immuno-contraceptive potential of major antigenic determinants of chicken riboflavin carrier protein in the female rat," *Vaccine*, vol. 19, no. 9-10, pp. 1172–1179, 2000.

[38] E. D. Day, G. A. Hashim, D. J. Ireland, and N. T. Potter, "Polyclonal antibodies to the encephalitogenic neighborhoods of myelin basic protein: singular affinity populations neutralized by specific synthetic peptide probes," *Journal of Neuroimmunology*, vol. 13, no. 2, pp. 143–158, 1986.

[39] J. L. Bret-Dibat, D. Zouaoui, O. Dery et al., "Antipeptide polyclonal antibodies that recognize a substance P-binding site in mammalian tissues: a biochemical and immunocytochemical study," *Journal of Neurochemistry*, vol. 63, no. 1, pp. 333–343, 1994.

[40] M. Esumi, Y. H. Zhou, T. Tanoue, T. Tomoguri, and I. Hayasaka, "In vivo and in vitro evidence that cross-reactive antibodies to C-terminus of hypervariable region 1 do not neutralize heterologous hepatitis C virus," *Vaccine*, vol. 20, no. 25-26, pp. 3095–3103, 2002.

[41] B. Chaba, P. Kumar, W. Haq, L. Sabhnani, and D. N. Rao, "Influence of immunoadjuvants and a promiscuous T-cell determinant on the immunogenicity of RESA peptide antigen of *P. falciparum*," *International Journal of Immunopharmacology*, vol. 20, no. 6, pp. 259–273, 1998.

[42] I. Hilgert, P. Stolba, H. Kristofova et al., "A monoclonal antibody applicable for determination of C-peptide of human proinsulin by RIA," *Hybridoma*, vol. 10, no. 3, pp. 379–386, 1991.

[43] V. Tripathi, K. T. Chitralekha, A. R. Bakshi et al., "Inducing systemic and mucosal immune responses to B-T construct of F1 antigen of *Yersinia pestis* in microsphere delivery," *Vaccine*, vol. 24, no. 16, pp. 3279–3289, 2006.

[44] P. Kumar, S. Biswas, and D. N. Rao, "Potentiation of immune response against the RESA peptides of *Plasmodium falciparum* by incorporating a universal T-cell epitope (CS.T3) and an immunomodulator (polytuftsin), and delivery through liposomes," *Microbiology and Immunology*, vol. 43, no. 6, pp. 567–576, 1999.

[45] H. Hillen, S. Barghorn, A. Striebinger et al., "Generation and therapeutic efficacy of highly oligomer-specific β-amyloid antibodies," *Journal of Neuroscience*, vol. 30, no. 31, pp. 10369–10379, 2010.

[46] A. Nowakowski, C. Wang, D. B. Powers et al., "Potent neutralization of botulinum neurotoxin by recombinant oligoclonal antibody," *Proceedings of the National Academy of Sciences of the United States of America*, vol. 99, no. 17, pp. 11346–11350, 2002.

[47] R. Robert, M. P. Lefranc, A. Ghochikyan et al., "Restricted V gene usage and VH/VL pairing of mouse humoral response against the N-terminal immunodominant epitope of the amyloid β peptide," *Molecular Immunology*, vol. 48, no. 1–3, pp. 59–72, 2010.

[48] W. Liu and Y. H. Chen, "High epitope density in a single protein molecule significantly enhances antigenicity as well as immunogenecity: a novel strategy for modern vaccine development and a preliminary investigation about B cell discrimination of monomeric proteins," *European Journal of Immunology*, vol. 35, no. 2, pp. 505–514, 2005.

[49] D. J. van den Heuvel, R. P. H. Kooyman, J. W. Drijfhout, and G. W. Welling, "Synthetic peptides as receptors in affinity sensors: a feasibility study," *Analytical Biochemistry*, vol. 215, no. 2, pp. 223–230, 1993.

[50] C. Li and J. P. Allain, "Chimeric monoclonal antibodies to hypervariable region 1 of hepatitis C virus," *Journal of General Virology*, vol. 86, no. 6, pp. 1709–1716, 2005.

[51] M. Skok, E. Lykhmus, S. Bobrovnik et al., "Structure of epitopes recognized by the antibodies to α(181–192) peptides of neuronal nicotinic acetylcholine receptors: extrapolation to the structure of acetylcholine-binding domain," *Journal of Neuroimmunology*, vol. 121, no. 1-2, pp. 59–66, 2001.

[52] E. Hanan, S. A. Priola, and B. Solomon, "Antiaggregating antibody raised against human PrP 106–126 recognizes pathological and normal isoforms of the whole prion protein," *Cellular and Molecular Neurobiology*, vol. 21, no. 6, pp. 693–703, 2001.

[53] S. M. Taubenfeld, Y. Song, D. Sheng, E. L. Ball, and G. R. Matsueda, "A monoclonal antibody against a peptide sequence

of fibrinogen gamma chain acts as an inhibitor of factor XIII-mediated crosslinking of human fibrin," *Thrombosis and Haemostasis*, vol. 74, no. 3, pp. 923–927, 1995.

[54] A. J. Sytkowski and J. W. Fisher, "Isolation and characterization of an anti-peptide monoclonal antibody to human erythropoietin," *Journal of Biological Chemistry*, vol. 260, no. 27, pp. 14727–14731, 1985.

[55] S. Subramanian, P. R. Adiga, and A. A. Karande, "Immunocontraceptive efficacy of synthetic peptides corresponding to major antigenic determinants of chicken riboflavin carrier protein in the female rats," *American Journal of Reproductive Immunology*, vol. 44, no. 3, pp. 184–191, 2000.

[56] A. Helg, M. S. Mueller, A. Joss et al., "Comparison of analytical methods for the evaluation of antibody responses against epitopes of polymorphic protein antigens," *Journal of Immunological Methods*, vol. 276, no. 1-2, pp. 19–31, 2003.

[57] L. Sabhnani, M. Manocha, K. Sridevi, D. Shashikiran, R. Rayanade, and D. N. Rao, "Developing subunit immunogens using B and T cell epitopes and their constructs derived from the F1 antigen of *Yersinia pestis* using novel delivery vehicles," *FEMS Immunology and Medical Microbiology*, vol. 38, no. 3, pp. 215–229, 2003.

[58] J. M. H. van den Elsen, L. M. A. van Unen, L. van Bloois et al., "Thermodynamic analysis of the interaction between a bactericidal antibody and a PorA epitope of *Neisseria meningitidis*," *Biochemistry*, vol. 36, no. 41, pp. 12583–12591, 1997.

[59] O. E. Obeid, C. M. Stanley, and M. W. Steward, "Immunological analysis of the protective responses to the chimeric synthetic peptide representing T- and B-cell epitopes from the fusion protein of measles virus," *Virus Research*, vol. 42, no. 1-2, pp. 173–180, 1996.

[60] E. D. Day and G. A. Hashim, "Affinity purification of two populations of antibodies against format determinants of synthetic myelin basic protein peptide S82 from S82-AH- and S82-CH-Sepharose 4B columns," *Neurochemical Research*, vol. 9, no. 10, pp. 1453–1465, 1984.

[61] R. Moreno, F. Pöltl-Frank, D. Stüber et al., "Rhoptry-associated protein 1-binding monoclonal antibody raised against a heterologous peptide sequence inhibits *Plasmodium falciparum* growth in vitro," *Infection and Immunity*, vol. 69, no. 4, pp. 2558–2568, 2001.

[62] M. K. Mustafa, A. Nabok, D. Parkinson, I. E. Tothill, F. Salam, and A. Tsargorodskaya, "Detection of β-amyloid peptide (1–16) and amyloid precursor protein (APP770) using spectroscopic ellipsometry and QCM techniques: a step forward towards Alzheimers disease diagnostics," *Biosensors and Bioelectronics*, vol. 26, no. 4, pp. 1332–1336, 2010.

[63] J. T. Downs, C. L. Lane, N. B. Nestor et al., "Analysis of collagenase-cleavage of type II collagen using a neoepitope ELISA," *Journal of Immunological Methods*, vol. 247, no. 1-2, pp. 25–34, 2001.

[64] B. E. Thomas, M. Manocha, W. Haq, T. Adak, C. R. Pillai, and D. N. Rao, "Modulation of the humoral response to repeat and non-repeat sequences of the circumsporozoite protein of *Plasmodium vivax* using novel adjuvant and delivery systems," *Annals of Tropical Medicine and Parasitology*, vol. 95, no. 5, pp. 451–472, 2001.

[65] M. Kaur, H. Chug, H. Singh et al., "Identification and characterization of immunodominant B-cell epitope of the C-terminus of protective antigen of *Bacillus anthracis*," *Molecular Immunology*, vol. 46, no. 10, pp. 2107–2115, 2009.

[66] A. R. Neurath, S. B. H. Kent, and N. Strick, "Specificity of antibodies elicited by a synthetic peptide having a sequence in common with a fragment of a virus protein, the hepatitis B surface antigen," *Proceedings of the National Academy of Sciences of the United States of America*, vol. 79, no. 24, pp. 7871–7875, 1982.

[67] M. Ramakrishnan, K. K. Kandimalla, T. M. Wengenack, K. G. Howell, and J. F. Poduslo, "Surface plasmon resonance binding kinetics of Alzheimer's disease amyloid β peptide-capturing and plaque-binding monoclonal antibodies," *Biochemistry*, vol. 48, no. 43, pp. 10405–10415, 2009.

[68] Y. Song, S. M. Taubenfeld, D. Sheng, and G. R. Matsueda, "Characterization of a monoclonal antibody directed against the carboxyl-terminus of human factor XIII. An epitope exposed upon denaturation and conserved across species lines," *Thrombosis and Haemostasis*, vol. 71, no. 1, pp. 62–67, 1994.

[69] P. J. Cachia, D. J. Kao, and R. S. Hodges, "Synthetic peptide vaccine development: measurement of polyclonal antibody affinity and cross-reactivity using a new peptide capture and release system for surface plasmon resonance spectroscopy," *Journal of Molecular Recognition*, vol. 17, no. 6, pp. 540–557, 2004.

[70] G. Ofek, F. J. Guenaga, W. R. Schief et al., "Elicitation of structure-specific antibodies by epitope scaffolds," *Proceedings of the National Academy of Sciences of the United States of America*, vol. 107, no. 42, pp. 17880–17887, 2010.

[71] C. Partidos, C. Stanley, and M. Steward, "The effect of orientation of epitopes on the immunogenicity of chimeric synthetic peptides representing measles virus protein sequences," *Molecular Immunology*, vol. 29, no. 5, pp. 651–658, 1992.

[72] M. W. Steward, C. M. Stanley, R. Dimarchi, G. Mulcahy, and T. R. Doel, "High-affinity antibody induced by immunization with a synthetic peptide is associated with protection of cattle against foot-and-mouth disease," *Immunology*, vol. 72, no. 1, pp. 99–103, 1991.

[73] J. Anglister, C. Jacob, O. Assulin, G. Ast, R. Pinker, and R. Arnon, "NMR study of the complexes between a synthetic peptide derived from the B subunit of cholera toxin and three monoclonal antibodies against it," *Biochemistry*, vol. 27, no. 2, pp. 717–724, 1988.

[74] D. T. Nair, K. Singh, N. Sahu, K. V. S. Rao, and D. M. Salunke, "Crystal structure of an antibody bound to an immunodominant peptide epitope: novel features in peptide-antibody recognition," *Journal of Immunology*, vol. 165, no. 12, pp. 6949–6955, 2000.

[75] M. García, M. A. Alsina, F. Reig, and I. Haro, "Liposomes as vehicles for the presentation of a synthetic peptide containing an epitope of hepatitis A virus," *Vaccine*, vol. 18, no. 3-4, pp. 276–283, 1999.

[76] G. Zeder-Lutz, D. Altschuh, H. M. Geysen, E. Trifilieff, G. Sommermeyer, and M. H. V. Van Regenmortel, "Monoclonal antipeptide antibodies: affinity and kinetic rate constants measured for the peptide and the cognate protein using a biosensor technology," *Molecular Immunology*, vol. 30, no. 2, pp. 145–155, 1993.

[77] R. Vita, B. Peters, and A. Sette, "The curation guidelines of the immune epitope database and analysis resource," *Cytometry Part A*, vol. 73, no. 11, pp. 1066–1070, 2008.

[78] U. Hobohm, M. Scharf, R. Schneider, and C. Sander, "Selection of representative protein data sets," *Protein Science*, vol. 1, no. 3, pp. 409–417, 1992.

[79] U. Lessel and D. Schomburg, "Creation and characterization of a new, non-redundant fragment data bank," *Protein Engineering*, vol. 10, no. 6, pp. 659–664, 1997.

[80] T. Noguchi and Y. Akiyama, "PDB-REPRDB: a database of representative protein chains from the Protein Data Bank (PDB) in 2003," *Nucleic Acids Research*, vol. 31, no. 1, pp. 492–493, 2003.

[81] P. Motte, G. Alberici, M. Ait-Abdellah, and D. Bellet, "Monoclonal antibodies distinguish synthetic peptides that differ in one chemical group," *Journal of Immunology*, vol. 138, no. 10, pp. 3332–3338, 1987.

[82] E. Nardin, "The past decade in malaria synthetic peptide vaccine clinical trials," *Human Vaccines*, vol. 6, no. 1, pp. 27–38, 2010.

[83] S. W. W. Chen, M. H. V. Van Regenmortel, and J. L. Pellequer, "Structure-activity relationships in peptide-antibody complexes: implications for epitope prediction and development of synthetic peptide vaccines," *Current Medicinal Chemistry*, vol. 16, no. 8, pp. 953–964, 2009.

[84] G. Nudelman and Y. Louzoun, "Cell surface dynamics: the balance between diffusion, aggregation and endocytosis," *IEE Proceedings Systems Biology*, vol. 153, no. 1, pp. 34–42, 2006.

[85] G. Nudelman, M. Weigert, and Y. Louzoun, "In-silico cell surface modeling reveals mechanism for initial steps of B-cell receptor signal transduction," *Molecular Immunology*, vol. 46, no. 15, pp. 3141–3150, 2009.

[86] A. K. Dunker, C. J. Brown, J. D. Lawson, L. M. Iakoucheva, and Z. Obradović, "Intrinsic disorder and protein function," *Biochemistry*, vol. 41, no. 21, pp. 6573–6582, 2002.

[87] J. L. Pellequer, E. Westhof, and M. H. V. Van Regenmortel, "Correlation between the location of antigenic sites and the prediction of turns in proteins," *Immunology Letters*, vol. 36, no. 1, pp. 83–99, 1993.

[88] G. D. Rose, L. M. Glerasch, and J. A. Smith, "Turns in Peptides and Proteins," *Advances in Protein Chemistry*, vol. 37, pp. 1–109, 1985.

[89] H. J. Dyson, R. A. Lerner, and P. E. Wright, "The physical basis for induction of protein-reactive antipeptide antibodies," *Annual Review of Biophysics and Biophysical Chemistry*, vol. 17, pp. 305–324, 1988.

[90] S. A. Plotkin, "Correlates of protection induced by vaccination," *Clinical and Vaccine Immunology*, vol. 17, no. 7, pp. 1055–1065, 2010.

[91] M. H. Van Regenmortel, "Basic research in HIV vaccinology is hampered by reductionist thinking," *Frontiers in Immunology*, vol. 3, article 194, 2012.

[92] S. S. Coughlin, "How many principles for public health ethics?" *Open Public Health Journal*, vol. 1, pp. 8–16, 2008.

[93] E. J. Emanuel and A. Wertheimer, "Who should get influenza vaccine when not all can?" *Science*, vol. 312, no. 5775, pp. 854–855, 2006.

[94] A. P. Galvani, T. C. Reluga, and G. B. Chapman, "Long-standing influenza vaccination policy is in accord with individual self-interest but not with the utilitarian optimum," *Proceedings of the National Academy of Sciences of the United States of America*, vol. 104, no. 13, pp. 5692–5697, 2007.

19

Wavelet Packet Entropy for Heart Murmurs Classification

Fatemeh Safara,[1,2] **Shyamala Doraisamy,**[2] **Azreen Azman,**[2] **Azrul Jantan,**[2] **and Sri Ranga**[3]

[1] *Department of Computer Engineering, Islamic Azad University, Islamshahr Branch, Islamshahr, Tehran 3314767653, Iran*
[2] *Faculty of Computer Science and Information Technology, 43400 Serdang, Selangor Darul Ehsan, Malaysia*
[3] *Department of Cardiology, Serdang Hospital, 43000 Kajang, Selangor Darul Ehsan, Malaysia*

Correspondence should be addressed to Fatemeh Safara, fsafara@yahoo.com

Academic Editor: Tatsuya Akutsu

Heart murmurs are the first signs of cardiac valve disorders. Several studies have been conducted in recent years to automatically differentiate normal heart sounds, from heart sounds with murmurs using various types of audio features. Entropy was successfully used as a feature to distinguish different heart sounds. In this paper, new entropy was introduced to analyze heart sounds and the feasibility of using this entropy in classification of five types of heart sounds and murmurs was shown. The entropy was previously introduced to analyze mammograms. Four common murmurs were considered including aortic regurgitation, mitral regurgitation, aortic stenosis, and mitral stenosis. Wavelet packet transform was employed for heart sound analysis, and the entropy was calculated for deriving feature vectors. Five types of classification were performed to evaluate the discriminatory power of the generated features. The best results were achieved by BayesNet with 96.94% accuracy. The promising results substantiate the effectiveness of the proposed wavelet packet entropy for heart sounds classification.

1. Introduction

Accurate and early diagnosis of cardiac diseases is of great importance which is possible through heart auscultation. It is the most common and widely recommended method to screen for structural abnormalities of the cardiovascular system. Detecting relevant characteristics and forming a diagnosis based on the sounds heard through a stethoscope, however, is a skill that can take years to be acquired and refine. The efficiency and accuracy of diagnosis based on heart sound auscultation can be improved considerably by using digital signal processing techniques to analyze phonocardiographic (PCG) signals [1–3].

Phonocardiography is the recording of sonic vibrations of heart and blood circulation. PCG signals can provide valuable information regarding the performance of heart valves, therefore it has a high potential for detecting various heart diseases [4, 5].

Two loudest heart sounds are the first and the second sounds, referred to as S1 and S2. The time interval between S1 and S2 is called systole and the time interval between S2 and next S1 is called diastole. Normal heart sounds are low-frequency transient signals produced by the heart valves

while pathological heart sounds, such as heart murmurs, are high-frequency, noise-like sounds [6]. Heart murmurs are produced as a result of turbulence in blood flow through narrow cardiac valves or reflow through the atrioventricular valves. Congenital heart defects or acquired heart valve diseases are often the cause of abnormal heart murmurs. Aortic stenosis, mitral regurgitation, aortic regurgitation, and mitral stenosis are among the most common pathological types of murmurs. These categories of murmurs were considered in this paper to be distinguished from normal heart sounds. Figure 1 illustrates the phonocardiogram of one normal and two samples of pathological heart sounds.

Research on PCG signals utilizing signal processing techniques is on the rise because of the ability of PCG recordings to represent important characteristics of the heart sounds. A large number of these studies have been focused on investigating the possibility of the PCG signal classification towards the diagnosis of heart valve disorders [7–11].

In general, two major processes are needed prior to actual classification, signal analysis and feature generation. Different signal analysis techniques are employed in the literature such as discrete Fourier transform (DFT), short time Fourier transform (STFT), Wigner distribution, Hilbert

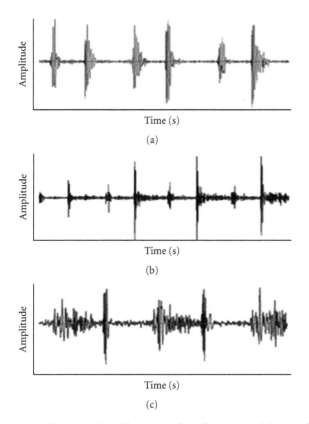

FIGURE 1: Three samples of heart sounds and murmurs: (a) normal heart sound, (b) aortic regurgitation, and (c) aortic stenosis.

transform, continuous wavelet transform (CWT), discrete wavelet transform (DWT), and wavelet packet transform (WPT). Of these, the Fourier and wavelet family of transforms have been more widely used for PCG signal analysis. However, with medical applications, wavelet transform has been found to be one of the best transform for analyzing transient and nonstationary signals, such as PCG [3]. This is because the wavelet provides a reasonable resolution in both the time and frequency domain. Therefore, in this paper, WPT is used to analyze PCG signals. This is further discussed in Section 2.

Feature generation has a crucial role in obtaining high classification accuracies. A number of features based on wavelet transforms have been defined in recent studies to classify different types of heart sounds and murmurs. For instance, Ahlstrom et al. [12] extracted energy and entropy from DWT of the PCG signals in order to classify systolic murmurs. A series of studies were also conducted by Choi et al. [3, 13, 14] whereby new features based on the wavelet transform were defined, such as the normalized autoregressive power spectral density curve, the mean of wavelet packet energy, standard deviation of wavelet packet energy, the maximum peak frequency, the position index of the wavelet packet coefficient corresponding to the maximum peak frequency, and the ratios of the wavelet energy and entropy information.

In our preliminary study [15], temporal, spectral, and geometric features were combined for heart sound classification. The feature set included zero-crossing rates as the temporal feature, and spectral roll-off, spectral energy entropy, spectral flux, and spectral centroid as the spectral features. Geometric features were added to this feature set, namely, summation of the first order derivatives, summation of the second order derivatives, curve length, area under curve, and centralized mean square values.

It is clear from these studies that entropy and features defined on entropy have been successfully utilized for heart sound classification. New entropies have been also defined and used in biomedical signal analysis. In the study by Vitulano and Casanova [16], entropy was introduced as a feature for analyzing one-dimensional signal. The entropy was measured as the ratio between signal perturbation and the total signal energy. The experimentation carried out on mammographic signals with different pathologies. Linear transformation has been performed to transform 2D mammographic signal into 1D signal. This entropy, introduced by Vitulano and Casanova [16], is adopted for this study to generate discriminative features from PCG signals. This has not been previously examined for heart sound classification.

Heart sound classification performed by most studies included classifying normal heart sound and murmurs. Several studies further investigated classifying various categories of murmurs. Neural network is a powerful classifier that was widely used in the past. Ahlstrom et al. [12] used a feed-forward neural network to evaluate a large number of linear and nonlinear features proposed based on DWT and achieved 86% accuracy in classifying systolic murmurs. Neural network was also used in another work by Ahlstrom et al. [17] to differentiate innocent murmurs from aortic stenosis, and a sensitivity of 90% and a specificity of 88% were obtained. Babaei and Geranmayeh [18] utilized a multilayer perceptron neural network (MLP) to investigate the potential of the main statistical characteristics of PCG signals for distinguishing murmurs and acquired 94.24% accuracy for classifying AR, AS, and PS (pulmonary stenosis).

Support vector machine (SVM) is another classifier that was commonly used. Two studies by Choi et al. [3, 14] were reported based on WPT and SVM classifier. In the former study, normal heart sounds were distinguished from murmurs with 96% sensitivity and 100% specificity [14]. In the later one, normal heart sounds were differentiated from regurgitation types of murmurs with 99.78% specificity and 99.43% sensitivity [3]. Choi and Jiang [13] also utilized autoregressive power spectral analysis and multisupport vector machine for PCG signals classification and achieved 99.5% sensitivity and 99.9% specificity to classify normal heart sounds from pathological ones. In addition to MLP and SVM that have been widely used for heart sound classification, KNN, BayesNet, and decision tree classifiers were included to evaluate the discriminatory power of the generated features.

The rest of this paper is organized as follows. In Section 2, the background theory of WPT and the entropy is provided. Details of processes followed for heart sound classification are explained in Section 3. Experiments including data collection and results of classification through generated features are discussed in Section 4. Final conclusions and potential extensions are given in Section 5.

2. Wavelet Packet Entropy

Wavelet transform is a powerful technique in analyzing non-stationary signals such as PCG signals [6]. The main advantage of wavelet transform is its varying window size that is narrow for high frequencies and wide for low frequencies. Therefore, wavelet transform is much more powerful than the other time frequency analysis techniques such as DFT and STFT, not only for providing useful time and frequency information, but also for its adaptive time and frequency resolution [19].

Selecting appropriate wavelet transform for a given application is also important. WPT was exploited in this paper, instead of CWT and DWT that were widely used in the past studies. A comparison between DWT and WPT by Debbal and Bereksi-Reguig [20] showed that DWT was more suitable than WPT in filtering of clicks and murmurs while WPT provides comprehensive information for a better understanding of the time-frequency characteristics of the cardiac sound.

One of the quantitative measures associated with WPT is entropy. Entropy provides valuable information for analyzing nonstationary signals. The background theory of WPT and the definition of the entropy used in the current study are explained in this section.

2.1. Wavelet Packet Transform. WPT is an extension of DWT whereby all nodes in the tree structure are allowed to split further at each level of decomposition. With WPT, both the approximation and detail coefficients are decomposed into approximation and detail components, in comparison to DWT that decomposes only the approximation coefficients of the signal as shown in Figure 2. Therefore, features can be generated based on approximation and detail coefficients at different levels to obtain more information. The WPT of a signal $x(t)$ is defined as follows:

$$x_p^{n,j} = 2^{j/2} \int_R x(t) \psi_n \left(2^{-j}t - p\right) dt, \quad 0 \le n \le 2^S - 1, \quad (1)$$

where n is the channel number, j is the number of decomposition level, or scale parameter, p is the position parameter, $\psi_n(t)$ is the mother wavelet, and S is the maximum decomposition level. After decomposing signal $x(t)$ by WPT, 2^S sequences can be produced in the Sth level. The fast decomposition equation for this kind of WPT is

$$x_k^{2n,j+1} = \sum_{p \in Z} h(p - 2k) x_p^{n,j},$$

$$x_k^{2n+1,j+1} = \sum_{p \in Z} g(p - 2k) x_p^{n,j}, \quad (2)$$

where $h(i)$ and $g(i)$ are wavelet quadrature mirror filter coefficients.

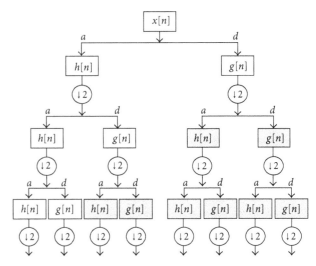

FIGURE 2: Wavelet packet tree with corresponding high-pass and low-pass filters (a = approximation coefficients, d = detail coefficients). The shaded nodes indicate the node not to be produced by DWT.

Three levels of the wavelet packet decomposition with the high-pass and low-pass filters were illustrated in Figure 2. This structure can be continued further to decompose the following approximations and details to reach to a proper level for representing PCG signals of desired murmurs. From the literature, it can be concluded that levels 6 to 8 were generally chosen for analyzing PCG signals of different pathological heart sounds [3, 12, 14, 20, 21].

2.2. Entropy. Different types of entropy such as log, norm, Shannon, sure, and threshold can be used to characterize the heart sounds. However, for this study the entropy introduced by Vitulano and Casanova [16] for analyzing 1D signals was utilized. They have transformed the 2D mammographic signal into 1D signal through linear transformation and then applied the entropy on the 1D signal to generate features for differentiating mammograms with different pathologies. They did not utilize any signal processing technique to analyze the signal prior to extract entropy features from the signal. In the current study, the PCG signals were first analyzed with WPT and then entropy features were generated from the wavelet packet coefficients.

Vitulano and Casanova [16] defined the signal "crest" as the part embraced between lines parallel to the abscissas axis, in which the ordinates are m and M, m is the absolute minimum and M is the absolute maximum of the signal. Therefore, the signal crest included all the points $x(t) \in X(t)$, so that

$$m \le x(t) \le M, \quad (3)$$

and crest energy is defined as

$$E_c = \sum_{i=m}^{M} x_i, \quad i \equiv [m, M]. \quad (4)$$

Signal entropy can be defined based on E_c as

$$S = 1 - \frac{E - E_c}{E}, \quad S \equiv [0, 1], \tag{5}$$

where E is signal energy, E_c is crest energy, and S is signal entropy.

Signal entropy S is defined based on one-dimensional signals and it has a potential to be applied on the other dimensional signals such as PCG signals.

3. Methodology and Materials

Classification requires a sequence of processes to be performed, including preprocessing, signal analysis, feature generation, and classification. Each process is discussed for heart murmur classification in this study.

3.1. Preprocessing. The preprocessing of PCG signals carried out in this study includes resampling, filtering, normalization and segmentation.

3.1.1. Resampling. Feature generation algorithms are highly dependent on the frequency sampling of the electronic stethoscope. Sampling frequencies 4, 5, 10, 20, 25, 40, and 50 kHz can be seen among the heart sounds obtained from online resources and sounds available in the market as auscultation training CDs. In order to remove the heterogeneity of the collected PCG signals, the original signals in the core frequency sampling were mapped into a new 4 kHz. The signal was considered as a time series and new samples are produced by application of the truncated sinc function interpolation.

3.1.2. Filtering. To remove noise from PCG signals, a band-pass finite-duration impulse response (FIR) filter was adopted with preliminary testing. Kaiser window with cut-off frequencies of 25 and 700 Hz was used because heart sound signals are in the range less than 700 Hz [2, 14, 21]. The frequency range of 49–51 was also removed to eliminate the power line noise.

3.1.3. Normalization. The amplitude of heart sounds depend on the pressure on skin measured by electronic stethoscope as well as the setting of the amplifier of the stethoscope. Equation (6), a commonly used normalization equation, was used in this paper to reduce amplitude variations as

$$x_{\text{norm}}(n) = \frac{x(n)}{\max(|x(n)|)}, \tag{6}$$

where n number of data points, $x(n)$ is the PCG signal, and $x_{\text{norm}}(n)$ is the normalized signal to be used in this work.

3.1.4. Segmentation. PCG recordings were segmented into their systoles and diastoles. The exact onset and offset locations of each systole and diastole were determined manually under the supervision of a cardiologist.

3.2. PCG Signal Analysis. Following the discussion in Section 2, WPT was utilized for PCG signal analysis. A wavelet packet tree was constructed and the coefficients were calculated for terminal nodes of the tree. The appropriate decomposition level was determined based on the following equation:

$$R = \frac{0.5 * \text{FS}}{2^{\text{DL}}}, \tag{7}$$

where R is the resolution, 0.5 is the Nyquist coefficient, FS is the sampling frequency, and DL is the suitable decomposition level with desired resolution. Since PCG signals were resampled into 4 KHz, resolution of 31.25 Hz would be achieved at level six using (7) that is a reasonable resolution for this study.

After determining the level of decomposition, four types of mother wavelets were examined as potential mother wavelets: The Mayer, Symlets, Coiflets and Daubiches. This was performed by computing the error existing between the original signal and the synthesis signal (i.e., wavelet packet transform of the signal). The error was calculated by the following equation that was defined by Cherif et al. [2]:

$$E_{\text{error}} = \frac{\sum_{i=1}^{N} |S_{oi} - S_{ri}|}{N}, \tag{8}$$

where S_o is the original signal, S_{oi} is the sample of S_o, S_r is the synthesised signal, and S_{ri} is the sample of S_r. Using the above equation, the lowest error was obtained for Daubiches which was chosen as the mother wavelet for analysing the PCG recordings.

3.3. Feature Generation. Features are representatives of the underlying signal and proper choice of features results in higher classification accuracy. As stated in Section 1, entropy was successfully used as a feature for heart sound classification. In this work also the entropy was utilized to generate discriminative features from PCG recordings. However, the entropy introduced by Vitulano and Casanova [16] (explained in Section 2.2) was exploited, instead of common entropies such as Shannon and log [3, 12, 22].

Systole and diastole segments of each PCG signals were represented in the sixth decomposition level of WPT with Daubiches8, as described in the previous section. There are 2^6 terminal nodes in the 6th decomposition level. The entropy was computed from the coefficients of all terminal nodes and 64 entropies were obtained for each segment. Then a feature vector including all 128 entropies was constructed. In order to reduce the dimensionality of the feature space, principal component analysis (PCA) was applied to feature vectors. Number of features to be selected was determined by trial and error. Thirty two features were chosen from each feature vector to be fed into classifier.

3.4. Classification. The discriminatory power of the generated features was evaluated via KNN, BayesNet, and decision tree classifiers in addition to SVM and MLP that were widely used in previous studies.

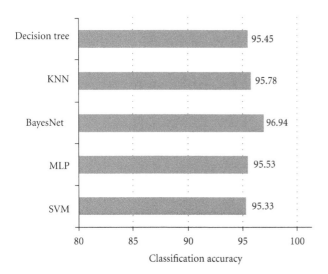

FIGURE 3: Accuracy of PCG signals classification using the wavelet packet entropy.

4. Experiments

The classification accuracy using wavelet packet entropy was evaluated with a collection of 350 heart sounds as discussed in the following section. A standard data collection for PCG signal is not available and the PCG signals from various sources were collected.

4.1. Data Collection. A data set of 350 heart sounds comprising 50 normal and 300 murmurs was employed. For murmurs, 80 MR, 100 AS, 50 AR, and 70 MS were obtained. Pathological heart sounds were collected from auscultation training materials where the sound categories were explicitly specified. Evaluation was performed based on the annotations provided. For the normal category, sounds were recorded using Welch-Allyn Meditron electronic stethoscope.

4.2. Results. Classification accuracy reflects the potential strength of generated features to differentiate underlying signals from each other. For each of the 350 heart sounds prepared for this study, a feature vector comprising thirty-two features was generated (Section 3.3) and classified. The classification accuracy was determined using a 10-fold cross-validation. The classification accuracy of each classifier is presented in Figure 3. Although the accuracies cannot be benchmarked against other studies due to the lack of standard data collections, the accuracies obtained following the experiments in this study are quite high showing the feasibility of using wavelet packet entropy for heart sound classification. The best and worst accuracies were achieved by BayesNet and SVM, with 96.94% and 95.33%, respectively.

Despite the small difference between the accuracy of classifiers, the results of the classification establishes the feasibility of entropy introduced by Vitulano and Casanova [16] for classifying PCG signals.

5. Conclusion

The feasibility of using the entropy for heart murmur classification was shown in this paper. The entropy was previously introduced for analyzing mammographic signals. It was defined as the ratio between signal perturbation and the total signal energy. In this study, the entropy was calculated from wavelet packet coefficients of PCG recordings as a feature to be used for classifying heart sounds. High classification accuracy of 96.94% is achieved by BayesNet classifier that indicates the viability of the entropy as a feature to describe PCG signals. A more extensive comparative study would be required to evaluate the proposed features against other features introduced for PCG signal classification on the same PCG database. In this study, normal heart sounds were differentiated from four types of murmurs. The heart sound categories would be expanded to include different murmurs.

References

[1] Y. Chen, S. Wang, C.-H. Shen, and F. Choy, "Intelligent identification of childhood musical murmurs," *Journal of Healthcare Engineering*, vol. 3, pp. 125–140, 2012.

[2] L. H. Cherif, S. M. Debbal, and F. Bereksi-Reguig, "Choice of the wavelet analyzing in the phonocardiogram signal analysis using the discrete and the packet wavelet transform," *Expert Systems with Applications*, vol. 37, no. 2, pp. 913–918, 2010.

[3] S. Choi, Y. Shin, and H. K. Park, "Selection of wavelet packet measures for insufficiency murmur identification," *Expert Systems with Applications*, vol. 38, no. 4, pp. 4264–4271, 2011.

[4] C. N. Gupta, R. Palaniappan, S. Swaminathan, and S. M. Krishnan, "Neural network classification of homomorphic segmented heart sounds," *Applied Soft Computing Journal*, vol. 7, no. 1, pp. 286–297, 2007.

[5] L. Jia, D. Song, L. Tao, and Y. Lu, "Heart sounds classification with a fuzzy neural network method with structure learning," in *Advances in Neural Networks*, vol. 7368 of *Lecture Notes in Computer Science*, pp. 130–140, 2012.

[6] B. Ergen, Y. Tatar, and H. O. Gulcur, "Time-frequency analysis of phonocardiogram signals using wavelet transform: a comparative study," *Computer Methods in Biomechanics and Biomedical Engineering*, vol. 15, pp. 371–381, 2011.

[7] W. C. Kao and C. C. Wei, "Automatic phonocardiograph signal analysis for detecting heart valve disorders," *Expert Systems with Applications*, vol. 38, no. 6, pp. 6458–6468, 2011.

[8] M. Salama, A. Hassanien, J. Platos, A. Fahmy, and V. Snasel, "Rough sets-based identification of heart valve diseases using heart sounds," in *Proceedings of the 7th international conference on Hybrid Artificial Intelligent Systems*, pp. 667–676, 2012.

[9] S. Sanei, M. Ghodsi, and H. Hassani, "An adaptive singular spectrum analysis approach to murmur detection from heart sounds," *Medical Engineering & Physics*, vol. 33, no. 3, pp. 362–367, 2011.

[10] Y. L. Tseng, P. Y. Ko, and F. S. Jaw, "Detection of the third and fourth heart sounds using Hilbert-Huang transform," *BioMedical Engineering OnLine*, vol. 11, article 8, 2012.

[11] S. Yuenyong, A. Nishihara, W. Kongprawechnon, and K. Tungpimolrut, "A framework for automatic heart sound analysis without segmentation," *BioMedical Engineering Online*, vol. 10, article 13, 2011.

[12] C. Ahlstrom, P. Hult, P. Rask et al., "Feature extraction for systolic heart murmur classification," *Annals of Biomedical Engineering*, vol. 34, no. 11, pp. 1666–1677, 2006.

[13] S. Choi and Z. Jiang, "Cardiac sound murmurs classification with autoregressive spectral analysis and multi-support vector machine technique," *Computers in Biology and Medicine*, vol. 40, no. 1, pp. 8–20, 2010.

[14] S. Choi, "Detection of valvular heart disorders using wavelet packet decomposition and support vector machine," *Expert Systems with Applications*, vol. 35, no. 4, pp. 1679–1687, 2008.

[15] F. Safara, S. Doraisamy, A. Azman, and A. Jantan, "Heart sounds clustering using a combination of temporal, spectral and geometric 8 features," *Computing in Cardiology*, vol. 39, pp. 217–220, 2012.

[16] S. Vitulano and A. Casanova, "The role of entropy: mammogram analysis," *Image Analysis and Recognition*, vol. 5112, pp. 863–872, 2008.

[17] C. Ahlstrom, K. Höglund, P. Hult, J. Häggström, C. Kvart, and P. Ask, "Distinguishing innocent murmurs from murmurs caused by aortic stenosis by recurrence quantification analysis," in *Proceedings of the Enformatika Transactions on Engineering, Computing and Technology*, pp. 1305–5313, December 2006.

[18] S. Babaei and A. Geranmayeh, "Heart sound reproduction based on neural network classification of cardiac valve disorders using wavelet transforms of PCG signals," *Computers in Biology and Medicine*, vol. 39, no. 1, pp. 8–15, 2009.

[19] Y. Chen, S. Wang, C.-H. Shen, and F. K. Choy, "Matrix decomposition based feature extraction for murmur classification," *Medical Engineering & Physics*, vol. 34, no. 6, pp. 756–761, 2012.

[20] S. M. Debbal and F. Bereksi-Reguig, "Time-frequency analysis of the first and the second heartbeat sounds," *Applied Mathematics and Computation*, vol. 184, no. 2, pp. 1041–1052, 2007.

[21] M. R. Homaeinezhad, S. A. Atyabi, E. Deneshvar, A. Ghaffari, and M. Tahmasebi, "Optimal delineation of PCG sounds via false-alarm bounded segmentation of a wavelet-based principal components analyzed metric," *International Journal for Numerical Methods in Biomedical Engineering*, vol. 27, pp. 1711–1739, 2011.

[22] A. Sengur and I. Turkoglu, "A hybrid method based on artificial immune system and fuzzy k-NN algorithm for diagnosis of heart valve diseases," *Expert Systems with Applications*, vol. 35, no. 3, pp. 1011–1020, 2008.

20

Detecting Cancer Outlier Genes with Potential Rearrangement Using Gene Expression Data and Biological Networks

Mohammed Alshalalfa,[1] Tarek A. Bismar,[2] and Reda Alhajj[1]

[1] Department of Computer Science, University of Calgary, Calgary, AB, Canada T2N 1N4
[2] Departments of Pathology, Oncology and Molecular Biology and Biochemistry, Faculty of Medicine, University of Calgary, Calgary, AB, Canada T2N 1N4

Correspondence should be addressed to Mohammed Alshalalfa, msalshal@ucalgary.ca

Academic Editor: T. Akutsu

Gene alterations are a major component of the landscape of tumor genomes. To assess the significance of these alterations in the development of prostate cancer, it is necessary to identify these alterations and analyze them from systems biology perspective. Here, we present a new method (EigFusion) for predicting outlier genes with potential gene rearrangement. EigFusion demonstrated excellent performance in identifying outlier genes with potential rearrangement by testing it to synthetic and real data to evaluate performance. EigFusion was able to identify previously unrecognized genes such as *FABP5* and *KCNH8* and confirmed their association with primary and metastatic prostate samples while confirmed the metastatic specificity for other genes such as *PAH*, *TOP2A*, and *SPINK1*. We performed protein network based approaches to analyze the network context of potential rearranged genes. Functional gene rearrangement Modules are constructed by integrating functional protein networks. Rearranged genes showed to be highly connected to well-known altered genes in cancer such as *AR*, *RB1*, *MYC*, and *BRCA1*. Finally, using clinical outcome data of prostate cancer patients, potential rearranged genes demonstrated significant association with prostate cancer specific death.

1. Introduction

Genetic alterations in cancer are the most challenging factors that might lead to aggressive behavior of cells. Among the most prevalent forms of genetic alterations observed in cancer cells are gene fusions, gene amplification, and gene deletions. Recurrent translocations generally fall into two categories: functional rearrangements that result in a change in gene's activity due either to a change in protein quality or quantity and the other category is silent translocations that have no effect on gene's activity. Functional translocations can be categorized into two subtypes; one that leads to fused transcripts resulting in new proteins with different activity like *BCR-ABL* in leukemia [1] and *EML4-ALK* in lung cancer [2]; on the other hand, it can lead to change in a transcript quantity by translocating a strong gene promoter to the intact coding region of an oncogene like *TMPRSS2-ERG* [3]. Another functional genomics rearrangement is genomic

deletion which results in loss of DNA segment that might harbour functional genes. *PTEN* is a well-studied genomic deletion in prostate cancer that is anticipated to trigger a cascade of genomic rearrangements [4]. Figure 1 gives a schematic description of the four rearrangement types.

Identifying gene rearrangements in general and gene amplification and deletions in particular has been a challenge during the past decade as it requires deep DNA sequence analysis of many cancer samples and their paired counterparts [5]. Though sequencing cancer genomes can reveal very precise results about gene fusion or deletions, it is not an easy task to obtain sequence data, as this needs fresh tissue and still relatively expensive. Another method to detect gene rearrangements, namely gene fusion, is to design special oligo microarray which covers all possible genomic rearrangements [6]. This method requires some knowledge about the predicted gene fusion variants and all possible exon-exon junctions. Recently, RNA-Sequencing

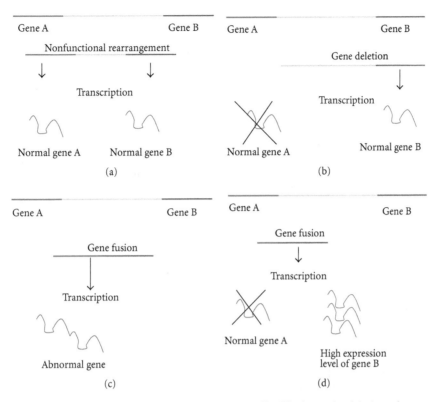

Figure 1: Gene rearrangements, common gene rearrangements in cancer cells. (b) Shows the deletion of some genes at the DNA level which leads to depletion of corresponding mRNA. (c) Represents the fusion of two genes that leads to fused mRNA and fused proteins. (d) Represents special rearrangement type that fuses a strong promoter of gene A to the 5' of gene B. This leads to underexpression of gene A and overexpression of gene B.

have gained attention to identify novel gene fusions [7]. Sequence reads that align across a gene fusion boundary (so-called split reads) are a strong source of evidence for gene fusions in paired-end RNA-Seq data. A number of algorithms and tools have been proposed to find split reads such as PERAlign [8], MapSplice [9], and deFUSION [10]. The only advantage of RNA-Seq-based algorithms is that they are able to discover fused transcripts (Figure 1(c)), but they are unable to discover rearranged genes at the DNA level (Figure 1(d)) as these types of rearrangements are not reflected in the RNA sequence. Despite the high accuracy of the above-described data types to discover gene rearrangements, obtaining and analyzing (RNA-Seq, oligo-microarray, deep sequencing) data is very expensive and extremely challenging as it depends on sequence assembly and alignment algorithms.

Another source of information to identify potential functional gene rearrangements or gene alterations that affect gene expression is microarray gene expression data that we will use in this work to discover gene rearrangements. Unlike sequence data that can be easily interpreted to identify gene rearrangements, microarray gene expression data requires preprocessing steps. New direction to detect genomic rearrangements is to use bioinformatics approaches applied to gene expression data [11]. This problem is different from the detection of biomarker genes in several aspects. Biomarkers are differentially expressed in almost all samples, while gene rearrangements occur in only a subset

of samples. Many studies showed that common biomarker extraction methods such as t-test, SAM, and so forth are not proper for detecting gene rearrangements [12, 13] as these studies attempt to maximize the difference between all cancer samples against all normal samples. Since fusion genes and gene deletions are rare genomic events leading to over expression in subset of cancer samples, new specialized computational approaches are in need to solve this problem.

Several methods have been proposed to identify rearranged genes from gene expression data (methods are described in supplementary file available on line at doi:10.1155/2012/373506). In the context of this work, we use outlier genes to refer to potential rearranged genes or altered genes. All previous methods consider each gene individually when ranking genes. However, ranking based on the global properties of the genes would reduce error rates. Herein, we show that all existing methods detect biomarker genes as outlier genes; a drawback of existing methods that we solved in our approach by proposing a new transformation function. The second advantage of the proposed method is simultaneous detection of potential gene amplification and potential gene deletions. None of the previous methods were reported to detect gene deletions, though they can be modified slightly to achieve the task of gene deletion detection. Thus, proposing different methods that can assess the over expression of a subset of genes is highly desirable for detecting gene rearrangements using microarray gene expression data.

In this paper, we use cancer cohorts (microarray gene expression data of hundreds of samples) to identify outlier genes that are overexpressed or underexpressed in subset of cancer samples using gene expression data. Outlier genes with overexpression are anticipated to have potential gene rearrangements, and outlier genes with underexpression are anticipated to have potential deletion. We propose EigFusion method that ranks outlier genes based on their effect on the gene expression matrix largest eigenvalue when removed from data; this effect could be due to gene overexpression in subset of samples or underexpression in subset of samples. After identifying outlier genes with potential rearrangement, outlier genes are characterized from a systems biology angle. Network is constructed to link potential rearranged genes by integrating functional protein networks to identify modules enriched with potential rearranged genes. Finally, we assess the clinical significance of the predicted rearrangements using clinical and survival data.

2. Materials and Methods

2.1. Existing Statistical Methods. Here we define annotations for the gene expression data, genes, and samples that we will use across this paper in both the existing methods and the proposed method section. Let X_{ij} be the expression values for genes $i = 1, 2, ..., m$ and samples $j = 1, 2, ..., n$. We assume that samples are grouped into two groups $S1$ and $S2$. In our work, $S1$ represents cancer samples and $S2$ represents normal samples.

In this work, we used all existing methods that are designed to tackle this computational problem. Cancer Outlier Profile Analysis (COPA) [14] is considered as the first algorithm that lead to the discovery of *ERG* rearrangement in prostate cancer. Outlier sums [15] were introduced to improve the *r*th percentile factor of COPA. The outlier robust *t*-statistic [12] is very similar to OS but it replaces the overall median by the median of normal samples. Another algorithm is the GTI algorithm [16] that weights the proportion of outliers by a robust measure of how outlying the outliers are in a single group. The previous four methods test for genes that are overexpressed in a subset of cancer samples regardless of the expression value of the remaining subset from cancer samples. This might lead to false positives as the remaining subset in cancer samples should be normally expressed. The methods are described in details in the supplementary file. Thus, there is a need for a more robust method that is not single genes based, is able to discriminate between biomarkers and outlier genes, and is not sensitive to the portions of cancer samples in the dataset. As a consequence, we propose EigFusion as an effective method to identify outlier genes with potential gene rearrangements from microarray gene expression data.

2.2. The Proposed EigFusion Method. A new method called EigFusion is proposed to predict genes that are overexpressed (potential fusion genes or amplified) or underexpressed (potential deletion genes) in subset of samples using gene expression data. EigFusion standardizes the gene profile

based on a newly defined median value for cancer samples. One of the important factors to determine in standardizing the profiles is to decide on the median. COPA and OS use the overall median, but ORT uses the median of normal samples. We think the median might be very crucial to distinguish between outlier genes and biomarkers. Thus, in here, we use the median of cancer samples to standardize the gene expression values across all samples. As a result, genes with high expression values in all cancer samples can be filtered out. Since some rearrangements might be more frequent for some genes and might occur in more than half of the cancer samples, we define three median values for each gene. The first one is the median of cancer samples ($median^{S1}$), we then divide cancer samples into two groups: values greater than $median^{S1}$ and values less than $median^{S1}$. We used the average of the medians of the three groups, we call it $AVGmedian^{S1}$. We defined the transformation function as

$$\hat{X}_{ij} = \frac{X_{ij} - AVGmedian_i^{S1}}{median\left(\left|x_{ij} - median_i\right|\right)}, \quad (1)$$

where $median(i)$ is the median of $gene(i)$ whole profile.

After transforming the expression values, genes were ranked using the following formula:

$$Score_i = \frac{E\left(\hat{X}_i\right) * \left(E\left(\hat{X}_i^{S1}\right) - E\left(\hat{X}_i^{S2}\right)\right)}{E\left(\hat{X}_{m \times n}^i\right)}, \quad (2)$$

where $\hat{X}_i$ is the transformed expression profile of $gene(i)$ across all samples and $E(\hat{X}_i)$ is the largest eigenvalue of transformed $gene(i)$ after converting it to matrix by multiplying it by its transpose, $E(\hat{x}_i^{S1})$ is the largest eigenvalue of $gene(i)$ in cancer samples, $E(\hat{x}_i^{S2})$ is the largest eigenvalue of $gene(i)$ in normal samples, and $E(\hat{X}_{m \times n}^i)$ is the largest eigenvalue of the matrix that have all the genes across all samples without $gene(i)$. The eigenvalues are large when the expression values are high; thus, when genes have high expression values in subset of cancer samples, they will be ranked high.

2.3. Gene Expression Data Simulation. Synthetic gene expression data was generated from a standard normal distribution $N(\mu, \delta^2)$. Gaussian noise ϵ was added to the expression values. Expression values of 1000 genes across 200 samples were simulated, and 10 test genes were added to evaluate the performance of the algorithms. Test genes were generated by adding a constant u (the maximum value in the data) to the expression of k cancer samples in the test genes, where k is chosen to be 2, 5, 10, 20, 50, 80, 100, 120, or 150; test genes are represented as $test_k$. For example, $test_{10}$ means that there are 10 cancer samples with added constant u; this gene represents an outlier gene that is amplified in 10 cancer samples. We also divided the 200 samples into cancer and normal groups. We used different sizes for the cancer group; we used size 20, 50, 100, 120, 150, or 180 samples. The aim from this variation in the size of the cancer samples is to evaluate the performance of the algorithms at different ratios of cancer to normal samples and assess the statistical

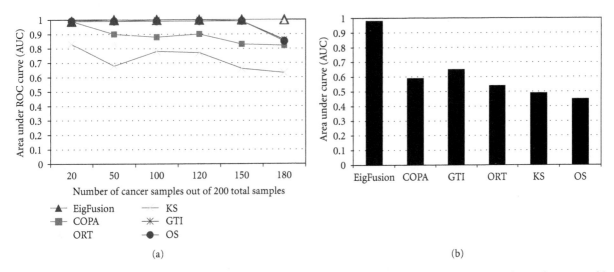

FIGURE 2: Evaluation of EigFusion performance on synthetic and real cancer data, AUC values are used to assess the performance of fusion gene detection methods. ROC curves were plotted as 1-specificity versus sensitivity of the methods. We plotted ROC curves for each method in several cancer samples size (*x*-axis) and found the area under the curve (AUC) as a measure of performance. (a) Using synthetic data, COPA and KS showed poor performance over all cases; on the other hand, ORT, GTI, and OS showed that poor performance is affected by the ratio of the size cancer samples to normal samples. (b) Applying all the methods on real prostate data (Singh data) showed that EigFusion outperforms the other methods.

power of EigFusion algorithm. In addition, test genes and size variation are critical to show the drawbacks of existing methods and how EigFusion can overcome the drawbacks of the existing methods.

2.4. Protein Module Rearrangements Enrichment.

We next integrated functional protein networks to assess if rearranged genes are functionally related and form modules. Functional gene rearrangements are anticipated to have effect on proteins associated with them. We integrated the identified potential rearranged genes with a functional protein interaction (FPI) network that covers more than half of the human genes and has more than 180,000 interactions. FPI was constructed from several data sources (Reactome, KEGG, CellMap, human PPI) as described in [17]. Modules with enriched rearranged genes were further characterized. Reactome FI cytoscape plugin was used to visualize and cluster the rearranged genes network [17].

3. Results

3.1. EigFusion Performance Evaluation on Simulated Data.

The receiver operating characteristics (ROC) curve was used for evaluating the performance of the different statistical methods and compare them with the proposed method. ROC curves were constructed using sensitivity and specificity rates for each method under each cancer samples' size; a variable that we used to assess the performance of our method to distinguish between biomarkers and potential rearranged genes. ROC curves showed to be not very sensitive to false discoveries. Therefore, we used three statistical measures to assess the false discovery rate of the methods. We used false positive discovery rate (FPR)(FP/FP + TP), false negative

discovery rate (FNR)(FN/FN + TN), and f-measure defined as

$$f - measure = 2 * \frac{precision * recall}{precision + recall}, \quad (3)$$

where precision is (TP/TP + FP), and recall is (TP/TP + FN).

FP is detected when the method ranks a gene in the top 10 when it is supposed to be ranked very low in the ranking list. For example, when the cancer sample size is 50 or 100, most algorithms (excluding EigFusion) ranked $test_{50}$ and $test_{100}$ genes, respectively, at the top of the list. We consider this as a false positive because these genes are supposed to be biomarkers as they have high expression in all cancer samples. None of the other methods were able to distinguish between biomarker genes and rearranged genes because they standardize expression profile with respect to overall median. When normal sample size is greater than cancer sample size, the median will be biased toward normal samples. Therefore, biomarker genes will not be filtered out as they will satisfy the IQR threshold and they will be ranked high. FN is detected when the method ranks positive test genes, which have high expression in less than half of the cancer samples, at the bottom of the ranking list.

We compared the performance of EigFusion, Kolmogorov-Smirnov (KS) statistics, OS, ORT, COPA, and GTI under different cancer sample sizes (Figure 2(a)). COPA was implemented as the 80th percentile of expression values after transformation of all data points using overall median and median absolute deviation for a given gene. We used 80th percentile as it is a medium value between the 90th and 70th percentile values that are most commonly used in COPA, plus it showed to give best results on synthetic data. The other methods were implemented as explained in [16]. As shown in Figure 2(a), EigFusion, GTI, and OS have high

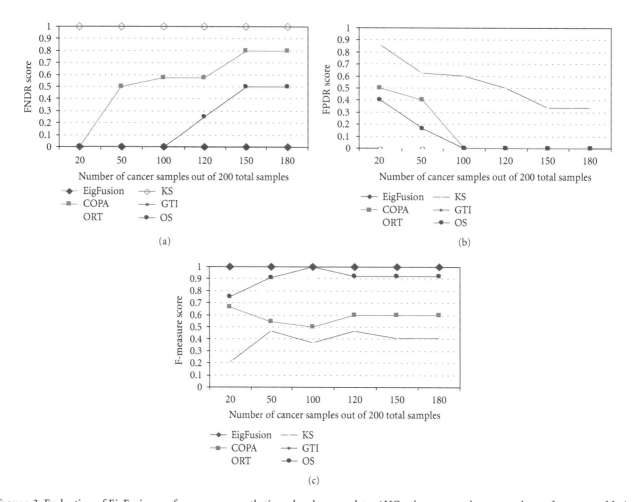

FIGURE 3: Evaluation of EigFusion performance on synthetic and real cancer data, AUC values are used to assess the performance of fusion gene detection methods. We used the (a) positive FDR (PFDR) and (b) negative FDR (NFDR) to assess FDR of each method under different cancer samples proportions. EigFusion showed to have zero FDR and f-measure value of 1. (c) We further assess the performance of the methods on real cancer data. We used Singh prostate cancer data with embedded test genes with different cancer proportions. We assessed the performance of each method based on their ability to identify $test_{10}$ and $test_{20}$ test genes.

performance across all the variation in the cancer sample size. ORT performed poor when cancer samples size were smaller than normal samples size, but the performance was improved when cancer samples size is larger than normal samples size. KS showed the poorest performance as it is not designed for gene fusion extraction. This supports our hypothesis that traditional biomarker extraction methods are not suitable for outlier gene detection task. Previous works [13, 16] showed that traditional methods like t-test and significant analysis of microarray (SAM) are not suitable for the functional gene rearrangement detection problem; thus, our results are in agreement with pervious work.

EigFusion method showed to be very sensitive to the number of outlier samples; samples that harbour amplified genes or deletion. It can detect genes with outlier percentage of 1%, unlike the existing methods that require larger outlier percentage as they sum the values greater than IQR. When the cancer sample size was more than 50, most methods ranked $test_2$, $test_5$, and sometimes $test_{10}$ at the bottom of the list. EigFusion showed to be very sensitive to such cases. We think this is very important as most of the gene fusion cases

are very rare and occur in less than 5% of cancer patients [3]. Results in Figures 3(a) and 3(b) showed that EigFusion has zero false discovery rate compared with the other methods. Though we could not compare the performance of EigFusion to GTI and OS using AUC values as they showed very similar performance, f-measure (Figure 3(c)) showed a distinguished profile for EigFusion.

3.2. EigFusion Performance Evaluation on Prostate Cancer Data with Embedded Test Rearranged Genes.

To test the models on real cancer expression data, we used gene expression data of 12600 probes in 59 prostate cancer samples and 87 normal samples [18] with embedded test genes. We used five test genes that have 10, 20, 30, 40 or 50 samples with rearranged genes. Good models should rank $test_{10}$ and $test_{20}$ high as they have small subset of samples with potential fusion. The other test genes have high expression in most of the samples and thus should not be ranked high as they would lead to false positive discovery. We showed that EigFusion outperformed the other methods on real data (Figure 2(b)) and it ranked $test_{20}$ in the top of the list and *test*$_{10}$ in fifth position. GTI ranked *test*$_{20}$ in second position but was unable to rank *test*$_{10}$ in the top 100. COPA also ranked *test*$_{20}$ in the 20th position but was unable to rank *test*$_{10}$ in the top 100. The other methods were unable to rank neither of the test genes in the top 100.

3.3. EigFusion Is Effective in Distinguishing between Biomarker Genes and Rearranged Genes.

We compared the transformation function proposed in this work with COPA transformation function as they both transform all data points, unlike ORT, OS, and GTI that only deal with values in the O_i set. We chose the case when cancer samples size is 50, as an example, and we compared the effect of the two methods on the *test*$_{50}$ gene (Figure S1.C). In this case, *test*$_{50}$ is a biomarker gene and should be ranked low. EigFusion standardizes the expression profile of genes based on the number of cancer samples, unlike COPA which standardizes the expression values based on the overall median regardless of the ratio between cancer and normal samples. EigFusion clearly shows how it can filter out biomarker genes.

3.4. Applications of EigFusion to Cancer Gene Expression Data.

We next demonstrated the affectivity of EigFusion on real cancer data that harbour ERG rearrangement in around 50% of the samples. First SAM failed to detect ERG gene as outlier. EigFusion was applied on prostate cancer gene expression data as it is among the most heterogeneous types of cancer, both histologically and clinically. We used MSKCC Prostate Oncogenome Project data [19] which has 179 samples (131 primary, 19 metastatic, 29 normal). Our goal is to predict potential rearranged (amplified, deleted) genes that occur in primary cancer samples, and metastatic. To statistically assess the significance of the results, we randomly permutated the the sample labels for 100 time and then find a *P* value for each gene. Only genes with *P* value less than 0.001 we selected.

TMPRSS2-ERG gene fusions have been reported in approximately 50% of over 1500 clinically localized prostate cancer samples [3, 20]. This fusion replaces the 5' end of *ERG* with the 5' untranslated region of *TMPRSS2* which results in overexpression of *ERG* gene and downexpression of *TMPRSS2*. EigFusion is able to rediscover *ERG* fusion as the second top gene in the list (Figure S1.A). *SPINK1* is another gene that was predicted to be overexpressed, it plays a significant role in prostate cancer development. Tomlins et al. [21] first showed that high levels of serine peptidase inhibitor Kazal type 1 (*SPINK1*), which occurs in about 10% of patients with prostate cancer, were correlated with higher rate of cancer recurrence. We also found that *ERG* and *SPINK1* fusions have low cooccurrence rate (less than 2%) which agrees with the latest research findings about the role of *SPINK1* in *ERG*-negative rearranged prostate samples [21].

We also identified other amplified genes which are potential candidates for rearrangements, such as *FABP5* (Figure S1.B) *KCNH8*. Many other genes such as *PAH*, *TOP2A*, and *CDH17* (Figure 4) showed to be amplified mainly in metastatic samples. We compared the set of rearranged genes

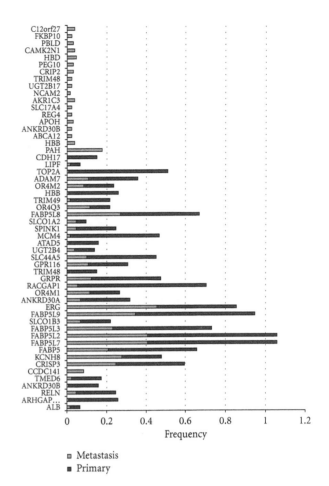

FIGURE 4: Genes altered in prostate samples, 54 genes are selected as overexpressed in subset of samples (primary or metastatic). Some genes showed to be overexpressed in only metastatic samples (genes with all red bars). Other genes showed to be overexpressed in both primary and metastatic but not normal samples (genes with red and blue bars). The frequency on the axis is the fractions of samples with rearrangement (overexpression in subset of samples) over all samples size. The red bars for example represents the frequency of gene rearrangement in primary samples.

from Taylor data with genes from Singh data [18]. We identified that *ERG*, *TFF3*, *FABP5*, *SPINK1*, *ISG15*, and *MRP4* as amplified genes representing potential rearrangements.

We further characterized gene rearrangements that are related to *ERG* fusion by grouping samples based on their ERG status: fusion-positive (ERG1) and fusion-negative (ERG0). We found several genes (*SPINK1*, *ETV1*,*PHA*, and *TFF3*) that are overexpressed only in subset of ERG0 samples. Also *FABP5* family showed to be more amplified in ERG0 samples, *KCNH8* and *GPR116* are more amplified in ERG1 samples (Figure S2). This is very essential to enable us to group prostate samples into subgroups: each with specific potential rearrangement signature, which may have prognostic implications. We also applied EigFusion on independent prostate cancer data [22] (455 samples) of known ERG fusion status. The samples were classified as 352 *ERG* fusion-negative prostate cancer samples (ERG0) and 103 *ERG* fusion positive prostate cancer samples (ERG1). We

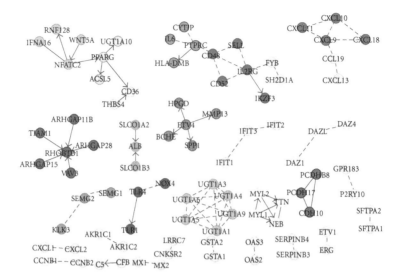

FIGURE 5: Integrating the discovered potential rearranged genes with functional protein interactions revealed functional modularity of the rearranged genes with enriched pathways.

detected 18 potential oncogenic rearrangements associated with *ERG* negative samples. Interestingly, we found that *ETV1* is associated with *ERG0* and has very low co-occurrence rate with ERG1. On the other hand, we found 25 potential gene rearrangements associated with *ERG* fusion positive. Interestingly, *SPINK5* was among the genes associated with *ERG* fusion.

We have also identified genes that are underexpressed in subset of the *ERG* fusion-positive samples. These genes could be the 5' partner of the gene fusions or could be deleted in the corresponding samples. We found also several genes underexpressed in subset of cancer samples like *KLK3*, *FOLH1*, *SPON2*, *A2M*, and *PCP4*. KLK3 has already been identified and used as a diagnostic biomarker. Thus, the other genes might be as important as KLK3. These genes could be either deleted in the corresponding samples or fused to one or many of the overexpressed genes.

We next asked if EigFusion can also be implemented to deal with other types of cancer. EigFusion was applied to ovarian cancer and leukemia gene expression data. We identified 94 putative rearranged genes in ovarian (Figure S3.A) and 88 genes in leukemia (Figure S3.B).

3.5. Rearranged Genes Are Functionally Associated. We next asked if the predicted rearranged genes are functionally associated and if they are enriched with particular biological processes. This is important to identify outlier genes that have influence on its neighbors. Thus, it helps to identify outliers that are influenced by rearranged genes. We integrated FPI network and the predicted set of potential rearranged genes to conduct core pathway analysis, based on the success of EigFusion in revealing common pathways alterations in prostate (Figure 5), ovarian (Figure S3.A), and leukemia (Figure S3.B) cancer. Results revealed that rearranged genes tend to form modules and share biological pathways. The tendency to form modules showed not to be random as we randomly selected 500 genes for 100 times and we did not

observe any module enrichment in any of the 100 trials. Table 1 describes that enriched pathways for the rearranged genes in the three cancers using EigFusion. We analyzed the pathways for all interacted genes and not individual modules. Wnt-signaling and cadherin signaling are commonly altered. Ovarian samples are altered in *KRAS* which is a member RAS/RAF cancer pathway. Another gene is *GNAZ* which is a member of the G protein complex that are involved as modulators or transducers in various transmembrane signaling systems. Leukemia samples are altered in integrin pathways and ERBb receptor family that are part of the epidermal growth factor (EGF) receptor family of receptor tyrosine kinases. Leukemia samples are also altered in RAS/RAF pathway at *RAC1* gene, a GTPase which belongs to the RAS superfamily of small GTP-binding proteins. We have also used the top 100 genes identified by COPA and GTI (supplementary file) and found that the two lists did not show any significant enrichment of biological pathways.

3.6. Identified Outlier Genes Are Associated with Perturbed Cancer Pathways. We next investigated if the predicted outlier genes are associated with master regulators that have been known to be altered in prostate and ovarian cancer. We integrated the copy number alteration (CNA) datasets to conduct pathway analysis of known altered cancer pathway. A search for altered subnetworks in functional protein networks identified several known pathways. Putative rearranged genes in prostate (Figure 6) showed to be highly associated with cancer master regulators *AR*, *KLK3*, *ERG*, *RB1*, *TP53*, *MCM4*, *FOXD1*, *PTK2B*, *NCOA2*, and *NCOA1* [23, 24]. Other genes like *FABP5*, *PCP4*, *SPON2*, *PAH*, *FOLH1*, *KCNH8*, *SPINK1*, and *GPR116* did not demonstrate any functionally associated modules, nor they are associated with master regulators. Genes rearranged in ovarian cancer (Figure S4.A) are highly linked to vital genes like *MYC*, *BRCA1*, and *PAX6* that were also altered in ovarian cancer. This provides further understanding of the deregulated

TABLE 1: Pathway enrichment analysis for rearranged gene, *P* values are in (), FDR < 0.005.

Prostate	Ovarian	Leukemia
Drug metabolism (<0.0000)	Receptor-ligand complexes (<0.0000)	Integrin cell surface interaction (<0.0000)
Retinol metabolism (<0.0000)	Cadherin signaling pathway (<0.0000)	Focal adhesion (<0.0000)
Toll-like receptor signaling (<0.0000)	Regulation of B-cell development (0.0001)	ECM-receptor interaction (<0.0000)
Estrogen responsive protein (0.0003)	Wnt signaling (0.001)	Wnt signaling pathway (<0.0000)
Receptor-ligand complex (0.001)	Protein kinase (0.001)	Signaling by PDGF (<0.0000)
Signaling by Rho GTPases (0.004)	Signaling by FGFR (0.002)	Formation of platelet plug (<0.0000)
P53 signaling (0.005)	PPAR signaling (0.004)	Regulation of bone mineralization (<0.0000)
FOXA transcription (0.005)	Calcium signaling pathway (0.004)	Pathways in cancer (0.0001)

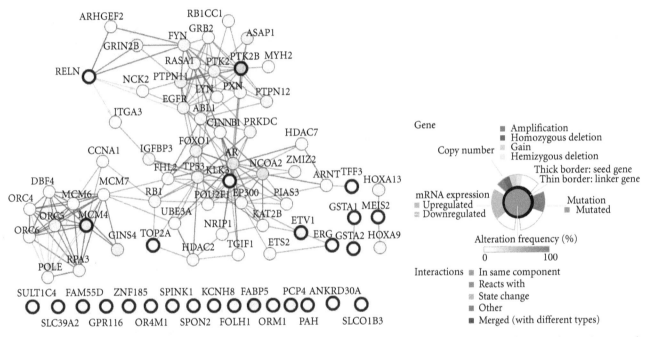

FIGURE 6: Functional modules of altered genes in prostate. Analyzing the rearranged genes by integrating functional protein networks and copy number alteration data revealed modularity of rearranged genes and high association with master regulators of well-known dysregulated pathways in cancer, such as AR, P53, and KLK3. Nodes with solid black border are identified by EigFusion.

pathways in cancer. We noticed that not all the identified rearranged genes are altered at the copy number level, but they are associated with altered genes. This indicates that these genes might not be altered but regulated by altered genes. We also conducted this analysis on the outlier genes identified by COPA and GTI. GTI genes showed to be associated with P53, MYC, RB1, and FYN. COPA genes are associated with TP53, MYC, RB1, and ACTA1. None of them showed any association with AR gene unlike EigFusion that showed that AR is most significant hub gene.

3.7. Validation of Outlier Genes Using Copy Number Variation Datasets. After discovering rearranged genes in both prostate and ovarian cancer, we validated the genes using copy number alteration (CNA) datasets for the same sample set from which mRNA gene expression data was retrieved. We selected the top 27 (altered in more than 10% of samples) genes rearranged in prostate cancer and investigated the copy

number alteration from CNA data (Figure 7). Approximately half (49%) of discovered genes were altered at the copy number level. We also observed that some of the genes were amplified and some were deleted. This shows that EigFusion can indeed identify amplified and deleted genes simultaneously. We then validated the prostate genes on ovarian CNA data. Interestingly, we found that most of prostate rearranged genes are also rearranged in ovarian cancer (Figure 8). We also found that the most significant genes identified by COPA and GTI have 19% and, 29% respectively, CNV. We then validated the ovarian rearranged genes using ovarian CNV and found that most of the discovered genes using EigFusion are copy number altered genes (Figure S4.B). Figure S4.B only shows the genes with the highest alteration rate. Ovarian genes did not show any significant alteration in prostate CNA data. Leukemia putative rearranged genes were not validated using CNA due to lack of CNA dataset of the same samples.

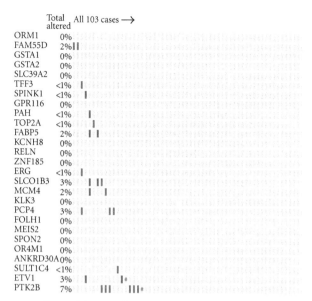

Total
altered   All 103 cases ⟶

Gene	altered
ORM1	0%
FAM55D	2%
GSTA1	0%
GSTA2	0%
SLC39A2	0%
TFF3	<1%
SPINK1	<1%
GPR116	0%
PAH	<1%
TOP2A	<1%
FABP5	2%
KCNH8	0%
RELN	0%
ZNF185	0%
ERG	<1%
SLCO1B3	3%
MCM4	2%
KLK3	0%
PCP4	3%
FOLH1	0%
MEIS2	0%
SPON2	0%
OR4M1	0%
ANKRD30A	0%
SULT1C4	<1%
ETV1	3%
PTK2B	7%

▌ Amplification ▌ Homozygous deletion ▪ Mutation
Copy number alterations are putative.

FIGURE 7: Validating prostate potential rearranged genes using prostate CNA revealed that half of genes are amplified or deleted in set of samples.

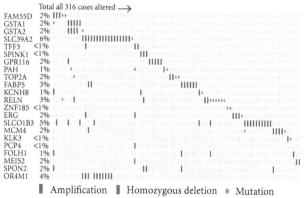

Total all 316 cases altered ⟶

Gene	altered
FAM55D	2%
GSTA1	2%
GSTA2	2%
SLC39A2	6%
TFF3	<1%
SPINK1	<1%
GPR116	2%
PAH	1%
TOP2A	1%
FABP5	3%
KCNH8	1%
RELN	3%
ZNF185	<1%
ERG	2%
SLCO1B3	5%
MCM4	2%
KLK3	<1%
PCP4	<1%
FOLH1	1%
MEIS2	2%
SPON2	2%
OR4M1	4%

▌ Amplification ▌ Homozygous deletion ▪ Mutation
Copy number alterations are putative.

FIGURE 8: Validating prostate rearranged genes using ovarian CNA revealed that most of prostate rearranged genes are altered in larger portion of samples compared with prostate CNA.

3.8. Survival and Clinical Analysis of Patients with Putative Rearrangements. We further characterized the association of the predicted rearrangements and survival data (death versus no death) and clinical data (aggressive versus not aggressive). Aggressive samples are defined as samples with high Gleason score and are in cluster 5 as defined in Taylor et al. [19]. We represented genes with putative rearrangements as vector V defined over $[0, 1]$ of length m, where m is the number of samples. $V(i) = 1$ means that sample i includes a potential fusion. Death and aggressiveness were also represented as two vectors of length m. $V(i) = 1$ when the sample corresponds to death outcome or aggressive cancer. We found the hamming distance between the genes

and the death and aggressive vectors to find how gene fusion is correlated with clinical outcome. We found that *ERG* is highly associated with death and aggressive cancer. 84% of samples with *ERG* fusion have death outcome and around 82% are aggressive samples. *MCM4* showed very significant association with death; 90% of samples with *MCM4* fusion have death outcome. *KCNH8, SPINK1, and GPR116* also have significant association with death (Figure 9).

Survival analysis (Figure 9) showed that samples with rearrangements in the identified 19 genes, that are altered in more than 10% of samples, showed to be at higher death risk than samples with no rearrangements ($P = 0.00128$, HR: 2.87). We reduced the gene set to *ERG, FABP5, KCNH8, SPINK1*, and we found that samples with rearrangements in these genes are even at higher risk of death ($P < 0.0000001$, HR: 4.12). ERG and SPINK1 are already associated with outcome; however, FABP5 and KCNH8 have not been associated with outcome. Here we showed that including FABP5 and KCNH8 as prognostic biomarkers improves aggressive cancer detection. Interestingly, rearrangements in prostate samples showed to be associated with survival in ovarian cancer. Ovarian cancer patients with rearrangements in prostate genes are at higher death risk ($P = 0.03$, HR: 1.4). We further used the Swedish prostate cohort data to assess if the rearranged genes are associated with cancer specific death. We only found the expression of 16 genes in the Swedish cohort. Clustering the gene expression data highlighted three distinct subgroups (low, intermediate, and high risk) (Figure 10). High risk patients are at higher risk for disease specific deaths compared to low risk patients ($P = 0.005$, HR: 1.89). No significant separation was observed between high and intermediate or low and intermediate groups.

4. Discussion

Here we argue that microarray gene expression data is a valuable source of information to discover outlier genes with potential functional gene rearrangements that have effect on the expression level of downstream genes. Since gene rearrangements are rare genetic translocation that affects a small sample of cancer patients and not all of them, it is feasible to discover genes that are overexpressed (amplified or fused) or underexpressed (deleted) in subset of cancer samples. Genes that are overexpressed in subset of samples are anticipated to be amplified or fused, and genes that are underexpressed in subset of samples are anticipated to be deleted. Unfortunately methods like SAM, *t*-test, *and so forth* that are developed to extract differentially expressed genes are not suitable to detect outlier genes. Previous works that aimed to identify gene rearrangements using bioinformatics approaches were limited to the identification of potential fused genes overexpressed in subset of samples and assessing the performance using synthetic data with embedded test genes. Herein, we followed the same approach by testing our EigFusion method on synthetic data with embedded tests. One might argue that real expression data does not follow certain distributions as in synthetic data. To address this point, we used real prostate cancer data with synthetic tests to test and compare methods. Unfortunately, there is

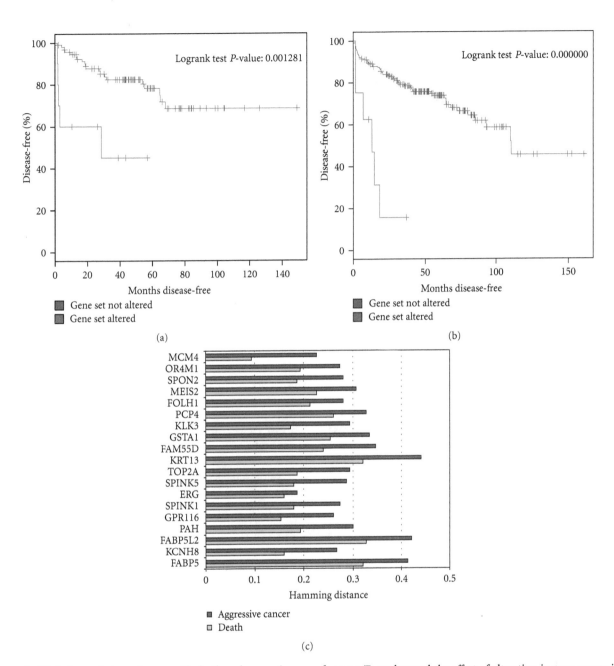

FIGURE 9: Clinical association of genes with death and aggressiveness of cancer. To understand the effect of alteration in gene expression, Kaplan-Meier survival curves are plotted to two sets of genes. (a) Is KM curves for all genes in figure top 25 genes altered. Samples with alterations demonstrated high risk disease. (b) Is KM curves using only ERG, SPINK1, KCNH8, and FABP5. Alterations in these four genes showed higher risk compared with the whole set of genes. (c) Hamming distance is used as a measure to find genes that have high association with death and aggressive cancer. Both death and aggressiveness were represented as vectors of samples. Distance shows how much gene's rearrangements vector differ from clinical vectors (death, aggressive). For example, ERG has distance of 0.16 to death vector; means that 84% of the samples of ERG fusion have death outcome.

no benchmark data that could be used in this study for performance evaluation purposes.

We compared the performance of EigFusion with all the methods in the literature that we are aware of that deal with outlier gene detection. One key factor that we considered and was not considered before is the size of cancer samples with respect to the size of normal samples. In this work, we showed that the ratio of cancer samples to normal samples significantly impacts the FDR. Existing methods such as COPA suffers from several drawbacks; first, the user defined rth percentile. Second, COPA is individual gene based method, and, most importantly, it fails to distinguish between biomarkers and genes with potential rearrangement especially when $S2$ is greater than or equal to $S1$. This is because the median will be biased toward normal samples. ORT, OS, and GTI also suffered from the same drawbacks. ORT showed to prefer high cancer proportion, unlike COPA that showed a decreasing performance as the cancer samples

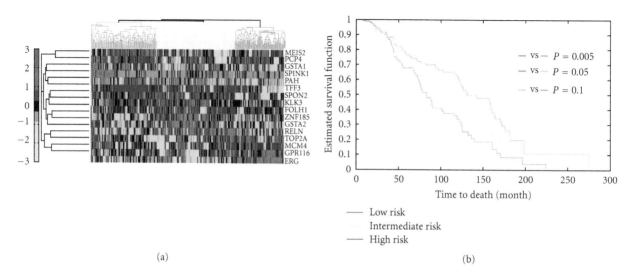

(a)

(b)

FIGURE 10: Hierarchical clustering of prostate rearranged genes. Validating the prostate rearranged genes on Swedish cohort revealed three prostate tumor subgroups with distinct rearrangement profile and different cancer specific death profiles.

proportion increases (Figure 3). Based on Figure (3), ORT has zero FPR, but high FNR. This is because it is able to give a low rank to all genes that have high expression in all cancer samples, and has high FNR because it was unable to detect fusion genes when the cancer sample size increases. GTI and OS performed equally and they are the closest to EigFusion; however, GTI and OS are unable to discriminate between rearranged genes and biomarker genes when the cancer samples are less than normal samples (Figure 3), and they are unable to detect rearranged genes when cancer samples size increases (Figure 3). Both OS and GTI showed to have high FPR when cancer samples are less than 100, and high FNR when cancer samples are more than 100, they perform best when the samples are equally grouped into normal and cancer samples. They both showed not to be affected by the variation in the size of cancer samples. They ranked the same test genes in the same order regardless of the cancer samples size variation. EigFusion is a new method to detect rearranged genes that we proposed in this work which showed to have better performance compared with other existing methods. EigFusion is able to overcome one of the drawbacks of the other methods, which is distinguishing between rearranged genes and biomarkers genes. EigFusion identifies both overexpressed and underexpressed gene in the same run. Thus, we think EigFusion is more generic to be used to identify genetic rearrangements in general that result in gene expression change. We also stress on the impact of cancer samples size with respect to normal sample size, that should be considered in any gene rearrangement prediction problem.

In our study, we aimed to characterize outlier genes and their potential functional gene rearrangements in several tumor types: prostate, leukemia, and ovarian. We first focused on functional gene rearrangements in prostate cancer patients (primary and metastatic) compared with normal samples (Figure 4). We found that large portion of these gene rearrangements occur in metastatic samples;

only *CCDC141* showed to be overexpressed in primary cancer. *FABP5* gene is overexpressed in both primary and metastatic cancer. *FABP5* is associated with psoriasis; it is a chronic immune-mediated disease that appears on the skin, breast cancer, and metastasis. Examination of the clinical implications of *FABP5* rearrangements revealed that samples with *FABP5* rearrangements are at higher risk of death (P value = 0.0000001) compared with ERG rearrangements (P value = 0.18). Furthermore, *FABP5* is overexpressed in samples that have *TARP* and *KLK3* underexpressed, which indicates that *FABP5* might be fused to *TARP* and *KLK3*. *TARP* gene is embedded within an intron of the T-cell receptor-gamma (TCRG) locus, which encodes an alternative T-cell receptor that is always coexpressed with T-cell receptor delta [25]. *TARP* was identified to be expressed in a prostate-specific form of TCRG mRNA in human prostate and demonstrated that it originated from epithelial cells [25]. This clearly shows that there is specific rearrangement or alternative splicing mechanism that leads toward aggressive cancer. Further characterizing *FABP5* and *TARP*, they are rearranged in ERG0 samples, which means that these two genes could be used to define distinct group of prostate cancer. Several studies showed that *C-FABP or E-FABP* is a metastasis inducing gene overexpressed in human prostate carcinomas [26]. *KCNH8*, another significant gene identified in this work harbours a binding site for ELK-1 transcription factor, which is one of the ets- transcrption factors family to which *ERG* belongs, in its promoter. This might explain the association between KCNH8 and ERG.

One of the problems bioinformaticians face is validating the proposed computational algorithm. In this work, we validated the identified potential rearranged genes using CNA datasets for the same samples from which microarray gene expression data was conducted. Large portion of the genes were copy number altered, either amplified or deleted in both prostate and ovarian cancer. Validating prostate genes on CNA of ovarian data showed interesting result; altered genes in prostate are also altered in ovarian but not the opposite. We also found that ovarian samples have higher alteration rate than prostate samples. Most of the ovarian genes are altered in more than 8% of the ovarian cancer samples; however, prostate genes are only altered in around 2–4% of prostate samples. This reveals that ovarian cancer is more heterogenous than prostate cancer.

Several other findings have emerged from our analysis, largely based on the opportunity provided by integrated analysis of functional protein networks. Putative rearranged genes are functionally related and form modules that are enriched in biological pathways, mainly RAS/RAF and cadherin signaling pathways. A second finding is that integrating functional protein networks with CNA data provides insights on to the dysregulated pathways. EigFusion was able to identify elements (rearranged genes) in dysregulated pathway, but integrating CNA and functional networks gave more insights into the dysregulated pathways as other altered genes, that EigFusion was not able to retrieve, were identified. Thus, we believe that integrating EigFusion with functional protein networks and CNA data would reveal and give detailed insights into the dysregulated pathways. One of the findings we were able to retrieve using the integrative approach is the nuclear receptor coactivator NCOA2 that was previously shown to alter AR pathway in primary prostate tumors providing mechanism for its potential role as a prostate cancer oncogene [19].

Survival analysis revealed that patients with rearrangements in the identified set of genes are at higher risk of cancer specific death. Using rearranged genes in prostate cancer helped to identify three subgroups with distinct outcome and different rearrangement profile. Using ovarian rearranged gene expression did not show significant prognostic value. Overall, these discoveries set the stage for approaches to the treatment of prostate, ovarian, and leukemia in which rearranged genes or network are detected and targeted with therapies selected to be effective against these specific aberrations.

5. Conclusion

Discovering cancer rearrangements can ameliorate the dysfunctional components in cancer cells. EigFusion successfully detected outlier genes with potential amplification or deletion genes (rearranged genes) in subset of cancer samples in both prostate and ovarian using gene expression data. EigFusion is the only method that is robust against variations in cancer sample size. Several genes like ERG, FABP5, SPINK1, KCNH8, and PAH are highly associated with outcome data. This set of genes could be used as prognostic biomarkers for prostate cancer. ADIPOQ and LY6H are discovered to be rearranged in 14% and 23% of ovarian samples, respectively. Using CNA to validate the rearranged genes demonstrated that ovarian cancer patients have higher rate of alterations per sample. Most ovarian cancer patients harbour multiple several genes altered. Integrating functional protein networks assisted to reveal the modularity of the rearranged genes. This ameliorates the

functional dysfunctional genes as components rather than single genes. Genes with rearrangements helped to identify three prostate cancer subgroups with distinct outcome. Finally, gene expression data is a valuable and widely available source of information to discover gene with potential rearrangements.

Acknowledgments

The authors would like to thank NSERC for funding. T. A. Bismar is supported by the Young Investigators Award of the Prostate Cancer Foundation, USA.

References

[1] A. de Klein, A. G. van Kessel, G. Grosveld et al., "A celllular oncogene is translocated to the Philadelphia chromosome in chronic myelocytic leukaemia," Nature, vol. 300, no. 5894, pp. 765–767, 1982.

[2] M. Soda, Y. L. Choi, M. Enomoto et al., "Identification of the transforming EML4-ALK fusion gene in non-small-cell lung cancer," Nature, vol. 448, no. 7153, pp. 561–566, 2007.

[3] C. Kumar-Sinha, S. A. Tomlins, and A. M. Chinnaiyan, "Recurrent gene fusions in prostate cancer," Nature Reviews Cancer, vol. 8, no. 7, pp. 497–511, 2008.

[4] J. A. Squire, "TMPRSS2-ERG and PTEN loss in prostate cancer," Nature Genetics, vol. 41, no. 5, pp. 509–510, 2009.

[5] M. F. Berger, M. S. Lawrence, and F. Demichelis, "The genome complexity of primary human prostate cancer," Nature, vol. 470, pp. 214–220, 2011.

[6] R. I. Skotheim, G. O. S. Thomassen, M. Eken et al., "A universal assay for detection of oncogenic fusion transcripts by oligo microarray analysis," Molecular Cancer, vol. 8, pp. 1–2, 2009.

[7] H. Edgren, A. Murumagi, S. Kangaspeska et al., "Identification of fusion genes in breast cancer by paired-end RNA-sequencing," Genome Biology, vol. 12, no. 1, article R6, 2011.

[8] Y. Hu, K. Wang, X. He, D. Y. Chiang, J. F. Prins, and J. Liu, "A probabilistic framework for aligning paired-end RNA-seq data," Bioinformatics, vol. 26, no. 16, pp. 1950–1957, 2010.

[9] K. Wang, D. Singh, Z. Zeng et al., "MapSplice: accurate mapping of RNA-seq reads for splice junction discovery," Nucleic Acids Research, vol. 38, no. 18, article e178, 2010.

[10] A. McPherson, F. Hormozdiari, A. Zayed et al., "Defuse: an algorithm for gene fusion discovery in tumor rna-seq data," PLoS Computational Biology, vol. 7, no. 5, Article ID e1001138, 2011.

[11] M. A. Rubin and A. M. Chinnaiyan, "Bioinformatics approach leads to the discovery of the TMPRSS2:ETS gene fusion in prostate cancer," Laboratory Investigation, vol. 86, no. 11, pp. 1099–1102, 2006.

[12] W. U. Baolin, "Cancer outlier differential gene expression detection," Biostatistics, vol. 8, no. 3, pp. 566–575, 2007.

[13] L. Li, A. Chaudhuri, J. Chant, and Z. Tang, "PADGE: analysis of heterogeneous patterns of differential gene expression," Physiological Genomics, vol. 32, no. 1, pp. 154–159, 2007.

[14] S. A. Tomlins, D. R. Rhodes, S. Perner et al., "Recurrent fusion of TMPRSS2 and ETS transcription factor genes in prostate cancer," Science, vol. 310, no. 5748, pp. 644–648, 2005.

[15] R. Tibshirani and T. Hastie, "Outlier sums for differential gene expression analysis," Biostatistics, vol. 8, no. 1, pp. 2–8, 2007.

[16] J. P. Mpindi, H. Sara, S. Haapa-Paananen et al., "Gti: a novel algorithm for identifying outlier gene expression profiles from

integrated microarray datasets," *PLoS ONE*, vol. 6, no. 2, Article ID e17259, 2011.

[17] G. Wu, X. Feng, and L. Stein, "A human functional protein interaction network and its application to cancer data analysis," *Genome Biology*, vol. 11, no. 5, article R53, 2010.

[18] D. Singh, P. G. Febbo, K. Ross et al., "Gene expression correlates of clinical prostate cancer behavior," *Cancer Cell*, vol. 1, no. 2, pp. 203–209, 2002.

[19] B. Tylor, N. Schultz, H. Hieronyymus, and W. Gerald, "Integrative genomic profiling of human prostate cancer," *Cancer Cell*, vol. 18, pp. 1–12, 2010.

[20] A. D. Darnel, C. J. LaFargue, R. T. Vollmer, J. Corcos, and T. A. Bismar, "TMPRSS2-ERG fusion is frequently observed in gleason pattern 3 prostate cancer in a canadian cohort," *Cancer Biology and Therapy*, vol. 8, no. 2, pp. 125–130, 2009.

[21] S. A. Tomlins, D. R. Rhodes, J. Yu et al., "The role of SPINK1 in ETS rearrangement-negative prostate cancers," *Cancer Cell*, vol. 13, no. 6, pp. 519–528, 2008.

[22] S. R. Setlur, K. D. Mertz, Y. Hoshida et al., "Estrogen-dependent signaling in a molecularly distinct subclass of aggressive prostate cancer," *Journal of the National Cancer Institute*, vol. 100, no. 11, pp. 815–825, 2008.

[23] J. Momand, H. H. Wu, and G. Dasgupta, "MDM2—master regulator of the p53 tumor suppressor protein," *Gene*, vol. 242, no. 1-2, pp. 15–29, 2000.

[24] S. S. Myatt and E. W. F. Lam, "The emerging roles of forkhead box (Fox) proteins in cancer," *Nature Reviews Cancer*, vol. 7, no. 11, pp. 847–859, 2007.

[25] H. Maeda, S. Nagata, C. D. Wolfgang, G. L. Bratthauer, T. K. Bera, and I. Pastan, "The T cell receptor γ chain alternate reading frame protein (TARP), a prostate-specific protein localized in mitochondria," *Journal of Biological Chemistry*, vol. 279, no. 23, pp. 24561–24568, 2004.

[26] E. A. Morgan, S. S. Forootan, J. Adamson et al., "Expression of cutaneous fatty acid-binding protein (C-FABP) in prostate cancer: potential prognostic marker and target for tumourigenicity-suppression," *International Journal of Oncology*, vol. 32, no. 4, pp. 767–775, 2008.

Permissions

The contributors of this book come from diverse backgrounds, making this book a truly international effort. This book will bring forth new frontiers with its revolutionizing research information and detailed analysis of the nascent developments around the world.

We would like to thank all the contributing authors for lending their expertise to make the book truly unique. They have played a crucial role in the development of this book. Without their invaluable contributions this book wouldn't have been possible. They have made vital efforts to compile up to date information on the varied aspects of this subject to make this book a valuable addition to the collection of many professionals and students.

This book was conceptualized with the vision of imparting up-to-date information and advanced data in this field. To ensure the same, a matchless editorial board was set up. Every individual on the board went through rigorous rounds of assessment to prove their worth. After which they invested a large part of their time researching and compiling the most relevant data for our readers. Conferences and sessions were held from time to time between the editorial board and the contributing authors to present the data in the most comprehensible form. The editorial team has worked tirelessly to provide valuable and valid information to help people across the globe.

Every chapter published in this book has been scrutinized by our experts. Their significance has been extensively debated. The topics covered herein carry significant findings which will fuel the growth of the discipline. They may even be implemented as practical applications or may be referred to as a beginning point for another development. Chapters in this book were first published by Hindawi Publishing Corporation; hereby published with permission under the Creative Commons Attribution License or equivalent.

The editorial board has been involved in producing this book since its inception. They have spent rigorous hours researching and exploring the diverse topics which have resulted in the successful publishing of this book. They have passed on their knowledge of decades through this book. To expedite this challenging task, the publisher supported the team at every step. A small team of assistant editors was also appointed to further simplify the editing procedure and attain best results for the readers.

Our editorial team has been hand-picked from every corner of the world. Their multi-ethnicity adds dynamic inputs to the discussions which result in innovative outcomes. These outcomes are then further discussed with the researchers and contributors who give their valuable feedback and opinion regarding the same. The feedback is then collaborated with the researches and they are edited in a comprehensive manner to aid the understanding of the subject.

Apart from the editorial board, the designing team has also invested a significant amount of their time in understanding the subject and creating the most relevant covers. They scrutinized every image to scout for the most suitable representation of the subject and create an appropriate cover for the book.

The publishing team has been involved in this book since its early stages. They were actively engaged in every process, be it collecting the data, connecting with the contributors or procuring relevant information. The team has been an ardent support to the editorial, designing and production team. Their endless efforts to recruit the best for this project, has resulted in the accomplishment of this book. They are a veteran in the field of academics and their pool of knowledge is as vast as their experience in printing. Their expertise and guidance has proved useful at every step. Their uncompromising quality standards have made this book an exceptional effort. Their encouragement from time to time has been an inspiration for everyone.

The publisher and the editorial board hope that this book will prove to be a valuable piece of knowledge for researchers, students, practitioners and scholars across the globe.

List of Contributors

Hassan Taghipour and Heydar Ali Esmaili
Department of Pathology, Tabriz University of Medical Sciences, Tabriz, Iran

Mahdi Rezaei
Department of Theoretical Physics and Astrophysics, University of Tabriz, Tabriz 51664, Iran

Scott Horton, Amalie Tuerk, Daniel Cook and Prasad Dhurjati
Colburn Laboratory, Department of Chemical and Biomolecular Engineering, University of Delaware, Newark, DE 19716, USA

Jiadi Cook
Resident in the Department of Family Medicine, Christiana Care Health Services, Wilmington, DE 19805, USA

Olga Papadodima and Aristotelis Chatziioannou
Metabolic Engineering and Bioinformatics Program, Institute of Biological Research and Biotechnology, National Hellenic Research Foundation, 48 Vas. Constantinou Avenue, 11635 Athens, Greece

Allan Sirsjo
Division of Clinical Medicine, School of Health and Medical Sciences, Orebro University, Orebro SE-701 82, Sweden

Fragiskos N. Kolisis
Biotechnology Laboratory, School of Chemical Engineering, Zografou Campus, National Technical University of Athens, 15780 Athens, Greece

Chiquito Crasto
Department of Genetics, University of Alabama at Birmingham, Birmingham, AL 35294, USA

Chandrahas Narne
Department of Computer and Information Sciences, University of Alabama at Birmingham, Birmingham, AL 35294, USA

Stephen Barnes
Department of Genetics, University of Alabama at Birmingham, Birmingham, AL 35294, USA
Centers for Nutrient-Gene Interactions, University of Alabama at Birmingham, Birmingham, AL 35294, USA
Department of Pharmacology and Toxicology, University of Alabama at Birmingham, Birmingham, AL 35294, USA
Targeted Metabolomics and Proteomics Laboratory, University of Alabama at Birmingham, Birmingham, AL 35294, USA

Mikako Kawai
Department of Pharmacology and Toxicology, University of Alabama at Birmingham, Birmingham, AL 35294, USA

Landon Wilson
Centers for Nutrient-Gene Interactions, University of Alabama at Birmingham, Birmingham, AL 35294, USA

Andrea Manconi and Luciano Milanesi
Institute for Biomedical Technologies, National Research Council, Via F.lli Cervi, 93, 20090 Segrate, Italy

Giuliano Armano
Department of Electrical and Electronic Engineering, University of Cagliari, Piazza d'Armi, 09123 Cagliari, Italy

Eloisa Vargiu
Department of Electrical and Electronic Engineering, University of Cagliari, Piazza d'Armi, 09123 Cagliari, Italy
Barcelona Digital Technological Center, C/Roc Boronat 117, 08018 Barcelona, Spain

Navadon Khunlertgit and Byung-Jun Yoon
Department of Electrical and Computer Engineering, Texas A&M University, College Station, TX 77843-3128, USA

Anna Divoli
Pingar Research, Pingar, Auckland 1010, New Zealand

Preslav Nakov
Qatar Computing Research Institute, Qatar Foundation, Tornado Tower, Floor 10, P.O. Box 5825, Doha, Qatar

Marti A. Hearst
School of Information, University of California at Berkeley, CA 94720, USA

Mohammed Alshalalfa
Department of Computer Science, University of Calgary, 2500 University Dr. NW, Calgary, AB, Canada Biotechnology Research Center, Palestine Polytechnic University, Hebron, Palestine
Ian Roberts, Stephanie A. Carter, Cinzia G. Scarpini, Konstantina Karagavriilidou and Nicholas Coleman
Department of Pathology, University of Cambridge, Tennis Court Road, Cambridge CB2 1QP, UK

Jenny C. J. Barna
Department of Biochemistry, University of Cambridge, Tennis Court Road, Cambridge CB2 1QW, UK

Mark Calleja
The Cavendish Laboratory, University of Cambridge, J. J. Thomson Avenue, Cambridge CB3 0HE, UK

Hamed Bostan and Mohd Shahir Shamsir
Faculty of Biosciences and Bioengineering, Universiti Teknologi Malaysia, 81310 Johor Bahru, Johor, Malaysia

Naomie Salim
Faculty of Computer Science and Information Systems, Universiti Teknologi Malaysia, 81310 Johor Bahru, Johor, Malaysia

Zeti Azura Hussein
School of Bioscience and Biotechnology, Faculty of Science and Technology, Universiti Kebangsaan Malaysia, 43600 Bangi, Selangor, Malaysia

Peter Klappa
School of Biosciences, University of Kent, Canterbury, Kent CT2 7NJ, UK

Manrique Mata-Montero
Department of Computer Science, Memorial University, Canada

Nabil Shalaby
Department of Mathematics and Statistics, Memorial University, Canada

Bradley Sheppard
Department of Computer Science, Memorial University, Canada
Department of Mathematics and Statistics, Memorial University, Canada

Gumpeny Ramachandra Sridhar
Endocrine and Diabetes Centre, 15-12-15 Krishnanagar, Visakhapatnam 530 002, India

Padmanabhuni Venkata Nageswara Rao
Department of Computer Science and Engineering, GITAM University, Visakhapatnam 530045, India

Dowluru SVGK Kaladhar and Sali Veeresh Kumar
Department of Biochemistry and Bioinformatics, GITAM University, Visakhapatnam 530045, India

Tatavarthi Uma Devi
Department of Computer Science, GITAM University, Visakhapatnam 530045, India

Sofie Van Landeghem and Yves Van de Peer
Department of Plant Systems Biology, VIB, Technologiepark 927, 9052 Gent, Belgium
Department of Plant Biotechnology and Bioinformatics, Ghent University, Technologiepark 927, 9052 Gent, Belgium

Kai Hakala, Samuel Ronnqvist and Filip Ginter
Department of Information Technology, University of Turku, Joukahaisenkatu 3-5, 20520 Turku, Finland

Tapio Salakoski
Department of Information Technology, University of Turku, Joukahaisenkatu 3-5, 20520 Turku, Finland
Turku BioNLP Group, Turku Centre for Computer Science (TUCS), Joukahaisenkatu 3-5, 20520 Turku, Finland

Mohamed Amine Fnaiech and Hazem Nounou
Electrical and Computer Engineering Program, Texas A&M University at Qatar, P.O. Box 23874, Doha, Qatar

Mohamed Nounou
Chemical Engineering Program, Texas A&M University at Qatar, P.O. Box 23874, Doha, Qatar

Aniruddha Datta
Department of Electrical and Computer Engineering, Texas A&M University, College Station, TX 77843, USA

Syed Toufeeq Ahmed
Department of Biomedical Informatics, Vanderbilt University, Nashville, TN 37232, USA

Hasan Davulcu, Sukru Tikves and Radhika Nair
Department of Computer Science and Engineering, Arizona State University, Tempe, AZ 85281, USA

Zhongming Zhao
Department of Biomedical Informatics, Vanderbilt University, Nashville, TN 37232, USA
Department of Cancer Biology, Vanderbilt University School of Medicine, Nashville, TN 37232, USA

Anne E. Thessen and Dmitry Mozzherin
Center for Library and Informatics, Marine Biological Laboratory, 7 MBL Street, Woods Hole, MA 02543, USA

Hong Cui
School of Information Resources and Library Science, University of Arizona, Tucson, AZ 85719, USA

Mario Flores and Yufei Huang
Department of Electrical and Computer Engineering, University of Texas at San Antonio, San Antonio, TX 78249, USA

Tzu-Hung Hsiao
Greehey Children's Cancer Research Institute, University of Texas Health Science Center at San Antonio, San Antonio, TX 78229, USA

Yidong Chen
Greehey Children's Cancer Research Institute, University of Texas Health Science Center at San Antonio, San Antonio, TX 78229, USA
Department of Epidemiology and Biostatistics, University of Texas Health Science Center at San Antonio, San Antonio, TX 78229, USA

Yu-Chiao Chiu and Eric Y. Chuang
Graduate Institute of Biomedical Electronics and Bioinformatics, National Taiwan University, Taipei, Taiwan

Salvador Eugenio C. Caoili
Department of Biochemistry and Molecular Biology, College of Medicine, University of the Philippines Manila, Room 101, Medical Annex Building, 547 Pedro Gil Street, Ermita, Manila 1000, Philippines

Fatemeh Safara
Department of Computer Engineering, Islamic Azad University, Islamshahr Branch, Islamshahr, Tehran 3314767653, Iran
Faculty of Computer Science and Information Technology, 43400 Serdang, Selangor Darul Ehsan, Malaysia

Shyamala Doraisamy, Azreen Azman and Azrul Jantan
Faculty of Computer Science and Information Technology, 43400 Serdang, Selangor Darul Ehsan, Malaysia

Sri Ranga
Department of Cardiology, Serdang Hospital, 43000 Kajang, Selangor Darul Ehsan, Malaysia

Mohammed Alshalalfa and Reda Alhajj
Department of Computer Science, University of Calgary, Calgary, AB, Canada

Tarek A. Bismar
Departments of Pathology, Oncology and Molecular Biology and Biochemistry, Faculty of Medicine, University of Calgary, Calgary, AB, Canada

Printed in the USA
CPSIA information can be obtained
at www.ICGtesting.com
JSHW051439221024
72173JS00006B/1522

9 781632 394453